Songs from the Alley

SONGS
from the
ALLEY

▨▨▨▨▨▨▨▨▨▨▨▨▨▨▨▨▨▨▨▨▨▨

KATHLEEN HIRSCH

TICKNOR & FIELDS

New York

1989

Library of Congress Cataloging-in-Publication Data

Hirsch, Kathleen.
Songs from the alley / Kathleen Hirsch.
p.   cm.
Bibliography: p.
ISBN 0-89919-488-5
1. Homeless women — Massachusetts — Boston — Biography.
2. Homelessness — Massachusetts — Boston — Case studies.   I. Title.
HV4506.B67H57   1989   88-36736
362.8'3 — dc 19   CIP
[B]

PRINTED IN THE UNITED STATES OF AMERICA

V 10 9 8 7 6 5 4 3 2 1

The author is grateful to the Archives of the Archdiocese of Boston
for permission to quote from the letters of Father Anderson
and Father McElroy, and to the Massachusetts Historical Society
for permission to quote from the annual reports of the Penitent
Females' Refuge. The quotation on page 119 is copyright © 1988
by the New York Times Company. Reprinted by permission.

For
Mark
and my parents

The people that walked in darkness have seen a great light:
They that dwell in the land of the shadow of death,
   upon them hath the light shined.
Thou hast multiplied the nation, and not increased the joy:
They joy before thee according to the joy in harvest,
   and as men rejoice when they divide the spoil.

Isaiah 9:2—4

We have all known the long loneliness and we have learned that
the only solution is love and that love comes with community.

Dorothy Day

There's a town out there where life always wins.

Gabe Francis, on a street corner in Boston

Contents

Prologue

WELL AFTER COMPLETING most of my research for this book, I came upon the following passage by the turn-of-the-century social reformer Robert A. Woods. It so eloquently articulated the ideals I have attempted to bring to my investigation of homelessness that I quote it in full here.

> To secure acquaintance and knowledge so complex, detailed, and intimate meant involving one's self with people sufficiently to be taken within the reserves of family and neighborhood life and thought. It called for accurate and minute familiarity with the local pattern of streets, houses, and institutions, as well as sustained participation in many-sided associations and interests. Science itself demanded that such an onset be characterized not only by alertness but by sympathy. Only those who can go among men and women with affection can understand the tissue of objective causes and inward motives which bind people together. Scientific disinterestedness calls for, not the separateness of the observer, but suspended judgment in the midst of action. The explorer of society must gain his facts largely as a byproduct of humanized participation in enterprises formerly quite alien to him.[1]

The Pine Street Inn is one of the nation's oldest, and Boston's largest, shelter for the homeless. Three years ago I approached its directors, asking to be allowed to spend an indefinite period of time inside the institution as a volunteer and observer and, later, as a journalist recording the experience of shelter life for homeless women.

Boston seemed the ideal setting for my project. The size of its homeless population, roughly 5,000, is typical of many medium-sized American cities, not — like the massive numbers and unparalleled complications that plague New York City — unique. Boston also boasts the most enlightened and aggressive homeless policies in the nation. In 1983 the state enacted sweeping changes in its welfare, housing, and social services programs with the aim of eradicating homelessness. The city had just elected a mayor whose primary human services concern was the plight of the homeless. Raymond Flynn became chairman of the U.S. Conference of Mayors' Task Force on Homelessness and Hunger, and a nationally recognized expert on homelessness. What better place, then, to examine how well our policies were helping the victims of our greatest national shame?

I set out to see for myself, away from the strident voices of advocates and policy planners, and all who had a political stake in the issue. Away from easy answers. I wanted to enter the subculture of homelessness as completely and with as few preconceptions as possible and, by earning the trust of the women who moved in it, to accrue an intimate understanding of their pasts, self-perceptions, and current preoccupations, and the institutional resources they could draw on in solving their individual crises.

Many journalists before me had made the same request, I was told, and all of them had been refused. It was my good fortune that after months of soul searching and deliberation, the Pine Street Inn's administration decided to let me in. "We were getting bigger and bigger," one administrator said later. "We felt, maybe it is time to have someone come in and show us how we're doing."

From that moment on, I was welcomed into the Pine Street community. There is hardly a shelter task I didn't perform during my months there, from serving dinner and washing dishes to overseeing showers, stocking the supply cupboards, and participating in staff meetings. I escorted homeless women to welfare offices, hospitals, and detoxification facilities. At all hours of the night and day I conversed with guests and the unflagging staff.

The staff, the administration, and current and former board members extended to me a degree of trust and confidence that far exceeded what any journalist hopes for. Every question I asked and every request I made for analysis and information were answered thoughtfully and candidly. This, and the countless small kindnesses — a cup of coffee when I was beyond the point of fatigue, the ready humor, and the selflessness with which I found myself surrounded — moved and sustained me more than I can say.

Outside the shelter, much of my time was spent in the city's parks and alleys, in the waiting rooms of bus stations, at subway stops, in the public library, over coffee in cheap diners, and on heating grates, trying to grasp the tenor and flow of days and nights on the street, and the lives of the individual women who subsisted there.

Though I never attempted to live the life of a homeless woman, regarding this more as a guise than as an enlightening research tool, for two years I became a virtual stranger to family and friends. Immersed in a process so isolating and — what I hadn't anticipated — so internalized, on several occasions I experienced a loss of orientation to my own world. During these brief and desolate epiphanies in the dark along deserted city streets, I saw what it was to be anonymous, unconnected, and unable to escape from the feelings of vulnerability and hopelessness this engendered. Stripped of life's sustaining illusions, I saw how easily any one of us can become lost in America.

Amanda and Wendy, the two main characters in this narrative, chose me as much as I chose them. It was the special connection I felt with each of them from the start that prompted me to work increasingly closely with these two — not because they represented "typical" homeless women. I quickly learned that there are no typical homeless people, only common suffering. Amanda and Wendy were both articulate and thoughtful about their circumstances, and as time went on, I began to see that they offered invaluable windows onto two worlds of vitally important contrast: between those homeless who accept the system of services society currently offers and who try to meet their own needs, with varying degrees of success, by using the shelters; and those who refuse, or have been refused by, our system, and for whom we need approaches not yet conceived.

The subject of physical, sexual, and emotional abuse comes up over and over again in the lives of the women I got to know. In fact, if any common thread unites them, it is this. Reported abuse is extremely difficult to corroborate by more than one source. Juvenile records, where they exist, are not generally accessible to researchers. I queried acquaintances and experts as to the reasonable likelihood of the women's accounts, and I have reported their stories factually as they told them to me, adding, where available, the relevant perspectives of others.

The events and conversations recounted in this book are real and accurate as I observed them or as they were reported to me by at least one source. They have not been manipulated in any way, nor has natural sequence been tampered with for purposes of narrative impact.

Complete candor in these accounts was essential to the portrayal of the underlying causes and effects of homelessness. However, nothing could be further from my objective than to cause the subjects of this book, through public exposure, greater pain and heartbreak than they have already experienced in their lives. Their privacy is precious to them. To protect it, I have changed the names of all of the homeless, their families, acquaintances, and those shelter staffers who requested it, as well as certain minor details and distinguishing characteristics, including the names of hometowns.

Boston, Winter 1988

SHORTLY BEFORE SEVEN on a Saturday morning, the number 47 bus pulls up to an icy stop several blocks from Kenmore Square and admits a solitary rider. Amanda Daley is dressed for work in running shoes, size-twelve boy's jeans, and a turtleneck. Over these she has pulled a hooded blue sweatshirt and a new pea jacket recently purchased at an Army-Navy store downtown. Her once glossy walnut hair is now amply grayed, clipped into functional waves around a face that has also begun to gray and go a little gaunt with time. Lines trace out shadows under hazel eyes, and even in moments of repose, her mouth doesn't relax its hold on some long habit of sorrow. She is thirty-six years old.

She gazes through window grime as the bus travels down Brookline Avenue past the hospitals — Beth Israel, Harvard Medical School, and Children's — that sprawl in all directions into the thin neighborhoods that survive on the periphery. By midday these streets will be choked with ambulances, interns, visitors, and the ubiquitous sidewalk vendors who hawk sausages and pretzels. But now they are quiet, wintry and calm, as the driver turns down Avenue Louis Pasteur, past the Isabella Stewart Gardner Museum, headed into the poor, mostly black neighborhood of Roxbury. Amanda mulls over what she'll have for breakfast, which she eats every morning in the Goodwill store cafeteria. Two eggs, bacon, toast, and a glass of milk ought to hold her until lunch, she thinks.

Now, too quickly, it seems, the School of the Museum of Fine Arts appears directly in the bus's path. Amanda narrows her eyes and forces

herself to look away. She'll have coffee this morning, she thinks, groping back to thoughts of breakfast. She needs all the energy she can
get as she struggles to hold ninety-three pounds on her meager five-
foot frame.

After breakfast she'll head over to the retail clothing department
and start to rack a fresh binful of the garments that Morgie's collects
from all the Goodwill donation drops in the city. These are cleaned,
tagged, and sold at discount prices to the poor, many of them living
in the housing projects and tenements that back up to the store's
property. She'll be able to do one bin, certainly, before the store auction begins.

At this thought, her hands go clammy. She's tried not to let herself
dwell for even one minute on the auction, the weekly event where
final-sale and choice specialty items are sold. But the auction has been
on her mind since Monday. In the process of unpacking a fresh load
of donations — refugee toy trucks, glass olive trays, dried-out vinyl
handbags, and washed-out clothes — she'd uncovered a handmade
wooden dollhouse. As if, she would think later, it had found its way
to her.

The bus turns at the Museum School and passes alongside it for
half a block. Then it is behind her. She has crossed an invisible border, as specific and palpable as her own heartbeat. She has entered
what she still thinks of as *her* territory, her streets, the neighborhoods
where her friends are. Down Tremont, in any number of alleys, her
buddies, long since roused by the sun, have drifted farther back into
the South End for the day, toward the Pine Street Inn or the Salvation
Army or one of the few lunch counters where they can still get a cup
of coffee and a roll for under a dollar.

Others approach from the opposite direction, setting out from the
shelters where they've spent the night, heading downtown. She sees
Denise, carrying her soft plastic attaché, the very image of the maiden
librarian, with her gentle, downturned face and the patient smile that
Amanda never once saw fade in all the months that they both slept at
the shelter. A little farther along she sees Joanie, her expression angry
and pinched, as it always is from the constant strain of shelter life.

Amanda glances down Washington as the bus crosses it. There, in
the boarded-up, tax-delinquent properties, the unlit parks, and trash-
filled fire escapes, the rituals of survival continue as she knew them.
She catches a glimpse of one of the street women who never uses the

shelters, up at the intersection. The woman must have come from City Hospital, judging from the direction she is moving in — weaving, more precisely — in a thick plaid jacket and a pink scarf, as if she can't see two feet in front of her.

Amanda recalls the hardness of the shelter beds as vividly as if she'd slept in one just last night, and the endless standing in lines — for showers, for food, for warmth. And the walking, for miles, adrift in the city, just to be free of lines and restive, crowded lobbies. And the anonymity and confusion and fear that for six years thrust her into a world that is all but invisible to those who are just now waking up, on this drab weekend morning, to the music of their clock radios and their automatic coffee makers.

Amanda knows that she will never again belong completely to the busy flow of the visible city. How could anyone in that world understand her love for a man like Thomas, her joy in the darkest recesses of a vacant building? How could she ever account intelligibly for her return to the filthiest and most obscure streets of the city, in search of the mother whom she had been seeking since childhood? She knows with certainty that a part of her will remain forever bound to the society of those who are lost and who, in their own need and loneliness, reach out to comfort one another. Among them Amanda began, for the first time, to understand what it is to be loved.

Now the thought of the dollhouse comes back to her. She tries to be reasonable with herself. For one thing, the dollhouse is crudely built, an amateur job of painted plywood and pressboard slapped together with tacks and Elmer's glue. It is in serious need of repair. The wallpaper has begun to pull away from the walls in many rooms, the staircases are all but detached, and the roof is only very tentatively held in place. The exterior will require several new coats of paint. The furniture she will want to buy or build for it, the china and glass accessories, the lamps, quilts, and reading chairs, could easily consume a lifetime of days off, and money she doesn't have.

But the biggest hurdle is space. She'll need to have a more or less permanent place for the dollhouse. In the small room, with its single window, that she has only very recently begun to call home, she's taped a few pieces of calendar art to the wall, mostly pictures of kittens. Also the MBTA bus schedule and a postcard that one of her co-workers sent her from a holiday in North Carolina. She's picked up a few odd dishes and several used paperbacks.

Now she can see the new Goodwill store ahead. It is a two-winged, contemporary brick office and retail complex on the edge of the ghetto, built on land set aside by the city's redevelopment authority twenty years ago for an industrial office park that never fully materialized. Morgan Memorial is the newest enterprise in that stymied urban revitalization scheme. Earlier, the Digital Equipment Corporation set up a small satellite operation in the depressed, high-crime area.

The bus draws up to the curb and stops to let her off. She is hungry this morning and glad to be going indoors. Just months ago she didn't have this option. She breathes in the cold air. She's made up her mind. She will pay whatever she must to make the dollhouse hers.

AT THREE A.M. only withered leaves resound in the concrete cavern. Rats swim in under the loosened lids of engorged dumpsters and emerge below, scenting human feces down the way. It isn't moonlight that shines here, between the back of the public library and a block of restaurants and liquor stores that front Huntington Avenue. It is the searchlights of a high-priced parking lot where Jaguars and Mercedes bed during the day.

It's been a bad winter, brutally cold. Directly across the street from the lot, on the library's heating grates, all that remains of those who usually huddle here is a pile of abandoned blankets and a litter of empty bottles. Most everyone fled shortly after midnight, driven out by the bone-numbing cold. Only one bundled mass of rough gray army blanket remains slightly fuller than the rest. The sole of a sneaker suggests itself inside the woolen womb. At the other end, matted white hair grows in against peroxide. And only those who know Wendy's habits would think to check on such a bitter night, to see whether she is crazy enough to have stayed outside.

Roused, she talks quietly for a while, glad for the company. From time to time she glances down the street, but the face she wants to see doesn't appear there. She pulls blackened hands out of the sleeves of her plaid wool jacket and warms them over the current of hot air, her face a study in the claims of the streets, knife wounds and razor scars. When she grins, it is without benefit of front teeth. She is thirty-two years old.

She's out here, she explains, because she wanted to be with Kurt. But he got so cold that he finally headed for the all-night men's shelter, leaving her alone on the grates. He took the rest of the vodka, too. Her vodka. And the black knit cap some nice woman had taken off her own head and given to Wendy the day before. He'd ripped her off.

"And he tells me that he loves me." She laughs disdainfully. Her voice lifts into a mocking falsetto. " 'Let's go in. It's a wee bit cold. I don't feel comfortable.' I hate whiners. Especially after all these years I've been out here. Through all the shit, you know?"

She fumbles among the orphaned bottles. Now that she's awake, her hands have begun to tremble. If she doesn't find a few drops, she'll be in trouble long before eight A.M., post time at Danny's Liquors.

"You get the inners," she explains about the shakes, "before you get the outers. And then you get the heebie-jeebies." She pauses, as if intending to say more. But suddenly she is crying, silent tears that run down her cheeks and into her open palms.

"I'm so afraid," she whispers.

Once more she checks the entrance to the alley. Then she starts to sob without restraint. Her broken cries make a weird circuit down around the cavern and back. They stop her. She drops her hands back into her lap and searches them.

"I'm losing my soul," she says softly.

Now it is almost seven-thirty, and she's been up to the Auditorium trolley station, where Kurt said he'd meet her. When she didn't find him there, she walked the seven blocks back to the library at Copley Square. Some of the other guys have come back already, but not him.

She did end up at City Hospital last night, but only for an hour or so. She guesses it was around four when the all-night outreach van finally came by the library. Only the fact that the heat blowers had gone off convinced her to let them take her to the hospital's emergency intake shelter. At intake she spent an hour sitting on a metal folding chair. She refused a bed when they offered one. She refused to stay for breakfast.

At five o'clock she pushed her way back across the bags and tied bundles stowed by the hospital door, setting out in the subfreezing morning to find Kurt. Her feet were raw and sockless in an ill-fitting pair of second-hand sneakers. She's had nothing in her stomach for the past twenty hours except a liter of vodka.

Almost two and a half hours later, she's ready to give up, put her hand out to passing pedestrians, and start earning the day's keep.

ONE

Home

ONE

Dollhouse Dreams

THE DOLLHOUSE was the most beautiful object in Amanda's childhood home. Secured high on a sideboard in the large kitchen, out of reach of the clumsy, eager fingers of little girls, the dollhouse was a museum of homely comforts, with its matching miniature armchairs, quilted bedspreads, postage-stamp-sized petit point rugs, and dwarf Limoges tea cups and saucers. The many-roomed dream house held her captivated for hours.

Amanda had always been admonished to look but never touch. This treasure was Mother's own, one to which *her* mother had devoted years of pin money, pinched from the pension check. With wonder, Amanda scrutinized rooms so perfectly papered and furnished, so warm with the purpose once lavished on them, that it seemed sometimes to her child's mind as if the life that went on in those rooms was more real than what passed for life below, in the prosy world of sneaker laces and homework.

Lost to the cold and silent kitchen around her, she waited for something that never happened in those tiny rooms — she didn't know what, only that it would be something of great moment. At length her attention would lapse, and as she turned away, she would imagine herself a dwarf, carefully retreating on tiptoe through the silent house so as not to disturb her mother.

The house was always so quiet. Her uncommunicative mother kept to herself in the cellar, despite Amanda's efforts to draw her out. She tried to do nothing that would make her mother angry, to be as unobtrusive as possible. For she loved her mother, despite her moods, and hated to be separated from her.

The only time her mother, Renata, emerged from her obscure melancholy was when she spoke of earlier days, when she had had every reason to believe that she would live the life of an artist. Then her dark eyes would gleam, and her restored laughter would infuse the kitchen with sunlight.

That was the one sad thing about the dollhouse, Amanda would reflect. For all its diverse rooms, no place had ever been made in it for canvases, paint brushes, or an easel.

In the days just after the war, the young bohemians at the Boston Museum School were mostly female, girls in black leotards and long straight hair and cigarette holders, bringing Beat to an institution long the stronghold of Brahmins, a finishing school for aristocrats. The new generation of students lounged outside the studios, smoking. They listened to jazz. They flirted with the few remaining male professors who hadn't gone off to war. And they did all of this boldly, sweeping their hair out of their eyes and lying recklessly about their ages.

The Museum School was riding high on the crest of the boldest wave in painting ever to have washed into the provinces north of Manhattan. The movement was led by the painter Karl Zerbe, a recent Jewish refugee of the German Expressionist school who had come to the Museum School determined to awaken America to the vision of his German colleagues Max Beckmann and Oskar Kokoschka. Zerbe and his protegés, young artists like Hyman Bloom and Jack Levine, were creating such a stir in Boston's claustrophobic art world that they were soon regarded as a new American school of painting, the Boston school.

These were heady days, when country girls could meet sleek, detached city girls from Brookline and Hyde Park, who seemed to know all the ropes even if, in fact, they didn't. Together they drew from live models. They made lithographs, studied the market for design jobs, and were cautiously naughty, knowing full well, most of them, that one day some man would walk them into marriage and propriety. Most of them.

One of the city girls stood out. She was tall, slender, and remote. Her deep, intelligent eyes and her somewhat gaunt features conveyed a savoir faire that was almost too Olympian. Renata Stevens kept others at bay. She disdained anything off-the-rack — clothes, phrases, concepts, personality. In every instance she designed her own. Renata refused to make do. She rarely laughed, and she never engaged in girl talk. She sketched and painted, and she read voluminously.

"She was very, very intellectual," one of her classmates remembers. "And very cool. All of these long words, multisyllable things. I could never talk to her because I couldn't understand what she said most of the time."

Renata was a stranger among friends, in a crowd of rebellious and spirited girls. She was accepted because she was interesting in her intensity and because, after all, they were artists and eccentrics all, in their dreams.

Born in 1922, Renata Stevens was an only child. Her father had died of tuberculosis when she was three, leaving her self-sufficient mother to raise her on the outskirts of Boston. Not even her daughters know for certain what Renata's childhood was like. Later, contemporaries speculated that she had suffered profoundly from isolation and overprotection. They guessed that she hadn't had much to do with children her own age, and perhaps hadn't been comfortable with them when she did, since her interactive skills were weak. She never developed an ego strong enough to cope with challenges when they came her way. Smothered, perhaps, by the hopes and ambitions of her mother and the spinster aunt who helped raise her, she may have compensated for her social weaknesses early in adolescence by erecting an almost impenetrable façade of intellectualism.

One early incident suggests something of Renata's budding intensity, which manifested in an almost suicidal willfulness. Her mother had sent her off to a boarding school in rural Maine. As family lore has it, Renata became upset about some shortcoming in school life and walked out. A solitary twenty-mile trek through snowy wilderness in the dead of winter brought her to a relative's home over the border in New Hampshire. Almost miraculously, she arrived unharmed. Renata had made her point.

In 1945 Renata arrived at the School of the Museum of Fine Arts to study illustration, determined that her life would never be pedestrian. When she wasn't painting or bent over her delicate, studied drawings or her original, blousy shirt patterns, she was buried in books. Occasionally she dated Jack Daley.

Jack was one of the new breed showing up in increasing numbers at the school, drawn by Zerbe and the foment his ideas had produced up and down the East Coast. Like the other returning war vets who were "sieging the citadel," as one of them liked to put it, Jack was there on the GI Bill. He had done his stint in the Pacific.

Jack had a calculating, cocky personality, arrogant in an off-handed, attractive way that seemed to fit his Black Irish good looks, dark hair, and somewhat wary blue eyes. Resettled into civilian life and quickly comfortable in his new, unstructured habitat, Jack assumed the role of the thinker among his buddies, who spent endless hours engaged in tavern badinage. At the end of these sessions, it was always Jack who deployed the evening's best, and typically final, line. He believed he could bluff his way through anything he set his mind to. And he usually had the talent to pull it off.

Jack's chief liability was an underlying sense of inferiority, a result, perhaps, of his small physical stature (he wasn't five foot five) and of his childhood years under the thumb of a domineering father. These handicaps had produced a cockfighter, quicker to challenge than to negotiate, a man who often preferred the bravura of his own day-dreams to the sober duties of the everyday.

As a painter, Jack Daley had promise. Among the competitive group of young artists striving for recognition by Zerbe and the galleries, he was one of a handful of advanced students allowed to conduct studios for the newcomers. Graduates of the school had two options: to try to support themselves by their art alone or to teach. Student assistants received good training for the latter career, as did those who took courses in engineering at nearby Tufts University. Like many of the male students just out of the service, Jack enrolled there so that he could teach high school drafting. Going into his third year, he set his sights on winning a coveted traveling fellowship that would finish off his education with a year of painting in Europe.

When he announced one day in the midst of these activities that he was planning to marry Renata Stevens, his friends laughed. At least Jack hadn't lost his sense of humor — this was the funniest thing they'd heard in weeks.

No one thought of marrying Renata. "She was harsh and sarcastic and witty, and cutting and sophisticated and very intimidating," one friend recalls.

But Jack apparently saw in Renata's cool what he thought he needed. And she, perhaps, needed what she took to be his self-assurance. Looking back years later, the same group of friends would see in this union the tragic attraction of two dreamers, people completely unequipped to deal with their own frailties, much less with life. Said one, "Something, somewhere along the line in both their lives, wrapped them up so tight into themselves, you kind of wonder, when they got together and got married, was this their first and only act of giving?"

They were married on Valentine's Day, 1948, and with two other couples set up a communal household in a dilapidated three-story house near the Museum School. The couples divided the single-family dwelling into three two-room units, one on each floor. There was only one bath, and hot plates and toasters served as the cooking facilities. When plugging in an iron or turning on a lamp, it was essential to yell a warning, over the music, to the other floors. Fuses blew often.

Renata and Jack occupied the middle floor. While Jack put in arduous days in his studio, Renata, who'd finished her academic program, worked on commissions for book illustrations at the drafting table that took up a corner of the front room. But the squalling babies downstairs broke her concentration. Their mother, married to another museum student, seemed to have forgotten that there was more to life than sun suits and baby talk, and Renata spent less and less time socializing with her housemates.

Soon her friend on the top floor announced that she too was going to have a baby. Renata viewed the developing pregnancy with detachment. Her friend carried to term, but the child died hours after birth. The couple returned home from the hospital empty-handed and shattered by the loss. Jack and Renata were sitting on the front steps when they arrived.

Renata trained a cold, level eye on the woman. "Oh," she said, "home so soon?"

In the evenings, when Jack was home, Renata was happier. She could engage in serious art talk with the men and relax with a beer. She still looked forward to a year in Europe if Jack won the scholarship, and beyond, to a bohemian, peripatetic existence in some of the more interesting ports of the world.

"Renata is an artist," one of the men in the house once observed during those social evenings. "She's kind of a bluestocking. She has some aspirations for gentility. You look at Renata, you're looking at Virginia Woolf."

The nights were often late ones, dominated by poker, Cole Porter, and gin. The combination caused its share of problems. One of the other wives remembers once being pressed into joining the fray. "I don't gamble at all. And I didn't drink at all. There I was, odd one out, and they wanted me in on it. I didn't know anything. There I am with all these cards in my hand. I didn't care. I couldn't take it seriously. I didn't want to be there. The game progressed. I went around, paying half attention, and I let it pass. It went around again. I passed. Well, it ended up I was holding such a beautiful hand and the pot was getting bigger and — Jack's reaction! I never saw him get so angry! I just cringed. 'Are you for real?' I asked. It was only a game, you know? As time went on, I realized that he was serious about gambling."

He was more serious about art, however, and his quirks were usually forgiven. That spring he won the traveling fellowship. The future that had drawn the couple together, and in which they had invested all their energies, was at last within reach.

But Jack was never to use the fellowship. For one thing, the painting department lacked the cash to fund it that year. For another, Renata was pregnant.

Unplanned for and resented, Renata and Jack's first daughter, Jane, was born in early December, 1948. Thanks to Jack's father, Renata had the best hospital care money could buy. Afterward the couple responded to the disappointment of their altered status by proceeding, as much as possible, as though it hadn't happened. Travel abroad might have been out of the question, but the artist's life was not. The Daleys stayed in their sparsely furnished two-room flat, and Renata resumed her life there, making as few adjustments as possible.

If Renata had previously proved to be a domestic disappointment, now she courted outright disaster. With typical distraction, she believed an advertising pitch that Tide detergent was running at the time, claiming that no rinsing was required with the cleanser. Renata proceeded to simply wash her baby's diapers without rinsing them and, as soon as they had hardened on the indoor clothesline, put them back on her. The child developed a severe diaper rash and was rescued only when one of the two other women in the building, hearing her incessant cries, came into the flat and discovered the source of her pain.

Within two years Renata was pregnant again. All three of the men found themselves at the same juncture at this time: responsibilities began bearing down; they had to get jobs. The other two started lining up interviews for teaching positions. But Jack, faced with the challenge, was paralyzed, much to his friends' surprise.

"Jack was brilliant. Great wit," one of these men said years later. "But he and I went for a job interview at a teachers' employment agency, and I saw that man in absolute fear. His lip was trembling. He was white. He was unable to answer, except monosyllabically. He came apart." His friend was astonished at an insecurity so successfully masked all those years. The other two men got teaching jobs. Jack was unemployed.

Jack's crisis of confidence wasn't surprising, considering the accomplishments of his father and siblings. His father, a self-made man, was a well-known contractor for large corporate projects throughout Boston's South Shore. Jack's older brother had gone to Annapolis. Jack was immensely proud of him; he was always trying to fill his brother's shoes, but in his own eyes never quite succeeded. His other brother became a prominent scientist, and his sister a dean at a major university. Then there was Jack, the artist.

Now he had a wife and a second child on the way and no means of supporting them. At this point Jack's mother, a force in her own right, intervened. Grandmother Daley insisted that the city was no place to raise children and that Jack must move his family to the suburbs.

"He wanted to be a teacher," Amanda says, years later. "But her word was law. My Grandmother Daley did not have a tendency to keep her nose out of her kids' business. And, like a pair of fatheads, my parents did what she told them to. Looking back at it, I think they should have had a lot more spunk and just done what they wanted to do." Instead, Jack allowed his father to use his construction contacts to get him a job with the state as a road construction surveyor.

Amanda Daley was born at 6:42 P.M. late in July of 1951 at Boston Lying-In Hospital. Where her sister's "nursery" had been a corner of a room dominated by her mother's drawing table, Amanda came home to a tidy, tiny red ranch house on an eighth of an acre of land in a subdivision miles from anything except more of the same.

This was the Betty Crocker version of the American dream, in which artistic aspirations were viewed as mere hobbies, to be indulged only when the housework was done. Renata was so overwhelmed by the normalcy of it all that she began to shut out what she couldn't deal with. Isolated in alien surroundings, she spent most of her time working at her drawing table in the cellar, struggling to maintain her inner life.

The nursery was cheerful enough, done up in pastels and ginghams. But the parents' interest in their second child soon paled. On

Amanda's first visit to the pediatrician, the doctor informed Renata and Jack that she should be put in a body cast to counteract a potentially serious spinal deformity that could stunt her growth. Renata and Jack joked about this in the presence of friends, defending their shaken illusions of superiority by making their daughter the butt of their black humor. More serious still, they refused to heed the doctor's advice. Though Amanda escaped any severe handicap, her lack of physical coordination plagued her childhood, and her slight body never fully developed.

Poor judgment degenerated into cruel neglect. When a friend dropped in some months later, she discovered the baby lying unclothed in the crib on sheets of old newspaper. Almost a year later, at an afternoon reunion of the three women who had shared the Boston house, Amanda remained slumped near Renata's feet while the other children played. As the group was breaking up, one of the mothers saw Renata pick Amanda up. The little girl's legs remained completely immobile, tensed in the same semi-seated posture, and her face was oddly wrinkled, as if she regularly stayed for hours in the same position, her cheek pressed against the mattress of her crib. Clearly, Amanda was not often touched or attended to. She didn't know the first thing about play.

At this point Renata's mother stepped in, either because she was still trying to protect Renata from the ravages of life or because she was becoming aware of her daughter's shortcomings as a parent. Whenever Jack was away on business, which was increasingly often, Renata would stay at Nanna's house with the two children. Amanda's memories of these times, and of being cared for by her grandmother, are happy ones. The drafty old house was charming, and it contained, in those very early years, the chief attraction in Amanda's life: the wonderful dollhouse. Under Nanna's supervision, the two girls could play with it freely without fear of straining Renata's nerves.

Nanna set up a trundle bed for the sisters in her back room. If Amanda woke up first, she'd go straight to the dollhouse. At the sound of her footsteps Nanna would get up and prepare breakfast while Amanda played among the pretty miniature things.

If Jane was awake, they would play quietly together. But when, inevitably, they forgot to whisper, the results were predictable. "All I can remember is having my mother absolutely furious, yelling," Amanda says.

On such occasions Nanna would snatch up the girls and tell Renata to go back to bed. Then she would get the children dressed and take them into town, stopping at the library or running a few errands, so that by the time they returned, Renata would be up, having had some quiet time to herself.

After three years as a company man, whatever residual hopes Jack had had about making a creative mark on the world had gone into the neat little Cape Cod house he built one town away from their ranch. He drew the blueprints and acted as his own contractor, ordering all the windows, lumber, and supplies. "He knew how many sticks were going to have to go into that house," a friend said. "And what was ordered was used. There was nothing left over." Much of the work he did with his own hands, on weekends and evenings. He built the chimney alone, brick by brick. Though the house remained far from complete inside when the family moved in, Jack was rightly proud of his accomplishment.

The Daleys' new home, set behind pines on a wooded lot at the edge of Sharon, typified what was happening in the town in the mid-fifties. Until then Sharon had been an established New England village, where residents who weren't natives still felt like newcomers thirty years after they'd arrived. But now it was being transformed into a bedroom community by families like the Daleys, people with jobs in nearby Plymouth or Brockton, or as far away as Boston. Many of them were war vets, with high school educations and young families, who had grown up in the city and had put together just enough money to buy a house outside of it. They wanted the fresh air, clean streets, and good schools of the suburbs at an affordable price.

Sharon was special. Broad, acre-zoned properties and well-situated shingled Capes backed up to woodland and brooks. The town's center consisted of little more than a Congregational church and a petrol pump; beyond were stables. A white-trimmed grammar school sprawled comfortably on several acres of country land, surrounded by baseball diamonds and playing fields. In the late fifties, in response to the influx of newcomers, a high school was built; about sixty percent of its graduates went on to college.

"There are poor people who live here," allows one terse old-timer. "And there are some wealthy people. But it's not a poor or a wealthy community. It's middling, you know?"

Amanda first saw the two-story white Cape from the back seat of Grandfather Daley's dark green Chrysler. Its proportions pleased her. She would have her own room. Best of all, Nanna's dollhouse was coming with them.

When they moved in, Jane entered school. Amanda spent her days alone, wandering through the new house. Playmates were hard to come by, with just a few scattered houses within a mile or so, but Amanda knew nothing of playmates in any case and amused herself by playing alone in the dirt pile out back. Here too Renata spent most of her time in the cellar. When Amanda was certain that this was where she was, she grew confident enough to approach the fabulous dollhouse.

It was set up on the sideboard in the kitchen — the one finished room — with strict instructions from Renata not to touch. Fantasizing about the dollhouse was Amanda's chief comfort. She liked to imagine that a visitor would come through one of the doors and keep her company. Or that one day in the miniature kitchen cookies would be baking as good as those that Nanna made. In the dollhouse there would be no unhappiness and no departures. The undefined tension that she felt everywhere in her real house would be resolved. For Amanda, those hours full of fantasy were the happy times.

"And then," she adds, "there was also the shit I had to put up with."

For Jack, the house did not prove a lasting recompense for all that he had thrown away. He spent more and more time on the road. When he was gone, Amanda bore the brunt of Renata's frustration and resentment, and her violent mood swings kept the little girl always off guard.

"I didn't know what was going to happen next," Amanda recalls. Sometimes Renata yelled at Amanda, sometimes she spanked her, and sometimes she just stayed in bed all day, incapacitated by vague ailments.

When Jack wasn't on the road, he spent much of his time down at the American Legion post. After a few hours there, he'd return home, the cockfighter prepared to spar.

One night when Amanda was nine, she was doing her homework at the kitchen table, struggling with an addition problem, when Jack came in. Capriciously drunk, he decided at that moment that he was going to teach his daughter how to add dollars and cents — a difficult concept for her, and a sensitive one for him. From the moment he began, she could make no sense of his explanation. Impatiently he wrenched her off the chair and flung her against the sideboard.

"You're stupid!" he shouted. "You can't add dollars and cents yet, and you're nine years old?"

She heard small objects rattle and crash in the dollhouse behind her before she felt the pain. Blows began falling on her shoulders, and as she collapsed on the floor, her father struck her in the stomach and thighs.

Her mother stood by, watching in silence. Amanda had no place to run to. The beating continued until Amanda almost lost consciousness and only came to an end when her father broke his hand.

Amanda wrapped her battered body around a table leg. Somewhere far away she could hear her father swearing in pain. Disoriented and terrified, she loosened herself from her fetal curl, stood on shaky legs, and urinated all over herself.

After that moment she would not be able to remember many things that were done to her during the eight years she remained in her father's house. A certain order of memory just went dead.

And Rufus Makes a Family

THE CHAFED and grass-stained rabbit had fur of blue, a cottonball tail of pink and, knotted around its neck, a crushed sateen ribbon of white. Wendy had named him Rufus.

He'd been a gift from her Papa — a small gesture, considering the great happiness she had brought to his old age. Balding and merry, and unable to have children of his own, Papa had wed the spirited Lila late in life. Now all his time belonged to the bright-eyed step-granddaughter who had invented for the two of them a secret world of Sunday afternoons. There were tomahawks to make and tea parties to attend. And, to seal the pact, there were names for just the two of them to use when no one else was around. Papa called her Tudybeak. Rufus made them three.

Outside of this charmed circle lay only a house made hollow by absence, a front door that no father would ever open.

There had been cause for fear even stateside during the war. German submarines were sinking ships off the eastern seaboard, and merchant vessels had to enter and leave Boston Harbor in the safety of convoys. Boston women of the comfortable classes "knit for Britain." They pressed tin cans for recycling, purchased groceries with war ration books, and went to work to support their families in the local war industries.

For those women who had just gotten by in peacetime, the war was especially hard. They had to make do with last year's clothes a year or two longer. They hoarded packets of Lucky Strikes, and went to bed every night with their curls safely pressed between the long thin spokes of hairpins.

Those who lived close to the navy yards in Chelsea and Charlestown had a more intimate view of the war than most Bostonians. They grew used to seeing returning veterans, shell-shocked and hard-drinking, who spent time at the nearby naval hospital, trying to forget. These men, known in naval jargon as NPs, the neuropsychiatric patients, predominated in the hospital population. Between 1937, two years before the attack on Pearl Harbor, and 1943, that population had swelled tenfold.

The streets remained full of war stories even after VJ Day. As late as 1950, victory continued to sustain some of the romance of the sea, and war-poster visions of adventure drew younger enlisted men, boys who'd missed combat by fortune of birth, to the barracks of Chelsea. William Domaine was one such young man. He hailed from southern Michigan, and upon his arrival in Charlestown, fell in love with a waitress named Molly.

Molly Jackson was the illegitimate daughter of Lila Burroughs and a barfly named Frank, who'd come together one night outside a saloon in Louisville, Kentucky, and had parted shortly afterward. Lila was a woman of will: she'd set out from home in rural Kentucky in the early 1930s to become a barmaid in the big city. As time went on, she was able to send half of her wages back home to the farm. And as more time went on, she sent back three children, all born to different men.

Molly was the second child, and the only girl. Her Appalachian childhood in the middle of the Depression quickly taught her one ironclad rule: if you didn't work, you didn't eat. Provided a parching summer sun didn't burn the young shoots before their time, a small vegetable plot and a coop full of chickens kept her grandmother's larder full. But it was a meager life, and by the age of seven Molly and her brother Bob were pulling their own weight, harvesting tobacco leaves with their hands and selling them, one by one, for a few pennies along the side of a country road.

Sitting there, often without benefit of shade, Molly would think of her mother in Louisville. It was hard to know what she meant to the barmaid who'd gone off and left her. Her illegitimacy marked her like a brand. Lila's caprice, and then her abandonment, seemed to Molly a scar that must have been obvious to everyone. She was an object of suspicion among peers and an easy mark for adults. Not to have a father meant that you were not safe in the world. People took liberties that they never would have attempted with a more protected child.

Then, when Molly was ten, Lila descended on the farm, scooped up her three offspring, and took them north with her to Charlestown. At the age of twenty-nine, she had met and planned to marry the love of her life, Papa, an Italian bachelor years older than her, who worked as a purchasing agent for the navy.

The family took a flat next door to St. Mary's convent on Monument Hill. Molly was baptized and from that point on was reared as a Catholic in the straitlaced atmosphere of the wartime town. Her life revolved around her studies. After years without books or the leisure for them, she became an avid reader and eagerly made the brief daily walk to the brick parochial school whose hillside view took in the entire sweep of Boston below.

But too soon again there was no time for books. If you didn't work, you didn't eat. Molly began to earn what she could. Following in her mother's footsteps, she became a waitress.

William was the son of a French Canadian father and a mother from the Micmac Indian tribe, which once dominated the eastern sections of Quebec, Nova Scotia, and northern Maine. Dazzled by William's dark coloring and peat-brown eyes, set off by his military whites, seventeen-year-old Molly fell in love. In the winter of 1951 their union was recorded in the Boston Registry of Marriages, sanctioned by a local minister, witnessed by a few relatives, and immortalized in a scrapbook of greeting cards and snapshots. In William, Molly placed her trust and her future. She believed that he would lead her out of her illegitimate past and keep her safe.

In less than a year she gave birth to a son. The next year another son, and the next year another. From one year to the next, the family moved from Massachusetts back to William's native Michigan, from one ill-furnished flat to another, leaving little behind except unpaid bills.

They were poor. Earning a living for the family was left to Molly; William proved too lazy to find a job. He was also abusive, and routinely cheated on his wife. When their second baby died at the age of one year, there wasn't even enough cash for a tombstone. This was to haunt Molly for years, not just because she buried a part of herself along with her baby boy, but because her marriage died then, too. She knew that she had loved disastrously. By the age of twenty-one, Molly Domaine felt like an old woman.

It may be that Molly hated her last gesture of weakness for her husband and that she transferred her bitterness to the life that was soon growing within her. Wendy was born shortly after three on a cold December morning in 1955, back in Massachusetts at the Chelsea Naval Hospital, a healthy, brown-eyed baby. For Molly the child was like a bad joke, come into the world to mock her, another female who would grow up to mirror her pain and vulnerability, who would no doubt be wounded as she had been, and who would give birth to other girls, perpetuating the curse of a life without love. Wendy was marked for grief.

The scarred family staggered back to Michigan. Then, after seven years of marriage, Molly said no more. She moved out just before Christmas and shortly afterward made her way back to Massachusetts, taking the children with her.

Five hundred miles away, back in Massachusetts, Wendy waited for her father to appear at the empty windows of their new house, to discharge the loaded, accusing silences when her mother returned from a day of burdened determination, struggling to keep her children sheltered and fed. Wendy, alert to even the slightest shift in the emotional barometer, drew in the residual poisons. She felt perpetually anxious and heavy with guilt. Soon she started to transform the events of her life into a private mythology that could give meaning to, and at least partially rationalize, a grief too primal for words.

For her half-breed father, the lost piece of her heritage, she would in later years orchestrate a brilliant "return." But now, more immediately, she needed to give her own secret name to the betrayal that linked her to her mother.

"My mother hated me from the minute I was born. She probably hated me before I was born. See this?" she asks, pointing. "My mother did this to me. Burned me with a clothes iron when I was three months old."

As Wendy tells it, this was when the force of her mother's inchoate feelings exploded in a moment of savagery. She says she remembers lying in her crib, aware of her mother ironing shirts several feet away from her, when suddenly she saw the dull hot metal coming toward her, twisting until its point was about to penetrate her rib cage. In her description of this hellish image, Wendy gives her burnt flesh the odor of dead roses. She shrieked in terror and pain as a brand formed on her chest in the shape of a crude cross, marking her forever with her mother's curse.

Molly's memory of the accident is very different. She shuts her eyes and shakes her head, remembering. "The bassinette tipped over and her chest hit the radiator," she says. "The children, in playing, had knocked it over. They were all upset."

Her grandmother's husband seemed like a savior sent to banish these nightmares of her infancy. When he wasn't working, Papa would spend all his time with the child. He read her stories and took her out in the back yard to play. The relationship was so essential to Wendy that she created for them a fantasy world as idyllic and unblemished as the other one was horrifying. It was an Eden that admitted only her, Papa, and Rufus, the rabbit — and, when necessary, little Granny.

Life at Papa and Granny's house in the small rural town near Plymouth, where Wendy lived with her mother, was well suited to her needs for an absolute love she couldn't get at home. Away from her brothers Mark and Jeff and her mother, with no competitors for the attentions of the older couple, she thrived on her frequent visits.

"They wanted to adopt me," she says now. "See, we were a family. The three of us."

To her, Molly was the woman who always came home exhausted at the end of a thankless day of waiting on tables, disappointed every night when she finished counting her meager tips at the kitchen table.

"I wasn't around much — I couldn't be — I had to support them," Molly recalls. "Only once in my whole life did I accept welfare, and that was the first Christmas I was alone with the children, in Michigan. But my mother was always with them. I never never left them alone by themselves. Wendy was too young to understand then. But later I tried to explain, many times, why I couldn't be a cuddly mother to her. By the time I got home, I was so exhausted. And there was dinner to cook. So many demands."

Who would love her?

Papa loved her.

Papa taught Tudybeak the alphabet, and one day he showed her how to read and write her own name. Joyously she carved the magical letters into the tops of Granny's new living room end tables with a screwdriver. Papa, the indirect author of the spree, rescued Wendy from Granny's wrath. She wasn't even spanked.

"Sometimes I wonder," her mother says, looking back, "if she wasn't too spoiled. Every bump and scrape was fussed over. Maybe that established a pattern. I've wondered that many times, believe me."

Papa was to teach her something else that she wouldn't comprehend for many years. He told her that the one enduring law of nature was the law of repetition. What goes around, comes around. As Papa explained it to her, it meant that everything that happened in life would eventually come back again, good and bad alike. And he tried to persuade her that for every bad thing that happened, something good would always follow.

"I was his pride and joy," Wendy affirms. "I could do no wrong in his eyes. If you'd known him, you'd have thought he was my natural grandfather, not in looks, but by his actions."

But the idyll was to end.

"I was raped," Wendy says, "when I was five."

The man she accuses was her mother's new husband, Henry Fayre.

Stories of early sexual abuse riddle the family history. Wendy's Uncle Bob, now an old man, still claims with rage in his voice that he was a victim of his stepfather, Papa. "I was abused by that man mentally, physically, and sexually until I left home."

Molly would admit years later to her daughter that *she* was raped at the age of sixteen by *her* grandfather.

Corroboration doesn't come easily. The relentless patterns of violation in Wendy's family are revealed only in subtle changes of tone used for certain stories, the nervous drift of eyes, the unfinished sentences. Was it Papa who sexually assaulted Molly, as he did her brother Bob? Did Papa make inappropriate advances on the young Wendy? Or was it, as Wendy claims, her new stepfather?

There are no conclusive answers. But, given the devastating consequences and the almost textbook pattern of self-destruction that was to trace itself out in Wendy's life, there is reason to believe that a rape did occur. It was real enough for Wendy.

Henry Fayre, born outside of Hattiesburg, Mississippi, had never known anything but squalid poverty. Growing up in a hard-scrabble state in the midst of the Depression, the son of a chronic and severe alcoholic, he'd kept himself alive as best he could, living on raw fish caught in nearby streams when he had to. There was no time in this

family for much demonstration of affection. Until he was a grown
man he never owned a new pair of pants. Every toy and Christmas
present he ever received came from the Salvation Army.

Henry Fayre is one of those men who on first glimpse seems to have
been hardened into virtue. He is slow to speak and humble. His face
is prematurely creased, and his large head always slightly bowed. He
is a gentle man. He seemed, to Molly, to be a mender of hearts.

When Molly met him in 1960 on a blind date, he was working as an
electrician and contributing fifteen percent of every weekly paycheck
to the Salvation Army, a habit he would continue through his entire
working life. On weekends, for relaxation, he fished. Several years
Molly's junior, Henry had never married. But as the pair spent more
and more time together, Henry knew that he wanted to keep Molly
safe, help her raise her children, and have one of his own with her.

According to Molly, Henry proved true to his word in the course
of a marriage that has lasted nearly thirty years. As a husband and
father, he loved to give gifts. As if making up for all the years of a
boyhood without sentiment, he is partial to inspirational greeting cards
and soft-focused photographs of seascapes with stirring poetry super-
imposed on them. When times were hard, Molly says, Henry was there.
He thought nothing of putting cardboard in his shoes rather than let
Molly's children go wanting.

Before Henry Fayre came along, the traumatic burn, combined with
the powerful fantasy world in which Wendy had enclosed herself with
Papa and Rufus, seems to have made her forget any time she spent
with her mother. Her account of being raped marks the transition in
her life occasioned by Molly's remarriage. In later years she would
add to this, almost as a parable, the story she remembers of a custody
dispute over her between Lila and Papa and her mother and Henry.

"I remember, in the courtroom. I had to go in with my grandfather.
We go into the judge's chambers. There's my mother with her new
husband, whom I did not know at all. And the judge's ruling [to her
mother, referring to the burn trauma] — 'Well, you seem to have made
a clean breast of things and gotten your head together.'

"They're pulling me away from my grandfather. I'm screaming.
And there's my poor grandfather, crying. My grandmother's crying.
I'm crying. And my mother is literally dragging me. I'll never forget
what my Papa said. He looked at the judge and he said, 'You know,
you've just made the worst mistake of your life. You've just destroyed
this little girl's life.' "

And so Wendy went home with her mother and, in her own mind, her terrorizer.

Tears coursed down the face in the bathroom mirror.

"Ugly!" She glared at it. "You're ugly! Why are you so ugly?"

This was what her mother told her, and Wendy believed her. She knew it was true — ever since the day she'd been forced to do things that made her afraid to remember. That was when she was five. After that she had become ugly. Now she was six, and it seemed as if her mother had forgotten her name. She was so lonely.

The streaming eyes stared at their own image. "I hate you!"

The bathtub was almost full. She got in and lay down on the bottom. She let out her breath. But she could not die.

Instead, Wendy became a model daughter. When she returned home from elementary school at the end of the day, she looked after her new baby stepbrother and cleaned up after the older boys. The events of the preceding year had left her a quiet and undemanding child, eager to please and instantly responsive to the needs of others. A perfect little girl.

When she was nine, Wendy Domaine's family moved to within two miles of Amanda Daley's. The two girls grew up less than four streets apart, separated by a mere town line: a two-lane road that converged on the shopping mall, where both girls spent countless hours window gazing. They ate at the same fast-food restaurants, bought groceries at the same food store, and no doubt walked the same country roads. Yet the two never met. Until they both ended up on the streets of Boston, they would have seemed, to most casual observers, just two suburban girls, no different from the rest.

The new town of Easton was somewhat stigmatized as the poor cousin of its closest neighbors. Not far away the teen-aged sons of South Shore families drove their parents' Mercedes to school every morning and didn't give a thought to part-time jobs. By contrast, everyone in Easton worked. Easton was a shoe factory town that had at one time supplied wares and domestic help for those better-heeled neighbors. By the mid-1960s, only a few of the factories remained; here and there on country roads, structures resembling large chicken coops, white-washed and many-windowed, still employed a small number of town residents.

But if most of the factories had long since moved south, little else in Easton had changed. The town still had a single aging shopping

center and a Main Street dotted with family restaurants operated by
the same couples who'd opened them thirty years earlier.

As soon as they were old enough, teenagers in Easton got after-
school jobs to augment their parents' incomes. Most of the men were
blue-collar tradesmen; their wives, unskilled laborers who kept alive
the spectral leather and textile factories. A few military families, personnel for the naval air station not far away, more or less completed
the population.

If Wendy had had a mind to, she could have grown up with a chip
on her shoulder, for the outside world always seemed to look down
on the citizens of Easton. She could have felt cheated, not only out
of the Mercedes and the easy affluence of her neighbors, but also
out of the myriad extracurricular opportunities available in nearby
towns where committed teachers and mothers who didn't work outside the home channeled youthful creativity into useful civic projects.

Occasionally the problems of Easton's unsupervised young people — random vandalism and gang activities — got serious enough to
warrant a brief visit from the state police. To the generation of youngsters growing up with Wendy, Easton seemed to be a town on the way
down. A good percentage of them would, like their parents, become
nurses, carpenters, and law enforcement officers, but they would move
away and never come back.

Nine-year-old Wendy's new home was a ramshackle two-family house
with an iron stovepipe jutting out of the tarpapered roof. Several small,
multilevel additions had been tacked onto the rear. Out in the back
yard a small wooden shack listed, and out front the window trim bore
several different shades of paint. It was easily the most irregular house
on a street that lacked sidewalks, where the houses, though separated
by fir trees and telephone poles, were still close enough that the
neighbors kept the blinds drawn on either side. Even here, where
respectability was the norm and tidy front lawns were trimmed with
lilies of the valley and forsythia bushes, Molly and Henry's children
would be a little bit different.

Wendy's bedroom looked out across a sea of white tombstones, the
town cemetery. She observed the move to the new house by quietly
locking herself in the bathroom one afternoon. She took out Henry's
razor and, facing out the window, imagined that she was slitting her
wrists.

THREE

▨▨▨▨▨▨▨▨▨▨

Magdalens and Madonnas

JANE ENGLISH was born to a place bleached by brine, where crying gulls stitched back and forth between the close-moored, essential boats, a place bound to civilization, it sometimes seemed, by nothing more than fishing nets and rum.

Approaching by sea, English captains recorded a beauty of inlets and spires and gentle hills under skies not unlike those of Dover and Bristol. And they wrote of a populace that was at once guarded and endowed.

By 1775 sixteen thousand sailors, fishermen, and artisans had made Boston the British empire's fourth largest town and one of its most prosperous. Daily its wharves were thronged with merchants meeting shipments of tea or West Indian sugar cane. The raw material that didn't go to one of Boston's numerous distilleries to be made into rum was disbursed by middlemen and clerks who handled its distribution, auction, and finally sale, to shops like the one run by Elizabeth Perkins on King Street, which also dealt in dishes and glassware, anchovies, Cheshire cheese, rum, brandy, wine, velvet, corks, walnuts, and garden seeds.[1]

The Revolution changed little in Boston proper. It wrought no physical damage. George III's troops moved out to battles in the towns just weeks after the conflict began. When the Declaration of Independence was read in 1776 from the balcony of the State House, it was to a restored populace whose children remained anchored — physically, economically, and politically — to the port.

Boston remained a warren of lanes that ran like erratic rivulets uphill from the docks. The city covered about one square mile and supported, besides its homes, nineteen churches and a handful of public buildings: a jail, a courthouse, a workhouse, an almshouse, and the State House. Government was efficient and lean. Nine selectmen and a handful of fire wardens and constables kept the peace. Twelve overseers of the poor administered the city's largest budget item, poor relief.

Despite the colony's contribution of a disproportionate number of early political leaders to the cause of nationhood, government never even remotely competed with commerce as a favored occupation for Bostonians. The same captains who had recognized the city's natural beauty accurately read in its human grain the most homogeneous and politically conservative populace in America. By the time the war finally ended in 1783, Paul Revere had long since returned to his smithy and John Hancock to his office by the docks, and the city's merchants — many of them former Loyalists and members of the pro-British elite — were more concerned about the effects of independence upon business than about the Bill of Rights.

With no natural resources of its own to export, Boston relied exclusively on the skill of its merchants and shippers to secure Boston as the entrepôt of the shipping trade. Until 1773, the year of the Boston Tea Party, the city served as the control point of a lucrative trade between Africa and the West Indies, shipping slaves in one direction and rum in the other, in exchange for British tea and favorable trade agreements. Many shippers amply fortified their open-market income with smuggling. After the war, punitive British tariffs and the abolition of slavery in British possessions destroyed the city's principal economic activity. On the now quiet wharves the merchants were forced to find, or create, new markets in order to survive. Just a few feet behind them, the town's local economy, supported by grocers, butchers, tailors, cobblers, carpenters, and seamstresses, suffered a brief recession in response to these pressures. But Boston's tradesmen were stable enough to withstand the secondary economic shocks with surprisingly few losses.

Matthew Parke, one of these merchants, had fought in the Revolution as a captain lieutenant of the marines in naval service on the frigate *Alliance*. In 1781 he married Judith Cooper, the daughter of Boston's Baptist minister, and settled down to live as a grocer. A son, William Cooper Parke, was born the following August. The next month Judith died.

No records describe the arc of Parke's life over the course of the next fifteen years. His name disappears from the city directories. He may have returned to sea or resettled temporarily or left the boy with another family. But at some point his wandering ended. On December 8, 1796, he and Jane English were married by the Reverend Samuel Stillman at Boston's First Baptist Church, on what is now Stillman Street in Boston's North End. Second marriages were not uncommon. The female mortality rate in colonial New England was so high that many men married twice, among them Paul Revere and Nathaniel Hawthorne. Jane became stepmother to Parke's fifteen-year-old boy and moved to 2 Fleet Street, close to her husband's grocery on the north side of the town dock.

Jane's life, as the wife of a man who owned a home separate from his business, was probably typical of the lives of middle-class women of her day. Mornings most likely were spent feeding the chickens, tending her small garden, and straightening the open-hearth kitchen and parlor of her four-room home. Women up and down the street were doing the same, while vendors passed by with horse-drawn carts of vegetables and fish. Residential, commercial, and social spaces in the North End of Parke's day were so tightly interwoven, they were often indistinguishable. Many merchants lived above or behind their shops, and the rest, like Parke, lived close enough to their workplaces that they could return home for lunch every day.

Class distinctions were few. Even the wealthiest residents, who had taken over the mansions, walled gardens, and orchards of the former colonial governors and commanders — merchants like Barnard, Haward, and, soon, Revere himself — lived just around the corner, down Moon Street on North Square. Unpainted wood-frame homes with thatched roofs served almost everyone. Only leaded casement windows and additional stories set the well-to-do apart from the poorer families in the community.

Poverty was viewed as a temporary condition, a result of hard times. Poor relief was straightforward. Those in need received assistance at home — fuel, food, and money — paid for out of the poor tax levied separately from other taxes on every Boston household. The few homeless, and those too desperate to sustain themselves at home, stayed at the almshouse.

The only private "resource" for the poor in Parke's day came in the form of cooperative aid societies. They were small, members-only organizations, usually based on ethnic ties. Ten such cooperatives existed in Boston in 1800. Unlike the almshouse, and "outdoor relief," which was distributed to those poor who weren't sent to the almshouse (both of these adapted from English institutions), cooperatives offered a radically different approach to neighbors in need.

"Sensible that such is the uncertainty of human affairs that it is no uncommon sight to observe those persons who once lived comfortably greatly reduced, which may as well happen to us as them — for this reason, we have formed ourselves into a Society for the relief and assistance of each other under like circumstances." Thus the preamble to the Massachusetts Charitable Society's constitution, composed in 1762, stated the cooperatives' first principle.[2]

Members of cooperative societies contributed monthly to a fund, the interest from which was distributed to those in need, usually in the form of loans to be repaid as soon as possible. Cooperatives transformed charity from "the gift of the rich to the poor" to something more mutual and interdependent; in the words of one social historian, "a happy sharing of small resources."[3]

Cooperatives also performed a self-policing role among their members. "No prophane or dissolute person or openly scandalous shall have any portion herein or be a member of the society," declared the founders of Scots Charitable Trust.[4] The dissolute might count on the indiscriminate, soulless benevolence of the public dole, but not on the cooperatives, whose "happy sharing" wasn't wasted on those who wouldn't reciprocate. Most of the recipients of cooperative aid, the records show, were unmarried women or widows.

After her morning chores, Jane Parke would stroll up to the city's major commercial street, King Street (now State Street), and mingle there with other women, catching the conversation and gossip of men, side-stepping oyster sellers seated on stools in the narrow streets, buying herbs, posting letters, and attempting to avoid the carts that moved through the lanes at breakneck speed.

Jane could not vote, of course. She had no independent legal status. And, except for the few spinster schoolteachers and widows of her acquaintance, none of her women friends had any more of a public life than she did. Outside her domestic life, the only place Jane Parke was allowed to participate in the larger historical and political currents of her time was at church.

The church was taken even more seriously in Boston than politics, if not business. Almost every Bostonian attended church services twice on Sundays and read the Bible daily. And it was here, in the church, rather than in politics or commerce, that eighteenth-century Boston women were able to contribute to America's progress in work of broader scope than their accomplishments as wives and mothers.

This wasn't, as we might expect, charity, efforts to personalize or to augment outdoor relief. The work of Boston's church women was far weightier than seeing to the corporeal needs of the family next door. In 1800 Jane Parke was one of fourteen women from the Baptist and Congregational churches to embark on a venture of spiritual trade, a sort of moral counterpart to the city's mercantile ventures, exporting Christianity and notions of social progress to the pagan reaches of the globe. The founders determined to invest their monies (and prayers) directly in missionaries and their principal wares: Bibles and other tracts to be carried to the heathens. The fledgling Boston Female Society for Missionary Purposes elected a board of officers, decided on dues and a meeting schedule, and in so doing ardently believed that they were forwarding the designs of both God and country.

But even as these ingenuous merchants of the soul were dispensing prayers to the exotic ends of the planet, other forces at home were stirring turbulent social waters that would in time dramatically redirect the Society's energies.

The February 1789 launching of the *Astrea,* bound from Boston Harbor for Canton loaded with copper, iron, cloth, snuff, and tobacco, may have gone unobserved by the average Bostonian, but impossible to ignore was its return in May 1790.[5]

When the cargo was unloaded, there arrived on shore almost unbelievable luxuries. Teas, of course, but also exquisite porcelains, satins, and silks, live birds of paradise, apples, melons, and otter skins. The merchants' post-Revolutionary quest for a new trade triangle had finally been rewarded in the pathway to China.

The ship owners who guided these fortunes into port weren't from the old trading families. Many were from the northern county of Essex, more conservative and commercially aggressive than their predecessors. They had quietly begun to fill the power and commercial vacuum left after the war, and it wasn't long before the potential of the China trade, under their stewardship, became obvious to Boston's bankers.

In 1790 the city had only one bank; by 1810 it had twenty. Over the next decade, banks opened at the rate of six per year, and Boston became a financial center second only to New York.[6] Thousands of related businesses and small industries arose in the wake of this wealth, most of them just outside of the city.

In Boston proper, one effect of this sudden affluence was to spawn class consciousness. Though the city remained a dignified enclave of self-employed artisans, craftsmen, and merchants, their ranks began to divide. For the first time in Boston's history, sharp class distinctions were emerging.

As the new merchant princes rose in Boston's financial ranks, they demanded homes in the latest style, with imported wallpapers and furnishings, and impressive views of the city. They no longer wanted to live near the docks. The same year that the Boston Female Society for Missionary Purposes was established, Boston's greatest architect, Charles Bulfinch, began building luxury townhouses along Tremont Street on the Common. In time these were joined by other costly residential developments like Tontine Crescent and, later, Colonnade Row. The merchant princes also demanded fine accommodations for the influential dignitaries, like General Lafayette, who began to arrive. They built the extravagant Exchange Hotel, with 212 rooms on four floors, opulent even in its day. All of this development shifted the city's architectural and social axis from Jane Parke's old North Square neighborhood and the piers to Tremont and Park streets and the Common. With a population of 25,000 (almost double what it was on the eve of the Revolution), Boston was becoming a city both cosmopolitan and communally estranged.

"The town of Boston is so grown you would scarce know it for our native place," Bulfinch's mother wrote to her brother in 1804. "Almost every spot of land is coverd with brick buildings, and the paved streets and hackney coaches make us very noisy."[7]

Where an earlier generation had laid a social groundwork of intellectual discourse from pulpit and political platform, founded the American Academy of Arts and Sciences, the Boston Library Society, and the Massachusetts Historical Society, the merchant princes added to the city's attractions by repealing a 1750 law prohibiting theater productions. Theirs was a society that valued wit, manners, and money. Ralph Waldo Emerson complained that, "from 1790 to 1820, there was not a book, a speech, a conversation, or a thought, in the state."[8] But one of the signers of the Constitution, Elias Boudinot of Pennsylvania, who visited Boston in 1809, disagreed. "I never enjoyed myself, in so large a company, with such entire satisfaction. The greatest hilarity prevailed, with Innocency & Mirth. Seldom has more brilliant wit, from every guest, with more decency of manners, prevailed in a Social Circle."[9]

The old neighborhood ties no longer held. Puritan New England with its Calvinist determinism, with its rigid, if homogeneous, social structure, had vanished. However, democracy did not eradicate all hierarchies; it didn't, obviously, create economic equality. It merely conferred on every individual a *legal* equality in relation to his neighbor. In the context of Boston's history, democracy quickened the individualistic, entrepreneurial strain in its character, as it slowed the pulse of interdependence and citizens' perceptions of themselves as members of an ordained human community. All were now free to pursue their fortunes as aggressively as they could. They moved into and out of cities, ventured into Canada for furs and out to the territories. Those moving up and down Boston's social ladder were virtual strangers. And all of them were oriented toward a single value: wealth.

"It was in the nineteenth century that Boston matured as a city based upon a rigid family structure pivoted upon material wealth," wrote the cultural historian Brett Howard. "Money was the chief essential. 'Money is power,' exclaimed one minister from his pulpit. 'Every good man and woman should strive for power. Tens and thousands of men get rich honestly. But they are often accused by an envious, lazy crowd of unsuccessful persons of being dishonest and oppressive. I say . . . Get rich! Get rich!' "[10]

To have watched this transformation from the bottom of Fleet Street must have been a dizzying experience. Jane Parke, her husband, and their neighbors had been left in the dust and commotion of the workplace, as the city's rich and powerful moved away from the docks and hired intermediaries to handle their business. Without the stimulation and community feeling of their presence, the old streets must have seemed oddly vacant and, in some dim sense, threatening.

City leaders hadn't abandoned all sense of moral obligation to old neighbors and those less prosperous than themselves. They still met in church and on King Street. And in 1799 Bulfinch designed, gratis, a replacement for Boston's old almshouse, which had stood since 1643 on the corner of Park and Beacon streets. Bulfinch's new structure, on Leverett Street at the edge of the Mill Pond alongside the Charles

River, was an important enough source of civic pride to be glowingly
noted in the City Directory the following year as "a new elegant and
commodious Alms-house."

But by the time it was built, this seemed an inadequate, if not irrel-
evant, civic gesture. For, along with a new breed of rich, a "new poor"
had been developing. Little of a definitive nature could be said about
them, except that their needs weren't being addressed by the almshouse or by old-fashioned outdoor relief.

The new poor had their own community on the back side of Beacon
Hill. The edge of civilized Boston ended far short of it, by the shore
of the Mill Pond, where such citizens as Daniel Webster lived. Beyond
that, even as late as the early 1800's, Beacon Hill was remote, a graz-
ing area demarcated by a wooden post erected by the Puritans. There
was no reason to go there.

The third and furthest summit of Beacon Hill, Mount Whoredom,
supported "a disreputable community along its sunless northern
slope."[11] There, as the name suggests, the poor plied their many illicit
trades on pasture land owned, ironically enough, by clergymen of the
First Church. At night they retired, after days spent in begging and
petty thieving, to a cluster of close, filthy shacks on steep, dark alleys
at the bottom of the hill, in what came to be known as North Slope
Village.

The flight from unprofitable rural farms to Boston during the post-
war recession, which had affected the farmers far more than city merchants, was finally making itself felt in Boston. The new poor were no
longer old neighbors, citizens down on their luck. They were un-
knowns with no local ties. They begged, slept in public places, were
unkempt, smelly, and often drunk. Both men and women, begging
for spare change, accosted decent citizens as they strolled through the
Common.

Despite these obvious symptoms of distress, until real estate developers seized upon the scheme of gentrifying Beacon Hill, the residents of Mount Whoredom were more or less left to their own devices, paying for their transgressions only with an occasional night in
jail. To the developers, the vagrants were a nuisance but not a deter-
rent. Bulfinch and his real estate investors did what any self-respect-
ing entrepreneurs would do: they changed the name of Mount
Whoredom to Mount Vernon and incorporated into their design a
buffer zone to protect the rich from the poor, in the form of horse
stables behind every Beacon Street mansion.

The stables provided, at best, a temporary barrier. The residents of Mount Whoredom in time only became more visible. They were obvious to Jane Parke, Mary Homer, and other women of the Female Society when they shopped a mere quarter of a mile away on State Street. The ragged, uneducated street people were too poor even to attend church properly clad. They were lost to their self-destructive way of life, one that had generated its own subculture, caste system, and rules of conduct, and seemed to be producing successive generations of the same.

The members of the Female Society were appalled by such conditions in their midst. "That they [the Society] had too long slumbered over these miseries, was now deeply felt," wrote the secretary, Mrs. M. L. O'Brien, in 1801.[12] Why send Bibles to Tibet when moral encouragement was so badly needed at home? And what was the meaning of progress, when so many were languishing in its very midst, in their own city?

The society took stock and, in a bold and innovative step, "the design was formed to send a missionary to these poor outcasts, if one Christ-like could be found who would go into these highways of sin, and urge them to flee from impending ruin."[13] To this project the ladies of the Boston Female Society committed a full year's dues.

On June 19, 1818, the Reverend Mr. Davis descended the back side of Beacon Hill. His findings were to prove decisive for Boston's nineteenth-century poor. Squalid children blocked his path. Inside one door he found five gravely ill adults lying on the dirt floor. Other North Hill Village residents, drunk and unconscious, had collapsed against the exterior walls of the makeshift shacks that crowded the fetid alleys. Those who were still conscious played cards, fought, and drank until the evening, when the community's petty thieves returned with the day's loot and began to hawk their wares. North Hill Village offered the entire litany of urban poverty: overcrowding, hunger, disease, squalor, underemployment, illiteracy, and crime.

"Here, week after week, whole nights are spent in drinking and carousing," Davis informed the Female Society. "And as the morning light begins to appear, when others arise from their beds, these close their doors."[14]

Exactly how many people the village supported in 1818 is impossible to guess. Only one population was counted, for out of the cornucopia of social ills that the Reverend Davis observed, one alone struck an acutely raw nerve. "Here, in one compact section of the town," he reported, "it is confidently affirmed and fully believed, there are three hundred females wholly devoid of shame and modesty."[15]

As if to confirm his worst impressions, not long after his arrival Davis was asked to preside over a wake in a brothel. Throughout the affair the madam, who was "past the meridian of life," released a torrent of profanities and "similar enormities" from one corner, while the mother of a recently deflowered fifteen-year-old, indifferent to the soul of the deceased, clung to the hem of the minister's coat and wept out her tragic tale. It was all too much for Davis. The distraught preacher wrote to his patrons up the Hill, "Think, O think, ye affectionate mothers, how would your hearts be wrung with anguish, and your eyes run down with tears, in view of your amiable daughters, the objects of your tenderest solicitude, ensnared by the wiles of the ungodly, and falling victims to the vile lusts of brutes in human forms."[16]

The shock with which his impassioned report was met on Federal Street can only be surmised. "The Society appropriated days to fasting and prayer," Mrs. O'Brien chronicles. "Many tears were shed, and many prayers were offered, and they were not in vain."[17]

Within a year a Magdalen Asylum was founded, under the direction of a newly created all-male board. Financed wholly by private contributions from local citizens, merchants, and churches, the asylum opened its doors three years later as the Penitent Females' Refuge.[18]

Seventeen "miserable, houseless, abandoned beings" spent the first year sheltered not far from their former haunts on Ship Street. The following year the Society moved the women into Paul Revere's former estate, just a stone's throw from Jane Parke's home. The asylum, under the management of "two elderly, discreet, Christian people," remained there for the next twenty years.

As soon as they arrived at the refuge, the homeless women were inducted into a regimen as earnest as it was unbending. In accepting shelter, they were required to observe the rules. Everyone rose at five for morning prayer. After breakfast and room inspection, they spent the day earning their board by performing work contracted by the refuge administrators with local households: needlework, spinning, quilting, rugmaking. Later in the day they attended Bible classes, learned "the common branches of education," and maintained the refuge — cleaning, doing the laundry, and preparing the meals. During their few free moments, the women were encouraged to read great literature. They were in bed by nine o'clock.

Though the superintendent and two full-time staff members were paid, the asylum relied heavily on volunteers from the Ladies' Auxiliary (the Society's new name), each of whom visited once a week to teach the women skills and conduct their Bible studies. The auxiliary also donated all the clothing for the women.

No other visitors were allowed, and the women could not leave the property, except under the most extreme circumstances, so adamant was the administration about maintaining the purity of the environment. The organization's constitution stipulated, "Piety, Industry, and Economy, shall be the governing principles of all the arrangements."[19]

Conversion and conformity were the goals, along with preparation for one of the few acceptable roles available to poor single women: as maids for well-to-do families. But the opportunity to earn "an honest and reputable living" came only when "proof be given that their repentance is sincere."

The annual reports are filled with success stories. These stress, interestingly, those converts who best learned to control their tempers.

> S.K. was one of the most degraded. For some misdemeanor she was confined in the House of Correction. While there, she heard, for the first time, of the religion of the Bible, from the weekly visitants, by one of whom she was induced to go to the Refuge when her imprisonment expired. She was, at first, discontented. The change in her situation was very great. Her temper, which was violent, had never been under the least control. She was ignorant; could neither read nor write. A dissolute mother had hastened her ruin. Now, with excited sympathies, behold this lost one sitting beside her compassionate teacher, first learning the alphabet, at length able to read in the Bible of the blessed God who made her and gave her an immortal soul. Behold her now, with new feelings, seeking earnestly the salvation of her soul, of the very existence of which, but a few months before, she was confessedly ignorant. She became deeply sensible of her sinfulness; at length, it was hoped she believed in him who died to save sinners. She gave the best evidence of a radical change, by living a religious life. At a suitable time she was placed at service in a religious family in the country, where her penitence and her hopes were to be tested. There she gave great satisfaction. Her temper, from which most was feared, seemed entirely under control.[20]

The more docile and tractable the woman became, the more credible did her "repentance" seem. Over and over one reads of those whose "gratitude is ardent," or of the converts whose "constant effort" it was "to do every thing to please" the superintendents.

The volunteers were more than satisfied with their efforts. "The inmates have received the remarks made to them with fixed attention, and not unfrequently, with deep feeling, whether of reproof, caution, or exhortation; the practical effects of which have been observable on subsequent visits," according to a Ladies' Auxiliary report of 1828. "Their improvement in neatness and industry, have been accompanied, in many cases, with efforts at self-government, and the cultivation of good dispositions; the better feelings of their nature being awakened by these disinterested efforts to improve their present condition and promote their future happiness."[21]

Once returned to the unthreatening path of mere poverty, the women were again considered worthy of charitable, sympathetic acceptance.

Why didn't the many schoolmistresses on the Society's board — Mary Webb, Mary Doubt, and Elizabeth Haskins — press for a school for the women in their own neighborhood, where they might have learned a trade? Why didn't they support several women with cash from their annual dues? The Society's answer was brief but definitive. "To remain where they are," wrote the ladies in 1817, "would expose them not only to sufferings, but to a liability to relapsing into sin."[22]

The first price of Boston's economic advancement had been the rupture of the threads of community. Old neighborhoods went into decline as new ones were formed. The primitive but seemingly effective safety net protecting the poor had broken. In New York, Philadelphia, and even in the newer inland cities, the same phenomenon was occurring. And increasingly, social critics were linking modernity and madness, social chaos and crime.

As David Rothman would observe one hundred and fifty years later in *The Discovery of the Asylum,* the emerging lifestyle of the new republic "seemed willfully designed to produce mental illness. Everywhere the [reformers] looked, they found chaos and disorder, a lack of fixity and stability."[23]

The manifest poverty of North Hill Village, tangible and threatening, became a focal point for this generalized anxiety in Boston. The Female Society hardly needed the ardent Mr. Davis to suggest to them that "multitudes, evidently in different professions and employments, clad in a manner indicative of affluence and high life, as soon as the sable curtains of the evening are drawn around them, pass and repass from one end of the street to the other; and beyond all doubt contribute much in different ways to the support and encouragement of the abandoned and the prostitute." They didn't need to be told that "from this sink of sin, the seeds of corruption are conveyed into every part of the town."[24]

Moreover, this subculture of poverty was now perpetuating its own evils. No longer, it was felt, could the family, the church, and the school counteract the corruptions wrought in taverns, gambling saloons, and houses of ill repute.[25] For the first time in the New World, the suspicion was dawning that poverty wasn't merely the result of a sudden reversal. Much less was it simply one's ordained place in the social order. Poverty might in fact be a by-product of certain forms of social organization and of social change. Progress might create circumstances in which personal "sin" became almost inevitable.

But if society itself was the cause of this problem, who was to solve it, and how?

The refuge was one of the earliest private charities in America to depart from the philosophy of the cooperatives. Its vision was at once radical, utopian, and nostalgic. The directors believed that it was necessary to isolate and contain the problem (in this case as it manifested itself in poor women driven into sin) apart from the society from which it had sprung. By creating inside the asylum a self-contained community guided by standards of discipline, order, and faith similar to those of an earlier era, they believed that they could transform the victims of social dislocation. The asylum-shelter was intended to be a total environment, offering housing, job training, positive associations — a place where women could redeem their self-esteem and acquire the skills necessary to reenter mainstream society as productive wage earners. It was a social laboratory in which the vulnerable, the wayward, and the deviant were to be rescued, rehabilitated, and molded to the norms of the community.

Bostonians thought that the idea was insane. In the ninth annual report, the secretary of the Society noted, "Their project was derided as visionary, and even the purity of their motives was suspected. With scanty pecuniary resources, with little sympathy, even from the christian public, amid the sneers of the vicious, and the scoffings of the abandoned, regarded as fanatics, with no one to bid them 'God's speed,' they persevered in the path of duty, though every step was on thorns."[26]

The asylum's earliest advocates, like Jane Parke, weren't society leaders. The first officers of the Penitent Females' Refuge were a tailor, a stonecutter, a cabinetmaker, and a merchant clerk. This was a purely grassroots, private-sector initiative, and as such it established the precedent for every subsequent poverty reform movement in America up to contemporary times.

If the ardent "little people" of the refuge's directorship were at first derided, the refuge model increasingly seemed to make sense. The abstract and anonymous force of "society" had overrun "community," the network of mutual and personal support, in determining the quality of life in the nineteenth century. The era of manageable poverty was past.

And relieving poverty was getting expensive. By 1820 a third of Boston's city budget was going to poor relief. Rather than alleviating the condition, relief seemed only to be sustaining a permanent underclass, most notably the growing community on Beacon Hill. As time went on, the chronic poor became more entrenched and more detached from the values of mainstream Boston.

In 1822 Josiah Quincy headed America's first investigation of welfare reform and concluded that the preferred mode of assistance was no longer outdoor relief, on which so many marginal families had depended, but instead institutional homes like the refuge.

"The most economical mode is that of Alms Houses," the Quincy report concluded, "having the character of Work Houses, or Houses of Industry, in which work is provided for every degree of ability in the pauper; and thus the able poor made to provide, partially, at least, for their own support; and also to the support, or at least the comfort of the impotent poor."[27]

This was a total reversal of public policy. Until that time in Massachusetts, only one of every four relief recipients spent time in an almshouse. But the Quincy committee argued that, based on surveys across the state and on published accounts of Britain's experiences, the current system of outdoor relief was sapping the character of the Commonwealth's poor and the finances of its taxpayers.

Workhouses would resolve two nagging problems that had gotten out of hand with outdoor relief: first, the impossibility of separating the able-bodied poor from "the pauper, who, through impotency, can do absolutely nothing,"[28] and second, the drastic variation in local relief practices, a corrupting influence in itself.

The poor begin to consider it as a right; next, they calculate upon it as an income. . . . The stimulus to industry and economy is annihilated,

or weakened; temptations to extravagance and dissipation are increased, in proportion as public supply is likely, or certain, or desirable.
The just pride of independence, so honorable to man, in every condition, is thus corrupted by the certainty of public provision; and is either
weakened, or destroyed according to the facility of its attainment, or its
amount.[29]

The committee concluded that "the pernicious consequences of the
existing system are palpable, that they are increasing, and that they
imperiously call for the interference of the Legislature, in some manner, equally prompt and efficacious."[30]

In contrast to outdoor relief, the committee found that in Massachusetts and in England, "In every case, where means of work were
connected with such houses, in united districts, and when they have
been superintended by the principal inhabitants, they have been greatly
beneficial."[31] They were cheaper, they corrected the laziness of their
inmates, and they checked the spread of poverty.

Over the next twenty years, sixty Massachusetts towns constructed
almshouses, and many others refurbished old ones, using the model
of the early private asylums. By 1840, Massachusetts had one hundred
and eighty almshouses to house those who previously received relief
at home, or survived on the streets. They sat on 17,000 of the Commonwealth's green acres, land valued at close to a million dollars. In
a parallel development (and relying on the same rationales), peniten-
tiaries and state hospitals were being built to house the criminal and
the insane, society's other two deviant groups.

The almshouse envisioned by the Quincy committee would meet
every conceivable need:

> To rehabilitate, as well as comfort the poor. To the feeble, the old, the
> weak, and the sickly, the almshouse would offer compassion. To the
> unemployed, the able-bodied victims of hard luck, it would, either in its
> own quarters or in conjunction with a workhouse, provide the oppor-
> tunity for labor, and thus dispense relief without enervating the recip-
> ient. To the vicious, the idle, who wanted nothing else but a dole it
> would teach the lesson of hard labor, insisting that anyone who receive
> public funds spend his day at a task. The almshouse would serve all
> classes of the poor.[32]

An important part of the almshouse's explicit program was a kind
of moral intelligence, which was to be communicated to the poor
through the attitudes of the staff, the example of the more advanced
inmates, the language and policies of the institution, and prayer.

But small, private, community-based asylums, modeled on the Penitent Females' Refuge, where such attitudes may have been conveyed through close one-to-one relations, soon gave way to large public facilities governed by inflexible behavior codes and safety and health regulations. The buildings themselves became a subspeciality among architects and contractors. Numerous examples of asylum architecture survive today. They were located away from the rest of the population or in rural areas where the inmates could do some farming.

"Rehabilitation" in the context of these human warehouses meant little more than adapting to a narrow range of work options: weaving, sewing, and spinning for the women, and farming for the men, an activity that left many of them idle during the winter months. In some almshouses a passion for the curative effects of work was such that if nothing better was available, inmates were forced to haul bricks or wood from one corner of the lot to another and back again.[33] Inmates also performed most of the chores — washing the dishes, doing the laundry, and cleaning.

Rehabilitation also meant, as it had at the Penitent Females' Refuge, learning to obey rules. A bell woke inmates at five, another bell sent them to breakfast. There they took assigned seats, ate within the prescribed amount of time, and went off to their workshops. As the institution's policies calcified, inmates were forced to observe silence while they worked. And, in time, no one was allowed to leave the asylum without permission. Only scheduled, and limited, family visits were allowed. Alcohol was forbidden.

The results of the asylum policy in solving the problem of urban poverty were abysmal. By the end of the Civil War, four out of every five persons who received extended relief remained within an institution.[34] But by then most poor houses were so overcrowded and mismanaged and dangerous, so full of the sick and the illegitimate offspring of casual encounters, that no one really believed in their promise anymore.

In retrospect, most students of poverty agree that supporters of the poorhouse had no clearly defined vision to begin with. Society wanted the asylums to shelter the poor but not to be so comfortable that residents would lose the incentive to get out (or be enticed there by its ease relative to the streets). The result was a program of half-hearted "assistance" that constantly ran afoul of the conflicting agendas of social control: the dread of promoting idleness and of making life too easy for the undeserving.

Inmates were poorly nourished, received inadequate health care, and had no privacy. They became weak and ill and even more dependent on the system than they'd been as recipients of outdoor relief. Poorhouse advocates believed in rehabilitation but never offered the job training or services that would have equipped inmates to become truly self-sufficient. Despite the workshops and various educational programs that were tried, fewer and fewer paupers left asylums "reformed" or equipped for employment that would lift them out of poverty. The poor kept coming, and many returned again and again. The asylums had created a generation of institutionalized people whose only common bond was their poverty and their dependence on a demeaning system of assistance.

Demoralized staff, with no expertise beyond a desire to help the poor, experienced high burnout rates. Those whose jobs were the result of political influence lacked incentive and social status. They usually didn't last long. Activists and advocates continued to split hairs over regulations and the extent to which indoor relief should be the dominant public relief policy,[35] but they had long since ceased to have any real effect on poverty or the lives of asylum residents.

In time an emphasis on discipline and custodial attitudes replaced those of an earlier therapeutic environment. The conflicting motives of rehabilitation and deterrence had clashed without resolution for too long, and in the end deterrence and punishment won out.

In the 1840s Boston began to receive waves of European immigrants. Before that time the average rate of immigration was 2,000 people a year. By 1849 it had swelled to 28,917 a year. By 1880, forty percent of Boston's poorhouse population were immigrants, most of them Irish.

One lasting legacy of the poorhouse era was the creation of the professional social worker. The country's first school of social work, the Harvard-Simmons School, was founded as a direct response to the growth of poorhouses. Local and national conferences began to give the poorhouses, and their employees, the trappings of legitimacy, and soon whole curricula evolved to train the keepers of the poor in the proper attitudes, approaches, and criteria for judging and rewarding conformity.

At the Penitent Females' Refuge, where the small scale and personal approach minimized the more grotesque effects of public policy, the results were still dismal.

"The managers have indeed found great difficulties in their way," the board admitted, specifically, "their inability to carry complete conviction to the minds of those, whom they have attempted to exhort & warn to *flee from the wrath to come.*"[36] The board's policy of "temporary shelter" had resulted in a revolving-door phenomenon. After three years the managers decided that they would take only those women who were willing to stay at least a year.

But even with longer periods of shelter and training, the success rate didn't improve. By the Society's own admission in 1831, only a quarter of the women stayed a full year at the refuge and did not return. More than a quarter couldn't tolerate the inflexible rules and left after less than three months, and a third of them "relapsed."

In spite of these dim results, surprisingly little changed at the refuge, except its currency as an institution. Stonecutters were replaced on the board by judges and affluent merchants. But the assumptions, programs, and means of assessing "repentance" remained the same.

In the early 1840s the refuge fell on hard times that might have occasioned a reappraisal of its policies. A fund-raising flyer acknowledged, "Other plans had been devised by Christian charity, less complicated and expensive." Nevertheless, "experience had proved the necessity of the healthful discipline, the moral culture, and the *strict seclusion*, of the Refuge."[37] The refuge couldn't be abandoned. It had become a mirror of the social service industry it had helped to create.

In 1854 the board wrote, "Our higher aim has been the restoration of the lost image of God."[38] But rather than change its less-than-successful programs to attain that lofty goal, by adding a greater range of job-training programs, for example, the board lamented the degree to which that image had been lost in its charges. "Many . . . are in a deplorable state of ignorance, not only of the common rudiments of education, but the ordinary duties of domestic life," bemoaned one report.[39]

When the refuge's own vision of what was possible for the women failed, they blamed the women. And never once did the annual reports make mention of the most common cause of their graduates' demise: the sexual advances of the husbands and sons of the households in which they were employed.

By 1900 the philosophical influences of Darwin and Freud once again revolutionized the way society thought about its poor. Not surprisingly, one begins to read about the problems of "mental culture" among the "inmates." Perhaps, the Society's reports now began to intimate, some of their wards were too mentally ill to cope with the program they offered.

"We know also that mental culture given to a person who is really depraved only increases the power of doing evil," they wrote. "Also some have been really feeble-minded, and would better be in institutions specially designed for such."

It is ironic that if Jane Parke had lived today she probably would have died homeless. Matthew, her husband, died of consumption in 1813 at the age of sixty-seven, leaving $2,237.22 in his personal estate — a pittance, even in those days. His only heir, William, never executed his will. Jane remained in Boston for several years and finally followed her stepson, who was then a merchant's clerk, his wife Susan, and their three children to Portsmouth, New Hampshire.

However, her stepson didn't take her into his home. She died, alone and penniless, in a rooming house in 1828, owing her landlord two years' back rent (tallied as 104 weeks) "including the last sicknings," and her stepson some $250, debts which forced William to sell the old property on Fleet Street and several other parcels. In her will Jane bequeathed to her nieces, the next generation of Parke women, "clothing, beds, bedding, furniture and Plate." But her nieces never received these goods: even these humble mementos went to settle debts incurred in loneliness and poverty.

FOUR

Top of the Dirt Pile

AMANDA WAS OUT of school for a week after the beating that broke Jack Daley's hand. She was black and blue from her knees to her waist.

"At that point," she was to say years later, "I figured out that I was going to have to rely on Number One. Me."

The violence, now inescapable, was a secret too horrible to think about and too humiliating to confide to anyone else. Unbeknownst to others, and censored from the family's acknowledged life as soon as it had spent itself, violence nevertheless became the most real thing in Amanda's childhood. It was to escalate, shift its tactics and focus many times over the years, but it never went away. No matter how good or docile Amanda tried to be, she could not defuse her father's irrational fury.

"He would get absolutely nasty. I mean, he started throwing furniture around. Or people. He hit just me. He'd scream at my mother."

The year the beatings began, Amanda was out of school so often that she had to repeat the fourth grade.

The ride on the school bus was a long one for those children who lived near the town line, and especially for Amanda.

"Cooties!" One of the boys would begin taunting her as soon as enough of them had assembled on the leather seats.

"You have lice in your hair!"

The scene repeated itself every morning and afternoon: her books snatched and thrown helter-skelter under the seats, the punching and slapping, the pulled hair. Sometimes she could barely breathe, sometimes she thought she would die simply from having cried so hard and so often.

"Her hair was never combed," one of her schoolmates on that bus now recalls. "It was dirty. The same clothes all the time. The same outfits. Dresses, skirts, that sort of thing, but maybe two or three outfits that were alternated all the time. Like she got out of bed in the morning and just went to school. Nose always running. That kind of thing, just basically unkempt."

Another remembers, "Amanda always had a kind of wounded-bird thing about her, and the pecking order was always very much there to do a number on her in any situation. She didn't move like normal kids. She held herself a little oddly. I remember watching her walk. It was almost a limp, or something odd about the gait. The way she held her shoulders, her hands. Not relaxed."

She never fought back against her tormentors. Her slender body wedged between two seats, hands and knees on the floor or pressed up against the window, she curled herself into a ball and cried. Jane, sitting several seats away, never turned her head in her sister's direction. Many mornings, by the time she arrived at the school door, Amanda had thoroughly wet herself.

The teacher was screaming at Amanda, making an object lesson of her in front of the class. She had committed an insignificant offense, accidentally spilling a box of paints. Now she sat at her desk, crying and crying. And the teacher just kept screaming.

A classmate recalls: "These kinds of things would happen to Amanda. She would be selected out. When you think about the wolf pack hunting the deer, they find the one that doesn't quite fit in and they go for it. Amanda was always the one who got selected, whether by the kids on the school bus to tease on the way home, or on the way into school, or at the lunch table. If you heard a commotion and found out that somebody got their lunch tray tipped over before they finished their lunch, you weren't surprised if you found out it was Amanda Daley."

No friends came home to play at the end of the day, and they wouldn't have been welcome if they had.

"My mother would have a fit if they came in," Amanda remembers. "It was just basically understood that she didn't want them around."

Jack Daley's house remained unfinished, though it wasn't until years later that anyone realized the appalling conditions Amanda returned to every day. The upstairs rooms had been divided, but the studs were still exposed in many places and no wallboard had been hung. Other rooms had been dry-walled but never taped, much less painted; seams and nails punctuated the flat white. Window sills were rotting because they had never been painted, and the floors had already begun to warp; Jack hadn't ever bothered to seal and finish them. The front yard remained an untouched expanse of dirt and stones. Weeds thrived unchecked for months, and saplings grew up wherever they took hold.

Renata had never learned to cook. She boiled pork chops and grilled almost everything else on a hibachi on the floor inside the kitchen door.

On the rare occasions when children did manage to penetrate the interior of the Daley home, they found encyclopedias instead of toys.

"There was a globe," one guest remembers. "We didn't have that. The impression I got from Amanda was that they tried to stress the academic. There seemed to be a focus on this intellectual upbringing. A 'You don't need toys, you're a small adult' attitude. I wasn't convinced, myself, and I don't really think Amanda was, even though I think that was the ethic that they were trying to make her believe. This is what you are. Your mom and dad are very intelligent and somewhat superior and therefore you are going to be very intelligent and somewhat superior."

Christmas was a single book and an orange.

"This was at a time," remembers the same woman, "when television commercials were at you to get a Barbie doll and a Betsy Wetsy, and this, that, and the other. I can imagine she felt terrible. First day back from holiday, the only thing you talk about is what you got for Christmas. She tried to explain it to me that this austerity was part of their appreciation of the holiday, or for austerity's sake, or something. I remember scratching my head and thinking, Either that, or the folks really don't care, or they're trying to convince you that you're having a good time eating your orange and reading your book."

Amanda's sister Jane adapted to all these unarticulated cues, at least to all appearances, brilliantly. Jane cultivated the image of a highly intelligent and slightly eccentric artist, reminiscent of Renata as a young woman.

"She was dark. Dark hair like her father's, and I think she had dark eyes," one classmate remembers. "She wore leotards and the dark plaids. But she wasn't quite as beeboppy as Mom. She had one foot in whatever fashions were going on at the time. And I think she sewed, because she'd wear clothes that, although not quite store-bought, had the semblance of what was going on. I saw the slightly Nehru jacket effect as we were going into the sixties. She didn't have the white go-go boots. I'm sure she wasn't allowed to wear those. But she was really trying. And I think she had more friends at school. She was classified as a brain. Very, very highly intelligent. If they had had a debating team, I'm sure she would have been on it. I don't know how many friends she actually brought over to her house, but I always got the feeling that she seemed to be a couple of paces ahead of Amanda. Somewhere along the line, she picked up on something that Amanda had missed. More normal of the two, if you want to use the word normal. Yet there was something different about Jane. That difference was still there, the influence of the Daley, separate-way-from-the-mass-of-society difference that they wanted to establish."

Amanda continued to be "a second-hand-Rose kind of kid," even as she grew more able to attend to her own appearance. One classmate remembers, "When I think of Amanda, I picture her in a white blouse with a plaid skirt that had suspenders, little buttons at the waist. Knee socks, I think. I don't think I ever saw her in nylons, even throughout high school. It was always the skirt, penny loafers, a good Catholic school-type outfit. Nothing ever stylish."

There was only one bit of relief in this relentless dreariness, and it was a significant one for Amanda. She was permitted to join the Camp Fire Girls. Renata had been a Camp Fire Girl. Possibly, encouraging Amanda to mirror her own happy childhood experiences was the extent of her ability to mother.

Amanda's Blue Bird troop leader still remembers Renata. "When I first met her, she and Amanda came up and we chatted. But it wasn't a friendly chat and I don't know that she ever strolled up again. You couldn't get *to* her. You couldn't become friendly with her."

Blue Birds and Camp Fire Girls were placid ports of normalcy and acceptance in her otherwise unrelenting drift in isolation. For one afternoon every week, Amanda could spend a few hours in a kitchen where cookies were being baked or puddings made or greeting cards decorated, "simple things that everyone could get involved in," as her troop leader says. "Basically she was a good little child. Very quiet, stayed by herself. You'd have to draw her in."

Amanda had no difficulty throwing herself into the troop's tasks and working for achievement beads, as generations of Camp Fire Girls had done before her. It was her one hope of sharing something with her mother, and she desperately wanted Renata to be proud of her.

"I did pretty good at it," she says. "We earned all sorts of beads to do anything. Keep your room clean for a month. Do the dishes for a month without complaining. You name it, we did it. I had a good time."

Amanda's Fly-Up Night was a moving experience for the many mothers who'd watched her progress through Blue Birds. On Fly-Up Night a higher-ranked girl "ties" each Blue Bird with the Camp Fire Girl scarf and gives the younger one her hat. The Blue Bird tosses her beanie into a ceremonial wastebasket and is declared a full-fledged Camp Fire Girl.

Amanda's memory of the event is still vivid. "All the Blue Birds are lined up on one side of the auditorium stage, and the oldest Camp Fire group in town — you're talking probably Individual Torch Bearer rank, at this point — welcome in the new members of the Camp Fire troop. I remember my name being called, and I just marched across that stage. All I remember is applause, and saying to myself, Why are all these people clapping?"

In the summers Amanda went to camp for a month. Though the camp was just one town away, it took her a distance not measured in miles. Thirty years later she remembers every detail of the experience.

"The cabins had screens all the way around. There were eight beds, seven campers and one counselor. We were outside pretty much all day long. I took nature, was in carpentry, archery, swimming. I learned a lot about the skies and stuff. Sunday mornings we had church outdoors. That was nice and peaceful. Sundays you walked around wearing a white shirt and scarf, and, if you had one, you could wear the vest, the whole gear."

As a Camp Fire Girl, Amanda designed and built a birdhouse, learned to identify different trees, mastered bird calls, and created pictures of various cloud formations. And she was introduced to one other skill that would prove valuable in later years: she learned the rudiments of building furniture for dollhouses.

By junior high school, Amanda's omnipresent stack of books had so increased that she had to carry a satchel. While the other girls were spending their free time lounging in the hallways or outside study hall, gossiping and planning their weekends, Amanda could be seen lugging the enormous book bag around with her.

And she continued to be the butt of easy cruelty. "Sixth and seventh grades — that's a bad age group anyway. They're mean to one another. The kids did give her a hard time," one former teacher admits.

Amanda would linger after school waiting for Sue, the gym teacher, to finish team practices. Sue was one of the few teachers who encouraged her, and for the first time in her life, Amanda found herself participating in group activities in gym, even though the other kids didn't want her to be on their teams. Groping for alliances, unable to voice either feelings or need, Amanda would wait alone for Sue in the locker room until it was nearly dark outside and the teams came in, the equipment was put away, and the lights turned off. At that point, there was nothing for Sue to do but offer her a ride home.

Sue remembers those rides out to the house at the end of town. "Everything was always dark. You could never see in there. The blinds were drawn. They were just very quiet and into themselves. You never knew what they were like. I don't think I ever met the parents."

After a moment's thought, she continues, "She was just very pathetic. Really pathetic. And I felt so bad for her. I think if it was now, I'd try to do something. Back then it was so different. I don't know if they had many counselors. Now there are so many different people helping in school."

The normal activities of her adolescent classmates were alien to Amanda. The family didn't own a TV. "They weren't allowed to use the telephone — receive calls, or make them," says one former neighbor. "Imagine a teenaged girl not allowed to use the telephone."

The rest of her classmates were beginning to discover close dancing and cigarettes. Not Amanda.

"Parties?" a classmate says. "Oh, no. God, no. She was alone all the time. She didn't have any friends."

One afternoon during these junior high school years, a classmate happened by and saw Amanda crawling along the top of the dirt pile behind the house, pushing a toy truck.

When Amanda was twelve, Renata began to hear voices. A neighbor remembers sitting in her living room one afternoon entertaining a friend when Renata rushed up the driveway.

"We'd just sat down, when all of a sudden up the driveway came

Renata," the neighbor recalls. "She was quite upset. Nothing would do! She had to talk with me. Okay. Here I was entertaining, and she just didn't regard my friend at all, she was so upset. She started talking about the voices coming out of the woods in back of her house. 'I got so frightened I just had to leave the house,' she said. She just drove around and around. Finally she came here, to me. She said, 'It sounds like somebody talking on one of those megaphones in my woods, and they're hollering back and forth. I think maybe somebody's injured, or something's going on.' "

When the neighbor called the local emergency squad, she was informed, after checking, that nothing was happening in the woods.

The same neighbor had already been subjected to one harrowing experience with Renata earlier that year. Renata had discovered that the woman was hosting a birthday party for her son and would be baking one of her renowned cakes. Since Renata didn't know how to bake, she asked if she might come down and watch her.

"We hardly spoke, once a year maybe," said the woman. "Anyway, she insisted. 'Is there anything I can do?' I said, 'Well, maybe you can look after little Billy while I cook.' "

Renata accepted the assignment of watching the one-year-old. So as not to be underfoot, she took Billy into the living room.

"I was in my flour," the woman recalls, "doing this and that. All of a sudden there was a knock on the door, and a complete stranger came by with my baby in his arms!"

The stranger had been driving past the house and had narrowly missed running over the tiny child.

"He had been in front, right on the edge of the road, lying on his belly!"

Renata meanwhile was sitting in the living room, reading magazines.

"She was devastated," the woman remembers. "She was so apologetic. She never forgot it. No matter what I said, she could never forgive herself. She was very upset about it. I always thought of her, truly, as being a child herself."

Some weeks after the incident with the imaginary voices in the woods, Jack had Renata committed to a psychiatric hospital. "All of a sudden," he told their friends, "one morning, she sat up in bed and started talking, and it was all garbled. I couldn't understand a word."

No one even remotely connected to the situation failed to wonder what effect Jack's drinking had had on Renata's fragile psychological constitution. Alcohol had become an integral part of his daily life, an addiction that went unchecked because everyone he knew drank too. Hard drinking — behind closed doors, alone or with one's spouse or the guys down at the Legion post — was de rigueur in the Daleys' neighborhood. In time, almost every youngster of Amanda's age within a half mile of her house had to cope with at least one parent with advanced alcohol dependency, one of these women says now.

"People didn't socialize as a neighborhood," she recalls. "Everybody was into their own thing. People after work would go to the Legion for an hour or so, then go home to their kids and continue drinking. There was a very high incidence of alcoholism on that street."

Renata's hospitalization brought a virtual halt to the girls' outside activities. Jack, who had no health insurance — gambling on the odds that he'd never need it — now was forced to mortgage the house to pay Renata's psychiatric bills. His drinking got worse. He was in several automobile accidents. Finally, he totaled his car. Without insurance to replace it, he had to do without one for a time.

Jack was losing control of his life, and he knew it. As his rage and frustration mounted, he took more of it out on his younger daughter.

"You should respect me," he yelled at her one night at dinner, "because I'm your father."

"I looked at him and I said, 'You've never really served in the role of being a father. Not from my point of view.' "

After Renata returned from the hospital less than a month later, the couple became virtual recluses. On the few occasions when they left the house, it was clear to everyone that they were losing their grip on reality. They approached one of their old Museum School friends about a scheme whereby Renata would do paintings of antique objects and old houses to augment the family income. Realizing the futility of that scheme, the friend offered instead to take Renata to her workplace and help her get a job. Jack wouldn't hear of it.

When Jane graduated from high school almost two years later, she started laying plans to get as far as possible away from her childhood and everything associated with it. But Jack, already irrational, did everything in his power to obstruct her desperate fight for independence. He forbid Amanda to speak to her.

"I had basically been told, you cannot have anything to do with your sister. This was my father, 'I don't want you to say anything to her. She's garbage. She's trash. She's this, that, and the other thing.'"

Jane locked herself in her bedroom and read. She emerged only to eat, and when she did she drew more abuse from her father. The stress was too much for Amanda.

"One day I was in gym class and I just sat down and cried my eyes out," Amanda remembers.

Later that day her parents received a concerned call from the school. "When I got home that night, my father was in the worst mood I'd ever seen him in. He was completely smashed. And he was picking up things and throwing them, saying shit like, 'If I ever find that daughter of mine in this house, I'm going to break every bone in her body.' He told my mother to get rid of 'that little goddamn sucker' — meaning me."

Renata was allotted a brief period in which to get her out of the house. Amanda, her face streaked with tears, was hustled into the car with her sack of books on her lap. Her mother headed south toward Nanna's. When they arrived at the foot of the familiar driveway, Renata leaned over, opened the door on Amanda's side, and waited for her to step out. Then, without a word, she sped off.

"I remember going inside," Amanda says, "and just crying."

That same night Jane was thrown out of the house in Sharon.

Amanda spent a week at her grandmother's house, then returned to the embattled scene in Sharon. Salvation was soon in sight — but not soon enough. When Jack's father stopped by one night some weeks later, "he found my father using me like a punching bag against the side of the house." The man Jack feared more than any other in the entire world felled his son with one blow. Then he turned and struck Renata.

At last a savior had appeared. Grandfather Daley sent Amanda, now seventeen, to a private Catholic boarding school in nearby Plymouth. Amanda felt secure under the protective eye of the sisters during her two years there, but it was too late to catch up socially with her peers.

"I don't think she ever joined the mainstream of adolescent society," one of the sisters remembers. "She was always looking at it longingly, hoping she could be more a part of it."

Amanda spent most of her time withdrawn into a book and anxiously making sure that some authority figure was close by.

"She'd just be there all the time," one of the dorm mistresses remembers. "She was like a shadow. We knew we were too late to mold her, but we tried to make the short time she was with us happy."

The summer before her senior year, Amanda was allowed to return home. She hadn't been there long when Jack's car was stolen from the front yard. After it was recovered, Renata was too frightened to drive it ever again. And once more she started behaving erratically.

On the Fourth of July, during a family picnic at Jack's parents' house, Renata at one point turned to her husband and exclaimed in a loud voice, "Gee, Jack, just think! I don't have any underwear on!"

Days later Amanda came downstairs to discover her mother stalking around the house. She was stark naked, and as she moved from room to room, she was spewing forth a torrent of unintelligible phrases.

"There was my father putting on a big brave front, and there was my mother flitting around the place. What the hell was going on? Nobody would tell me. My grandfather showed up one afternoon. He was the one who called Glenside Hospital. I remember bawling my eyes out when he came, asking him, 'What's wrong?' "

Renata received shock treatment. No one went to visit her, not even her own mother. As soon as she was able to, Renata checked herself out, but her personality had been completely transformed.

"She became a different person," her daughter says. "She was a lot quieter. She did not scream or yell as much."

In 1972 Amanda's adolescence officially ended. She received her high school diploma on May 29. Her father, perhaps subconsciously trying to cast her off once and for all, told friends that she had entered a convent and was going to take the veil.

▨▨▨▨▨▨▨▨▨▨

FIVE

From Margin to Mainstream

FROM THE MOMENT she woke up in the morning until the moment she went to bed at night, Esther Barrows thought about the family. Not her own. A single woman earning a pittance, with just a room in a lodging house in the poorest section of Boston, Esther was preoccupied both with the family as a universal unit — and a fragile one in industrial America — and with the hundreds of impoverished examples around her. Their welfare was her all-consuming charge. Esther almost couldn't look out her window on East Canton Street without seeing abandoned children playing in the gutters or emaciated young mothers with insufficient means of feeding their babies. She had come to realize that in the America of 1910, devoting oneself to being a good neighbor could constitute a "work" — enough of a work to last a lifetime, if one had the stamina and the spirit for it.

Hundreds of miles away, on the South Side of Chicago, the tenements were also crowded with recent immigrants. There another college-educated woman, Jane Addams, was dedicating her life to a proposition that she had arrived at after several years of intense reflection: "That the things which make men alike are finer and better than the things that keep them apart, and that these basic likenesses, if they are properly accentuated, easily transcend the less essential differences of race, language, creed and tradition." [1]

Addams and a handful of like-minded reformers in Boston and New York were busy importing to America's most blighted alleys and impoverished city blocks the Oxford-born notion that democracy would survive the ravages of modern industrial life only if rich, poor, and in-between joined hands in the common enterprise of community.

Poverty was no longer the outcast condition, made more strange by distance and the impenetrable stone walls of asylums. It was as close as the uneducated, hungry family cramped into the tenement next door.

When Jane English and her Revolutionary-era female friends established the Penitent Females' Refuge with the fire of missionary reform alive in their breasts, the South End of Boston was still a dream under the waters of Boston Harbor. On the desolate, narrow, and often flooded horse path that extended from downtown to Roxbury, between marshes and open ocean, the only life along the route was the final paroxysms of those who swung from the gallows there. Public hangings made grim sport out on Washington Street — or the Neck, as it was called. Only two households had settled that far from the center of the city. A world apart, they sat facing the harbor alongside a brickyard, a copper mint, and a few old war fortifications.

But in 1804 the first of several massive landfill projects was under way, transforming the South End into a majestic showcase for the city. The city chartered a group of investors who owned portions of the wetlands and now called themselves the Front Street Company. Their initial project was to construct the South End's first cross street, which they named Dover. The group then proceeded to fill in nine acres on the ocean side of Washington Street and lay a road parallel to it, which they called Harrison Avenue.

A second development company was chartered. The South Cove Company was an auxiliary of the Boston-Worcester Railroad, which wanted to build terminals and rail yards near downtown. It filled in a large area for this purpose, then proceeded to build the largest hotel in the country nearby, sparing no modesty in naming it the United States Hotel.

The developers' fondest expectations weren't disappointed. By 1850 the South End's six hundred acres embraced a fully developed infrastructure of streets and charming squares built on the English model. Blocks of three-story brick bowfronts with gardens overlooked gated parks. Union and Chester parks, Franklin, Worcester, and Rutland squares immediately became some of the city's most prosperous addresses. The Back Bay, Boston's second major landfill project, would not exist for another twenty years. For the moment South End homes were much sought after by the many out-of-towners who were moving into Boston as industry increasingly centralized capital and business there.

But by the end of the century those charming streets had become known as Hell's Half Acre. Many a luxury townhouse had been a tenement for nearly twenty years. Washington Street harbored the greatest concentration of brothels, saloons, and speakeasies in New England. And the immigrant families who dwelled nearby fought a losing battle to keep their children innocent of their influences.

This rapid deterioration began with the influx of tens of thousands of European immigrants to America beginning in the mid-1840s. Between 1846 (when Boston's total population numbered 99,036) and 1855, 230,000 immigrants arrived in port. Fifty thousand of those who stayed in Boston were Irish.[2] They made up two-thirds of all the foreign families living in the South End, and soon were joined by Swedes, Syrians, German and Russian Jews, Poles, Italians, and southern Blacks. By 1898 ninety-seven percent of the population within a half-mile of Dover Street was either foreign-born or of foreign parentage.[3]

Those residents of the South End who observed the dramatic shift taking place moved out before the influx totally undermined their property values. The single-family homes they left behind became residences for fifteen families or more. These uprooted and desperate newcomers often shared a single sink per floor and one toilet, on average, for fifteen to thirty people. Their back yards, if not already swallowed up by a second tier of hastily constructed tenements, became garbage fills. None of the dwellings had proper sewage or bathing facilities.

Mary Antin, an immigrant whose family arrived in the South End late in the 1890s, depicts what the area had become by then in her memoir *The Promised Land*:

> On Wheeler Street there were no real homes. There were miserable flats of three or four rooms, or fewer, in which families that did not practice race suicide cooked, washed, and ate; slept from two to four to a bed, in windowless bedrooms; quarreled in the gray morning, and made up in the smoky evening; tormented each other, supported each other, saved each other, drove each other out of the house. But there was no common life in any form that means life. . . . The yard was only big enough for the perennial rubbish heap. The narrow sidewalk was crowded. What were the people to do with themselves? There were

the saloons, the missions, the libraries, the cheap amusement places, and the neighborhood houses. People selected their resorts according to their tastes.[4]

The heads of these families, many of them unskilled and unable to speak English, or prevented from pursuing on American soil the rural livelihoods of their homelands, could find only menial work. The men took jobs at the docks or the railroads, at Boston Gas and Electric, as municipal laborers, or as clerks. Many of those who couldn't find work succumbed to the refuge of the saloon. Cynical tavern keepers exploited this vulnerable group, enticing them in at midday with free lunches and in the evening with a barrel of beer just outside the door. The South End developed its first significant homeless population: four shelters slept four hundred men each night.

Many of the women were forced to work, either because their alcoholic husbands didn't or because a single paycheck wasn't enough to make ends meet. The women of the South End became Boston's domestic servants, waitresses, cooks, laundresses, dressmakers, and, if they were young, attractive, and lucky, stenographers in its downtown offices. Before they left in the morning, they bought the family's milk and bread at the often unhygienic open-air markets nearby. Produce was purchased from carts in the streets. On Saturdays, usually after working a half-day shift, they went to the Salvation Army and the cut-rate installment-plan stores to shop for what few pieces of clothing and furniture they could afford.

While families struggled to improve their imperiled existence by working in shops and factories, competing forces undermined their efforts at home. Pickpocketing was a way of life for the neighborhood's many ragtag bands of unsupervised boys. When they reached their teens, boys were drafted into gangs. Those with already seasoned tastes found gambling, prostitution, and alcohol a few easy dollars and doorsteps away. At night, while exhausted parents slept, the South End became a carnival of vices, offering anyone who ventured outdoors boundless reserves of music, liquor, and sex at countless all-night theaters, "hotels," and restaurants.

The twenty-two churches in this pocket of sin didn't seem to wield nearly as much influence on the South End's 50,000 souls as its sixteen saloons, eleven pawn shops, two striptease clubs, and numerous dance halls. Families that had risked everything in coming to America were being threatened with disintegration, not by disaffection but by

the stresses of survival. And neighborhoods were being destroyed —
not by poverty, as astute observers saw it, but by alienation and lack
of common interests and collective purpose.

No legal mechanism or simple welfare policy would repair the invid-
ious erosion of values occurring in America's industrial era slums. In
England a generation earlier, a succession of Oxford philosophers,
ministers, and even artists, including Thomas Carlyle and John Rus-
kin, had come to a similar conclusion about the poor in London's East
End. These men had a deeply rooted reverence for political democracy and an idealistic view that spiritual development was one of the
aims of a worthy society; they believed that nothing as static as law or
as indifferent as financial support would restore the essential sense of
community to urban civilization. A more subtle, integrative, and par-
ticipatory solution was needed, the Oxford group decided.

In 1883, after some twenty years of discussion, thought, and exper-
imentation, a solution seemed to be found. It was the inspiration of
Samuel Barnett, who had become chaplain of St. Jude's, the poorest
parish in London's Whitechapel district. Barnett opened a residence
there for university men willing to live and work in the impoverished
environs of St. Jude's for a period of time. Toynbee Hall, as the residence was named, had as its raison d'être the ongoing process of community building: "to reestablish on a natural basis those social relations which modern city life has thrown into confusion"[5] on the very
streets and in the tenements where those in need of fellowship lived.

Once social relations were reestablished, they would provide the
basis for neighbors to come together for assistance and protection of
their common interest. In the view of Barnett and his group, one
common interest was the very relations being established; the settlement house was both a means and an end in itself. Any "service" that
its residents rendered to the community escaped the pious affecta-
tions of charity because they were reaping as well the benefits of a
society based on the value of cooperation.

Jane Addams, meanwhile, back in America, was two years out of
Rockford College, a women's college in Illinois, and was studying to
be a doctor. Reared in a home where Abraham Lincoln had been a
beloved influence and an occasional correspondent, by a Quaker father who'd served for sixteen years in the Illinois Senate, Addams had
early on decided to pursue a career working with the poor. While in

medical school, however, her health failed. Her plans interrupted, she was sent abroad on doctor's orders to recover. While she was in Europe, in 1888, she ran across an article about Toynbee Hall. Immediately she wrote to Samuel Barnett and asked to visit.

Addams swiftly saw the applicability of the settlement house to the slums of Chicago. When she returned to the States, she at once began to look for a dwelling from which she could work out the practical philosophy she'd observed at Toynbee Hall. In a Chicago neighborhood of small merchants surrounded by a number of often hostile ethnic groups living in impossibly tight living quarters, Addams found her home. Wedged between a saloon and an undertaker, it would become the figurative nursery for a new community. She named the residence Hull House.

Addams began an evening reading club. She enlisted volunteers to run a kindergarten (the neighborhood's first), where mothers could leave their children all day while they worked, rather than alone in cribs or tied for safety to table legs. An after-school boys' club grew into a five-story activities center complete with shops, equipment, and recreational and study rooms. A girls' club organized language and crafts classes and cultural functions. Hull House sponsored evening coffees and social gatherings, and celebrated ethnic holidays. Where previously the different groups had found it in their best interest to keep to themselves, Hull House offered a congenial, neutral ground on which to test out friendships. It was a place where outsiders could acquire the skills to move into the mainstream culture and where residents could find effective advocates when city services were lacking or corrupt ward bosses attempted to manipulate them.

Such organized activities aside, some of Addams's most important tasks were those that no one else in the city cared to perform. She helped bury the dead and nurse the sick and see to it that the elderly people living at the paupers' home got a two-week visit in their old neighborhood every summer. She helped at the births of illegitimate children and provided a temporary haven for abused wives and for immigrant girls ensnared by prostitution.

While Hull House was in its infancy, a Boston man, Robert A. Woods, had become intrigued by the Oxford experiment. A graduate of Andover Theological Seminary, Woods was sent to Toynbee Hall by one of his seminary professors, William Tucker, who later became president of Dartmouth College. Toynbee Hall made as deep an impression on Woods as it had on Addams. When he returned to the United States, he delivered a series of lectures at Andover on the settlement house movement. Then he and his wife moved into a brownstone at 20 Union Park in Boston's South End, and on January 2, 1892, opened Andover House, the city's first settlement. Woods invited young men from Harvard to live with them and begin the work of establishing neighborly relations with the poor in Hell's Half Acre.

If Addams was to become the most prominent practitioner of the settlement house movement, Woods would be its leading apologist. The two met for the first time in the summer of 1892 at Plymouth, Massachusetts, where the Ethical Culture Society was hosting its first conference on philanthropy and social progress. It was with the conviction that they were renewing some of America's most basic concepts of community and opportunity that the small group stood close to where the Mayflower had touched ground more than two hundred and fifty years earlier.

Addams's conference paper, entitled "The Subjective Necessity for Social Settlements," laid out the manifesto of the American settlement movement: "Truth in action."[6] Settlement work, she claimed, closed the abyss between theory and action that was threatening America's social integrity. The well-off younger generation, pursuing idle pleasures and feeding the growing consumer culture, were becoming disconnected from any sense of civic responsibility.

Woods, whose lectures had just been compiled into a book, *English Social Movements,* set forth his conviction that settlements were the best form of charity work, because they drew on the energies and talents of the communities themselves. Far better than the (necessary) remedial charity that addressed acute material need (poor relief) or the paternalistic charity that relied on resources outside the community, what Woods called the "reconstructive" charity of the settlement house freed people's latent creative powers, reaffirmed community, and achieved lasting change.

The Plymouth group believed they'd discovered in the settlement house the key to making urban life work for rich and poor, educated and illiterate alike. Radically different from the theories of an earlier generation, this one drew the poor from the margins of society into the mainstream. It recast the image of the poor, focusing no longer on the unattached, errant drifter or the immoral prostitute, but instead on the impoverished, deserving family. And in concentrating its efforts on preserving the family as the seat of character, citizenship, and neighborhood life, this movement oriented much of its best resources to the needs of poor women.

The settlement house movement was uniquely matriarchal and feminist in the history of poverty work in the United States. A 1922 survey of 250 settlements revealed that of their 1,411 house residents, 1,090, or 70 percent, were women. Neither before nor after would women be the primary theorists, administrators, workers, and consumers of such a coherent system of social services. And never again would such services be so holistic, so well integrated into the daily life of poor communities or so cognizant of the role that nonmaterial goods — association, creative expression, and pride in heritage — play in sustaining the quality of life and the political health of a democratic society.

Hell's Half Acre was only too ready for the settlement house movement. Andover House was soon renamed South End House, and a women's residence, Denison House, was opened nearby. It was here that Esther Barrows made her home for twenty years.

Barrows was a trailblazer. She was the first applicant to the new Simmons School of Social Work and a member of its first class. During her required fieldwork practicum, she was assigned to work with the Associated Charities in the district around Union Park. Here she came into contact with Woods and soon became a resident of Denison House.

In return for a pittance, usually just room and board (which cost anywhere from $300 to $500 a year), paid for mainly through fellowships provided by Andover, Harvard, and Amherst colleges, Barrows and her colleagues made an average of three hundred house calls every week. Sometimes they just chatted. Sometimes they visited on some errand, informing a young mother that milk was far better for her baby than the beer she was giving him, or inviting the household children to participate in one of the festivities sponsored by the house, which by 1910 had a social center on Harrison Avenue.

The twenty-eight workers at South End House were augmented by one hundred "associates," volunteers who came in one or more times a week to teach a class or perform a specific service. In time the house residents received stipends beyond their board and costs, and the office workers earned salaries competitive with what they'd receive in regular office work. And the staff began to include salaried workers from the neighborhoods themselves.

The settlement's mission, however, never changed. Nor did its approach, which was to respond to people's needs on a one-to-one basis and to sponsor activities the neighbors thought would enhance the quality of life in the South End. The work wasn't always easy or pleasant. Those who died had to be buried, and children had to be fed; hot soup was carried door to door during influenza epidemics, and human chains organized in the dead of winter to distribute as many buckets of coal as the house could obtain from the yards. Settlement residents acted as the watchdogs of city agencies and as agents for tenants of poorly maintained hovels, pressuring absentee owners into making needed improvements. South End House set up an evening school where young men and women could learn vocational skills.

By 1914 Boston had thirty-three settlement houses; in many respects they embodied the social work ethos of the period.

One of the very few institutions to survive this era of constructive radicalism carried the concept of community building to lengths well beyond those imagined by Woods. Its founder, Henry Morgan, was iconoclastic, ingenious, and ambitious. He drew the best from the settlement house movement and the most effective from the temperance movement. He anticipated modern-day homeless shelters by a century. Yet the chief distinction of the institution that became his namesake lay in its merging of social programs with a profitable business enterprise that provided the poor with jobs in the community. Though political circumstances forced it to redirect its mission, today his creation still exists, as Morgan Memorial Goodwill Industries.

Morgan, born in 1825, was an itinerant preacher who made his way from abject poverty in Connecticut to camp meetings in the rural South. When he returned to the North, asylums and reformatories were among the few legitimate organizations that would give him a stump to preach from. Morgan's outspokenness and unorthodox ways, his charisma and legendary ability to convert sinners and drinkers, made him suspect among his peers. Wherever he went, his performances only made him more popular among the masses and more renegade within his own Methodist church.

On his arrival in Boston in 1859, his requests to preach at local houses of worship were refused; in defiance, he rented the Boston

Music Hall. A "genuine specimen of a live, jumping, nervous Yankee," the Boston *Atlas* described him the next day.[7] The papers carried his speech verbatim. It was the last time Henry Morgan would ever have to worry about an audience. In spite of itself, Boston approved. And Morgan decided to stay.

He convinced the city to give him the Franklin School building on Washington Street in the South End, which was already becoming an immigrant slum. His circuit preaching in asylums and reformatories had left him vehemently opposed to poorhouses and to delegating the work of dealing with the poor to surrogates. At the Franklin School, Morgan created the Boston Union Mission Society, a combined church and Sunday school. He set up a free vocational program and established the first night school in Boston, for boys who worked during the day. If they needed a place to sleep after classes, Morgan provided that, too. The inveterate preacher continued his stumping, now on street corners and saloons in the South End, convinced that "whole communities aroused to philanthropic action will accomplish more for preventing crime and reforming the fallen than a few paid officials in costly institutions."[8]

In time his trade school, staffed entirely by volunteers, was so successful that, much to Morgan's bitter disappointment, the city decided to take it over; Morgan foresaw that as an institution with paid instructors and vested interests it would cease to be the flexible program he'd created, and most of his poor students would no longer be eligible.

But by that time, 1868, Morgan's horizons had broadened considerably. The most renowned preacher in the city, he was that year elected chaplain of the State Senate. Though temporarily deprived of an operational base among the poor, he now had allies among Boston's bountiful, who could help him when opportunity arose. In the rapidly changing demography of the South End, this wasn't long in coming. The Church of the Disciples wanted to sell its South End building and leave Boston's Bowery. With the governor, William Claflin, acting as intermediary, and the Jordan Marsh & Company department store sponsoring a benefit to help raise the funds, Morgan purchased the building and renamed it Morgan Chapel. Until his death at the age of fifty-nine in 1884, Henry Morgan concentrated his energies on his church.

Morgan left no successor, and it is unlikely that anyone could have filled his shoes. Morgan Chapel went through five ministers in the

next nine years, conditions in the parish reducing three of them to
nervous breakdowns before they departed. Then in 1895 the chapel
found its ideal pastor in a young seminary student who was earning
his B.A. at Boston University's School of Theology.

Edgar J. Helms, originally a farm boy from Iowa, had banked
everything on the prospect of missionary service in Asia. Informed at
the eleventh hour that any overseas posting couldn't include his fian-
cée, Jean, he was advised to consider a different type of missionary
work, one closer to home. Helms was no newcomer to inner-city missions. Two years earlier, for his ministerial fieldwork, he had started
a settlement house in the North End. Modeled after Woods's one-
year-old South End House, the North End counterpart helped clothe,
settle, and find jobs for immigrant Italian and Irish families.

Helms decided to accept the challenge of leading Morgan Chapel.
He became the sixth pastor of the church no one wanted, not far from
Woods's settlement house, in a neighborhood grown as alien to Yan-
kee Brahmins as Calcutta or Delhi. There Helms found his new world.

Helms's congregation consisted of about three hundred derelicts
who were accustomed, by the precedent of his predecessors, to being
locked in the chapel for Sunday services in exchange for a free breakfast afterward. When they could, they slept in the pews at night, out
of the rain and the cold. No one else in the neighborhood dared, or
cared, to negotiate the hazards of the streets to perform so useless a
chore as praying. They were too tired, too hungry, too afraid, or too
drunk to bother. Morgan Chapel was the "tramps' chapel," and if five
able-bodied pastors hadn't been able to make more of it, no one was
putting money on the Iowan.

Helms did away with the enforced Sunday services. While he and
his wife cleaned the resultingly empty church, removing its cast-off
rags, trash, and stench of urine, Helms introduced himself around
the neighborhood by preaching on street corners. He knew that nothing would come of his chapel if people's stomachs remained as empty
as their futures seemed, if they had no decent shoes in which to walk
even as far as his front door. As soon as the sacristy was clean enough
to start having services again, it acquired a new weekday identity as
well, as a day nursery for the children of working parents. For the
tramps, displaced but not deserted, Helms made the baptistry over
into bathing facilities and had showers installed in the basement.

The tramps' chapel was becoming the people's church. Morgan

Chapel soon had a vitality it had never known. Activities kept it open from dawn until well after dark. With a donated soda fountain, Helms was even able to compete with the bars by opening a Temperance Saloon in the basement. Six nights a week, the pub was a haven for men on the wagon. There they were able to get out of the claustrophobic atmosphere of their tenement flats, play cards, read, and fraternize without resorting to the bottle.

And every Saturday night, while the neighborhood emporiums were doing a land office business siphoning off the workers' hard-won wages, Morgan Chapel provided a cheaper alternative for anyone who cared to attend: free musical presentations, recitations, and entertainment.

Mary Antin, one of the many children who attended, preserved for posterity the impressions of those evenings. "We were all a little bit stage-struck after these entertainments," she wrote, "but what was more, we were genuinely moved by the glimpses of a fairer world than ours which we caught through the music and poetry. . . . The total effect was an exquisitely balanced compound of pleasure, wonder, and longing."[9]

On such longing and promise Helms reinvigorated Henry Morgan's evening school, expanding the curriculum to offer classes in printing, penmanship, shoe repair, tailoring, cobbling, and carpentry, in addition to the Saturday industrial school that his wife had begun as soon as they'd reopened the church.

Helms encouraged the young to expand their skills into music and crafts. For ten to thirty cents a lesson, children could take up the violin, mandolin, or guitar. In time Helms identified the need for a summer playschool. He and his wife hired Lucy Wheelock, who later became a national leader in early childhood training; she began a year-round kindergarten and turned the chapel into a summer playschool for the children of working mothers. The children were served breakfast and lunch, supervised in games, and given a few rudimentary lessons.

In 1899 the old chapel was demolished and a new one, Morgan Memorial M.E. Church, was built with a $50,000 mortgage. It had two auditoriums, a gym, bathing facilities, game rooms, classrooms, and a proper nursery and kindergarten. An employment office helped neighborhood people find work.

Helms's improvement, if not resurrection, of his section of the South End was remarkable by any standards. In the short span of five years, the poor community had an activities center, its working parents had a safe place to leave their children, and young people had a place to learn trades instead of hanging around street corners seeking less licit livelihoods. The church's employment service found jobs for about six hundred people each year. It also succeeded in weeding bad tenants out of adjacent buildings, assiduously documenting illegal activity, finding decent replacement tenants, and confronting absentee landlords with requests for evictions that were hard to refuse.

If veneration for church and neighborhood was nurtured in the home, so too was home life dependent on a sustaining material and moral environment. Helms understood the symbiosis among home, community, and church that kept all three alive. The worst evil, and the one most relentlessly to be broken down, was isolation.

During the bleak winter of 1902, the country was experiencing its most serious depression ever. South End residents began turning up at the church doors desperate for anything Helms could offer: hot soup, rags, a few pieces of wood. But resources were few, and widespread starvation threatened.

Helms then took the most revolutionary step in his evolving scheme. He gathered all the castoff clothing he'd received as donations from Boston's well-to-do and opened the chapel to the multitudes waiting outside. Then he stood aside as they assaulted the piles of garments. What he saw horrified him. Normally decent people were scavenging like animals, without dignity or regard for the equally needy around them. Helms threw everyone out again, locked the doors to the chapel, and thought.

He perceived that this sort of charity would undermine everything he'd been trying to do in the parish, and concluded that he would have to sell the clothing, if only for a few pennies, in order to protect people's self-respect. And if he was going to do that, he realized, he'd have to also see that they could earn the money to pay for it.

Helms set off with a wheelbarrow into the streets and alleys of Beacon Hill, begging for cast-off clothing. Back at Morgan Memorial he set up workshops where residents were paid to clean and repair the donations. The workshops became auxiliaries to the industrial classes, the first place of employment for class graduates. The repaired clothing was sold in the Morgan Memorial thrift shop. It proved lucrative, and the cast-off retrieval system became popular throughout Boston. Soon the surplus coffee bags used for clothing collections were a standard feature in church basements all over the city.

The thrift shop proceeds began to support the children's programs at Morgan Memorial, allow Helms to give aid directly to needy parishioners, and pay workshop salaries. In 1905, three years after it had begun, the operation was employing more than 1,150 people and was incorporated separately as Morgan Memorial Cooperative Industries and Stores "for the purposes of giving temporary employment and providing training to those who are out of work and without means, giving especial attention to those who are handicapped and those who have dependents."[10]

The system was refined. New workers spent part of their first two weeks deciding on the training course they wished to pursue under supervisors who filled out biweekly progress reports. A portion of the first two weeks' wages went directly into a credit bank on which employees could draw in time of emergency. After the trial period, each worker was enrolled as a student in one of the trade programs and received a pay raise. While learning a trade, they worked in the workshops, and when they had mastered it, they were helped to find work in the open market.

Word of Helms's achievements spread rapidly. Morgan Memorial became known as the "Industrial Church." At the St. Louis Exhibition of 1904 Morgan Memorial won awards, and the next year in Liège, Belgium, it won the Grand Prix given by the International Jury in Social Economics, which raised the institution's profile at home and abroad.

Helms, meanwhile, was beginning to articulate the experiment's philosophical underpinnings. For the man who had decided on his career path after reading Horatio Alger's tales, this wasn't difficult. Wrote one of his biographers, John Fulton Lewis, "Helms was convinced that America had been a divine inspiration, giving Americans a priceless opportunity to provide a 'heaven on earth,' and that Christianity was the source of democracy's strength."[11] For Helms the democratic ideal and the Christian ethic of equality and brotherhood went hand in hand. "He abhorred the disdain which many Americans seemed to hold for immigrants." Moreover, and perhaps more important for the future development of Morgan Memorial, "he was alarmed at the practice of the business community and the growing labor movement to depersonalize their relations with the working man and to ignore 'service' to humanity by concentrating all resources on profits and organization."[12]

Helms himself wrote in 1927, "Christian civilization not only de-

mands productive industry where everyone able shall do his work, it
also demands that industry shall be carried on in a spirit of goodwill.
There should be work for everybody and everybody should work.
Louis Blanc's dictum, 'From every man according to his ability; to
every man according to his need,' is a fine statement of the Christian
industrial philosophy of the Goodwill Industries." [13]

Helms's workshops and industries were, he believed, a model for
the successful merging of democratic ideals with the aims of individual
fulfillment. "The Goodwill Industries are converted industries in
that they seek to be utterly unselfish. They exist for 'service,' and not
for profits." [14]

On these and related themes of social justice, Helms began to lecture
regularly. In 1907 he founded the Morgan Memorial School of
Applied Christianity, which offered forums and courses entitled "Religion
as Applied to the Political, Social, Industrial and Economic
Problems of the Present." A decade later the school was so successful
that it merged with Helms's alma mater to become the Boston University
School of Religious Education and Social Work, whose descendant,
the School of Social Work, still exists.

In 1910, through a restructuring by the Methodist church of the
management of Morgan Memorial, Helms became free to appoint his
own board and reorganize the industries independently from the
church. He created a national organization to promote community-based
cooperative industries around the country. Morgan Memorial
continued to grow. With the support of two wealthy New Hampshire
brothers, George E. and John H. Henry, a new six-story plant was
built in 1913. A second building was added five years later. A rug
factory, begun in 1906, that sold reconstructed Brussels and tapestry
rugs, was moved out to a two-hundred-acre farm in western Massachusetts
that the Henrys had donated to Morgan Memorial as a summer
camp for children. Now it also served as a rehabilitation work
center for recovering alcoholics and a country retreat for families in
need of a month out of the city.

By 1922 thrift shop sales were so healthy that accountants confidently
projected the year's income at $244,000. Morgan Memorial
now had ten thrift shops: the South End's main store and a bargain
basement, and stores in East Cambridge, East Boston, Charlestown,
South Boston, Roxbury, the West End, Lynn, and Fitchburg. Goodwills
(all independently incorporated) were also operating in Brook-

lyn, Philadelphia, Cleveland, Buffalo, Denver, St. Louis, Los Angeles, and San Francisco.

Helms never forgot that his industrial workshops were only one facet of the community he envisioned and of the "reconstruction" required in the lives of its inhabitants. Chronic alcoholism and a homeless, skid-row existence continued to keep some people from getting into Morgan Memorial's constructive network of services and jobs. They had their own circuit — from curbside to tavern, to jail and back to the streets of the South End again — and for some it seemed unbreakable. Helms began serving as chaplain at the Charles Street Jail, trying, on a one-to-one basis, to help men break out of this trap. He soon realized that if his efforts were to succeed, he needed a place for these men to live, off the streets and out of abandoned buildings, while they tried to get their lives back together again.

Helms became a pioneer of modern-day shelters for the homeless. In 1915 the long-time sheriff of the Charles Street Jail, Fred Seavey, died, leaving Helms a modest legacy with which to build such a residence. The Seavey Settlement opened as a fifty-bed facility that same year. Men who came to the door were referred to as guests of the house. They were given clean beds, showers, and, in the morning, laundered clothes and medical examinations. If they chose to stay, each man, with the help of a counselor, decided on goals that he would work toward. No time limit was ever placed on a guest's length of stay; rather, his continued welcome depended on his progress toward his own goals, which usually included some variant on the twin pursuits of sobriety and employment. As soon as he was able, each guest was given work at Morgan Memorial. As he began to achieve some of his objectives, a guest "graduated" from being a junior member of the house, to middle, and then to senior status, earning new duties and privileges at each step. Unsuccessful guests, who wouldn't work or weren't ready to stop drinking, were asked to leave after a few weeks.

Helms was soon given a thirty-one-room residential hotel for working women. Residents didn't have to be homeless and didn't have to commit to any program; the hotel was open to any woman who was unable to afford a decent place to live. The Eliza Henry House, midway between a lodging house and a shelter, included sixteen suites for young married couples who were working their way through school. This house was soon joined in the Morgan Memorial "family" by the Lucy Stone House in Dorchester. This house, a bequest from the family of the first Massachusetts woman to earn a college degree, was used for daily outings for mothers and their children from the South End.

As a final instrument for housing the destitute and homeless, the Henry family also helped organize the Massachusetts Housing Organization. The M.H.O. bought up South End lodging houses and renovated them, then made them available to Morgan Memorial for homeless individuals and families.

For Helms, the pinnacle of this service empire had to be a place of worship. The chapel continued to tie the people of Morgan Memorial to its original purposes. Helms still conducted Sunday services, and most social services were still based in the Shawmut Street church. But Helms, characteristically, nurtured larger dreams. While still a seminary student working in the North End settlement, he'd conceived the notion of one day building a church especially for poor immigrants. It would be an international and interdenominational house of worship, a spiritual counterpart to the secular democratic city, a place where newcomers could find and bear witness to the many faces of God that composed the soul of a pluralistic society.

In 1918 this church of the imagination became stone. The Church of All Nations opened its massive doors on Shawmut Street next door to the Seavey Settlement. The Cathedral of the Poor, as Helms referred to it, took on the force of manifest destiny in its facade, with stones from the Second Unitarian church in Copley Square, where Ralph Waldo Emerson had served as ninth pastor. A multilingual ministerial staff held church services in seven languages. Like Morgan Chapel, the church became the base for all of Morgan Memorial's services.

A member of the church outreach team was assigned to each South End neighborhood, and every ethnic group had a contact person. The outreach workers would try to involve new immigrants in the church's many departments — clubs for adults and young people, drama and music classes, and discussion groups. There were Bible classes for children, classes in English and composition for adults, and talks on how to make one's way in the American system.

The church activities meshed with the work at the Industries. New church members were given jobs if they needed them, and employees were expected to perform ten hours a week of religious or social work in the community.

By 1922 the Church of All Nations was ardently recruiting members from a population of 24,000. Morgan Memorial Industries employed 4,000 people, and the Seavey Settlement served 1,000 guests. But Helms, a man of uncanny foresight, was already predicting that by 1945 the South End's population would be half of what it was in 1922. It was time to expand elsewhere. Morgan Memorial's twenty-fifth anniversary report expressed the church's expectations: "It is not improbable that this form of Christian endeavor, working out in lines of reconstructive philanthropy and constructive social service in the spirit of Christian love, will in another quarter of a century occupy all corners of the earth."[15] Helms began making plans for an international tour that would take in Australia and the Far East, and further visits to encourage efforts he knew to be beginning in India, China, Mexico, South America, and Europe.

It was not the crash of 1929 but national recovery that proved cataclysmic for Helms and Morgan Memorial. In 1929 Goodwill Industries, operating in some 132 cities, earned $3 million in total national sales. The next year gross receipts dropped almost 11 percent, though collections increased by 53.4 percent. At a time when only five jobs were available for every hundred people across the country, Goodwill managed to keep most of their 37,000 employees on the payroll and succeeded in finding outside jobs for some 9,000 people. In the South the Methodist Episcopal church had to abandon the Goodwills because they no longer had the money to support them. Independently, these Goodwills continued and managed even in such straitened circumstances to give 2,000 people work.

At his first glimpse of New Deal thinking, Helms was cautious, to say the least. A memo sent in 1932 to the executive committee of the Bureau of Goodwill Industries posed a series of questions pertaining to lower operating costs, then noted: "Government and social agencies are now demoralizing the poor by insisting that supplies shall be given rather than that work should be required; how can we bring our idealism to bear upon this situation?"[16]

Helms believed that his approach worked and was better for people's dignity than mere charity, whatever its guise. For those who simply couldn't compete in industrialized society, he began researching the idea of farm colonies based on the Shaker model. However, despite his skepticism toward the New Deal, when Franklin Delano Roosevelt established the Federal Employment Relief Administration, and Congress in 1933 passed the National Industrial Recovery Administration act with plans to open sheltered workshops, Helms and others within Goodwill lobbied hard for the federal government to study their experiences and programs.

In response the NIRA (which was later declared unconstitutional) sent Helms a rather clipped missive informing him that as a "barter and exchange" business, Goodwill Industries wouldn't be eligible for federal operating grants as part of the relief act. Helms, stunned, argued that Goodwill was in every sense a workers' cooperative, not a barter operation. Moreover, its effectiveness couldn't be challenged. As the largest and most established operation of its kind in the country, it was turning every dollar's worth of goods into five dollars in benefits for the needy, producing the equivalent of twenty-five million dollars in wages for the unemployed during the Depression. The government wouldn't budge. When Helms then applied for operating funds under the barter and exchange provision of the relief act, he was refused.

Helms had spent thirty-five years quietly proving that effective work could be done in poor communities, given an integrated vision of need and sufficient grassroots support to respond to it. Now he found himself on the margin, his mission dismantled piece by piece. Goodwill Industries would have to find a new poor and a new geography if it was to survive.

▨▨▨▨▨▨▨▨▨▨

SIX

Bottomed Out

FREEDOM WAS EMILY BRONTË, the life of Marie Curie, and the fantasies of Paris. It was the morning. Once Wendy reached the end of the short gravel driveway and passed the gray mailbox and the last few houses along her country road, all she had to do was wait for the school bus, which ferried her to the school library and from there to the trimmed walks of the Luxembourg Gardens, with Colette or Proust as her guide.

The sanctuary that Papa and a plush bunny rabbit had once created, her own curiosity and imagination now enlarged. Wendy would read for hours, both in school and behind her closed bedroom door after she finished her homework at night, escaping into other lives in search of the shape to eventually give her own. Though Papa would remain her closest ally on earth, she was beginning to establish independent patterns of flight.

Early in her school years, she distinguished herself as the class "brain." A studious, shy girl who wore glasses and braids and seemed never to be without a book, she consistently earned straight A's. She needed no one to tell her that if anything was going to win for her a life commensurate with her dreams, it was her intellect.

But every morning had its afternoon. Back at home she invariably found the dishes waiting to be washed, the house to be cleaned, the domestic burdens that fell without second thought on the only daughter.

"I was the model daughter. Go to school, come home, clean house, do this, do that. Don't say mum, you know?"

There was Johnnie, her half brother, to look after and the table to be set for dinner.

"My mother was a lousy housekeeper," Wendy says. "But she constantly wanted this and wanted that and wanted this and wanted that, right? In other words, you couldn't please her."

Meanwhile her brothers played in the back yard. But something else hurt far worse than the inequality of hours at play.

"My brothers, they're getting C's and D's. I'm getting A's and B's. They're getting money for all their C's and D's. They — my parents — look at my report card and it's, 'Oh yeah, we knew she'd do that again.' "

Academic achievement had no place at home, where her real value, it seemed clear to her, was in the work she did after classes let out. Occasionally, when she was finished with her chores, she would join her brothers in their games.

"My brother always played the cop," she recalls. "He always used to shoot me."

Across the street lived a girl named Anne, part of a large Irish brood that met the world running. The bang of screen doors and the commotion of pursuing feet never ceased at the Kellys'. Anne had red hair and freckles and, like the rest of her siblings, a resilient humor that made it impossible to brood over life's slights for long.

To Anne it seemed natural that she and her contemporary across the street should become pals. But to Wendy, things were not that simple. Anne offered entry into a world Wendy had never known, perhaps the ultimate seductive fantasy: an untroubled childhood. The two became inseparable.

"Me and her were demons together," Wendy recalls, falling easily into the vernacular of those days. "She was my bestest friend."

It was Anne who supplied the pair with their first fashion magazines. For hours the two pored over glossy photos of teen idols, trying to crack the elusive code of Madison Avenue perfection.

"We did all this good shit together," Wendy giggles. "She had all these freckles, you know. We used to send away for all this stuff to try and erase them. I'd say, 'Annie, you know I don't think it's going to work. It's all a gimmick.' "

Together they bought their first bras, consulted about their periods, and gummed their eyelashes with their first mascara. As a pair they went on their first diet. When Anne took a babysitting job in the neighborhood, Wendy would bring her homework over and keep her company. The most flagrant naughtiness they indulged in was pooling their lunch money for a pack of cigarettes, which they smoked among the trees behind the cemetery until they both turned green.

In her heart of hearts, Wendy may have known that this happy lull wouldn't last, but it eased the lonely splendor of her academic standing and her Cinderella life at home.

Even Wendy's mother would shake her head fondly and say to her daughter, "What you can't think up, she will. And when you're together . . ." As Molly's words trailed off, it seemed to Wendy as though the stalemate life had forced her to accept years earlier might finally have been broken.

Had it not been for the aches that began to course up and down her legs at night, it might have been. The cramps began to disturb her sleep. Growing pains, her mother suspected. But at night, staring into the pitch darkness, trying not to waken anyone with her crying, Wendy, not quite twelve, feared something worse. Some mornings the pain was so bad she could hardly get out of bed. Then came the day when she realized with horror that she had begun to limp. She tried to camouflage her gait at school and kept to herself, sitting in out-of-the-way corners with her face buried behind a book.

But she couldn't outfox her growing deformity: another symptom soon appeared. Just above her right knee, a fleshy knot started to grow. Self-conscious and afraid, she watched the bulb that she could no longer hide, as it became larger and more hideous.

"You're ugly!" she heard a voice inside her head saying. "Why are you so ugly?"

One morning she awoke to such excruciating pain that she could not move. The doctor was called, and swiftly diagnosed her as having rheumatoid arthritis. Her other leg had developed a compensatory excess of cartilage growth, which would have to be removed.

When she told Anne the news, she didn't cry. Her face felt tight and her voice pinched; already Wendy was somewhere far away.

The next two years saw a succession of operations and recuperative stays in long-term-care hospitals, with wheelchairs and crutches and a pity that made Wendy want to break glass. Just as she had begun to learn how to move in time with the rock albums that she and Anne played in the basement after school, she was suddenly a cripple who had to be taught how to walk.

But the illness that condemned Wendy to exile in a sterile hospital among the terminally ill, completely out of touch with the adolescent world, offered unforeseen compensations. Exempted from normal life she had endless hours to read again, to write poetry and indulge in dreams about a future far away from the streets of Easton.

Wendy never forgot that her natural father was half French. Lying in her hospital bed, she thought of him often. And she thought about *his* father, and whoever, generations before, had stepped onto a boat at Le Havre or Brest to come to the New World. In those long speculative months, Wendy decided that she wanted to take up the quest of those generations and return to their source. She would win a scholarship after high school and study in Paris, perhaps settle there. Paris became the future that made the hospital ward, and Easton, worth enduring.

She would wheel herself down to the chapel and sit for long periods. "It was just nice and peaceful," she remembers. "I really didn't know anything about God or Jesus or anything like that. I wasn't raised in a Christian home. It was every man for himself."

One day when she entered the chapel, "there was this older lady sitting there. There was just a feeling of solitude and peace, you know? And she says, 'Pray, and God will take away — maybe not cure you — but at least he'll help you deal with it.' "

Wendy didn't forget her words. Returning to Easton physically healed at last she started attending services at the Baptist church in town every Sunday. Alone, she found solace in the church, in the sound of the minister's voice, and in the secure feeling of community around her.

"I started going to Sunday school. Then I got baptized. I used to go to the youth group, choir, the prayer reading. And on Sunday evening, I'd go to church."

But it didn't take long for the old domestic routines to reassert themselves. Molly was now working a seven-to-three shift in one of the local factories. She was home when Wendy returned from school. Nevertheless, Wendy says, it was she who was expected to do the chores. And she sensed that her mother resented the church activities that took her away from her household duties.

"I was about fourteen or fifteen, and my mother got tiffed at me for something. She'd make me really super angry, and I'd pray. Inside my head, right? 'Just remember, she's your mother,' and all this stuff. So one day she says to me, she says, 'You're no Christian. Never will be.'

"I just looked at her very calmly, and I said, 'A Christian is a person who believes in Christ. It doesn't mean they live a perfect life.'

"And another time, she took my Bible and slung it across the room. She broke the binding. Which hurt. I just picked it up. It was the Bible my grandfather used. I taped the binding with adhesive tape you use for wounds."

Finally, one night, Wendy remembers her mother delivering the remark that would shatter what remained of her fragile peace.

"I know why you spend so much time in church," she remembers Molly shrieking. "You're going there to get fucked!"

Wendy had tried to observe the secret world of adult love. But what she saw confused and disheartened and threatened her.

"My family is totally weird," she says. "The only closeness I ever had was with my grandmother and grandfather. I mean, I never seen my mother and stepfather kiss each other. I never seen any closeness. Never seen them sit down next to each other on the couch and watch TV together. I mean, I never seen them hold hands. I just never seen no affection at all expressed between the two of them. I'd go to other kids' houses, you know, and I'd see something different. And something clicks. Something's not right. I don't understand it. I never have. To tell the truth, I don't know if they have any sexual activity at all anymore. Even back then."

Wendy did not want to "get fucked." She didn't even want to be touched. And, as if to guarantee that she wouldn't be, she added another layer of fat to her body.

For years she'd been left alone. She had done her chores and read alone in her room and been mercifully free of any sense of encroaching danger. But her mother started working nights, partly to earn the money to pay for Wendy's orthodontic work. This left her alone with Henry Fayre and her three brothers. While Molly worked, secure in her vision of a benevolent, self-sacrificing husband at home, Wendy saw a different man. She says she was raped one night while she was reading in her bedroom, by Henry. And two years later, she says, the same thing happened again, this time at the hands of her older brother.

"My stepfather raped me when I was fourteen, and my brother raped me when I was sixteen," she says without elaboration.

These violent and frightening violations she kept segregated completely from what she continued to think of as her real life. Like the other distorted injuries of her childhood, they were nightmare visions that had to remain as far from consciousness as possible.

In her own mind, she was still a virgin, only now she was more terrified of boys than ever. By the time she turned fifteen, she had never had a boyfriend or been on a real date.

"You're so ugly! Why are you so ugly! I hate you!"

One day in her tenth-grade biology class, however, something snapped.

"Everything was getting, like, jumbled, you know?" she recalls. "I was sitting there in biology class, and it dawns on me, I'm the model daughter. They say jump, you jump. They say sit, you sit. When they want you, they take you out of the closet like a suitcase. When they don't want you, they put you back in the closet like a suitcase. I said, 'No more. This is it. I'm not going to be a robot anymore. I'm me, and I want to be myself. I can't be something for somebody else. I'm only me.' "

Wendy's rebellion kick, as she calls it, had begun. One night soon after this epiphany, Anne was babysitting. As usual, Wendy decided to join her and bring her homework along. That night would change her life.

"She was already getting drunk and doing dope, smoking reefer," Wendy says. Anne had always been a step ahead when it came to trying new things. When Wendy arrived, her friend took her into the kitchen and opened a cupboard.

"They had a liquor supply like there was no tomorrow," Wendy remembers. "Anne taught me how to water down the bottle to make it look the same, ya know?"

The girls helped themselves. Anne poured Wendy a water glass full of Seagram's 7. It was the first alcohol she'd ever tasted. She got drunk. Then she passed out.

After that, "I couldn't stop drinking. I was hooked from the word go."

Wendy had discovered a liquid magic that opened up whole new dimensions of freedom. "All my life, I'd been abused. All my life, I felt so inadequate. I was terribly shy. Ha! I found what makes me — oh ho, I found something. This works! And I was off and running."

Stolen moments became trysts with small, readily disposable pint bottles and breath freshener. She drank in the evenings and on the weekends in the privacy of her room.

"I managed to handle it. I didn't get the shakes or anything like that."

She tried hard to avoid making her mother suspicious. But now when she was with her girl friends, any fear of detection was neutralized by the fact that she had blossomed into a previously unknown Wendy, a gregarious, entertaining, and confident young woman. For the first time in her life, she felt likable. She even thought she liked herself.

It was just a matter of months before her life's fugitive dimension began to pull her in more deeply. She started selling her clothes to pay for her booze.

"My mother was buying clothes for me, right? Brand-new clothes with the tags still on them. 'Hey, couple dollars for this dress. Five bucks for this nice pair of jeans. Five bucks for this sweater.' I was boozin' it, ya know?"

At fifteen, when her drinking began, Wendy was a pretty girl with soft umber eyes, broad cheekbones, and full lips. She wore her hair long, with bangs that framed her heart-shaped face. Her only real shortcoming, not counting her extreme self-consciousness, was the extra weight she had put on right after her illness.

That summer she and Anne went to Florida to visit Granny and Papa in the retirement home they had moved to. When the girls arrived in Tampa, Wendy, who was five foot four, weighted 120 pounds; by the time she left three months later, she weighed barely 90. All summer long she lived on half a tuna fish sandwich a day, with a cup of tea in the morning and another cup at night. During the day she drank gallons of water.

"Every time I looked at myself, fat fat fat fat. That's all I could think of. I said, 'Granny, you gotta help me. I'm trying to cut myself down to twenty calories a day.' I'm talking about sicko. Within one month I lost thirty pounds."

Then one day at lunch time she was sitting at the kitchen table drinking iced tea when a reverse compulsion took over. She got up, opened the refrigerator, and ate almost everything in it without stopping. When she was done, she ran to the toilet and vomited it all up. For the rest of the summer, instead of reading and thinking about her future, Wendy spent most of her time binging and throwing up.

When she returned to Massachusetts in the fall, she was thin, still quiet, and still shy. Could anyone have seen the warning signs? On the surface nothing was unusual. Not once had she publicly stepped out of her role as a studious, unconfrontational teenager.

"I was quiet. It's not that I was rebellious or anything, or made any trouble. It's not like I was a disciplinary problem. I'd never been suspended in my life. My grades were always good. It's not like I was the typical fuck-up. I was fucked up in the head, but that's beside the point. I was basically quiet."

Now that she was thin, Wendy started refusing to wear her glasses, convinced that they detracted from her looks. She paid more attention to her beautiful long hair than to her grades. Every morning she was up at five to wash it and then meticulously blow-dry it into long, straight silky falls. "Every morning. Talk about a fanatic. It took half an hour. Just my hair. That didn't include my bath. Didn't include my make-up. I got to be a champ putting make-up on. Ten minutes was the most. Then I'd be strutting my stuff."

She'd begun to drink again after taking the summer off from booze. But she was still earning straight A's. And despite all of her tactics, she still couldn't break through her debilitating inhibitions.

"But here I am shy! I'm going through all this trouble for nothing."

Sean, who sat in front of her in American History class, wore braces too. They were both so shy that their orthodontia became one of the major topics of conversation between them.

"I was madly in love with this boy. You talk about a crush? He was so cute! I had this thing for Irishmen. But I'm shy as a bastard. So here's Sean. Shorter than me. Anyhow, we wind up going steady."

One day when Wendy was sneaking a cigarette in the girls' room, a friend teased her. "If you and Sean ever kiss you'll probably get locked together with them braces." That wasn't a worry. They never even held hands.

The Bloodhound Sensation was the biggest event of the school year, and for upperclassmen, the most dreamed-about, dreaded, and exaggerated affair of their high school career. Held at the end of the football season in the gymnasium, the Sensation was Easton Central High School's answer to the senior prom. The decoration committee put weeks of planning into color schemes and streamer draping; the refreshment committee rounded up willing mothers to provide the punch, and every girl hovered nervously by her telephone waiting to be invited.

Sean finally got up the nerve and called Wendy.

"I got all decked out," Wendy remembers. Her dress was turquoise blue, "and I had a plunge, baby, that went right down to here. I showed off my figure."

Upstairs, she brushed her hair so that it fell straight down her back, while her brother drove around to pick up Sean and came back to get her. When Wendy saw Sean coming to the door, she wasn't disappointed. He was a knockout in his dark suit, and it touched her deeply when he awkwardly presented her with the cellophane-wrapped florist's box that held the corsage of pink flowers he'd picked out without consulting her. The pair set off for the gymnasium on a high, if uncertain, note.

When she entered the crowded room, transformed for the night by dimmed lights and crepe paper balls, Wendy instantly grew tense. In all of her excitement and daydreaming about this night, she hadn't thought through actually spending four hours alone with someone she could hardly say hello to during the course of the school day. Even before Sean brought her the first of many glasses of sweet punch, any connection that she'd felt to the slender beauty in the turquoise gown in front of her mother's mirror had vanished. The night, she sensed all of a sudden, was going to be too much for her. Much too much.

She recalls the evening in minute detail. "I don't know how to dance. I don't know how to act. And I'm sober. Everybody's dancing and I don't know how to dance. He's shy, and I'm shy. You gotta understand, we never exchanged a peck on the cheek, or held hands. I'm talking about two severely shy people."

For the next four hours, Wendy stood close to one of the walls next to her date, unable to think of anything to talk about, depressed and lost. A part of her knew that she didn't belong there; a part of her wanted to, desperately.

"I felt like an idiot. It wasn't me. It's not me. I'm sorry. It's just not me. I wasn't comfortable. I got bad legs and I'm not exactly graceful. It just, I'm not—I won't even get married unless I'm wearing blue jeans. I don't need no dress! Who am I out to impress?"

On the way home, Sean bought her a hamburger. She was too depressed to touch it. Back in the house and out of her gown, she couldn't put the failed evening out of her mind quickly enough. She'd blown it once more. Possibly for the last time.

I hate you! the mirror said back, this time coldly, without tears.

After the Sensation, the entire tenor of Wendy's life changed. Now she and her mother couldn't be in the house together for five minutes without fighting. And even after she had slammed the door of her bedroom and flung herself on her bed, there seemed nothing left of her in the space where she had once spent so many hours in imaginary flights to Paris. What she needed now, she wasn't going to find in fantasy or in books.

By New Year's the fighting, accusations, and lies had reached a crisis stage. Molly was at her wit's end. She didn't know what to make of her daughter's explosive and unpredictable anger. Ever since the summer, when Wendy had been under her grandmother's exclusive influence, Molly had sensed that something wasn't right. But she didn't know what to do about it. Several times she'd taken Wendy for consultations with a psychiatrist, but he hadn't offered any useful insights for his expensive time. Wendy only seemed to be getting worse.

In January Wendy quit the part-time job she'd held for less than a month. "The company was moving anyway, to where I wouldn't be able to go to work. It was a pickled meat packing factory, and I was sixteen. I had to come home from school after a full day, clean house, run to my job, which was two miles away—I had to walk it. Then, after I got off of work, after five hours, I had to walk back two miles home, at night. I had to do my homework. And then next thing in the morning, I had to go to school."

The confrontation with Molly occasioned by Wendy's quitting was the last one they would have for many months. In the course of it, Wendy swears, Molly beat her up. Wendy didn't hesitate: she picked up the phone and called her grandmother in Florida.

"I was at the end of my rope," Molly admits. "I didn't know what else to do. So I said, 'Fine. Go down and stay with your grandmother.' "

Tucked inland, well behind the strip of two-star hotels, alligator keychain shops, and golf courses where tourists sample the peninsula's pleasures, Pinellas Park moves to another rhythm altogether. With its cinderblock and slab ranches set close together on small numbered streets crisscrossed by miles of shopping mall, Pinellas would just as soon be left to itself, to its Confederate license plates and pickup trucks and bird baths. Just a few miles away in one direction sprawls the headquarters of the Church of Scientology; in the other direction the

Black Hills region is the site of Josef Meier's annual Passion Plays. But
the people of Pinellas prefer the down-home sensibility preached from
their Baptist and Pentecostal pulpits.

When Wendy arrived, she enrolled in the regional comprehensive
high school, Northeast High, and settled down to be left alone. Like
almost everything else in this part of the world, Northeast High was
modeled on the shopping mall. It has two free-standing "super-store"
structures linked by causeways to the smaller "boutiques," the library
among them. Shoe-store-sized modules house the summer school offices and other auxiliary academic programs.

The social dynamics played out every day in the school's corridors
were similar to those Wendy thought she'd left behind in Easton.
Northeast High encompassed in its district the most affluent parts of
St. Petersburg, Snell Isle and Shore Acres, as well as the working-class
enclave of Pinellas Park. It was a demilitarized zone not only between
two neighborhoods but between two classes, so different as to qualify
as separate cultures: the culture of BMWs and back-yard pools, and
that of blue-collar, Bible-toting Southern Baptists.

And even more than Easton, Northeast High was awash in drugs.
Its halls and bathrooms served as a constantly shifting marketplace
for every narcotic on the Drug Enforcement Administration's list.
Tampa and St. Petersburg were second only to Miami as importation
points for South American cocaine and marijuana. Both substances,
as well as pills, angel dust, and LSD, were readily available and of the
highest quality money could buy. Drugs were the vehicle for social
exchange among groups from different schools. Where there were
deals to be made, a kid from Lakeview, at the other end of town,
wouldn't hesitate to enter Northeast territory.

Wendy, something of an old hand by now, and out of range of her
mother's censorious eye, didn't have to go far to find what she needed.
She stuck close to her Papa's home, did her share of pills, reefer, and
booze, began to run with boys, and was left alone.

Yet some internal, already precarious balance was in the process of
being destroyed. Not only was she no longer able to contain the contradictions in her life; after the Bloodhound Sensation, Wendy no
longer had the will to try.

By the time she returned to Easton for her senior year, she was no
longer on the college prep track, where she had been an A student,
one of a handful taking Advanced Placement English, third-year

French, and art. She drifted into the business courses: typing and stenography. She also drank heavily.

"My senior year was a very drunken year. I skipped four days every week. I signed my own notes, because me and my mother have the same kind of handwriting. And the fifth day — you gotta go the fifth day. If you're out five days, you've got to have a doctor's note. So I'd go in on the fifth day, but I'd make up my own notey-poo for an early dismissal. I'd go to the office, get my dismissal slip for right after homeroom, out the door. I had to! I couldn't stand it! I wanted to drink."

That year she missed seventy-six days of school. That she graduated at all was something of a technical oversight.

When the weather turned warm that spring, Wendy and Anne ran away from home. They hitchhiked to Boston and found their way downtown to the Common. It was a perilous caper for seventeen-year-olds, but they didn't care. Among the dope pushers and the bikers, the pimps and the drunks who hung out at the rise of the hill along Tremont Street, Wendy was willing to take her chances. What did she have to lose? As she describes herself then, "I don't know the ropes. I don't know where to go or what to do. And I'm not talking about selling myself. I'm talking about just hiding, ya know?"

She and Anne sat on a park bench smoking cigarettes. It wasn't long before a Puerto Rican man came up to them. He told them he wanted to get them a hotel room, to get them away from this scene. "You two are little lambs in a lion's world," he said.

"No funny business," Wendy insists years later. "He paid for a hotel room just to get us off the street. And this was just out of kindness. There are a lot of nice people in this world." Only as an afterthought does she remember that their benefactor also left them with a liter of vodka.

So the two of them sat, just hours after their arrival in the city, getting high on vodka in the air-conditioned comfort of Howard Johnson's. After a while, hungry, they went out for doughnuts and potato chips. Along with their snacks, they picked up two guys and returned to the room.

"Two young guys. No funny business," Wendy insists. "We have this big box of doughnuts, a color TV. I'm going to sleep."

The next morning the foursome took off for Nashua, New Hampshire. "We were right out of there. Here we are, these two young stupid broads. Don't know shit from shinola."

They made their way north as far as the small town of Claremont, where they drank and smoked dope and had sex until all three activities got to be crashing bores. Then one day Anne turned to Wendy and said, "Let's go back to Easton."

"What?" Wendy, still with a buzz on, thought Anne must be kidding. "I had nothing but grief back there."

"Let's go back," Anne insisted. "I want to see if my boyfriend still wants me."

Wendy reluctantly agreed. "We hitchhike back. Five hours." All the while, Wendy was thinking to herself, "This better be good."

At the gray mailbox she took a deep breath and started up the gravel driveway toward the door.

"I'm not scared, but at this point, hey, I'm taking no shit, you know?" She sat down at the kitchen table, tired and hungry. "All I want to do is just go to sleep."

Her stepfather walked in. When he saw her he just stood, hands on his hips, studying her.

"Wendy," he asked at last. "Are you on dope?"

"Gee, Dad," she answered, her voice bold with sarcasm, "I thought I was on a chair."

Then Wendy watched Henry Fayre drive his fist through the wall.

"Instead of hitting me," she realized.

After he'd calmed down and was sitting opposite her at the table, playing with a bottle cap, he said, "Answer me this one question. Just tell me one thing. Why did you come back?"

She didn't have to think long.

"I couldn't think of anything else to do," she admitted.

When she had arrived in Boston on her spree with Anne, Wendy was pregnant but didn't know it. Months before, she'd started to view pregnancy as the perfect resolution of all life's contradictions. Though it might have been the last option that a college-bound star pupil should have chosen, it was the most suicidal one that her angry half could inflict on herself. It would give her a few moments of affirmation as a sexually attractive person. And if, by becoming a mother, she cut off hope of fulfilling her academic potential, she would secure for herself a role and a companion in her child.

"I met this guy," she explains. "He was only six months older than me. A kid himself. The only people I'd ever heard say I love you were my granny and my grandfather. The only thing I ever got at home was, 'Get out of my way. You fucked up again, huh? You didn't wash the dishes too good, did ya?' I did nothing right, no matter how I tried.

"I used to sit there and think of different ways to kill myself. Which is the best way. Which won't hurt the most?

"He was the first person who said, 'I love you.' And I let him do it."

It was confusing, stressful, awful.

"It didn't feel like love, let me tell you. Maybe he wasn't experienced enough, I don't know. I didn't like it. I liked the foreplay. I had the feelings. But when I came down to the nitty gritty — oh no! It's an awful feeling, really. You're so insecure, and everything, and you don't know what the hell is up or down, and you don't know how to react. What am I supposed to say? Am I supposed to whisper sweet nothings in his ear? You don't know how to move. You don't know how to walk. You don't know how to talk. You want to be attractive and everything, but you don't know how the hell to even act! That first experience is a dilly."

Afterward she tried to kill herself.

"I took about a hundred aspirin. All it did was just tear my guts up."

But the longing to be loved, and the illusory security she hoped to gain, proved stronger than the pills. She kept trying.

However, by mid-March, sitting in a hotel room in Boston carrying his child, Wendy had long since lost the aim of motherhood in the momentum of her out-of-control flight, and the boy had long since gone his own way.

For Molly, all of the bitter years of her life with her first husband were resurrected in Wendy's pregnancy. Her daughter was so like him, now that Molly thought about it. And so like the part of herself that she mortally feared.

Wendy insisted. She wanted to have the baby. There wasn't the slightest chance that the father would marry her. Like her grandmother before her, she didn't want him anyway. Molly, beside herself, consulted the psychologist at Easton High. He told her he thought Wendy was not competent mentally, physically, or psychologically to give birth.

That decided it. One spring morning Molly flew with Wendy down to New York, prepared to drag her daughter, if necessary, to the abortion clinic where she'd made an appointment. Wendy would never forgive her.

"My mother forced me to have the abortion," she would say many many times over the years. "I wanted the baby. I was six months pregnant, too far along to have an abortion in Massachusetts. What they do is they stick a needle into your embryonic sac and take out the embryonic fluid, and they inject salt solution, and the baby convulses to death.

"I didn't know this. You actually give birth to a dead baby. The only thing wrong with that baby was it didn't live long enough to get big enough. It was fully formed.

"I didn't look. I didn't want to know if it was a boy or a girl. I can't forget. It hurt me. It really hurt, you know. I was forced to. See, I didn't know I had any rights. It tore me apart. I can't explain it. I wanted that baby. I wanted it."

Wendy and her baby would have been the only people who mattered in the whole world. It would have been enough.

"I didn't give a shit about the father! Okay, so the father was a kid. Same age as me. My mother is a sicko. At the same time, my brother got married, because he knocked my girlfriend up. My child would have been born two weeks before hers. And my mother loves that kid. She always says, 'Little Tommy is my flesh.'

"I feel like, 'What was mine? Shit?' You know what I'm saying? Every time I see that kid, all I can think of is, my baby would have been two weeks older than him. It's just a resentment and bitterness toward my mother."

High school was over. After Wendy finished her last final, she called her grandmother.

"Granny," she said, "I can't take it anymore."

"I'll call you back within an hour and let you know when the plane leaves from Logan," Lila answered.

Minutes later the phone rang and her grandmother informed her that she had made a reservation on the noon flight the next day.

"It was nonstop, Boston to Tampa. I couldn't take that many things. I had to make my grand escape, you know?"

That morning in May, Wendy put on two sweaters over a short-sleeved T-shirt. She was wearing blue jeans. As an afterthought, she tossed a sheepskin-lined dungaree jacket over the sweaters. She picked up her bag full of panties and bras, and as she headed for the front door, tacked a note to the refrigerator.

"I'm gone," it said.

SEVEN

The Margin Redrawn

BY THE TURN of the century, the neighborhood-based approach to the problems of poverty had supplanted asylums. Thanks to the efforts of Henry Morgan, the settlement house workers, and private agency caseworkers, most of the immigrants who came to Boston in the second half of the nineteenth century were integrated into the American mainstream, and impoverished families who existed "on the margin" were kept from falling over it.

Poverty as this era defined it was not the pauperism that had given rise to the almshouse or even to the asylum. It was now more broadly conceived as any obstacle to an individual's enjoyment of a reasonable quality of life. To late-nineteenth-century social thinkers, low economic status was but one such barrier. Others, taken for granted as indices of poverty by those who worked directly in the settlement houses and at Morgan Memorial Industries, included the inability to speak fluent English, chronic illness, alcoholism, orphanhood, and illiteracy.

By 1900 industrialization had created yet another face of poverty. Every major city in the North was collecting migrant workers — railroad workers and seasonal laborers traveling from the East Coast to Chicago and beyond — in need of temporary lodgings. Their numbers were beginning to plague the cities, which were ill equipped to house them. These itinerant laborers followed the work, put in endless days of toil when they could, and tended to be idle and drunk when they couldn't. Unlike the mill and mining companies, which supplied workers with at least rudimentary shelter, the railroads offered little or nothing. As a result, cities at the major terminus points were dense with nomads who lived like animals, forced into under-heated, unventilated flophouses and tenements without kitchens or plumbing — uprooted, malnourished, and prone to disease. These drifters didn't belong in the settlement houses. Yet they needed shelter; they were freezing to death on street corners and starving for lack of regular wages.

Charles Dawes was a Chicago utilities magnate, lawyer, and banker, a descendant of William Dawes, Paul Revere's companion on the night of his historic ride. Dawes, who later served in the McKinley administration, was vice president under Coolidge, and received the Nobel Peace Prize, read in the pitiful conditions of unsheltered workers a painfully personal message. Dawes had lost his only son, Rufus, to a drowning accident in 1912 at the age of twenty-two. Rufus had been especially sensitive to the needs of the poor (some accounts suggest that he may have been an alcoholic). To honor his son, Dawes determined to address the problem of the unsheltered workers crowded into Chicago hovels, the sort of people Rufus had often put up for a night in hotel rooms. Dawes decided to create for them temporary, affordable residential hotels.

The Rufus Dawes Hotel for Men opened in Chicago in 1914. Two years later in Boston, the Rufus F. Dawes Hotel, a Refuge for Unfortunate Men, was ready to accept guests for the night, close to the railroad station and just blocks from the Morgan Chapel. A nickel secured a bed in the dormitory-style lodging. The three-story brick building was designed to sleep 315, but Dawes had the foresight to install trundle beds to double the sleeping capacity during the winter months. The dorms were "absolutely fireproof," the hotel's literature advertised. They were waterproof as well: every morning the large dormer windows were opened wide to ventilate the rooms, and the walls and floors were hosed down. Nightly baths were compulsory, as were the "fumigating rooms" in which the men's clothes were placed to destroy whatever vermin they harbored. Pillows and mattresses were covered with oilcloth. After an aseptic night at the Dawes, breakfast could be had for three cents: two for coffee, and a penny for a dough-nut.

Dawes's concept was both novel and controversial. Even in those days, lodging houses charged more for their rooms than his hotel did. When he opened such a hotel in Chicago for women, however, Dawes drew his worst fire: critics were sure he had just created the city's biggest brothel. But Dawes didn't waver in his commitment "to take care of people whom no one else cares to take care of."[1] His hotel for women differed from the men's in that each guest had her own room, reflecting his determination that those who used his lodgings be treated with dignity. He asserted that having guests pay a small sum was essential to their self-respect.

> So much has been printed about the Mary Dawes Hotel that is calculated to mislead prospective guests and create wrong impressions, that my brother, Henry M. Dawes, who is my associate in the enterprise, and I desire to make this statement regarding its purposes.
>
> We are simply hotel keepers, and the Mary Dawes Hotel is nothing but a hotel run as a first-class, respectable place, different from other first-class hotels only in its cheaper prices. Since our guests pay for our service, we assume no right as hotel keepers to inquire into their private affairs. There is nothing in the fact that one becomes our paying guest, *either in our hotels for men or for women,* which should subject him or her to any other restrictions than if a larger rate per day were being charged.[2]

But numbers alone proved his idea worth defending. In its first two years the 303-bed Dawes Hotel in Chicago claimed to provide an astounding 294,222 lodgings.

And numbers had begun to matter. While settlement house workers were advocating the preservation of humanistic values, mechanized labor was developing its own analytical methodology, the quantification of social problems. Statistics, argues Daniel Boorstin in his social history, *The Americans,* gave social reformers the impetus to dispute more "sentimental" interpretations of poverty with a flurry of figures.

America's first national survey of its slums was undertaken in 1892 by the commissioner of labor. Fourteen years later Robert Hunter, a social worker from Chicago, published a study, called simply *Poverty,* in which he propounded the novel idea that the poor "could be defined as those Americans whose income fell below an established minimum."[3] Hunter's book became a national best seller, and his definition of the poor, based on income level, became the standard in American social policy for the rest of the twentieth century.

The Depression seemed to validate Hunter's idea. Redefined as simply a deficiency in income, poverty begged for a new philosophy of public (federal) activism to eradicate it. Reformers and advocates of an income-based definition of poverty pitted figures against each other, jockeying for dominance in the debate over various approaches to public welfare. Some, for example, preferred to set "maintenance income levels" and provide supplemental incomes to raise poor people to those levels. Others favored a more relative approach, identifying the poor as society's "bottom fourth" (or fifth or ninth), who should be brought closer to those higher up. Everyone agreed that combating poverty meant one thing: providing income for those who weren't earning enough in wages to maintain an acceptable standard of living.

Shattered in this climate was the broader conception of poverty as interconnected material and nonmaterial barriers to fulfillment, and with it the belief that the social and economic welfare was the province of small, private, nonprofit agencies and foundations. With the New Deal, the job of caring for the poor, the disabled, and the elderly went to the federal government. Social security, a legal minimum wage, the creation of public housing and federal jobs programs, all took the place of those services once offered almost exclusively by Morgan Memorial, the Salvation Army, and small neighborhood houses and church-affiliated centers throughout the country.

When Edgar Helms's bid for participation in the government's sheltered workshops was rejected, Morgan Memorial, like many organizations, had to redefine its mission if it was to survive. In 1934 the head of Buffalo's Goodwill, Glenn W. Leighbody, wrote to Helms:

> Recently I have discussed with some of the people interested in national relief [the question of specializing in helping the handicapped] and they are unanimous that within the coming months the Government will assume responsibility for the group we now have, known as social handicaps, which are nothing more than unemployed people, most of them inefficient, without trades or direction. I do not believe we will be allowed to compete in business, offering as a reason the fact that we are giving employment to unemployed people. I do believe that if we now set up our organization to take on handicapped people we will not only be allowed to continue but will be recognized as leaders and given assistance.[4]

It was thus that Goodwill Industries continued, as an organization serving the physically handicapped and, after World War II, the combat-disabled and mentally handicapped.

The Dawes Hotel withstood the Depression better than did the myriad settlement houses and relief organizations in the South End. For

South End residents the Depression meant the virtual collapse of this infrastructure. Besides the Dawes, only a handful of evangelical missions survived, and in 1940 Charles Dawes worked out a lease arrangement with the oldest and most prestigious of these, the Union Rescue Mission, to take over the operation of his hotel. The mission, which already ran a small settlement house, a summer camp for children, and after-school programs in a storefront on Dover Street, renamed the Dawes Hotel the Boston Industrial Home.

Beyond this, the Depression changed the character of the South End remarkably little. Its maze of streets still supported the vaudeville theaters where Al Jolson and Eddie Cantor played, the Coconut Grove nightclub and the Castle Theatre, the honkytonks and movie theaters, and more barrooms per square foot, it seemed, than the rest of the city combined. Squeezed in among its tawdry round-the-clock nightlife were the Armenian, Turkish, Syrian, Italian, German, and Irish families whose businesses, restaurants, kosher markets, and fish stores provided sustenance for the residents of the neighborhood's hundreds of rooming houses and residential hotels.

But by the end of World War II, the second and third generations and the families of war veterans were leaving the slums and going to the greener communities of the South Shore. Enticed by the low-cost mortgages offered by the Veteran's Administration and the Federal Housing Authority, the offspring and grandchildren of Boston's immigrants were leaving their parents in the city and becoming suburbanites. From their split-levels and ranches they could ride the "elevated" back downtown to their offices and see only the picturesque rooftops of the cramped tenements they'd left behind.

"The ride 'intown' was and is a place for wide-eyed anticipation," reminisced one editorial writer for the Boston *Globe* of that period. "Passengers could examine the Victorian rooflines, the pediments and curlicues that so handsomely obscured the panorama of anxiety and danger 30 feet below, of switchblades flashing and winos sleeping in doorways, deaf to the screeching wheels of the Elevated."[5]

By 1955 the South End had its first public housing project, 508 units along Washington Street next door to the Cathedral of the Holy Cross. But urban renewal began in earnest in the late sixties. Almost the first piece of business was to raze every building along Dover, the South End's oldest and now most infamous street and, in an attempt to obliterate past associations, to change its name to East Berkeley.

Blocks of tenements were leveled, and for a time nothing was erected in their place.

The neighborhood, already on the skids, went into a serious decline. The small-business economy that had supported roomers — the laundries, cheap diners, and remaining settlement houses — collapsed as the displaced population that had supported them was forced to find apartments farther from the downtown area. What had been a predominantly white, working-class community became a minority and welfare-dependent one. A handful of bars, like J. J. Foley's, the Turf, and the Red Fez, remained. So did a few old-time bootleggers and hookers and a number of tenacious merchants — mostly cigar sellers and purveyors of plaster statuary. The rest, by the late sixties, was a wasteland of broken sidewalks and boarded windows, young Hispanic families and old people who'd hung on, and a few white urban "pioneers" drawn by the superb, if deteriorated, rowhouses. What had been a cohesive district bound together as much by its rich diversity as by the loyalties of its various ethnic groups had taken on the appearance of an inner-city war zone just the other side of the Back Bay. Washington Street and its environs became a ghoulish midway of interracial violence.

"Businesses, of course, were driven out because of crime. Everybody was afraid to live there," Milton Friesen remembers. Friesen at the time was a newcomer, director of a Salvation Army shelter and a halfway house for alcoholics known as Harbor Light Center. Harbor Light had taken up residence in one of the former tenements several blocks from Dover. It fronted Washington Street across a lovely urban square known as Blackstone Park.

"Blackstone Park was considered *the* place to buy drugs," Friesen recalls. "It was the scene of a number of riots in those days. Clashes between black and white. It was a place with bootlegging problems. I remember, behind our building — all those buildings have since been torn down — you could get any kind of liquor, anything you wanted, twenty-four hours a day, seven days a week. There was a lot of fighting. It was a bad place."

The violence eventually became so rampant that police tried to enlist what few agencies they could in the area to help them.

"One summer the police came and asked permission to hide [for surveillance purposes] in our building," says Friesen. "The Salvation Army officer who made that decision had a real dilemma. Should you do that, or shouldn't you? What does that do to your constituency once it's over? The first summer he let the police in. The next summer he said no, because it had a real adverse effect on us."

Those landlords, many of them negligent absentee owners, who hadn't already given up and fled, did so now. Suspicious fires and deliberate destruction further scarred the community. By the end of the sixties, only speculators and a few white liberals committed to building new urban neighborhoods wanted property in the South End. Most other owners of lodging houses or brownstones just prayed for better days. Around them their neighbors were leaving as quickly as they could.

City government relocation efforts, aided by the few remaining settlement houses, found new living quarters for the 3,500 households displaced by urban renewal. But what these people lost, often forever, in the process may have been even more essential than a dwelling place. Their losses would bear directly on the problem of homelessness ten years later. They lost social cohesion, family ties, neighbors, relationships with familiar merchants, local clerics, and social service agency workers to whom they could turn in times of need. "Home," in this extended and crucial sense, was ceasing to exist for many Americans.

For residents of inner-city neighborhoods like the South End, home was lost. And the old sense of community didn't travel well to the suburbs. Suburbanites broke with many of the old bonds: to parents, to church, to the mutual aid societies and associations that had once kept generations, groups, and individuals in crisis from falling apart. Impoverished in ways that modern culture — still in thrall to a purely economic frame of reference for poverty — no longer recognized, the suburbs were creating the preconditions for homelessness as actively as were financially strapped sections of the inner city. Almost everywhere, Americans were evolving a culture of disconnection and estrangement, the groundwork for a culture of homelessness.

The problems of displacement created by these forces — the movement of younger generations out to atomistic suburbs, the abandonment of the elderly and the poor to the inner city, the resulting turf battles over the scarce jobs that remained there — wouldn't be felt at places like the Boston Industrial Home for another decade. At the Home business continued as it had when the Dawes family ran it, but with a new twist: evening chapel service every night.

"You didn't eat unless you sat through that sermon," Milton Friesen recalls. "Some of it was agony, because if you hadn't eaten all day, the aroma of that stew or soup penetrated to that chapel, and there you sat, listening to these long-winded preachers. The people who went to the altar, who responded to this altar call for salvation, were the first people who were fed."

Salvation at the Home was one of only two routes open to the chronic skid-row residents, many of whom were alcoholics, in the mid-sixties. The other route was going to "the Tombs." Every street drunk in Boston knew about the Tombs, the subterranean holding cells of the county court system. They epitomized the Dark Ages of alcohol awareness.

Public drunkenness was a crime, as it had been since 1835. The only treatment alcoholics received was at the hands of the criminal justice system. The way this worked depended utterly on the local police. Based on their familiarity with the drinkers on their beats, the constabulary would decide who ought to be picked up and when. The police in Station Four in the South End were pros at this selection process: up until the early 1960s the South End had the highest number of drunkenness arrests per square mile in the United States.

Processing took place at the precinct station: some regulars were allowed to sleep it off in one of the cells for the night. The chronic cases were usually sent to the Tombs. In the morning they appeared before a judge in municipal court. They could be released, but only into the hands of one of the Alcoholics Anonymous people who lingered like dubious guardian angels in the wings of the courtroom for any who might choose to reform. Most were sent out to Bridgewater State Hospital. Opened in 1866 as the commonwealth's work farm, Bridgewater by the late sixties was the only hospital in Massachusetts for the criminally insane. Conditions there were primitive at best. The cells, virtually unchanged since they were first built, were dank and in serious disrepair. Wrist restraints and solitary confinement weren't uncommon. Yet come winter, many South End skid-row denizens chose voluntary incarceration at Bridgewater as a way of escaping the cold for a few months. There, at least, they didn't have to pray.

But this state of affairs wasn't to last much longer. In 1959 Massachusetts established a Division of Alcohol, the first in the nation. Under its auspices a small number of outpatient clinics were set up to offer alcohol counseling in existing public health centers around the state. The same year the city hired a young man named Jim Scott to open the country's first dual-diagnosis ward for alcoholics suffering from tuberculosis at the state's chronic disease hospital in Mattapan. And Jack Donohoe, a recovering alcoholic, opened Hope House, an alcohol halfway house in the South End, which would soon expand into a network of residences for newly sober alcoholics.

Jim Scott's Mattapan program proved so successful in achieving long-term sobriety in its patients that he was invited to duplicate the program at Long Island Hospital, a Depression-era "dormitory" in Boston Harbor built to replace an almshouse that had functioned there for almost a century. Homeless men could get a bed in the Long Island dorm without going through the Tombs.

Scott knew much more about skid-row alcoholism than he had when he'd started two years before. He'd attended Rutgers School of Alcohol Studies and spent a month living on the Bowery to get a first-hand view of the conditions that he'd begun to suspect contributed to the seemingly inescapable trap of street alcoholism.

He found the Bowery, though larger, to be much like Boston's South End. It had a few missions, Dorothy Day's Catholic Worker house, a Salvation Army, and several flophouses, one of which became Scott's temporary home. What he discovered there was an atmosphere not so much of angry desperation as of resignation and defeat.

"You go into a place like that and your first admission is fear. Then, the second thing, you get frustrated and angry. Then, after that, it's just despair. There's nothing. No way out. I had a suitcase in Grand Central Station in one of those lockers. If I had not had that, and somewhere to go, I'd have been trapped there for good. I don't know how you get out," he says.

Scott returned to Boston convinced that the less time people were left to drift in Bowery-like conditions and the more incentives they could be given to get out, the sooner they could be helped and the more lasting would be the results, in terms of both sustained sobriety and solutions to their social and personal problems.

Scott took six men into an experimental program at Long Island and enlisted several Maryknoll seminarians from the nearby town of Hingham to help him run it. He painted and fixed up separate quarters and ensured that the men slept in good beds, had decent food and recreation. In addition to going through alcohol rehabilitation, they worked their way up into paying jobs at the shelter and then into mainstream jobs.

By this time, 1961, City Hospital also had the rudiments of an alcohol counseling program. Known as Room Five, it consisted of a small office just off the emergency room. Alcoholics could talk to a social worker there, although the best that could be offered to the thirty to forty who came through the door every day was a list of local AA meetings or a chance to get into Scott's Long Island program. If they weren't ready to get sober — and most of them weren't — they would soon retrace their steps up Harrison Avenue back to the Boston Industrial Home. Or they would remain on the streets and face the very distinct possibility of ending up in the Tombs.

Several bills had been introduced into the state legislature by advocates who knew that there was a better way.[6] They were attempting to decriminalize alcoholism and raise public awareness about the pathology of addiction. Alcoholism, they argued, shouldn't be punished by a jail term. It was a disease, and the government had a responsibility to offer chronic drunks a decent medical detoxification and rehabilitation program.

Nationally, similar sentiments were beginning to be voiced. In 1967 the President's Commission on Law Enforcement and the Administration of Justice published a major report on the limited benefit to alcoholics of spending time in prison and pointed out the waste in tax dollars involved. In response the Department of Justice created the Office of Law Enforcement Assistance Administration and offered grants to cities interested in creating alternative demonstration rehabilitation projects.

In 1968 the Supreme Court, in a landmark decision, *Powell v. Texas,* upheld a verdict of public intoxication, but its decision stated that alcoholism is a disease and should be treated medically, not criminally. However, the court went on, it declined to take the step of decriminalization, for one reason: cost. Both the majority and minority reports in the five-to-four decision were unanimous in the opinion that the nation couldn't possibly create enough agencies to care for the volume of alcoholics then being processed through the justice system. The court left this Gordian knot up to the states.

On the evening of January 1, 1968, the unthinkable occurred. The Boston Industrial Home, without warning, locked its doors, leaving more than three hundred men out in the cold with no place to go. Jim Scott, at Long Island Hospital, was beside himself. It had been general knowledge that the tenements around the Home were slated for urban renewal by the Boston Redevelopment Authority (BRA). But no one expected the shelter to close without adequate warning in time to relocate. Scott placed a frantic phone call to Father Jack White, in his rectory at St. Phillip's Church in the shadow of City Hospital, informing him of the catastrophe.

Jack White was an outspoken member of a new group called the Association of Boston Urban Priests. ABUP had come into being in 1967, fueled by the desire of young inner-city priests to confront racial and social injustice in the beleaguered parishes struggling to remain alive among the poor. The priests were getting involved in community organizing, trying to obtain for their neighborhoods everything from health care and social services to better representation in City Hall. A Boston *Globe* article had quoted one member as saying that ABUP was going to be "the voice of the poor." This is what prompted Jim Scott's desperate call to Jack White.

"This is a chance to put your money where your mouth is," Scott told White.

"We said sure," recalls Father Frank Kelley, another ABUP board member then. "Something had to happen, and we saw that if we didn't have this place, we were going to be in trouble. We didn't know a thing about running a shelter. But all of us said, 'Yeah, we can't do without this thing.' "

Scott proposed that ABUP be the legal entity for a shelter at the site of the former Boston Industrial Home. It would lease the building from the BRA for a dollar a year and would bill the state's welfare office for its services. Scott would hire a staff to run the shelter.

Scott rounded up Long Island's full-time administrator, a charismatic young seminarian named Jim Buckley, and the Room Five social worker, Bill Hartigan. "We're taking over," he told them. "I'll get some volunteers, and I think one of you would be great to run it." By the following Monday, Jim Buckley had become director of the shelter, renamed the Pine Street Inn.

Scott drafted an "active cousins club" of volunteers. They helped paint and repair the building, and at the end of their first year, they held a Christmas Mass in the lobby to celebrate, followed by a baked ham dinner, caroling, and dancing. Scott had succeeded, just barely, in keeping hope and a home alive for the South End's homeless men.

"Then," Jim Scott recalls, "Paul Sullivan came to see me."

Scott couldn't have known on that winter morning, when he looked up to see a slight man with a receding hairline and a bulbous nose approach him, that his salvage venture was about to become another man's obsession.

Paul Sullivan was thirty-one and just getting sober. He had come to the Pine Street Inn after drinking away more than half of his life. He'd lost every job he'd ever managed to get and had failed two serious suicide attempts. He had come because all he could see before him was endless broken headlights, and booze-sick dreams, and jail cells if he didn't.

Sullivan had been raised in lace curtain gentility in the Boston Irish stronghold of Dorchester, the second son of a successful clothing merchant and a beautiful, vain mother. May Sullivan had been the "Miss Boston" of her day, a model for downtown department stores.

May created around her a vibrant household, a magnet for her women friends and other people's children. Always generous with money, she was a revered member of her "club," a group that moved from house to house for luncheon, bridge, and the ubiquitous Manhattan cocktail. She was adored by the neighborhood children.

"She was the greatest mother in the world," her son Frank remembers. "She was warm, but dynamite — a coquette."

In her gregariousness, May was probably trying to compensate in part for the stern, unapproachable demeanor of her husband. Frank Sullivan was born in Middlebury, Vermont, the youngest of six brothers. As each of the boys came of age, he was loaned money by the older brothers to set himself up in a clothing business. Frank decided to try his luck in Boston and became the first brother to pay back his full share of the family pot.

"He was very structured," his son Frank remembers. "There was no way to love him. He was very strict. He was at work all day. He came home late. He worked six days a week. On Sunday he got up, went to the store, then he went to church, then came home, they made love, we had dinner, then went to bed early. We were tolerated. He didn't know how to hug you, but he loved you."

But there were cracks in the armor of this rigid, self-disciplined man. Frank Sullivan, in the parlance of the day, "had a bit of a sauce problem" and was prone to going off "on toots."

In this atmosphere, Paul grew up silent and diligent.

"Paul was extremely intelligent," his brother recalls. "He had wisdom. And he had tremendous patience. He was a mediator. He was my father's favorite. He saw Paul being somebody."

Paul was a member of the scholarship class at St. Mark's school, but he didn't have much of a life outside of that. Frank, by contrast, was the neighborhood sparkplug, and Paul followed his initiatives in almost everything.

"I went into Scouts," Frank says. "He did. I didn't enjoy Scouts, he didn't. He was a follower, he was not a doer."

Even before high school, Paul had decided on a career path: he wanted to be a veterinarian. But for reasons that his family still can't fathom, he was the only child in his class not to win a high school scholarship. For a boy whose entire life was devoted to his studies, this was a cruel blow. His father, who had the means, sent him to Cathedral High School all the same, following his brother.

Paul began to pass through the South End on his way to school every day, and he began hanging around its street corners after the final bell. By the end of his junior year his father was dead, and Paul had become a drinker.

"He used to go down to New York with the guys," his brother Frank recalls. "He always drank away — he didn't do it much at home. He'd come back and be sober. He might have a couple of belts after school, but you didn't know it."

Still an excellent student, Paul managed to maintain his grades and after graduation again followed Frank, this time to Northeastern University, where he obeyed his late father's wishes and studied engineering — for a semester. He earned straight A's in every course except drafting, which he failed. Reeling from the shock of this, he left school, fled to Florida, and found a job waiting on tables at a Boca Raton hotel.

"He drank and screwed up, had crazy experiences," Frank recounts. At the end of the tourist season, Paul returned to Boston, enrolled in the Boston College business program, and graduated four years later on the dean's list. Then he entered the navy.

Up until then Paul had never been a "stupid drunk." But by the time he got out of the service, he'd become reckless. After a summer on Cape Cod, during which he did virtually nothing but drink, he returned to Boston to live with his mother. Frequently over the course of the next six years she would call Frank in a panic after Paul had smashed the lights in the hallway or put a hole through the mirrored glass around the vestibule mail slot. One night he drove a brand new MG into the ocean. Occasionally, he even struck his mother.

The few construction jobs he got, he lost. He drove a UPS truck for a time. Then his alcoholism got so bad that he was out of work for what his family feared would be the rest of his life. That was when Paul tried to kill himself. First he attempted hanging from a clothesline in the cellar. Then he tried to shoot himself through the mouth. But the clothesline broke, and the shotgun failed to fire.

One day shortly after this, Paul stopped drinking. No one knows exactly what prompted his sobriety. Family members think that the death of an alcoholic relative finally convinced him. "He was dying and he sent for Paul," Frank recounts. "Paul went in to see him. He shut the door. He was in there for about an hour. He came out and he looked like death. The next day, two days later, he said, 'I'm not drinking anymore.' And he never did."

"Then Paul Sullivan came to see me," Jim Scott remembers. "He came looking for a job. I sent him over to Jim Buckley."

The Pine Street Inn in 1969 remained almost completely unknown outside of a small circle, tucked into its narrow alley in a part of the city that few had any reason to venture into. Shortly after Buckley hired Paul Sullivan, another newcomer brought the skimpy staff to four. Richard Ring, a slender and reserved twenty-three-year-old from Mattapan, was just out of the navy and interested in social work. His arrival enabled the Inn to stay open during the day.

For the most part the daily cycle of activity continued to conform to long-established patterns. The guests (the Inn retained the Dawes tradition of calling its residents "guests") showed up at Police Station Four late in the afternoon to receive tickets for their bed and meal from a welfare department employee. They made their way to the Inn four blocks away and found a seat on one of the wooden benches in the lobby, or got into line to shower and hand their clothes over to be put in the fumigating room overnight. The bed ticket got them a cot in the second- or third-floor dormitory; the meal ticket, breakfast at one of two greasy spoons nearby. Rules were minimal: no bottles and no violence. It wasn't necessary to impose a curfew: by seven at night those who'd bothered to seek a bed were ready to go to sleep.

With the withdrawal of the mission directors, the Pine Street Inn reverted to an earlier secularism — but with several important differences. The guests were openly referred to as alcoholics, and instead of paying a small sum for their beds, now they were on the dole. A private institution had become a semipublic one.

Sullivan quickly established a special rapport with the guests. In an era when most of Boston was garbed in love beads and tie dyes, Paul Sullivan arrived at Pine Street every morning in a jacket and tie. While a younger generation was tearing away all the trappings of conventional respectability, Sullivan insisted on addressing every street drunk as Mister.

"He'd meet with the drunks staggering in on their terms," Richard Ring recalls. "He'd meet the drunk who was sick on the right terms. He'd meet the drunk who needed help on the right terms. The guest that just needed a pat on the back — he would get it. The guest who needed ten bucks to get home, he gave it to him. He gave out cigarettes from the day's beginning to end. We didn't have anything else to give them then, other than a hot cup of coffee and a day-old doughnut in the morning. Paul did heroic stuff. Paul was pulling people out of dumpsters in the dead of winter — literally."

He was also rapidly becoming a fixture. Sullivan was there when Ring arrived in the morning and long after he left at night. He was there on the weekends. Almost overnight, it seemed in retrospect, Paul and the Inn became indispensable to each other.

"On any given day, Paul would hire a staff person, fix the leaky washers, help somebody out of a seizure, get somebody into a detox, deal with the cop on duty. Paul just did everything imaginable," recalls Ring.

When the treasurer took his first vacation, Sullivan decided that the books weren't being handled properly and had him fired on his return. Within a year of the Inn's reopening, Jim Buckley, who had received the Junior Chamber of Commerce's Outstanding Young Man of the Year award for his work at the Inn, had drifted away from the work and finally resigned. When Jim Scott offered Buckley's job to Ring, Sullivan, who had never fought for anything in his life, became a political gladiator.

"He met me in the basement of the t.b. clinic at Long Island," Scott recalls. "I was a little taken aback, to tell you the truth. He referred to Jim [Buckley] as a bastard, and he said, 'I did all the work and that bastard got the award.' There was a lot of bitterness on Paul's side.

Paul let me know that if he didn't get the job, he'd leave, and take the rest of the staff with him."

Ring acquiesced, as so many others would, in the face of Sullivan's incontestable passion and growing obsession. Scott had no choice but to accept Sullivan's terms.

That tensions would arise between Scott and Sullivan was inevitable. They turned out to be crucial, dividing the men over the direction the Inn would take and determining not only its course but the course of homeless policy in Boston and Massachusetts for the next twenty years.

Scott wanted to connect the Inn to an alcohol rehabilitation demonstration project for which he'd received funding, via the Mayor's Office of Justice Administration, from the federal Law Enforcement Assistance Administration. He hoped to house the Boston Detoxification Project in the basement of the Inn. Then he wanted to get existing agencies — the Salvation Army, Hope House, the South End Center, job counselors, welfare and social security counselors — to come to the Inn one day a week each "and try to talk to them [the guests], and get them out of the Pine Street thing and into a system, depending on what their need was," he says. The guests would be allowed to stay at the shelter as long as that was the only way they could function, but he saw the Inn as "transitional" in orientation.

Scott further envisioned a halfway house model for the Inn, moving newly arrived guests into smaller inns scattered around the city as quickly as possible. Not only did he believe that recovering from alcoholism would be easier in smaller settings, but he was convinced that the individual needs of the men could be more effectively addressed. Small shelters could offer group counseling, work programs, and what Scott called "social detox," a community environment in which long-time street people could become resocialized.

In 1971 the state legislature, after a long and divisive struggle, passed the Massachusetts Alcohol Treatment and Rehabilitation Law. The victory was a bittersweet one for those like Scott who'd advocated a comprehensive system of care, including outpatient aftercare. The law would result in only short-term detoxes — five to ten days. On the other hand it was a coup for those who argued that jail was still a necessary form of housing for homeless alcoholic men. This group successfully argued that detoxification per se bears no relation to long-term recovery from alcoholism. This being the case, they claimed,

detox centers would become just a different form of public intoxifi-
cation control, not real rehab centers. So while police, under the new
law, were no longer allowed to arrest public drunks, Bridgewater State
Hospital remained authorized (and funded) to take them in on a voluntary basis. When this version of the law was passed, Scott was even
more determined that Pine Street should become part of a comprehensive alcohol rehabilitation program, since the rest of the state-funded
system was destined, he saw, to be inadequate.

Paul Sullivan had vehemently opposed the decriminalization of alcohol, and he wholeheartedly opposed Scott's plan for bringing a
multiservice approach to the Inn. Sullivan wanted the Inn to be a
sanctuary, a place where alcoholics who were not ready for recovery
would feel welcomed and respected, not patronized, pitied, or pressed
by some social worker into doing what they couldn't, yet. Sullivan called
his lobby, with its smoke-tinged windows, grimy floors, and stiff benches,
"God's waiting room" and he would sit for hours there offering the
men conversation and a sympathetic ear.

Ironically, the passage of the bill he'd opposed expanded dramatically the demand for his shelter. Men just out of detox could no longer
count on the police station floor as a refuge on cold nights. Now the
only alternatives were Bridgewater or the Pine Street Inn.

Scott, concluding that Sullivan wouldn't give up control over the
Inn, turned his attention to the Boston Detoxification Project, which,
after lengthy negotiations with Sullivan, moved into the Inn's basement. Before long Scott resigned as president of the Pine Street board.

In 1973 Pine Street was incorporated independent of ABUP, though
several priests who had formed strong friendships with Sullivan stayed
on the board to help chart its course.

"We hammered out a philosophy of the place," Frank Kelley remembers. "We said we wanted to provide food, shelter, and lodging
to people who are homeless. That's it. We kept it simple. The vision
that Paul had was that we had this large social welfare system, which
people kept falling through the cracks of. We saw people continually
not getting what they needed from the welfare system, alcohol rehab,
through V.A., Medicare, Medicaid, you name it. Paul would talk about,
'We're here to catch people who fall through the cracks of society,
because after Pine Street, there's only the graveyard.' That's the way
things were. Being an alcoholic himself, he understood what life was
like on the street, and how important Pine Street was."

The Inn lived by its bed tickets. At month's end the chits were returned to Welfare, and the Inn was reimbursed fifty cents, later a dollar, per ticket. Sullivan revealed an astute business sense. He would bring in his own tools and fix the pipes. He made sure the building was properly insured. He even found one of the few churches in town that didn't expect a "donation" of fifty or a hundred dollars for a funeral mass, as well as the cheapest caskets for burying the men who died on the streets and were never claimed. He had a system for finding day-old doughnuts to distribute, and he recruited recovering alcoholics to donate their services to his cause.

Sullivan started hanging around the emergency room at Boston City Hospital several nights a week, talking with the nurses about men from the Inn who came to the accident ward. Soon Paul or one of his staff would call and go down for medical supplies.

"It wasn't too long after that, in 1972," recalls psychiatric nurse Randy Bailey, "that the emergency floor nurses started to go down to Pine Street, and they formed the clinic."

The clinic, open until ten or eleven each night, was run entirely by volunteer nurses. They treated cuts, bruises, and respiratory problems. Their supplies consisted of bacitracin, peroxide, and a few bandages.

Yet for all of Sullivan's ingenuity and moxie, the Pine Street Inn never had enough money. Friends in ABUP started putting the word out, and soon priests throughout the Boston area responded, bringing parishioners in as volunteers. They formed "meal groups" preparing and serving cooked dinners and donated clothing and bedding. But the volunteers did more than fill in the material gaps, which some days seemed overwhelming; even more important, they created a financial and political base of support that in time would prove critical to the Inn's existence.

These early supporters weren't inner-city activists but middle-class suburbanites. "The biggest social reform in the world wasn't too concerned about the homeless population," Frank Kelley recalls. "This was 1971, 1972, everybody was involved in the war, or racism, or feminism, whatever. But none of those folks were coming down to work at Pine Street. Nobody was too concerned about that as an issue. Our support was coming from ordinary working people — families, mainly — from churches and schools, who would come in and volunteer, wanted to do something about society. When those folks would come in and see what the situation was, they wouldn't turn away from it. They embraced it and worked with it."

In turn, Paul Sullivan brought something new and significant to the lives of these volunteers: a candor about alcoholism. Several nights a week he traveled to suburban churches to talk about the Inn. But what attracted the crowds was his riveting frankness about his own addiction. In making alcoholism fit conversation for many who had kept their own family secrets hidden, he carried a message that linked his audience not only to the Inn but often, intensely, to himself.

"He'd do it in a very direct, personal kind of way," Kelley said. "He had an enormous capacity to understand our emotions, how people feel about stuff. People would get access to his home number. They'd start calling him. Somebody has a booze problem at home, and they're calling him every night, or a couple of times every night."

The man who as a boy had been shy and passive now found himself a father figure, a crusader, and a confessor to Bostonians from every walk of life — businessmen, politicians, the clergy. He started to appear on radio call-in programs and became a well-known figure on television at holiday time. But he was impatient with ideology and with political radicals who tried to fit their theories to the Pine Street guests.

"You walk onto the floor at Pine Street, and all the ideas you had go right out the door," Kelley says. "You're in another world. It's just a madhouse. So you were very practical about what had to get done. In Paul's experience, the eyeball-to-eyeball, that one-on-one handling, of people starts to work the changes. It's much more significant than being committed to 'an issue.' "

In his assistant, Richard Ring, Sullivan had a perfect complement and foil. The two men couldn't have been more different. "Rich had the capacity to deal with the details of running the place that Paul never could," Kelley recalls. "Paul wanted to deal with people, and Rich saw the need for the organization and structure."

Ring was aware that urban renewal would soon force changes in the structures he'd worked so hard to keep running smoothly. The Pine Street Inn and its three hundred alcoholic men would soon have to move out of their comfortably obscure skid-row quarters.

The Pine Street Inn was still a man's world inside *and* out. The few women who showed up in the alley alongside the Inn late at night, mostly urban Indians of the region's dominant Micmac tribe, were generally chased away. Until 1973 nobody seemed to think of doing anything for these women. Then a feisty, impassioned young advertising executive named Kip Tiernan — who'd traded her business wardrobe for jeans, donned a large silver crucifix on a leather thong, and joined the social justice ministry at St. Phillip's/Warwick House — decided to see what could be done for poor homeless women.

After touring Chicago, Baltimore, and New York, spending time with Dorothy Day, investigating the Salvation Armies and the Morgan Memorials, she returned to Boston and told Father Jack White that she wanted to create a place where women could come together "simply because you were lonely and you didn't have anything."

There were homeless women out there, she told him, "but women were invariably at the back of every line. Even within the theater of poverty, women were in the back row." In 1974 she founded Rosie's Place, the city's first shelter for women, initially as a drop-in center in an old South End bakery several blocks from the Pine Street Inn.

Paul Sullivan helped Tiernan get Rosie's off the ground. He wasn't put off by its openly radical feminist agenda; the underlying concern, he knew, was the same as his. He offered the use of the Inn's laundry facilities, bedding, and advice. The existence of homeless and alcoholic women was beginning to attract the notice of Jim Scott as well. He helped open a halfway house for alcoholic women at this same time, 1974, under the aegis of the Boston Urban Sisters, ABUP's counterpart. Rich Ring left Pine Street to run it.

Rosie's shelter soon proved too small to accommodate a growing demand. The women who were turned away started showing up at the Inn, and one cold night the staff let them in.

"The men became very chivalrous and protective of the women," Frank Kelley recalls. "But then out came the knives, and you had a full-scale brawl in the lobby. Talk about disrupting something that was already chaotic. Paul was bullshit."

But the incident forced the issue. In subsequent conversations about moving the Inn to a new building, it was understood that Pine Street would have a women's unit.

In 1973 Paul Sullivan had invited Robert Walsh, the Boston Redevelopment Authority's South End project director, to become the Inn board's first president. Walsh, a former seminarian and a close friend of Frank Kelley's, consented. Sullivan had also attracted the interest and, soon, the friendship of Vincent P. McCarthy, a senior partner in the Boston law firm of Hale and Dorr, who specialized in real estate law and was a newly recovered alcoholic. Fortified by these powerful allies, Sullivan began the search for a new site. His options were limited by two major constraints. "One, we knew that no matter where we went, it would be a struggle" with the neighborhood, says Walsh. "Second, we didn't have any money."

The first of these constraints ruled out several attractive warehouses in South Boston, just across a short bridge from the Inn. Nothing would have been less wise politically than trying to locate the shelter in the Irish enclave that was the birthplace of both the state legislature's Senate majority leader and Boston's City Council president. The second constraint required that the building be as cheap as possible: preferably a foreclosed or tax-delinquent property. Given these restrictions, the South End was the most sensible choice, specifically the two-block-wide strip that had been the city's first landfill back in 1804, now an industrial corridor from Chinatown to Boston City Hospital and Massachusetts Avenue.

After considering three or four buildings, Sullivan and his advisers concluded that the former Fire Department training building, almost at the corner of Harrison Avenue and East Berkeley (formerly Dover) Street, answered all their requirements. It was large: five stories high and covering more than half a city block. It was only about four blocks away from the current Inn, two blocks from the back door of the Cathedral of the Holy Cross, and buffered from residential streets by commercial Washington Street.

"It was in nobody's backyard — simple as that," Walsh explains.

Also the price was right. The building was owned then by the BRA, which meant that it could be deeded, through the city of Boston, to the Inn for next to nothing. Sullivan would need money only for renovations and for operating the shelter, though that was no small expense for a tiny and obscure organization. Since its move was being forced by urban renewal, the Pine Street Inn was eligible for relocation money, as were the men who lived there. But this amount wouldn't begin to cover the costs of the move.

Sullivan went into high gear. Where earlier he had focused his efforts on hundreds of suburban church groups, now he penetrated the inner sanctums of city and state government. He courted lowly department assistants, wined and dined city councilors and cabinet secretaries, and drove hard bargains with those who might oppose him.

With a canny blend of conviction and finesse, Sullivan lodged inextricably in the minds of the city's and the state's most powerful figures the efficacy and necessity of his shelter. At the same time, as he'd done with so many others through the course of his personal odyssey, he forged unbreakable bonds of loyalty.

Still, government funding sources remained elusive until a sympathetic employee in the state's Department of Community Affairs, which oversaw all public housing authorities, suggested that the Inn apply for newly legislated funds under Chapter 689 of the Massachusetts General Law. But Chapter 689 authorized housing authorities to buy up property for the use of the elderly and handicapped. How could the Inn possibly fit these requirements? Some of the men were getting on in years, it was true, and not a few were physically handicapped, but it was hard to see how they might qualify.

The attorney on the Inn's board, Vin McCarthy, had the inspiration that broke what seemed an insoluble dilemma. Since 1971 Massachusetts had officially recognized alcoholism as a disease. To McCarthy's way of thinking, it was just a matter of adding to the fine print of state regulations alcoholism as a "handicap" that met the eligibility requirements for Chapter 689 funds. McCarthy's suggested addendum was approved by the Department of Community Affairs, and the Boston Housing Authority (BHA) obtained a tentative commitment from the department for $2.5 million to rehabilitate the Inn's new home, pending community approval and formal BRA designation of the site. The Pine Street Inn became Massachusetts 689-1.

Then all hell broke loose. The South End's sixteen community groups — loud, well organized, and combative — went wild. First, they argued, they had lived through the worst years of urban deterioration. Then they'd had to put up with the influx of social service agencies, halfway houses, pre-prison-release programs, shelters, and detox wards, the sprawl of an expanding public hospital, and the scores of poor that daily passed through their streets on the way to all of these.

"There were more social service agencies impacting the South End than any neighborhood in the city," Walsh says. "It was a social laboratory, and they didn't want any more. They couldn't understand why they had to have another one, particularly one which they found so offensive. It is a difficult thing for them to get up in the morning and have to step over somebody and come home and have to step over somebody."

The Inn negotiated. They would cap the number of beds at 350 instead of the 500 they'd originally planned for. One-third of the board of directors would be composed of South End residents. Further, the BRA agreed to see that offensive bars in the neighborhood were closed down.

Sullivan made house calls. By now his hair was beginning to go gray at the temples, he was pulled in so many directions at once in the struggle to keep his dream alive. He promised flophouse owners that his "boys" wouldn't cause trouble by frightening upstanding patrons away. He pleaded with residents. He cajoled, he wept, and sometimes he came close to blows.

The community, in desperation, organized two lawsuits. The first opposed the relocation on the grounds that the Inn was a medical facility and didn't have the proper licenses. The second was a zoning suit brought by an abutter. Both were dismissed. And on December 18, 1974, the leaders of the largest and most influential community group, SEPAC, the South End Project Area Committee, wrested an endorsement out of its membership, in effect putting the entire community's seal of approval on the project.

The next day the BRA held its public hearing. Representatives of various opposing factions jammed the hearing room, waving letters and making speeches. Prestigious clergy appeared to testify against the plan. But the opposition was silenced when Sullivan produced his trump card, a letter of endorsement from none other than the archdiocese's prelate, Humberto Cardinal Medeiros. That afternoon the Pine Street Inn won approval from the BRA, by a vote of four to one, to relocate its shelter to 444 Harrison Avenue in the South End.

"If we had tried to do it today, we couldn't," Walsh acknowledges fourteen years later. "Because the person they were rejecting was a much less objectionable person than the ones today, who are hostile, aggressive, younger, and not just classic derelicts. They're a mental patient, they're an addict, they're off their medication. Different guys."

Not long after this, Ralph Hughes moved to Boston to take his first job away from home, as a customer service representative for a rug cleaning company. In his free time the earnest young man read the *Catholic Worker* newspaper. On the streets he was aware of more and more homeless people. One day, returning from work, he got up his nerve, made his way over to the Pine Street Inn, asked for the supervisor, and told him he wanted to volunteer.

The supervisor, taken aback, told him, " 'Well, go ahead and sit in the lobby for a while. I have to go to a meeting now, but I'll talk to you when I come back.' "

When he returned two hours later, he was surprised to see Hughes still there. Ralph continued to come back every few days after work and keep the men in the lobby company. The staff quickly got to know him, and soon he was on the payroll.

"I thought it was such an honor," he says. "It was just what I wanted to do. The hell with the rug cleaning."

Paul Sullivan's door was always open, and Ralph often went in to see him. "He really was like a father to me in many ways. He always had the time," Ralph says. "Mostly I worked weekends. And he very often would come in, dragging the movie projector and the screen with him, either into or out of the building, because he was always doing dog and ponies [slide lectures] at church basements, or wherever. At nine o'clock at night he'd be coming back from a presentation. And he'd come by, drop that off, drop some clothing off, some blankets. Then he'd be out the door again. Or he'd be sitting at his desk, writing thank you notes, anything he could be doing during that time when he wasn't in meetings, or whatever, during the regular week."

One night at bedtime, Ralph was moving through the lobby, rounding up the stragglers. He approached one of the men sitting on a bench and gently said to him, "Hey, Jeff, time to go to bed."

"I wasn't kicking him, or grabbing him and pushing him off the bench, or anything like that. I just came up to him. The next thing I knew there was blood running down my wrist. He must have had a razor blade or something in his hand, and just slashed at me. It was his way of asking for help. Which is pretty much the way things happened those days, one way or another. We had another guy who, whenever he needed help, would go down on the Common and take off his clothes."

The deinstitutionalized mentally ill had arrived.

Massachusetts was a national model of deinstitutionalization. Between the mid-1950s and 1981, 22,000 patients were released from state mental institutions, and a network of community-based treatment programs, known as Community Mental Health Centers (CMHCs) was created — the only such program in the country. By the late 1970s many of the released patients had gone home to live with their families. Some 2,000 were known to be living in community residences, and upward of another 2,000 in short-term programs such as halfway houses. But it was no secret by then that many chronically mentally ill people were being discharged directly to the Pine Street Inn.

On the night he attacked Ralph, Jeff simply walked out of the building. When he returned the next day, the staff had him arrested. Jeff was tried and committed to Bridgewater State Hospital, where, it turned out, he'd previously been committed. He had a history of violent episodes.

"We realized that it was becoming less safe for everyone to work [at the Inn] and to live there," Ralph says. Increased staffing eased the tensions somewhat, but everyone saw the relocation to an expanded facility, work on which was progressing slowly, as the only change that would significantly improve conditions.

Late in 1977 Sullivan wrote to the director of the nearby Tufts Medical Center, outlining the desperate need for outpatient psychiatric services for his guests. The only facility that the Inn could use at the time, he explained, was the D Street Clinic in South Boston, in the heart of a white Irish working-class community where street bums would stand out even in the very best of circumstances. And 1977 was hardly the best of circumstances: Southie was still so ravaged by the tumult that followed the court-ordered desegregation of Boston's public schools that any outsider was suspect.

"The need for more adequate psychiatric care for the men at Pine Street is urgent," Sullivan wrote.

What ensued can only be described as a protracted political tug of war between the state and the shelter over which was responsible for the homeless mentally ill. The Department of Mental Health denied that their former patients were staying in the shelters. A 1979 Pine Street Inn study contradicted this. One-third to one-half of the men who stayed at the Inn, it found, suffered from mental illness, and only a quarter of them were receiving any treatment.

Once again Sullivan went into action. He invited Robert Okin, the commissioner of mental health, down to the Inn. He'd decided to ask Okin's department to fund a psychiatric nurse for the lobby. For Sullivan to admit this need wasn't easy. He didn't believe in intervention. But while his alcoholic guests were responsive to the type of persuasion he was highly skilled at, he felt unqualified to treat the mentally ill the same way. On the other hand, he was suspicious of the arbitrary and sometimes high-handed way the mental health system treated its clients. What Sullivan wanted was someone on site who could work with the truly needy mentally ill in the context of the Inn's noncoercive philosophy.

As a society, "we're very much into 'People have to get better. They have to function on a higher level,' " says Randy Bailey, at the time a psychiatric nurse at Boston City Hospital. "You learn very early in a professional psychiatric career that we don't have the cures to help the mentally ill in that process. With many of the very severely, chronically mentally ill, we can raise some levels of functions, but it's more a matter of reminding them to eat three meals a day or getting them to bathe."

Before he visited the Inn, Okin assigned Bailey to do a "needs survey" there. Sullivan showed the commissioner the results: more than two hundred of his men needed psychiatric care. The Inn then hired Bailey, through the Department of Mental Health, to assess guests and act as a liaison with local detox centers, the Solomon Carter Fuller Mental Health Center, which was closer than the D Street clinic to the Inn, and City Hospital's emergency room.

Late in 1980, under growing pressure from advocates for the homeless, the commissioner of mental health issued a universal "no discharge to shelters" order. The following month, a fifty-bed shelter specially designed for the homeless mentally ill was opened by the Department of Mental Health in an old school in Roxbury. All of the Parker Street Shelter's beds and clothing, and its first television, came from Paul Sullivan, who was a member of the advisory board.

Parker Street was run very much like Pine Street. The only requirement for admission was that the guest have been discharged from a mental institution, and have no history of violence and no active alcohol addiction. Parker Street was open all day, and each guest was assigned to a CMHC (though whether he or she used it was a matter of choice). Most important, no new guest was admitted until a permanent housing placement was found for a current guest.

The Parker Street staff discovered that almost every one of their first 147 guests had had permanent placements after leaving a mental hospital but had lacked adequate support systems to remain self-sufficient. Case management and continuity of care were crucial, yet the state seemed unwilling to fund the programs that would make this possible. Again and again advocates felt they were running into bureaucratic road blocks that betrayed a profound institutional indifference.

In October 1981 the disillusioned designers of the Parker Street Shelter formed the Massachusetts Coalition for the Homeless, following the model of the New York Coalition, formed the summer before. One of the New York founders was Kim Hopper, a young and gifted social researcher, who with Ellen Baxter had written the only contemporary work on homelessness, *Private Lives, Public Spaces,* several years earlier. Hopper came to Boston, bringing with him a young lawyer from the firm of Sullivan and Cromwell, Robert Hayes, who had begun volunteering his legal services for the homeless. Hayes and the New York Coalition were flush with success, having just won a consent decree from the city and the state of New York to improve conditions in the city's shelters.

Hopper and Hayes met with Carol Bower Johnson, who had recently resigned as director of the Parker Street Shelter. They told Johnson that to mobilize people around the issue of homelessness, numbers weren't as important as the appearance of numbers. Getting coalition members to agree on an agenda didn't matter for the time being. First get people and recognized organizations to agree to do something about homelessness, they advised her, then establish some committees and study groups. Only the public education committee really needed an active corps. Spreading the word and, especially, cultivating the media to make homelessness a legitimate issue should be the first goal, they said.

Similar groups had already formed in the Washington area and in Atlanta. The following spring, April 1982, at a conference on homelessness held at the Sheraton Hotel in Boston under the auspices of the National Conference on Social Welfare, a handful of friends and allies decided to form a National Coalition for the Homeless. At stake was the way homelessness and poverty in America would be defined into the next century. Ten days later the *New York Times* carried the story of this event:

> The meeting . . . wrestled with the overall question of how best to approach the problem of homelessness, whether to focus on such frequently cited causes as unemployment, shortage of low-cost housing and the so-called "dumping" of patients from psychiatric institutions or to try to treat the symptoms. . . . Mr. Hayes, the coalition counsel, urged modest goals and advocated "little more than a salvage operation" for now. He suggested that the "unacceptability to the American people of an army of ragged men and women living on our city streets" might be exploited as a means of getting them decent shelter.[7]

*

The relocation of the Pine Street Inn took six long and stressful years, but by the spring of 1980 the Pine Street Inn was on the map — for many Bostonians the most appealing cause in town.

"All of it was so real and apparently so different than the other kind of institutions," Ring said. "There was a truth and honesty to the whole thing. And that's what people responded to."

Contributions increased. The staff was expanded. By now some nine other shelters had opened in Boston and across the Charles River in Cambridge. Most of them were small, sponsored by churches, or run by grass-roots groups that had come out of the social activist movements of the late sixties. The city of Boston reopened an inactive wing of Long Island Hospital and put one hundred beds into it as a back-up for Pine Street. Though the staff people at the shelters knew one another informally, there was remarkably little interaction among the different managements, and no efforts to coordinate social or housing services. By 1980 a group of shelters existed, but it couldn't by any stretch of the imagination have been called a system.

On the eve of Pine Street's move, the Inn staff numbered fifty-three. Ralph Hughes, in the new position of men's unit administrator, oversaw the three shifts of his staff, the clinic, central services (which included the kitchen, maintenance, and transportation crew), and the forty-five-member live-in staff — formerly homeless men who received free room and board in exchange for work. The administration was composed of four people: Hughes, Sullivan, Ring, and an assistant director, Pat Murphy.

The Inn was open twenty-four hours a day and served three meals. (The 12,000 or so dinners a month were prepared by twenty-three volunteer food groups.) It had a psychiatric nurse and day counselors, and provided transportation to detox units and hospitals in the area. Paul Sullivan boasted that he hadn't bought a sheet or pillowcase for his 240 beds in five years.

At five o'clock on the morning of April 14, the homeless men of the old Pine Street Inn were wakened and assembled at the front door of the worn, soot-blackened brick structure. Rich Ring mounted a foot ladder, removed the sign that had identified the Inn to thousands of wayfarers, and handed it to Paul Sullivan below. Then Sullivan, followed by two hundred men, began the fifteen-minute trek through the quiet morning streets and across the bridge to the new Inn on Harrison Avenue.

Nothing had been spared in outfitting the new shelter. As it rose up in front of the groggy men, the brick building, with its original Italianate fire tower, a landmark on the Boston skyline, was immaculate. Inside, the freshly painted yellow lobby was a welcome change from their recently quit quarters. From its solid fire doors to its spacious dormitories and industrial-quality chrome kitchen fixtures, the new Pine Street Inn had been built to last.

Within twenty-four hours the new Pine Street Inn's women's unit was the largest shelter for women in the city. That night and for weeks afterward, women came to the door carrying their possessions in every conveyance imaginable — bags, suitcases, and grocery carts. Where had they been hiding? And how had they survived?

All the faces of poverty that had been hidden behind the doors of deteriorating public housing units or walled off behind the veneers of comfort in suburbia had shed their last inadequate defenses. Naked need came begging — those who'd lost their homes because of market forces, the mentally ill, the abused and beaten. But whether they came from the ghetto or from a glistening shore town, they shared the unmistakable stamp of impoverishment that, while no one was looking, counting, or measuring, had invaded American culture.

These women were socially isolated, without self-esteem or sense of community. They lacked the support systems needed to stay sane and connected. Denied or robbed of the dimensions that make "home" more than merely a roof and four walls, they'd ultimately lost even that lowest of common denominators. Their homelessness was no aberration of the American experience, but its inevitable and logical consequence.

On December 16, 1981, the U.S. Congress began its first hearings on homelessness, conducted by the subcommittee on Housing and Community Development of the Commitee on Banking, Finance, and Urban Affairs. The strategem of the National Coalition was to secure federal dollars for obviously needed emergency shelters and then to attack the sources of "mainstream poverty," primarily, in their view, the lack of affordable housing. The Coalition was beginning to meet with some success; the members' hopes — to play a key role in shaping Democratic housing policy in the late 1980s — no longer appeared idle.

The very same day at the Massachusetts State House, the Massachusetts Coalition, absent several members who were testifying in Washington, staged a Speak Out on Homelessness Day. Twenty-four hours later the state's welfare commissioner announced a plan to fund local nonprofit shelters on a partnership basis: the state would pay start-up costs and fifty percent of the operating expenses for six pilot shelters. Boston City Councilor Raymond Flynn filed an ordinance to establish an Office of Emergency Shelter. The day after Congress began its hearings, the Boston City Council started deliberating Flynn's proposal.

At the Pine Street Inn an era had ended. Though Paul Sullivan would continue to stamp his personality on the shelter in thousands of small ways, the Inn had become larger than him.

"We talked about that," his close friend, Frank Kelley, remembers. "He'd say, 'At one time it was all me. But it isn't. That's very clear.' The program had become much bigger than any one person. It wasn't Paul Sullivan's place."

Sullivan continued to do what he'd always done best. One morning he found a couple hunched behind a snow drift beside one of the nearby warehouses. They told him they'd been sleeping on the back porches of South End tenements for the past thirty years. When daylight came they would steal away, hiding their blankets until nightfall. If it got too cold, they'd crawl up behind the Inn, close to the dumpsters, for warmth.

"You're not going to get any sleep there," Sullivan insisted. "Come into the Inn. You can both live here."

But it seemed obvious to many that the enlarged institution demanded a different style of leadership now. After it relocated, the Inn started to close its doors during the day, except when the weather got too cold to send the men and women outside. Though it had evolved in its own way as an institution, the Pine Street Inn in many respects began to mirror the asylums of the early 1800s and the state mental hospitals of its own day. The staff-to-guest ratio, the policy of dispensing psychotropic medications, the style of serving meals, the hours and procedures, shift schedules, change-of-shift meetings, and the log book for keeping track of guests' "behavior" (staff would enter observations for the benefit of those on the next shift) were identical to procedures at most state mental hospitals in the 1970s.

By late in 1981 many of the old-time staffers, realizing that the Inn had entered a new stage of institutional maturity, from which retreat was impossible, had resigned.

EIGHT

Where?

IN THE SPRING OF 1972, Amanda Daley, just out of high school, found life anything but promising. It was banal, undirected, burdened. By then, her mother was a changed woman. The shock treatments had left her almost catatonic. At times it seemed as if she wasn't even there. Jack was gentle with his shattered wife in a way that Amanda had never seen him be before. He reminded her to take baths. Occasionally, he took her out for Chinese food. The world that the two of them had wanted to share from the very beginning was drawing a closed circle around them. Amanda knew she didn't belong there, but where she did belong remained a mystery.

Her sister, Jane, was living with Bill in an apartment in the Mission Hill section of Roxbury. Amanda liked Bill. A good ten years older than Jane, and previously married, he was by now a fixture; her sister had dated him since high school. Bill was earning his living driving a cab in Boston. The couple shared their flat with a friend who, as Amanda later described her, had "a drug problem and a drinking problem." The three agreed to let Amanda join them.

The Mission Hill section, just west of downtown Boston, is a series of steeply inclined roads lined with double-decker homes that have never been renovated. Most of the neighborhood is black and Hispanic, with a few white households. By the time Jane and Amanda lived there, the streets on either side of theirs had been nurturing an active drug trade for years. There were enough families around, however, that they never felt threatened by it. Like everyone else, they just learned to look the other way.

When Amanda first moved in with Jane and Bill, she had a job in one of the city's branch libraries. The want ad had sounded perfect: being surrounded by books was Amanda's idea of bliss, and she couldn't imagine any environment she'd prefer. But at the end of three short months, she'd quit. "It was one of the worst jobs I ever had," was all she would say later.

That summer in her spare time, which she had a lot of, she'd trudge up the steep incline of Tremont Street to the door of the Mission Church rectory. If Father Joseph was in, she'd say hello. Sometimes he'd take the time to talk to her. Father Joseph remembers Amanda as a tiny person who was always cheerful but who felt burdened by her sister's intensifying complaints that she wasn't pulling her weight around the house.

"She never asked for a dime," he says, though he knew she wasn't making any money. Once that summer Jane called him, pleading with him to persuade Amanda to get a job.

If the priest wasn't in or was too busy to talk, Amanda spent an hour or two chatting with Anna Ivanova, the housekeeper. With her ready ear, sympathy, and encouragement, Anna became like a mother to Amanda, and Amanda secretly started to call her Mom.

At home in the evenings life was quiet. Jane and Bill seldom went out. Amanda's link to the world beyond Roxbury was confined to her correspondence with Sister Mary Moore, and phone calls to her grandmother. In long, digressive missives to her former headmistress, Amanda would pour out her affection for the school and recall the memories that gave her so much happiness.

Her grandmother kept up a lively exchange of letters and phone calls with her granddaughter, and Amanda often took the bus to Plymouth for weekend visits.

Finally she found a job downtown, as a messenger for the Protective Insurance Company, a small, privately owned business that occupied three floors of an old brick office building in Kenmore Square. She would arrive promptly every morning and spend the next eight hours dashing between floors with messages, claims to be signed, and documents to be filed. Amanda liked the job and kept it for six years, longer than any other she was to have.

She got to know everyone at the company quickly. Wherever she went, she'd stop to chat. At lunchtime she liked to go outdoors and sit on one of the benches around the corner along Bay State Road, a gracious street of Georgian brownstones that runs through Boston University's urban campus.

The years can get lost quickly in such a life. If the six years during which Amanda was with the Protective were uneventful, they were also stable. Until the summer of 1978 the only thing that changed with some regularity was her address.

Around five A.M. on the Sunday before Thanksgiving in 1972, Amanda awoke to the smell of smoke and the scream of fire engines. Her building was on fire. In fact, the blaze had started in the room next to hers: their alcoholic roommate had passed out with a burning cigarette in her hand. The ladder trucks arrived just as the sisters had scrambled to the safety of the pavement in their pajamas. And at that moment Bill, his shift over, pulled up in his cab, striking a note that Amanda would find comic whenever she remembered the incident.

The household split up. Jane and Bill moved to Mattapan, and Amanda took a room in a boarding house on Marlborough Street in the Back Bay, within walking distance of the Protective. Thus began the happiest period of her working years. She liked living by herself and being answerable to no one. She did her job efficiently and well. At night she ate in the communal kitchen, then closed the door to her room and read or knitted until it was time to go to bed. No one put demands on her, no one yelled at her, and there was no pressure to conform. She wasn't isolated; someone was always around in the house if she felt like talking.

And Nanna continued to be a protective buffer against the world, as she'd always been for her youngest granddaughter. The month after the fire, Nanna's sister, her live-in companion for more than forty years, died. Though it was a devastating loss for Nanna, it didn't prevent her from fulfilling Amanda's request for a batch of Christmas cookies for her first office Christmas party. Shortly after the beginning of 1973, Nanna moved in with Bill and Jane.

Up to this point, Amanda had been able to build the beginnings of a life for herself. Every move — from the library to the insurance company, from Sharon to Jane and Bill's, then to her own room on Marlborough Street — had reflected her developing confidence and self-sufficiency. The only clear plan she'd had in mind when she moved to Boston was "to get the hell out of Sharon and just stay away from there. Just leave that whole part of my life. Bang. That's it." And to all appearances, it seemed that she was succeeding. She intended to establish her routine as a single career woman, maintain her good standing on the job, and wait and see what might come her way. Though she hadn't kept up with any of her schoolmates, she had several friends at the office. She wasn't in any hurry to get involved in a romantic relationship. There would be plenty of time for that.

For the next year, this vision held. Then in 1974, on a seemingly slender pretext, Amanda left the rooming house and moved back in with Jane and Bill and Nanna. She did so, she claims, because "the person living next to me decided to make a big pig sty out of their room."

Quarters were close in the five-room Mattapan apartment, so in September 1975 the foursome moved to Brighton, just a seven-minute trolley ride from Amanda's job in Kenmore Square. Their house, which had been the street's original tavern, had charm. Almost two hundred years old, it had the original gas light fixtures and broad-planked pine floors. At the end of the day Amanda could get off the Green Line several blocks from home and browse through the numerous boutiques and curio shops as evening closed in.

For a time, everyone in the house was lulled into believing that family spirit had prevailed and that Jane and Bill had done the right thing in taking Nanna in and helping Amanda out. The media said family support was dying in America. It certainly hadn't been part of their parents' life: Renata had virtually cut her mother off years earlier. There was no self-righteousness in Brighton because they were doing things differently, only a kind of surface faith that, for a time, made the arrangement seem so normal that it obscured the fact that Jane and Amanda weren't little girls anymore, playing dolls while their mother slept in another room. Buried were the deeper issues that were bound, in time, to erupt.

For Jane, who'd always been the one who tried to hold things together, the situation must have been frustrating at best. For all the years of struggling to be free of the burden, she had ended up with two fatally dependent people, as needy as her parents had been, whom she couldn't bring herself to abandon.

Amanda felt many pressures and a good deal of ambivalence as well. Her foray into independence hadn't gotten very far. Circumstances, she would say, had forced her back into the supportive net cast by her sister and Bill. She was grateful to have been taken in, but she didn't feel nearly as free to be herself as she had on Marlborough Street. Jane's attitude toward her swung from impatience to coldness and cutting sarcasm, a chilling echo of their mother. Jane made Amanda feel incompetent. And Amanda believed that, as Jane had missed the worst of what had happened in Sharon, she couldn't possibly understand Amanda's feelings or defenses.

"It was status quo as long as we stayed out of each other's hair," Amanda remembers. "But once we started, it was like World War III all the time." The emotional tension sometimes got so bad that she felt as if she were in Sharon all over again. She and Jane began to fight often. Bill tried to be the peacemaker — unsuccessfully. Too much was going on between the sisters to be resolved by a few kind words and determined efforts at self-control.

The only thing missing from this dark scenario was her parents. But not for long. One day Jack and Renata Daley showed up on the doorstep and announced that they were moving in. They were broke and had nowhere to go.

Jane and Amanda had not stayed in touch with their parents. Now for the first time they learned that their father's supervisors had repeatedly asked him to join AA. When he still couldn't own up to his alcoholism, the state finally fired him. By the time he and Renata showed up at their daughters', Jack had been out of work for months. His gambling had gone from bad to worse. Apparently now he had lost even the house on a bet.

"I was bullshit," Amanda remembers. "They had not once ever told Jane and me what was going on."

Several weeks after the pair moved in, Jane and Bill departed on a trip to England, leaving Amanda to cope with her parents.

"They expected us to let them move in, pay no rent, no heat, no lights, and none of the rest of it. There was no warning or anything at all. I had the following scenario: a cat that just had three kittens, three full-grown cats, parents, grandparent, all on my shoulders. Plus a job. He, my father, wasn't doing anything at all. I think they thought they were going to have a free ride."

Two weeks after her parents' arrival, Amanda came home one night to find them both sitting quietly in the living room. "Absolutely no word out of them. I said, hm, something's happened."

She went upstairs and found her grandmother lying on her bed in tears. Renata had discovered one of the cats sitting on a kitchen shelf. She had thrown it off and started berating Nanna for being a slob of a housekeeper.

Amanda remembers, "I hit the walls, the ceiling, the floors, the basement, both sides of the house, several times. Then I went downstairs and proceeded to chew those two bastards out. I said, 'You are going to pay me one hundred dollars a week to stay here. You're going to do your own cooking. If either one of you gets Nanna upset, you're going to be out of that door and in the street so fast your heads are going to spin. You touch any of my animals, the same thing's going to happen. You break a dish, you go out and buy a new one. Momma, none of this bullshit about having every single light on in the house. You're gonna help pay for the gas, the electric bill, everything else. I'm in charge of this house, not you two assholes. You're going to live on my turf, you'll live by my terms. You don't like it, leave.' It meant, basically speaking, that they didn't have any control over me anymore."

That moment still stands out in Amanda's mind as the most important in her life. It took all she had to express even a fraction of the anger she had been carrying since childhood. She was trembling with rage, and her voice was pitched so high that the neighbors could hear her. Her life, she believed, depended upon her taking control at that moment, asserting her will, and sticking up for her needs.

But when it was over, she was exhausted, physically and psychologically. Her parents didn't scream at her in response. They didn't argue. They remained for another month, then returned to Sharon, leaving behind a daughter whose victory felt hollow. Amanda discovered that expressing her anger hadn't restored her self-esteem. It hadn't made up for all that she had missed out on in life. And it didn't help her cope with what came next.

A week before her parents moved out, the Protective Insurance Company folded. Amanda's job was terminated. "They got taken over by the Holding Corporation of America," Amanda says, "which I humorously refer to as the Holding Corpses of Assholes."

After a month of casting about, depressed and aimless, Amanda accepted a job at the Prudential Insurance Company, where a number of the Protective staff had ended up. The downtown headquarters of the "Pru" were enormous and impersonal, a far cry from the family atmosphere at the Protective. But more oppressive than the corporate atmosphere was the responsibility of her job. Amanda was no longer a messenger; she'd been promoted to a job as a claims payer. For a year and a half she made valiant efforts to hang on, but the job was overwhelmingly stressful. Often when she left at the end of the day, her head was spinning.

"It was just too much pressure," she recalls. "I was earning five dollars an hour and seven-fifty overtime. That, and being told, well, you have to work from seven-thirty in the morning until eight o'clock at night, six days a week. Wait a minute. What about living?"

When she quit, she found a job as a cashier at a Woolworth's close to her home. That summer Amanda toiled through the hot days, then went home to a hot, empty house and three ornery cats. Jane and Bill were again off in England, and Nanna was at the Cape. She decided that at the age of twenty-nine she deserved a vacation, too. When Jane and Bill returned, she quit her job at Woolworth's. Taking her overtime earnings from the Pru, she boarded an airplane for the first time, bound for London.

Amanda walked the streets of London and viewed the sights for several days, then set out by train for her real destination, East Anglia. She wanted to visit the setting of the most wonderful story she'd ever read, Arthur Ransome's 1931 children's classic, *Swallows and Amazons*. In it the young Walker children create a magical kingdom of their own on an island far from the reaches of civilized society. Amanda found her fictional paradise and toured the countryside for two weeks, until she had to fly back to her own troubled reality again.

Back in Boston, jobless and increasingly unwelcome in Brighton, feeling as if everything was out of control, she drifted from one temporary job to the next through another winter, disconnected and lost. Things had gone badly at every turn. No matter how hard she'd tried, nothing had held together. She'd lost her best job and her only real apartment. Except for Nanna, there was no one to turn to.

She decided to get some counseling. Not knowing where to go, she called the Catholic Charities Bureau, which sent her to one of their social workers.

"The person immediately turned around and did a screw job on me," she says with bitterness. "She called my sister and told her what I'd said." Distraught and betrayed, frightened away from therapy of any kind, Amanda felt that she'd reached the end of trying.

On the evening of June 1, 1981, Amanda came home to a quiet

house. Nanna had left for her annual month-long visit to the Cape that morning. Bill and Jane were out doing errands. When she opened the front door, a familiar acrid odor met her. She went from room to room, trying to track it down. When she reached Jane's bedroom and saw Jane's freshly cleaned laundry piled on the bed, she started to laugh. Her pet cat, Kristie, had peed all over it. But the satisfaction of this arbitrary vengeance was brief. She knew before any words were exchanged with her sister that this would be the last straw.

The next morning she woke and packed her backpack. She stuffed in several notebooks, some underwear and socks, several pairs of pants, and her raincoat. A month shy of thirty, Amanda Daley was running away from home.

"I walked out the door and said, 'Sayonara, see ya later.' "

It was a sunny morning, and she had some money in her pocket. She walked the mile to Brighton Center and went into the Brigham's there, as she did every morning, for breakfast. Only today she wouldn't be turning the corner and passing through the familiar doors of the Woolworth's. After breakfast she would walk into Boston.

From Brighton Center one quickly leaves behind the busy, small-town congestion, the hodgepodge of opticians, dry cleaners, lighting shops, television appliance stores, fabric and junk shops, upholsterers, travel agents, and small savings and loans. A mile out, at Union Square, one can look directly down to the Citgo sign in Kenmore Square, and beyond, to the twin towers that dominate Back Bay's skyline — the Pru and the Hancock, familiar landmarks to Amanda.

She continued along the three-mile route, past car dealerships and the stereo and sporting goods shops interspersed with Boston University buildings. By the time she reached Kenmore Square, she had decided on her destination: the Boston Public Library in Copley Square.

All morning she sat in the reading room and read. By noon, when she emerged to find a place for lunch, the sky had clouded over and rain was beginning to fall. At the Burger King in Copley Square, she downed a hamburger and a Coke, then returned to the library. Later she watched high school students come in, chattering and buzzing as they worked on their final papers. She saw people who looked like they had nowhere else to go and found herself observing them closely, for the first time in her life. She had no idea where she was going to sleep that night. Running down to Nanna on the Cape wouldn't have solved anything. She had no friends she could call on. At five the library would close, and all she could focus on was the fact that out the window the sky looked like it was about to open up.

She closed her book and made her way down two flights of stairs, through the open gray marble lobby to a bank of pay phones. Scanning the phone book, she came across Runaway House Place, located, coincidentally, on Marlborough Street.

Amanda ran the five blocks to Runaway House and rang the bell. The man who let her in listened to her story sympathetically. He told her she could use the office phone to call the nearest women's shelter, Rosie's Place. Amanda had only once heard of Rosie's Place. She had never been inside a shelter. She had never even been in the South End. But on the other end of the line a woman was saying to her, "Don't worry about anything right now. Why don't you come over here and have some dinner?" Amanda, hungry and tired, realized that she didn't have much choice.

By now it was raining hard and almost dark. She found herself wandering down unfamiliar streets, completely disoriented. Many of the buildings looked abandoned. On brick walls she saw fluorescent messages spray-painted in Spanish. She kept close to the curb and avoided the alley.

At length she reached a street shadowed by the elevated T line. To her left was a housing project. Groups of black teenagers were hanging around outside a liquor store between her and the project, and young women loitered at the street corners. The only traffic was a slow procession of large, shiny cars whose drivers scrutinized the girls at the curb. But by then Amanda was too exhausted to be frightened. She just wanted to find a dry place to stay. A patrolman appeared, and Amanda asked him directions. In minutes she was opening the heavy pink front door to Rosie's Place.

Inside was bedlam. Women crowded around the dining room tables and the few chairs. Some were standing in lines, others had gathered in clusters, and still others were sitting on the floor talking to themselves. Dazed, Amanda inched her way in. Someone handed her a cup of coffee, and she made her way to a table, managed to find a seat, and slumped into it. Then she started to cry.

Opposite her a large black woman was cackling like a hen to herself, but as soon as she saw Amanda, she stopped.

"She came up to me, gave me a big hug," Amanda remembers, "and said, 'Okay, what's wrong?' I'll always remember it. And all of a sudden, there are three or four counselors, all these women, all of whom

I know very well now, were standing around saying, 'Okay, what's wrong?' I started to explain. They said, 'Don't worry about it. You're here. And we'll help.' "

Amanda had become a homeless woman. That night, because Rosie's beds were full, she was sent several blocks to the Pine Street Inn, where a bed was waiting. The next day she found a friend.

"I don't even know if she's alive or not," Amanda says now. "She was a thief. She could lie better than anyone I'd ever run into in my entire life. She was black, and she had so many problems that I don't know where to begin to describe her. I later found out that she was barred from every shelter in town. I trusted her because she knew the ropes. She adopted me."

The pair stayed together at Pine Street for three weeks. Amanda's companion-protector showed her what was safe and what wasn't, where to walk and what to avoid. Then Amanda contracted pneumonia. The emergency room physician at City Hospital told her she'd have to rest and remain indoors for a month. Amanda never saw her friend again.

Where to stay for a month was a problem. Besides Rosie's Place, which had a five-night limit, and the Pine Street Inn, where she wouldn't be able to remain indoors during the day, there was only Sancta Maria's, a small women's shelter nearby. But it too had a stay limit. That left Harbor Light on Washington Street, which had a number of residential beds for recovering alcoholics; Amanda was given special permission to use one of these until the middle of July, a week before her birthday.

The rest of the summer passed quickly. Amanda joined the small society of women who spent their days together in the parks and meal programs of the South End, and ended them more or less by chance at Rosie's or Sancta Maria's or Pine Street. The shelters were so close to one another, it hardly mattered which they chose.

One evening, as Amanda was sitting in the lobby at Pine Street, she looked up to see that Channel 5 was rebroadcasting a report on Rosie's Place that she had watched the previous summer from the comfort of her Brighton bedroom, with her cat, Kristie, curled up beside her. Spellbound, Amanda saw the faces of her new friends flash across the screen while the narrator's voice-over droned on. The images kept appearing: the bedrooms, where a year ago she never dreamed she'd sleep, the dining room where she now ate many breakfasts, lunches, and dinners.

"You never really know what is going to happen to you," she reflected as she watched. "You never really understand how the events in your day-to-day life will ultimately change your life, the way you live your life."

The experience of being homeless wasn't nearly as traumatic as she would have thought. The weather was warm, and people were kind and helpful. After recovering from pneumonia, she was feeling rebellious. With her long dark hair and horn-rimmed glasses, she looked like any other footloose young woman at large in the city of Boston. Protected by old-timers who were used to street life, she never experienced anything close to danger. And once past the first few hours of uncertainty, she felt that she'd done the right thing as far as her sister and Bill were concerned. She had all the time in the world — with no one breathing down her back, living among friendly, accepting people — to try to straighten out her life.

"I had a lot of stuff to think about," she says. "I was absolutely bullshit at my sister and the rest of the family. It was just the fact that somehow or other I'd figured out that something was wrong with the way we'd been brought up."

That summer, when she wasn't reading at the library or chatting with her new friends, she was writing down her reflections. By the end of three months, she'd filled two legal pads. Then one morning in early September, outside of the Pine Street Inn, Amanda looked up and saw her brother-in-law walking toward her, preoccupied, his eyes on the pavement.

"He'd been looking for me, but not really, you know. And he almost didn't know who I was. I says, 'Hi, Bill.' He looked around, and the expression on his face was one of the best I've ever seen. Shock, amazement, and surprise all rolled into one. He picked me up bodily off the sidewalk and gave me one of the biggest hugs I've ever gotten. He says, 'Where the fuck have you been? You completely vanished into thin air.'

"We met for about a week, and then he told me he wanted me to come home for the winter. Which, looking back at it, if I'd had it to do over again, I would have said, 'Uh-uh, I'll stay at Pine Street.' "

Amanda was different from her mother in one major respect: she had no focused aspiration, no developed talent. Aside from that, however, one wonders if their lives would have been so different if Renata had had a place to run away to. In many ways the daughter was beginning to mirror her mother, except that where Renata had run away to an internal place and found there not peace but madness, Amanda ran away into the world.

That winter she felt as out of place at Jane and Bill's as ever. In March she went back to Pine Street.

Two weeks after her return, Amanda was having lunch at Harbor Light when a staff member she knew there grabbed her arm.

"There's someone I want you to meet," she said. "I think you two would hit it off."

She couldn't have known how well. Thomas was in his late thirties, Amanda guessed, about eight years older than she. He was striking: five foot ten, with curly dark hair and engaging blue eyes, the son of an Italian father and an American Indian mother. But he had something more than good looks: Thomas had fire. He radiated an energy, intensity, confidence, and self-control that were magnetic. Amanda saw instantly that others were drawn to him and deferred to him. Thomas had lived on and off the streets for years and seemed to understand his power among street people. He knew precisely how and when to pull someone to him, how to make a person trust him. When he picked someone out of the crowd for any reason, that person became imbued with the reflected light of Thomas's aura. He was charismatic, intuitive, and kind.

But Thomas was something else, too — something that Amanda wouldn't discover for a time. He was hurt. His wife had cheated on him, he'd confided to a few trusted shelter counselors over the years. One day he'd come home from work and found her in bed with another man. He had beaten his competitor close to death, but the humiliation of that betrayal became an obsession. He would never let himself be hurt like that again.

That day at Harbor Light, and over the course of the next few weeks, Amanda and Thomas found themselves drawn to each other, though neither recognized at the time that part of the attraction was common experiences and complementary needs: his for a loyal woman to depend on him, hers for a protector. The destructive patterns that alcoholism and violence had etched into their individual psyches would return to torment and ultimately overwhelm them. But in April of 1982, disappointment and failure seemed part of the bleak past. The island kingdom that Amanda had sought in England they now discovered in each other.

They became inseparable. Thomas was staying downtown at a small mission for men called Kingston House. The mission, originally in the North End, had been part of the city's settlement house network until 1964, when it had closed its doors for fourteen years. Now, under the direction of Milton Friesen, the man who set up Harbor Light for the Salvation Army and ran it for years, a new Kingston House was getting off the ground.

Friesen and Thomas had known each other since the early days of Harbor Light. By 1982 Friesen had counseled Thomas during periods of unemployment and listlessness so often that he was like a father to Tom. He'd helped Tom get jobs, taken him in when he left them, and welcomed him back after he'd disappeared for stretches, drifting around the country. When Friesen agreed to set up the new Kingston House, he offered Tom and a few other street men the opportunity to sleep on the unfinished upper floor at night in exchange for helping him refurbish the dilapidated building during the day.

"He lived here for quite a while," Friesen recalls. "Probably seven months. In the beginning, we just had our doors open during the day for transient people. Then we were serving meals, and Thomas was helping me with that. He did anything for me. The upper floors were empty. It was just a crummy place to live, but there were a few people I allowed to live here who helped us run the place, and to have somebody here at night. They just put up a bed on an empty floor, and that's where they lived."

Soon, unbeknownst to Friesen, Amanda was living there too. It was the most exhilarating thing that had ever happened to her. Thomas would spend hours describing his travels around the country. He had been from one end of the continent to the other, he said, staying on Indian reservations all the way to California, then turning back again. He'd worked construction, he said, including that of her former office building, the Prudential tower. He'd worked for an accountant. Thomas had had more experiences than anyone Amanda had ever known. He read the newspaper everyday and thought about the issues. He was interesting to listen to, a man of strong political opinions. And, unlike anyone else in her life, he liked to engage her in discussions. What she thought genuinely mattered to Thomas.

That he had some very conservative ideas about women didn't bother Amanda in the slightest. In his view, "The man's the boss. If she loves me she'll certainly do what I tell her to do" — that was how Friesen summed up Thomas's outlook. It was fine with Amanda. She needed his strength or, a little like her father's bravado, what passed for strength.

Thomas was sober then and had been the whole time he'd lived at Kingston House. Though over the years his alcoholism had under-mined his confidence and sense of direction and had cost him regular employment, he tried to save others from having to deal with it. His drinking was always conducted in secret, away from the shelters.

"He was always clean," Friesen recalls. "I don't think I ever saw him drunk. That's not the Thomas I know. Even when he came back here [after a bout of drinking] I don't think he came back to this building until he was cleaned up. Always shaven and cleaned up."

Though Friesen saw Amanda during the day, he never suspected that she was staying after hours, jeopardizing the reputation of his institution. Instead he found himself wondering what she was doing on the streets.

"I never thought there was any reason for her to be on the street, you know. And while I cannot say that I ever thought, 'Why in the world are you associated with this man?' I think I would have thought, 'Why are you associated with this kind of a person, who lives this kind of an insecure, unproductive, no-future kind of a life?' But she was very much in love with him, I think."

In Thomas's appreciative presence, Amanda flourished. In fact, to Friesen she seemed transformed. "She's a tiny person, and I remem-ber being surprised on a number of occasions at her anger, and how vocal she was. She would talk and get very upset about some issues, social issues. She had some very strong ideas. I remember thinking, wow! She can really get on her soap box."

Thomas, for his part, only wanted Amanda to be happy.

"It was like I was starting something brand new," Amanda recalls.

They talked about getting married. Then in June they lied to Frie-sen, telling him they *were* married. This was because he'd discovered their living arrangement and was about to throw them out. Friesen stood firm.

"Thomas never got angry with me," Friesen says. "Even when I asked him to leave. He said, 'I know. I shouldn't have done it. Sorry. I understand, if your board finds out. You can't have this kind of reputation.'"

The couple took a room in Charlestown for a month. Then in July

they moved into an apartment in Everett, a working-class town just
north of the city.

Ellen Gallagher, a Harvard College sophomore, was on leave the fall
semester of 1983, coordinating a new shelter in the basement of Faith
Lutheran Church in Cambridge. After she announced plans for its
opening one day at the Harvard Square meals program, she looked
up and recognized Thomas. He'd been a frequent visitor to the lunch
program that fall, and Ellen remembered that his girlfriend had always been with him. Now Tom approached her, formally introduced
himself, and asked for a bed.

"My first impression," Ellen, a serious, sensitive young woman, recalls, "was, this is a scam. Why is he, this guy who's pretty put together, on the street?"

What happened to Thomas and Amanda between July 1982 and
December 1983 is a puzzle, whose pieces began to emerge disjointedly
in Thomas's confidences to Ellen over the next several months. Amanda
rarely speaks of that time and the memories she does voice are strangely
abstract ones. Their life was so private that the months seem to have
disappeared; in light of what happened later, Amanda may have willed
their virtual vanishing from her mind. That they lived together and
went through much suffering becomes clear only from other people's
recollections of brief encounters with the pair during that time.

After they moved into their Everett apartment, Thomas took a ma-
chinist's job at the U.S. Gypsum Company nearby. He kept the job
for eleven months, supporting them both until April 1983. That month
he became ill with lung-related disorders that resulted in his being in
and out of the hospital most of the rest of the year.

Amanda has said that Thomas suffered from a long-term heart ail-
ment and from asthma. And Friesen recalls that Thomas had had
some physical problems earlier: at one point he had walked off a desk
job Friesen had helped him get. "He just said he was tired and didn't
work anymore," Friesen recalls.

But when he arrived at Faith Lutheran in December, Thomas told
Ellen that he'd filed suit against U.S. Gypsum for asbestos poisoning.
He claimed to be represented by an attorney from the Indian Nation.
He told her that the company had offered him $540,000, but he'd
refused it, because he wanted not only money but justice.

"He wants attention brought not just to the damage he sustained,"

Ellen wrote in her journal, "but to the pain of those who came before and after."

He looked to Ellen to be fifty years old; in fact he was only thirty-six. He was consuming about twenty-two pills a day, with milk to protect his stomach. He said the pills enabled him to keep breathing and his heart to keep beating.

Thomas was no longer living with Amanda. She had moved back in with Jane and Bill in July, when the lease had run out on the Everett apartment. She was working again, as a clerk at Woolworth's. Remembering her life at that time, Amanda says, "You try to describe it to someone. How did I do it? I don't know. Going through five managers [at the store], five different systems of working in a store, going to the hospital, going home, sleeping."

Tom's illness had taken its toll on the relationship. Ellen recalls, "Some nights he'd come in and be okay. Other nights I have a very clear image of him, dying, totally out of breath, really in bad shape. His color would be all red. Or he'd go into the hospital to have those oxygen transfusions. And he'd always have to be doing that."

By July it must have been obvious to Amanda and Thomas that their living arrangement had become untenable. But apparently illness wasn't the only factor. While they were living in Everett, Thomas used to return to Kingston House alone to visit his old friend Milton Friesen. One time he confided that he wished he'd never met Amanda.

"I think Amanda was both good and bad for him," Friesen says. "She was good in the fact that there was somebody to love and be with, companionship. But there was a real ambivalent feeling, because for a while he would say, 'I'm so glad she came into my life because I don't know what I'd do without her.'

"I think she was very demanding. They would be talking about soon they'd be moving into this beautiful place — I think he had a grandiose idea of getting a beautiful apartment or a house somewhere for her. Those were her dreams, and of course in the state he was in they were unrealistic, but that was what he thought would happen, hoped would happen. And talking about having children, maybe on a farm. It was too far from any realistic goal. I think that probably got them into trouble a number of times."

For her part, Amanda, previously so docile, found that she could become distant and disdainful or almost irrationally enraged if Thomas failed to do things as she wished them done.

"They had some roaring fights," Friesen says. "She could get very angry. Thomas could too. I remember she told me off one time — that was after we had asked him to leave . . . I think that she took advantage of him. I really do. I think that she used him. That she was demanding, and that he wanted to fulfill her every wish. Maybe she had her job, but I think that he was superior to her. I really do. I certainly never, never, never would have placed Thomas here" — he lays his hand on his desk — "and her up here in any social or whatever criteria you want to use."

The relationship was also plagued by fears of betrayal and jealousy. Thomas would go back to Kingston House with tales that sound unbelievable to those who knew Amanda then. He told several people, including Friesen, that he'd discovered Amanda with another man on several occasions. And he said that she had been fired from her job for stealing.

Friesen remembers Amanda as being intensely jealous of any other relationship Tom had, including his friendship with Milton. She didn't want to share him with anyone. Outsiders portray a stormy love that over the course of time became overwhelmed by Thomas's fantasies, projections, and illness, on the one hand, and Amanda's demands, dependency, and struggles for control, on the other.

"It makes total sense," Ellen observes in retrospect. "She was raised with an alcoholic and she was engaging in co-alcoholic behavior: you have these two people caught in these negative patterns and each one is filling each other's negative needs."

What had drawn each of them to the other may also have been destined to tear them apart. They may have decided that if they were to preserve any affection, they simply couldn't live together, a decision that took hold because it was convenient for many secondary reasons as well. Amanda returned to the familiarity of her sister's flat; Thomas, after sleeping on friends' floors for a few months, to the neutrality of the shelter.

Faith Lutheran, the second church-run shelter in Massachusetts, was an exciting place to be in the winter of 1983. Like its predecessor at nearby University Lutheran, Faith Lutheran was the brainchild of Stewart Guernssey, a young Mississippi attorney who had come north to attend Harvard Divinity School in the fall of 1982. Guernssey raised $1,200 to run University Lutheran during February and March of 1983, then returned to Mississippi to practice law the following summer, leaving a committee to raise funds for a second shelter.

By the time Faith Lutheran opened on December 1, it had a six-month lease from the congregation and a $15,000 donation from the trust fund of an enthusiastic Harvard undergraduate. It also had what was at the time a radical agenda. Faith Lutheran would be a twenty-bed *community* shelter for both men and women, which meant that its residents would be able to live there night after night instead of competing for a place in the first-come, first-served policy that prevailed in most shelters. It was to be open from nine P.M. to nine A.M. every day, with dinner ready for residents when the doors opened. Guernssey hoped that Faith Lutheran would evolve into a democratically run community of homeless people.

Tom's old leadership abilities reemerged in full force. From the very beginning, Ellen recalls, "Tom pretty much ran the shelter. Tom could read people. Sometimes he'd tell you what his readings were. Oftentimes he was correct."

Tom was in his element again, unfettered by the snares of intimacy. "He had a sense of his own power," Ellen continues, "and of his ability to get people to do things that he wanted them to. 'You want me to get this place cleaned up? I'll get it cleaned up. Have it done in half an hour.' 'You want him out of here? I'll get him out of here.' Sometimes, to the point where I'd say, 'No, Tom, that's pushing it. We don't need to do that.'

"My image of Tom is of him parading up Broadway with several people behind him on his way to do laundry for the shelter. Stew would just give him the key. He'd do the laundry. We would just trust him to do these things. Tom had a position that Stewart never really could have [worked out] with the other homeless people. Even when Stew couldn't get things done, Tom could."

Guernssey agrees. "Tom was a natural leader. That showed itself very quickly, in terms of his taking responsibility for the manual stuff around the shelter, cleaning up, or cooking, or whatever needed to be done. He was also quite a commanding presence — tall and slender, a good-looking guy, and pretty well built."

Though Thomas was very different from Amanda's father, Jack Daley, they did share some qualities. "He was very authoritarian. He didn't put up with any nonsense and he ruled with an iron hand," Guernssey says. Indeed, if there was any source of conflict between Tom and Stew, it was over the enforcement of rules. Tom could sometimes go overboard.

Beneath the charisma and the kind, often vulnerable face Thomas showed those around him ran a deep fascination with violence that was intimately linked to his identification with victims. At a certain level Tom, feeling that he could never measure up, must have found solace in fantasies of violence, which by his own account he occasionally acted out. Though the face of the victim was what people usually saw, there was another side to Tom, and these paired faces seemed to meet in his sense of himself as an American Indian.

"His big thing was that he was an Indian," Ellen says. In talking to Guernssey, Thomas emphasized the prejudice against Native Americans that had contributed to his inability to hold jobs. With Ellen he'd reminisce about the Indian Nation, faulty rescue treaties, about a brother who wore warpaint and carried a tomahawk, "a tough Indian who will pound out anyone who speaks against his people." He spent hours in the library exploring Indian tribal history. Ellen remembers him talking about how violent and abusive the Indians were. " 'I'm proud of them,' he'd say. Then he'd laugh and jam a fist into his hand."

Thomas told Ellen he had grown up as one of seven children on a farm in rural Massachusetts, about halfway between Boston and Providence, Rhode Island, the son of an alcoholic father. By the time he arrived at Faith Lutheran, only three of the original seven children were still alive, he said. Two had been killed in Vietnam, and one sister had died young.

Ellen tried to fit the pieces together. He intimated that he may have had rheumatoid arthritis as a child. She wrote in her journal:

> Jack (one of the two brothers who died in Vietnam) taught him how to walk — how to throw away his crutches himself instead of standing in pain as others teased and broke them. In praising his brother he explained how Jack would consistently gather the offender, drag him up the street before Tom, and encourage Tom to beat him up. Nice. Tom promised he'd become a boxer and did — told me the story of progressing up to international competition, how he used to punch up his 3 taller bros. (Jack was 6'4").
>
> The "half-breed," as he repeatedly called himself, finished high school, took 2 years off — spent 1 riding around the country with $1,000 and his motorcycle — the next he spent on assorted Indian reservations. Describes a lot of fighting — a lot of barroom brawls, a lot of physical demonstration. Avoided a prison sentence (or charge) of attempted murder (though the reality existed "I tried to kill my wife after I caught her with a nigger") later "I left him as a pulp up against a tree", "heard he died a year later, suicide, I think (he hanged himself)." Oh yes, bi-

zarre tales. Only daughter Jennifer, 15, lives with Tom's aunt and uncle (in Califor.) He sees her once or twice a year. 7 years ago they parted. He explained "not knowing what to say to an eight year old girl." "If it was a guy it'd be different."

Tom told Ellen, though it was hard to imagine how he'd packed so much living in, that he'd been a Marine for nine years. He also revealed that although he'd avoided one prison term, he'd served two others: one for a year, and a second for six years, on undisclosed charges.

"Tom has surprised me greatly these past few days — A man I thought so quiet and peaceful now exposes a radical side of violence — of bitterness, of suffering and pain," Ellen wrote.

And yet the tender, vulnerable, and wounded side of him remained. "On cold days, the damage to lungs and respiratory system clearly shows," Ellen wrote midway through December. "Yesterday Tom looked very tired and uncomfortable. In response to 'Can I get you something?' he says, 'Yeah, a new pair of lungs.'"

On December 23 he reported that he was heading to the hospital for a report on his heart condition. Thomas was elated with the hospital's findings. "His heart is ok," Ellen wrote. "It's going back to normal. He called his family. Rode out to Worcester. Met all 17, including nieces and nephews, and told them the news."

Thomas's family wanted him to come home to the farm for the holidays and for a long stay, but he couldn't bring himself to leave the streets of Cambridge.

"I want to be here," he told Ellen, "with the street people. They're my friends."

On December 25, Amanda appeared at Faith Lutheran for the first time. She'd accepted Tom's invitation to spend Christmas Day. Tom was very happy that evening. He and one of the other residents, a man named Phil, had prepared a Christmas feast. They arranged the tables into a U-shape and decorated them with pots of poinsettias, trays of crackers, and assorted Christmas ornaments. The tree had been trimmed the night before and gifts exchanged.

Ellen remembers, "Tom and Amanda stuck pretty close together. Tom wandered around, listening to the piano player, trying to initiate singing. His high from the medical good news continued."

After that Amanda was a regular visitor. In fact, she took up the role she'd had beside Tom at Kingston House. To those at Faith Lutheran, she came to be regarded as a volunteer. Yet her relationship with Tom was often baffling to observers.

"It was very clear that Tom was entirely solicitous of Amanda's health and well-being," Stewart Guernssey recalls. "In his concern and care for her, in small ways around the shelter — getting her a soft drink or serving her a sandwich, always being sure that she was first in line as a guest."

Amanda was submissive. "But in a kind of spunky way, you know what I mean?" says Guernssey. "Very traditional female role, but with a little spark."

"I always got the sense that he was kind of protecting her," Ellen says. Yet certain aspects of their relationship made little sense.

"My initial impression was that she was — I don't know how to say this — that she was in a different league than Tom," Guernssey says. "That she was higher functioning than him. He was obviously on the street for some reason, the reason being somewhat unclear. In fact, it had to do with asbestos poisoning and heart problems and physical health. But while those things were clear, still it was not clear why he could not get social security, or something, to get himself together. There were some other mental-emotional problems, I concluded. Amanda didn't seem to have any of those. Amanda, essentially, was a volunteer at the shelter, although she had the concurrent role of being Tom's girlfriend. So, my thinking was, why is she making out with this homeless man? It was a couple of weeks later or longer before I came to understand that she herself had been homeless, and that Tom had helped get her off the streets."

And why wasn't Tom living with her? Looking back now to the spring of 1984, Guernssey says, "I think they would have been partners. Probably would have married, gotten jobs, and struggled in a working-class setting. I'm fairly convinced of it."

Ellen isn't so sure. "It didn't strike me as equal love, a partnership kind of thing," she says. "Amanda would go on her own way. If Tom was around she was going to be with Tom. It was nice and he was protecting her, but she wasn't following him around all the time. I got more a sense of Tom saying, oh Amanda this, Amanda that. He seemed to prize her. He seemed to really value her. I won't say she didn't value him, but there was also on some level a kind of detachment there from her to him."

And then, too, Ellen remembered Tom's refusing his family's invitation to spend the Christmas holiday with them.

"Now, when I think about homelessness in a more analytical way, that's what didn't fit about Tom," she said. "You got the sense of his strong family unit. They'd have fun together. I'm thinking, Well, he goes out and he must see them. Which still didn't fit with why he was here so reliably. A lot of people would take off for the weekend or have a family outing."

"I want to be with them, the street people, they're my friends," he had said to Ellen at Christmas. Many times he would remark, "These are my people. Street people are my people."

"I remember thinking, it doesn't seem like he's really a street person," Ellen says. "But he must have slipped onto the streets for a while and developed a certain kind of identification and then decided that's really where he belonged. But I always felt Tom could have gotten off any time he wanted."

Later, many would say that Tom wanted to die.

Throughout the spring of 1984 Tom and Amanda continued to move in separate, if intersecting, orbits — she in her working-class neighborhood and her clerk's job, he in the progressive mecca of Cambridge, commanding a community of drifters. Then in June, political events conspired to merge Tom's identification with street people and his need to be their savior.

Faith Lutheran's congregation decided at the end of May not to renew the shelter's lease. The community was stranded, with nowhere to go. "So we packed up and went to the Boston Common and camped out there for ten days," Stewart Guernssey recounts.

But the move was by no means the spur-of-the-moment affair that it might have appeared to outsiders. Guernssey, an attorney, researched permits, handled the media, and hired an attorney with extensive political contacts in the state Democratic Party, in case the group was sued. Most important, Guernssey had a political strategy.

On June 3 a group of about twenty from Faith Lutheran, and their sympathizers, erected a large tent at the foot of the Common along Charles Street near the Civil War monument, and settled in. Calling themselves the Boston Common Tent City, the group demanded that City Hall allow them to buy, for a dollar, an unoccupied, city-owned house to live in and that the state provide "active support" in the amount of $25,000 to rehabilitate it. They also demanded representation on a governor's advisory board on homelessness.

The camp-in on the Common existed in a sort of legal limbo. Had it not been for the sympathies of the city's newly elected mayor, Ray Flynn — who as city councilor had established Boston's Emergency Shelter Commission — they all could have been arrested for leafleting without a permit and inviting passers-by to join them.

"We didn't get anywhere for the first five days," Guernssey recalls. "The TVs came. Everybody was very nice. The mayor came the first day. Then the governor couldn't be upstaged, so he came running down to have his picture taken with the homeless. We set up a situation where we played one against the other pretty effectively."

But for all that, the first five days yielded no political victories. Not only were the politicians unresponsive, but the established shelters in Boston were furious with the group.

"They were bullshit," Guernssey says. "They were absolutely irate, because what we did was create a forum for homeless people to speak. And we didn't censor them. The homeless people said a lot of nasty things about big shelters that were probably all true — with, doubtless, some twist and some bend in the tone of what was said. But because we did that, the Emergency Shelter Commission, which in theory is the shelter's voice to the mayor's office, refused to endorse our getting a house for homeless people."

The group continued to demonstrate. They went to City Hall, and they took their signs displaying their motto, "Homeless not Helpless," to the State House. "We had pickets. We were singing old civil rights songs and stuff," Guernssey recalls. By now the group on the Common had grown to about two hundred people, but City Hall wasn't budging. More drastic measures were needed; they decided to march through Fanueil Hall Marketplace.

"There was a huge hue and cry," Guernssey recalls. "So that evening, we went through again. And the following day we went through again at noon. We sent word to the mayor's office that we were going to go through Fanueil Hall every noon and every evening until we got what we wanted." Within hours their demands were met: they were given a three-decker house in Dorchester.

"Ray Flynn was the hero of the whole thing," Guernssey says. "He overruled all of his aides who were trying to slow the process down and enabled us to get this house quickly."

The rest of the Boston shelter community was infuriated. "There were thirty other agencies who'd applied for housing from the city, and *one* had received it in the two years previous to our application. We were able to get into this house within three months."

Thomas led the demonstrators. Years later even the mayor would remember him as a dominating physical presence.

"He was the number-two person." Guernssey says. "Whenever I was off doing something [which was often], Tom was in charge." Despite his frail and weakening health, Tom insisted on sleeping out every night with his comrades. He wouldn't allow Amanda to participate in any way; he said it would be too dangerous for her. When a new element joined the original shelter group — young people who drank and did drugs and were generally disorderly — he was unhappy and threatened to walk out.

Two weeks into June, Thomas suffered a mild heart attack. By then the group had successfully negotiated its terms with the city. Because of his conflicts with some members of the group, Tom felt that it was time to part ways. Amanda had found a studio apartment in Brookline and arranged for Tom to move in with her.

Shortly after July 4 the Tent City group held a meeting. "Amanda and Thomas came to it, and Thomas got finally pissed off about these kids and walked away and said, 'I'm not coming back,'" says Guernssey.

Several weeks later he checked into Massachusetts General Hospital. On the last Sunday in August, Thomas died.

Ellen Gallagher received the news in Denver, where she was vacationing. Milton Friesen heard it at Kingston House. Everyone was shocked.

"I'd seen him about a week before," Friesen says. "He'd been here. He didn't look well. I remember standing inside at the counter, and he'd come, put his arm around me, and said, 'I'm so glad I've met you. You've helped me so much.' Just very tender. That's the last memory I have of him. But I never thought he was going to die."

Most of his friends hadn't realized how sick he was. But once the event sank in, it seemed to many that Thomas had willed his own death. For months he'd spoken of it as inevitable.

"I'll tell you the impression that I have of those last days," Friesen says. "Here was a person who perhaps all his life had had dreams and had never really seen the fulfillment of any of those dreams. And here was a woman in his life that he put on a pedestal. But that was not changing his life, either. The impression I have is that he wanted to die. I think that he was tired. Absolutely. Body and mind and soul and spirit."

Guernssey concurs. "Particularly toward the end, during the demonstration and afterward. He probably took some chances that he should have not taken with his health. He was having pretty severe heart problems by then, and nevertheless came and camped with us on the Common."

Ellen remembers that Tom had always talked about his premature death as something decreed.

"He got asthma, then he got heart trouble, then he got pneumonia," Amanda says. "He wouldn't stay in the hospital because he knew he was going to die. He didn't want to [stay there]. I knew he was going to die. But he wanted to come home and die. And I knew there was no possible way I was going to be able to cope with that. If I'd woken up one day and found him dead, I don't know what would have happened. That would have blown my mind, completely. I took him back to the hospital. Then we had a big fight because he wanted to come home again, and I said no. I said, 'You'll be dead, but I'll be still living.' "

Instead of allowing him to return to her room in Brookline, she called several of Thomas's friends from Faith Lutheran. "If you guys want to keep an eye on him," she told them, "make sure he eats, and make sure you take him back to the hospital. I have to work, and I can't deal with the idea that someone is going to die while I'm at work." They agreed.

Amanda went to see him in the hospital that last Sunday night in August. "We made up then," she recalls, "About an hour after I left, he died." The cause of death — an enlarged heart.

The following month the Tent City group moved into their house, which they dedicated to his memory.

Guernssey saw Amanda for the last time shortly after that. She'd come in to ask him to fill out a recommendation "for some kind of employee-of-the-year service award," he recalls, "because of her volunteer work at the shelter."

That year Amanda won the prize.

▨▨▨▨▨▨▨▨▨▨

NINE

Who?

THE FIRST THING Wendy did after she stepped off the plane at Tampa International Airport and arrived at Papa's door was to grab the pliers from the tool drawer and rip the braces out of her mouth. Then she got a job answering phones at an electrical supply company and plunked down two dollars and change for a pair of pantyhose and a tube of Revlon pink. Life had begun.

After fifteen years of waiting, she'd come home — and not a moment too soon. Papa, now in his seventies, had begun a long and losing battle with cancer. But his illness didn't stop the old man in those first summer months from dropping by the Howard Corporation every afternoon when his granddaughter got off work. Most nights they would head straight for one of the low-lit, beer-sour bars on their route home.

Often Granny had to come looking for them. The unflappable former Kentucky barmaid would come plunging through the door of the Anchor Lounge, playing her favorite part as Pinellas Park's self-styled skid-row rescue wagon.

Lila had made something of a local name for herself, driving to the corner of First Avenue and Fifth in downtown St. Petersburg to offer the first drifter she met a hot, home-cooked meal and a shower. After Wendy's arrival, Granny's mission became more elaborate. She would swing downtown, order her random dinner guest into the back seat of her car, then go off in search of Wendy and Papa. Her circuit complete, she would ferry all three of them home to meatloaf and mashed potatoes.

All her adult life, Lila Burroughs had extended herself for the dispossessed, and she wasn't about to draw the line at her own husband and granddaughter. The way her children figured it, Lila felt so guilty for being the cause of their unhappy childhoods that she was going to end her days performing acts of contrition on total strangers.

The lesson in all this wasn't lost on Lila's granddaughter. The more adrift you were, the more wounded and messed up, the more willing Granny seemed to be to take care of you. Seventeen-year-old Wendy took it all in. She continued to pull on her nylons, dab at her lashes with Maybelline, and get to her office job on time at least four out of five mornings a week. She never had so many beers with Papa that she was forced to call in sick. But she started to spend more and more of her time downtown with Granny at the John 3:16 Mission.

From the aluminum carports and trailer parks of Pinellas Park, it was a ten-minute drive to the quiet heart of downtown. Elevated on a foam pillow so that she could see over the steering wheel, Lila passed by mall after mall, all crowded with car washes and cactus plant nurseries, giant drug stores, and the occasional Pentecostal Holiness Church or low, concrete Christian school cloistered from the kitsch by five-foot chain-link and Dobermans.

After turning off Route 19, she drove some twenty blocks down Central Avenue toward the harbor and entered the old city. Downtown St. Pete's was slow and sunbaked, a tired port town of stucco walls the shade of dried coral, only listlessly resisting the pull back to wind-swept savannah. The cracked concrete released a hot, dry chalk as it crumbled around the bougainvillea. At this hour St. Pete's was closed up for the night and belonged to the drunks whose paths took them along the deserted grid of streets down to the piers. Beneath the second-story balconies of a few fleabag hotels the men sometimes waited for women to come out of the louvered doors and lean against the railings of rusted wrought iron.

By big-city standards, the town's skid row was modest, only a few hundred souls. But Wendy could see them in the evening, squatting against the base of vacant storefronts, drifting in pairs down to the water, passing pint bottles in brown paper bags on park benches. The police were virtually powerless to remove them from their turf or do anything but discourage the worst of their abuses against upstanding citizens: blocking the entrances to package stores, blatant solicitations for sex. About the only people in St. Pete's who had anything to do with the drifters were those like Lila, who, when she wasn't taking strangers home with her, passed out soup at one of the few missions scattered around the district.

When John 3:16 blew into town like a tuft of loose broom and took root there among them, no one paid much attention to the finer points of his redemptive plan. Most of the missions had a salvation component of one sort or another, but none of them preyed so hard on the soul that a man couldn't accept a bit of gospel along with the bread.

John 3:16 — the people of St. Pete's knew the man and his mission by the same name — set up shop in a rundown storefront on the backside of downtown near police headquarters. He started preaching a gospel of Food, Hope, and Soap to whoever cared to wander in and part with three panhandled dollars for a night of untroubled sleep. Large-hearted Christian women like Granny, who liked the sound of the evangelist's line, ladled soup and slices of bread and provided a touch of homey kindness. John 3:16 saw to the salvation.

At first it seemed harmless enough. John 3:16 went to the trouble of lining up jobs for the men, day labor on construction jobs and road crews. At the end of the day they would come back to bed and a bit of New Testament, and John would ask them to pass over a modest tithe for all of his efforts on their behalf.

Some of the older men were taken in for a time. But when they began waking up nearly every morning to find the spare change and few valuables gone from their pockets, they saw the light. God's mercenary offered the alibi that one of their own had been up all night rolling them. But soon John 3:16 was gone, run out of town.

"He was a man getting rich off these people," St. Pete's patrolman Joe Grunewald says now. "Putting them to work and getting their money." He laughs. "Went down to Miami and tried to open up another mission, and they threw him out of there."

Wendy began to accompany Granny after work on the old woman's missions downtown. What had Papa told her? That for every bad spell a good one comes along. For the time being, life was on the sweet curve of that loop, and she didn't have time to worry about what might come later.

At John 3:16, while it lasted, the drifters would roll their cigarettes between soiled fingers before lighting them, eyeing her silently, wondering what had brought this young girl to such a place. Although they never got an answer, they began to talk to her. For hours, bent over their coupled hands, they'd tell her stories of Bojangle lives, of nights spent passing from one jail to another, of years full of flatcars and honkytonks and back alleys and the women who'd stay with them for a time. Their stories moved Wendy. But something deeper than sympathy was quickened in her. The loneliness that trailed these men, that filled out their confidences, resounded within her. Here she felt attractive. Here she felt accepted. But more important than anything, among such lives she felt she could be understood.

Then she met Benjamin. He was easily the best-looking man to have drifted onto the scene, with his sullen way, rugged face, long blond curls, and blue eyes that didn't hide their desire for her. All the important criteria about Benjamin checked out. He didn't drink, and he wasn't a drug addict. The only time Wendy saw him commit a crime was later that summer when he stole a van just for the hell of it, so the two of them could joyride around town for a couple of hours. Perhaps most appealing was that he was twenty-seven, exactly ten years older than Wendy, not a kid like her last flame.

"I guess," she was to say of the ruinous relationship years later, "I just wanted somebody for myself."

Granny played matchmaker, happy to help fill the void she was sure had been left after Wendy's abortion. But it didn't take much prodding. In going with someone from the mission, it seemed obvious to Wendy, she wouldn't be leaving Granny but just gaining another companion.

"I happened to get drunk one night, see," she says of the night he proposed to her. "Nobody knew how bad — knew that I had a drinking problem. I kinda knew. But I didn't exactly say anything. Too young, you know. So I agreed."

By early fall Wendy was pleading with her mother, back in Massachusetts, to sign the consent form required for the marriage of a minor. Molly balked. She didn't trust Granny and sensed a terrible mistake in the making. To reassure her, Lila lied and said Benjamin worked at the mission. Papa, dying and no longer completely responsible, approved of the match.

Wearing a pair of faded blue jeans and a nondescript white blouse, Wendy was married to Benjamin Dalton on October 26, 1973, in the lobby of John 3:16. Granny had produced a minister for the occasion, one of her network of itinerant men of the cloth. Wendy moved into the flophouse apartment around the corner where Benjamin sometimes had a room. She was a wife now. Now she had someone.

With a stunning lack of irony, the young bride began to replicate her mother's early married life. She supported her husband by waiting on tables. She was conscientious. She worked hard, and she kept the apartment neat, priding herself on her housekeeping skills, so much better than Granny's or Molly's. She stayed away from the bottle. Since Benjamin didn't work, there wasn't enough extra money to actually fix things up, but in those honeymoon days, curtains and bedspreads didn't matter. They had each other.

But disillusionment wasn't long in coming. Returning home day after day, weary, her uniform soiled, sitting on the floor, lighting a cigarette and pulling the change out of her pocket to count her tips, as her mother had done on those countless afternoons in Chelsea with three squalling children pulling at her, it slowly dawned on Wendy that she, too, had a baby on her hands — only he was bigger than she was and ten years tougher.

She shakes her head now, trying to blot out the memory. "I swear to God I had more maturity in my little finger than he could have had in ten lifetimes. That bad. He wasn't a drunk, but he was a child! I had to support him, and I'm just out of high school!"

The tensions increased and began to rob the relationship of any real pleasure, and certainly of any future. With a self-protective instinct that her mother had lacked, Wendy vowed not to get pregnant by this man. Still, the lopsided arrangement continued, until one day Benjamin split without warning.

He was gone for three days. When he returned, it was with a confession.

Benjamin had lied when he signed the affidavit at the Pinellas County Clerk's office for their marriage license, swearing that Wendy was his first wife. In point of fact, Benjamin already had a wife, Emma Sue Dalton, age twenty-one. He also had a three-year-old son, Michael. The pair were just scraping by on $225 worth of welfare a month up in a small town in the foothills of the Hoosier National Forest.

The next thing Wendy knew, she was waking up again in a bed at Granny's, images from her brief, terminated marriage floating in incoherent sequences in her head. She never saw Benjamin again.

She moved through the next six months a zombie. The only thing that kept her going was nursing Papa, who was failing quickly. Wendy never left his side. She fed him, held his hand, and talked to him all day long. She plumped his pillows and washed his face. Throughout her childhood, whenever everyone else seemed to abandon her, Papa alone had given her consolation. Now he was the only connection to whatever self-worth that she had left.

By the spring Wendy had found another job, as a sales clerk. She began to go out on occasional dates with the manager of the drug store in the mall where she worked. He was a kind, down-to-earth, average man, who seemed genuinely interested in her. But while she took some comfort in his presence, she had no energy to give to anyone besides Papa. She saved her evenings for him.

Then Papa began to slip away from her. She couldn't slow the inevitable, no matter how hard she tried. "I was the only one holding his hand when he took his last breath," she recalls. In the other room Granny and Papa's sister, shattered, were gripping each other and weeping. "And here I am, not allowed to cry. I'm having to make phone calls to relatives. I gotta make the funeral arrangements. I was a kid. I felt like I was dying inside."

The rest of the family came down from Massachusetts, and in less than thirty-six hours Papa was laid out for an open-casket wake. For two days and two nights, Wendy stood by the coffin without moving or speaking. No one could budge her. Several times her mother tried to lead her away, but Wendy just ignored her.

Who would love her?

Toward the end of the last day of viewing, Wendy spoke for the first time. Molly had grown insistent, grabbing her daughter by the arm to try to pull her away.

"You get away from me," Wendy hissed. "Leave me alone."

Molly, frightened by the look in her eye, retreated.

Papa was buried the next day, a morning early in April, and with him the secrets that members of the family had never shared with one another. Wendy, standing at the gravesite, still hadn't cried, and she wouldn't.

Three days later she swallowed two handfuls of Valium and drove a razorblade hundreds of times across the flesh between her elbows and wrists.

Life became an odyssey marked less by the order of days, weeks, and years than by jail cells, detox wards, arresting officers, street alliances, and relationships that lasted for a brief, precious period before calamity once again set in.

Those who knew and loved Wendy would ask themselves over and over as the years went by, and snatches of stories traveled back to them (never, they were sure, the whole story), when *did* it begin, really? Increasingly, too, they asked what they were dealing with. Not surprisingly, interpretations ranged widely within the family.

In Granny's view, Wendy had always been an unloved kid, the black sheep in Molly's eyes, who had finally gone the way of her skid-row charges. In the years that followed, Granny believed every story Wendy told her, no matter how exaggerated or doctored. And she always, regardless of professional advice to the contrary, bailed her granddaughr out.

To Molly's brother, Uncle Bob, Wendy wasn't an alcoholic, she was just a bright kid who didn't want to work and craved center stage in the family's attentions. After countless nights, in the later seventies, of being awakened by a drunken, desperate call from Wendy in downtown St. Pete's, begging him to come get her before the cops did, Bob finally told her, "Don't call me anymore. I'm not going to pick you up if you're just going to keep on doing this. I have to get up and go to work in the morning."

To Molly, Wendy was a heartbreak and a mystery; she suspected that her daughter was seriously mentally ill. Molly worried that diagnosing Wendy merely as an alcoholic would mask deeper problems that would intensify if they weren't treated.

In Wendy's own mind, what she was dealing with was simple: it was about survival. The only man who'd really loved her had gone out of her life forever, and the man who'd said "I love you" had lied. She couldn't stand being so alone.

In the wake of her fraudulent marriage and Papa's death, the stories of the drifters began to sound like siren calls. Wendy ditched the drug store manager when she went crazy, not because he wouldn't have stuck by her but because he was too good. The shamed part of her refused to be worthy of decency; another part disdained it.

After recovering from her suicide attempt in one alcohol recovery program, she was shortly court-ordered into another one. When she got out less than a month later, she returned to what now seemed like home, to the mission crowd and the places they hung out.

She began to spend most of her time down along the side streets between Central and First, a short hike from the harbor, where the few thriving businesses were pawn shops making a killing on wrist

watches, a few wig and lingerie shops that catered to the black pros-
titutes who worked the avenue west of 20th Street at rush hour, and
the package stores, seedy and dim. In this narrow no man's land between decent St. Pete's and the ghetto, she could always find a few
regulars to sit with, at the shoe shine outside of Tony's Auto Repair
or at one of the sheltered bus stops. To belong, all she had to do was
shell out for the occasional bottle of Mad Dog 20-20, the local Vicks-
flavored, twenty-proof wine of choice. The liquor still worked its magic,
just as it had back in Easton with Anne. Wendy was a laugh a minute
when she was drunk, and since that seemed the only way to fight off
the biting, infinite loneliness in her gut, that's what she wanted to be.

During the day, if she wasn't down by the liquor stores, she'd drift
over to Mirror Lake, just behind the county courthouse. A small car-
avan of stragglers usually made their way there to sleep off the lunch
served at the St. Vincent de Paul soup kitchen around the corner.
She'd read beneath the low, generous shade trees or just sit and
watch the fountain, eventually dozing, one among many, safe in her
anonymity.

As night fell, she'd wander over to Williams Park, once the city's
preeminent square, taken over now by panhandlers like herself soliciting change for an evening at the Casa Blanca or Mastry's Bar. Mastry's was one of the few establishments where the denizens of skid row
were welcome. Dark, banked by the wall-long inventory of hard liquors and the sweet-tasting drinks that only the kids had any stomach
for, Mastry's was "neighborhood." It was family for the local businessmen and work crews and secretaries who stepped in to catch an in-
ning of the ball game or a few juke box tunes and a bag of Beer Nuts
on the way home. No matter what the hour, there was always a barfly
or two at Mastry's, nursing a draft.

Jay Mastry, not much older than Wendy, had just taken over the
tavern from his father. He had a soft place in his heart for the "planter
people," so named for the large concrete planters along Central Avenue where the drifters sat for a bit of shade when the sun was high.
For these frequently heat-dazed and unconnected folks, Mastry stocked
his cooler full of Mad Dog and Mr. Dude 44, a more lethal version of
the same. When they came in to buy the day's pint, he let them use
his toilet. For a few he agreed to be the forwarding address for their
government checks.

Mastry became confidant and banker, as well as intermediary between many of the regulars and their creditors or the cops. When his customers complained about too much panhandling right outside the door, he'd go out and apply his own effective and cordial methods of enforcement. The panhandlers would move on, returning only after sundown.

In the beginning Wendy spent only an occasional night out on the streets, and she'd be home before Granny woke up to know she'd been gone. But increasingly she began to press her luck, drinking and acting up until the police picked her up or the crowd she'd fallen in with moved on.

As Wendy became more seasoned, she began to meet some of St. Pete's skid-row fixtures. She got to know James Gaston, kingpin of the streets and a frequent target of the Myers Act, the state's protective custody law. It wasn't unusual for Gaston, a retired air force colonel in his mid-fifties, to be locked up three or four times a week. When he wasn't doing time himself, he was defending those who were in court. Some nights Wendy saw Fish, who, every time he got drunk, used to break into the S.S. *Bounty,* moored in the harbor, and climb one of the masts.

To Jay Mastry, watching the world from behind the oak counter of his bar, the girls on the street seemed so vulnerable. He relied on one of his sources, Charles Wheaton — a sweet, elderly alcoholic — to tell him what little he did know about them.

"They just go along with the guys like a guy," Charlie would tell him. "Drink right along with them, right out of the same bottle. If they're going to steal, they'll steal right along with them. Everybody has a relationship, sexual, sooner or later," he'd say.

"And they get together. They all have a place where they can crash. A lot of them have friends that get a pension. And the friend will get a place. Seven or eight of them will move in with the friend, supply the friend, whose money's all gone on the rent, with food and booze for the month. Until they get drinking too much, raise too much hell, and the cops come, and they bust it up and the landlord kicks them out. Then they go to another place, go in, try again, rent a place, pay cash, and then seven or eight people come in. I've seen it many times."

Charlie's favorite subject was the woman he'd loved for five years in spite of himself. When Jay heard Charlie talk about Karen, he knew that he might just as well be hearing about Joannie or Evelyn or Wendy.

"She uses me," Charlie lamented. "Everybody tells me. I don't think

I'm going to let her come back again," he'd tell Jay one day out of every ten. But Jay knew that Charlie was crazy about Karen. No matter what she did to him, he would let her come back. He'd visit her in jail and send her cigarettes. Whenever she and her young street lover, Jack, fought and he beat her, she'd come back to Charlie. She'd stop drinking for a day or two and then go right back to the street and to Jack.

Why? Jay would ask Charlie.

"Lust," Charlie would answer sadly. "Pure lust. She told me. Karen's been hit by two-by-fours and has gone back with that guy. And had a baby with him! Glutton for punishment, I guess. She drinks all she can get. They drink all they can get. They don't care if they stumble down, lay in the alley, dirty and drunk."

With sentiments such as these, Charlie would finish his commentary and leave, to furtively search the streets for Karen.

Jay would think of Charlie's stories whenever he saw a new girl hanging out with the group. He knew there wasn't much he could do to save her, but he tried at least to keep tabs on her and pass along what he knew to the sympathetic cops on the beat.

Wendy, a confused twenty-year-old initiate hanging on the fringes, was a spectral young sprite among the hard-core drunks. She could get nasty when she was drunk, but she was still a long way from being a knife-carrying tough, reduced to selling herself or relying on Fresh Breath mouthwash come Sunday when the liquor stores were closed.

All the same, the wounded cynicism of a man like Charlie wouldn't have dissuaded her from her new lifestyle. After her second go at a detox, Wendy briefly struggled along on the straight in an Anabuse program administered by the county at Bayfront Hospital.

"These meetings would last a half hour to an hour," she explained. "You'd take your Anabuse. If you drank on top of this stuff you'd get deathly ill. So I got to this meeting. I'm twenty years old, right, and I'm drunker than a skunk. I mean, I'm totally zapped. Then I turned around and looked at somebody and said, 'Do you like kielbasa sausage?' The lady that was running this particular meeting says, 'Wendy, are you going to come up here and take your Anabuse?' And I said, 'Hell, no. Not with as much alcohol as I got in me. What do you think I am? Stupid?' "

Wendy's welcome terminated on the spot. She returned to the streets, casting about for a toehold in her own existence, which was beginning to seem more and more inchoate. After several months' wandering failed to alter her sense that her life was unsalvageable, she tried returning to Massachusetts. But by the spring of 1976 she was back in St. Petersburg, looking for love.

"They keep coming back." Mastry would observe from his perch behind the bar. Looking out the window he'd see a familiar face back at the planters. "It's just a cycle, an endless cycle. I don't think I'll ever figure it out."

Soon after Wendy's return to Florida, she ended up in another detox program. This time it seemed as if the gods were smiling. One afternoon, when she looked up through the smoke-filled haze of the television room, she recognized a good-looking man whom she'd smacked with her handbag back in the Anabuse program. From across the room, he smiled.

"He looked pretty good," she recalled. "He hadn't gone downhill that bad yet. He grins at me. He's got this little smile. And I smiled back."

Vinnie Pearl, an Irishman with dark hair and intense blue-black eyes, reminded her of the boy who'd taken her to the ill-fated high school dance. So she had a thing for Irishmen, she thought. She pulled the oldest trick in the book.

"Does anyone have a cigarette?" she asked.

Vinnie got up from his chair and came over.

"What kind do you smoke?" he asked.

"Kools," she answered.

He left the room and returned several minutes later with a brand-new pack from the cigarette machine.

"You didn't have to do that," she told him.

"I know," he answered. "But I don't want to see anybody refuse you a cigarette when you need one."

Wendy saw that he was shaking like a leaf. His alcohol habit, she would learn, was relatively new: going on five years. But before that he'd been addicted to drugs for more than a decade.

Several days passed and they found each other again, this time at the group barbecue. Vinnie was still a bundle of tremors.

"I'm not the greatest eater," she recounted. "Never have been. But this poor guy can't even carry a plate, you know? I'm saying, Vin, will you please just sit down?"

They'd both found someone to take care of.

"I had my eye on him," Wendy said. "And he had his eye on me. I was a sweet young thing."

They discovered that they both loved card games and became partners for the nightly match of spades that took place in the lounge. Usually they won. In the confining circumstances of life in the ward, their courtship became a game within a game, some of it conducted in the language of bids, passes, and trumps. And some of it under the table.

One afternoon, unbeknownst to Wendy, Vinnie sneaked off the hospital property and bought a pint of vodka. That night after the card game, he drew her into the laundry room.

"Where the hell did you disappear to?" she said.

He kissed her. "Never mind. Come here."

He cracked the seal on the bottle and grinned.

"Start drinking, baby," he said.

They quickly killed the pint. As they drank they talked about how easy it would be to walk out the front door and across the lawn, out to Route 19 and into one of the many cheap motel rooms available there.

"We left the next day. We go right to a motel. You talk about drunk? Boy, did we get drunk."

Meanwhile Lila had returned to Pinellas Park after a month-long visit north. When she'd left, her granddaughter had been employed and living in an apartment of her own. When she returned, Wendy's phone had been cut off. Lila went around to her place, but no one answered, so she started making phone calls. It didn't take long to strike it right.

"So Granny comes up," recounts Wendy. After several drunken days in the motel room, she and Vinnie had had stabs of bad conscience. Together they had returned, repentant, to the detox ward. Granny arrived just after that.

"I'm still a quivering mass of shakes. She says, 'Wendy, I'll set you up in an apartment. I'll help you find a job. I'll fill your refrigerator and your cupboard with food, and I'll help you get clothes.' "

Quietly Wendy answered, "I can't do that."

"What do you mean?" her grandmother said.

"I love Vinnie."

Granny silently observed her.

"I'd rather stay on the streets with him than not be with him at all," Wendy went on.

Granny pulled herself up and said calmly, "I want to meet this Vinnie."

Wendy went to get her lover from the television room. Vinnie, still shaking, sat down in front of Wendy's grandmother.

Granny's eyes never left him. At length she asked, "Wendy, do you love him?"

"Yes," she said.

"Vincent, do you love Wendy?"

"Yes."

Granny sighed. "Then the case is settled. I'll get you both an apartment. Together."

"And that," Wendy concludes the tale, "is exactly what she did."

This was true love. The sobered pair settled into the efficiency that Granny financed in a pleasant, shady, residential section of St. Pete's, just north of downtown. Every morning they went out to work, she to a nursing home laundry, he to a job putting fiber glass on yachts. At night they played cards and made love.

Vinnie's family, up north, was less than thrilled by this turn in their son's life. Vinnie came from money. He'd been in the entertainment business in Manhattan until cocaine and, later, heroin had ruined him. He'd lost his job, his home, and his socially acceptable wife and hit the skids. When the amount of drugs required to maintain his addiction reached lethal levels, he'd switched to booze — vodka, mainly, and gin. Still, Vinnie's mother couldn't understand why he wouldn't simply take himself in hand and straighten up. She found the notion of his possible career failure intolerable and was continually calling him from New York to tell him so.

Despite her nagging, the couple persevered, struggling to beat the odds. Theirs was a venture into discipline and hope and a passionate embrace of the bourgeois values they'd both revolted against years before. More than anything Wendy had ever wanted, she wanted this to work. Her shift at the laundry was seven to three, the same shift her mother had worked back in Easton when she was growing up.

"I was up at five o'clock in the morning to have a little time to relax before I actually had to move. A cup of coffee or tea, whatever. Get my act in gear. Because I had to catch the bus at six-twenty. I can be quite responsible at times."

Wendy's years of training at home now proved reflexive: when she came home, she'd set about straightening up the house. It sometimes seemed as if the intervening years of madness had never happened.

"I'm a cleanliness nut. I know it seems impossible, but the kitchen would be totally clean. I'd have all the rugs vacuumed, everything dusted down and wiped down. The floors swept and mopped and the tub cleaned."

A day didn't go by that she didn't watch her lover struggle with sobriety. It was so hard for him, she could see — harder than for her. But he held on for the sake of their love, and soon they'd put enough money aside to move into an apartment of their own.

The apartment near Crescent Lake was the finest place Wendy had ever called home. "It was immaculate. Totally furnished. Frost-free refrigerator, electric stove, air conditioning in the bedroom. This was a beautiful apartment. It didn't have a tub, but it had a shower. That was okay."

Situated on a shaded, comfortable middle-class street lined with immaculate yards and elaborate landscaping, the white stucco apartment building could have passed for a large house. Its windows were trimmed in French blue. Magnolia bushes and willows bounded one side of the property, and a patio, where residents could sit on summer evenings and read the paper or play cards, bounded the other side. Just a block away was the lake, large and pristine, unpopulated most of the day and still unspoiled by the hideous high-rises that blight so many other areas of St. Pete's. In the afternoons Wendy could sit on its green shores until sunset and hear nothing but the passing footfall of others like herself, taking in the simple, astonishing pleasures of ordered existence.

"Oh, it was nice!" Wendy remembers.

Just as Wendy was beginning to believe in forever again, Vinnie got laid off. The man he had replaced at the boat company decided he wanted his job back.

"It totally devasted him," Wendy says. Once more, she was the sole breadwinner. "It was like his manhood had been stripped away. Here was this woman ten years younger, and she was keeping a roof over his head and feeding him and blah, blah, blah."

Vinnie started to receive food stamps, fifty dollars' worth every month, but that was all he could contribute to the household. Wendy tried to make it count more than it in fact did. She tried to include him in all the housekeeping decisions, the food shopping lists, the few leisure activities they could afford. But it didn't come close to making up for the loss of self-confidence that he had suffered.

"I'd say, 'Come on, Vinnie, help me plan out our stuff.'" But Vinnie sank deeper into depression and began to pull away from her.

Meanwhile, his mother, still denying the reality of her son's addiction, took what she saw as a fresh opportunity to ride him about returning to New York and getting another executive job.

"His mother just kept pushing him," Wendy said. "I told him, 'Vinnie, don't take a job unless you feel comfortable with it. I can be patient. I don't want you to work at a job that you're miserable at.' He wasn't ashamed of me working at a laundry. I mean, it was physical work. But his family just didn't understand. That's really what got him back."

Vinnie started to drink again.

"He drank suicidally," Wendy says. "His ego was totally shot. He lost all desire to live."

It wasn't long before Wendy joined him. And soon the fighting followed — noisy, brutal fights that began to disturb the neighbors above and below them. Drunk, Wendy would lean out the window and scream obscenities at the young mother upstairs. Blows could often be heard coming from Apartment 201, and weird, inexplicable complaints.

"Stop abusing my baby!" Wendy would wail. But there was no baby — at least, no real one.

The nightmares, the disappearing boundary between fact and possibility — all the fragments of her private wonderland of desire and pain — were quickened again by the alcohol. Neither she nor Vinnie could think in terms of cycles or any kind of order; they could only react, in recriminations and numbing disappointment.

Over the winter of 1977, destruction became the norm. If the neighborhood's serene side streets had proven a middle-class safety zone, free of temptations, the flanking thoroughfares offered all that Vinnie and Wendy needed in the way of liquor stores and drug action. Intoxicated, they would become violent — kicking, scratching, and biting. Vinnie twice tried to slit his wrists. The neighbors started calling the police.

Then one day in March, Wendy's worst fear returned: Vinnie would leave her. It was inevitable; she could feel it in the air of the now totally neglected apartment, suffocating her. Her breathing grew shallow. She was terrified.

By then they were consuming four quarts of gin a day. She was incapable of staying by herself. Whenever Vinnie went out for more gin, she would try to follow him or fight with him to stay with her a few minutes longer. Out of her mind with panic and alcohol, she started to bounce from drunkenness to detox. That month alone, Wendy checked into the Bayfront detox ward nine times.

On the morning of March 22 she was climbing the walls again. High on gin, she'd followed Vinnie out of the apartment and as far as the sidewalk when he went off to buy more liquor. There they'd run into Joe, one of their neighbors. Wendy begged Joe to take her, then and there, back to the hospital. She told him she was scared.

"Wendy's afraid I'm going to leave her," Vinnie joked callously. Then he turned and sauntered down the street.

Joe drove Wendy to Bayfront and stayed with her the better part of the day and into the evening, when the staff decided that they couldn't give one of their precious few beds to such a chronic recalcitrant. When Joe brought her back to the apartment, they found Vinnie, stark naked, passed out on the bed. Drinking himself into a stupor had become a nightly ritual. Wendy thanked Joe for having stayed with her all day and said goodnight.

Twice over the next several hours the police came by in response to calls from neighbors. Wendy had slipped out after parting with Joe and fortified her booze supply, and the usual arguments and scuffles had ensued. After the two warnings, the second just after 10 P.M., Wendy remembers that she fell asleep.

An hour later, Vinnie Pearl was dead. At 11:20 the police responded to their third call of the night, this one from Wendy. She was hysterical. When the police arrived, they found Vinnie Pearl's nude body lying across the mattress. His head was covered with vomit and blood. He had one black eye and a fresh cut above the other. Superficial wounds and bruises covered his body. Fresh teeth marks rose on his thighs. Strewn around the room lay the evidence of the melee that had culminated in this all-too-familiar domestic casualty: countless empty gin bottles, torn women's clothing, and blood. Everywhere.

Out in the hall, Wendy was beside herself. The police covered Vinnie's body with a blanket and radioed for a transport vehicle. Wendy was taken to headquarters and booked on suspicion of homicide, pending the autopsy.

Over the next several days, neighbors offered conflicting versions of what had happened that night. Some claimed they'd heard nothing. Others said they had heard only the couple's usual nightly arguments. One witness admitted to detectives that he'd heard moaning from their room less than an hour before the police arrived. Joe swore that there had been no wounds on Pearl's body when he had dropped Wendy off earlier that evening.

Wendy, described in the police report as the victim's common-law wife, stuck to her story. They had both fallen asleep after drinking heavily. When she woke up shortly after 11 P.M., she'd rolled over and tried to rouse Vinnie. When he didn't come to, she feared the worst.

The police had plenty of background on Wendy. She'd been picked up on drunk and disorderly charges any number of times and had an extensive file at Bayfront Medical Center. She admitted to having solicited for prostitution in order to pay for their booze, and she told them that both she and Vinnie had slashed their wrists several times recently in desperation, because the drinking had gotten so bad. She explained that the teeth marks were her effort to bring Vinnie to, the only thing that had worked on previous occasions. She had genuinely loved Vinnie, she insisted. Too much.

"My whole world centered around him," she told them and started to cry. "You really shouldn't let people get to you like that."

The truth hit her in a cold wave: it was Papa all over again. Her Vinnie, like Papa, had abandoned her.

The medical examiner determined that Vinnie's death was accidental, the result of an alcohol overdose. At the time of the autopsy, his blood alcohol level was a lethal .58.

As when Papa had died, Wendy lost control of her world.

"I was eating Valiums by the handfuls. I wouldn't eat. I was drinking. My brother had just come down. He stepped in and put me in the psychiatric unit of the hospital. They knew I'd eventually kill myself."

In her derangement she threatened to kill her brother's two children. When her brother sought to have her committed, the court gave her the option of either going to the state hospital or entering another alcohol program.

"I opted for the twenty-eight-day program," she recounted. "I drank the day before I left. How could I be happy? I was not happy. Nobody seemed to understand that I was grief-stricken. Okay, so the man wasn't a millionaire, and he wasn't the greatest. But he did the best that he could by me. I felt like my whole life had crumbled."

Three tortured years were to pass before geography and love again converged on anything remotely resembling security for Wendy. Until then the only thing that changed was her already potent burden of guilt. From the day she entered the court-ordered treatment program and got sober enough to view what had happened in a cold light, until 1980, when she left Florida for good, she maintained a constant flirtation with suicide. In her own mind, even though she had been cleared by the machinery of justice, she had killed her lover because she had bought the last bottle that he drank.

During these years, at various points between Massachusetts and Florida, she slit her wrists three times. Back north in Easton, after losing control on a drinking spree, she beat her head bloody against the walls of an ambulance while her mother looked on helplessly. The ambulance took her to a psychiatric ward that, because of strict commitment laws, wouldn't keep her against her will.

She lost another bedfellow when he hung himself with his own T-shirt in the St. Pete's city jail. She became attached to a Vietnamese engineer who managed to get her straight and get her a job at a plastics plant north of Boston. Eventually, though, she fled once more to Florida, sending him an anonymous telegram with the message that she was dead.

And at last she found her father. At the end of a journey to his home town in Michigan, bearing a paint-by-number landscape as her gift, she found the object of so many dreams. Only his face was hard to recognize now, the Indian in it emphasized somehow by all the years on booze. When he saw that time had never healed the cross-shaped scar on Wendy's chest, he wept.

Massachusetts had been a tragic place for Molly. In 1979 she and Henry Fayre sought sanctuary in Mississippi, there to endure and, God willing, to find some mitigating joy in the final years of their lives.

At 9:05 on Saturday morning, April 26, 1980, the St. Petersburg police received a complaint about a transient drunk lying on the sidewalk perilously close to the intersection of First Avenue South and Fifth, in danger of being run over.

When the officer arrived, he found Wendy, unable to stand up, incoherent, and very intoxicated. Her speech was slurred, her eyes glassy, watery, and red. As soon as she saw the policeman, she began to swear, and in the squad car she got even worse. At the booking desk she screamed over the usual station noise. Then she pulled the T-shirt she was wearing up around her neck and began to choke herself. When they handcuffed her, she dropped to the floor and began savagely to beat her head against the concrete until she drew blood.

At this point, on her tenth arrest for drunk and disorderly conduct, Wendy was "Bakered." The state of Florida, under the Baker Act, authorized involuntary commitment of individuals to psychiatric wards for observation and evaluation. Florida interpreted the criteria for commitment more liberally than did many other states. Social workers had more clout in arguing before judges that a person needed to be hospitalized because of behavior that potentially endangered his and others' personal welfare.

Wendy was taken to the emergency room of Bayfront Medical Center for treatment of her head wounds. A blood alcohol test revealed a level of .363. By three o'clock that afternoon, she was involuntarily committed to the comprehensive mental health program at Horizon Hospital.

The Critical Stabilization Unit to which Wendy was admitted was a locked ward, one of two at Horizon for potentially dangerous drug and alcohol addicts. Wendy would be observed there for seventy-two hours, after which, if the staff decided that she needed to remain hospitalized for psychiatric and alcohol treatment, she would have a choice. She could agree to stay voluntarily or be subject to further court-ordered hospitalization. Under the Baker Act, if she didn't agree to stay, the hospital had the authority to hold and treat her indefinitely while applying through the courts to do so, rather than having to release her, as was the case in other states, until they had obtained court permission.

After their observation, staff psychiatrists advised that Wendy, stabilized on Librium, remain in a twenty-eight-day treatment program. She agreed. She was transferred to one of the twelve specialized treatment programs upstairs, this one for alcohol addiction. (The hospital had programs for disorders ranging from depression and anxiety to special hearing impairment, as well as programs for abused children and geriatric patients.) The hospital did its best to make patients' stays pleasant and constructive. The bedrooms were cheery and large. The pool was used daily as part of the therapy program. A baseball field and volleyball and tennis courts out back behind the building were in constant use. There were certified high school classes for teenagers and a library from which patients could borrow books.

The program offered the usual encounter group meetings, the eve-

ning AA and NA (Narcotics Anonymous) meetings, and seminars on
the chemical effects of different drugs on the body. Wendy was taught
the same twelve-step program she had learned so many times before.
After a few days her intense cravings returned, and she began to sab-
otage her efforts at sobriety, telling herself that she was doing this
only to save herself from being chased out of the state.

It would be easy, she heard a voice saying, to walk off the hospital
grounds and head for one of the many cheap motel rooms in the
vicinity. But this time there was no Vinnie to do so with.

Less than two weeks after Wendy was discharged from the Horizon
Hospital program, at six-thirty on a Sunday evening, the St. Petersburg police were summoned to a domestic disturbance call in the
northeast section of the city. When the officer arrived at the address,
he found a cab idling out front. The driver explained that he'd picked
up an intoxicated woman downtown. She had instructed him to drive
here. He'd had the impression, the driver said, that she wanted to
move in with a man who lived here. Then the officer saw Wendy lying
on the sidewalk. Drunk, she identified herself as Ruth Malone and
said she'd just come to visit a friend who'd bought a new house.

Wendy had gained fifty pounds during her month in the treatment
program. Bloated, weighing 160 pounds, she didn't look good. The
officer explained that he had to arrest her under the Myers Act and
take her to jail.

The officer didn't need to point out to Wendy that the home owner
who'd called the police was none other than James Gaston, the king
of the streets, one of her earliest acquaintances and mentors, friend
and defender of the city's down and out. Even Gaston wanted no part
of her now.

Wendy lashed out. She started striking the roof of the police car
and pounding on the dashboard through the officer's open door. She
tried to break the cruiser's windows. She was finally locked behind
bars at 7:15 P.M.

TWO

In the World

Nothing

AT FOUR-THIRTY on a September afternoon, eight women wordlessly gather their belongings off the littered floor of the Pine Street Inn's lobby and, picking their steps around the few bodies prostrate there, wend their exhausted way down the day's final corridor, emerging onto a back street full of illegally parked cars and garbage bins choked with refuse.

The white Chevy van idling there will transport them to the basement of a church several miles away, where they will spend the night. Tonight, Friday, September 12, 1986, there is a new face among them. Flecks of gray pale the clipped brown waves, and the eyes are hollow. Amanda Daley, haggard, emaciated at seventy-four pounds, is lost once more.

The stench of recent vomit inside the van almost knocks her out. But no one else seems to notice as they settle in, least of all the driver, a hip-looking young woman at least a dozen years Amanda's junior, done up from head to toe in black — black boots, slacks and a black leather jacket. She tells Amanda that her name is Julie and, with everyone in, she slips the vehicle into drive and pulls away from the back of the Inn.

They turn onto Albany Street, a busy road that runs alongside the Southeast Expressway through the middle of downtown Boston. This stretch of Albany is a trick to navigate at rush hour on Friday. Its gallimaufry of parking garages, transmission shops, brick warehouses, the city's wholesale flower market and produce holds, and, at Massachusetts Avenue, Boston City Hospital — all are simultaneously disgorging their workers for the weekend. Julie, at the wheel, stays cool. A native New Yorker, she's earned her nonchalance in the capital of vehicular siege. She is buoyant and full of jokes, asking her passengers, as a sister would, how their day has been. She talks about the punk rock band she performs in on her nights off. She's eager to know who's seen any good movies and who has tickets to the Red Sox game this weekend.

Pressed into a corner at the rear of the van, Amanda recoils from the commotion. She feels suffocated by strangeness, by fetid human odors, and by an interior blackness that grows heavier and more impenetrable with each passing minute. Only a few hours ago she'd locked the door of her studio apartment on Beacon Street. She listened as the latch turned one last time, but she didn't linger. Once out the front door and onto the sidewalk, she moved rapidly under the rich overhang of autumn leaves, trying to get out of the neighborhood as swiftly as possible, before second thoughts arrested her.

She left everything behind: her books, her papers, most of her clothes, and her disintegrated past. Now she has no idea what is going to happen. Not tomorrow or next week, much less tonight. She doesn't even know where she is being taken.

As soon as she'd stepped inside the once familiar lobby of the Pine Street Inn, she'd recognized Mona.

"What the hell are *you* doing back here?" the counselor had boomed from across the room.

Amanda hadn't been able to find words.

"Go over to St. Paul's," Mona advised. "You'll be more comfortable there."

So that is what she is doing — not because she believes she'll be more comfortable, but just because Mona has told her to. She is nervous, depressed, and upset. More than anything, as the hours distance her from everything she's ever known, she is beginning to feel terror. She thinks she's going to throw up. She closes her eyes and fights back spew and tears.

At the corner of Mass. Avenue and Melnea Cass Boulevard, where Julie stops for a red light, the social and racial geography of Boston divide cleanly. A left turn would take them onto Route 93, heading south to the upper-middle-class suburban South Shore communities like the one where Amanda was raised.

Ahead, Mass. Avenue plunges into white Dorchester, an enclave of working-class Irish American families living in triple deckers and jealously guarding their turf from racial and economic disruption. Until now, Dorchester has been insulated from having to help meet the city's affordable housing crisis (and hence from having to integrate): Boston's rent control ordinances apply only to buildings of four or more units.

Behind them, Mass. Avenue runs through the gentrified South End, past former tenements, then on past some of the city's most august cultural institutions — Symphony Hall and the Christian Science Church — before crossing the Charles River, bisecting the Massachusetts Institute of Technology campus, and continuing into Harvard Square.

When the light shifts to green, the van turns right on Melnea Cass Boulevard, into Roxbury. And soon they are entering the most desolate street Amanda has ever seen. In the fading light of the gray afternoon, endless blocks of public housing stretch bleakly as far as she can see. Known colloquially as Orchard Park, the 774-unit project is one of the largest public housing complexes in Boston's black neighborhoods. The year before, Orchard Park's residents reported 232 crimes, ranging from motor vehicle theft to murder, earning it the dubious distinction of having the highest crime rate in the third largest public housing system in the nation.

Overgrown weed lots surround the project, fading into curbless, unpaved alleys that run off into the dusk and nowhere, strewn with burnt-out cars and stray dogs. On crumbling warehouse walls, spray-painted credos flash quickly by.

"Contras los reactionares se justicia," Amanda reads. "Let revolution finish it off."

The van arrives at the corner of Dudley Street, one of Roxbury's principal thoroughfares. The final mile to St. Paul's Church is a veritable drug supermarket, offering some of the best heroin and cocaine on the East Coast. Around and within the scattered retail businesses that have managed to survive — Costa's Barber Shop, the Ideal Sub Shop, La Borquineca grocery, D. A. Silva's Pizza and Subs — some $70,000 changes hands every day, in a trade controlled by fifteen-year-olds. The neighborhood is known to the police as "24/7": here, any drug is procurable twenty-four hours a day, seven days a week. Business is managed by competing gangs, who kill as a matter of course to establish and then defend their territories. The gangs, of black,

Jamaican, Dominican, and Vietnamese teenagers, each have their own distinctive style of street warfare, of dealing and hiding drugs, and of trying to beat the cops. But they all have one thing in common: their ruthlessness.

This district has more violent crime than any police district in the state, and most of it is drug related. In the words of a plainclothes drug officer who's worked the beat for years, "People like to shoot. If they have half a second they'll kill. The younger the kid, the more vicious. And they're totally without remorse."

At this late afternoon hour, clusters of young black men hang out at every corner. Not far away, girls no older than thirteen, wearing tight red pants and high heels, bounce babies on their hips; many are drug couriers from other parts of the city who have come down here to make some quick cash.

At the fifth crowded intersection, Julie turns right and the vehicle lurches into overdrive as it mounts a steep hill. At the top, above the failing two-family houses and broken sidewalks, Amanda can make out the stone tower of a church. Suddenly they come to the summit. It is as serene and beautiful as it is surprising, after what they've just passed through. In the center of rolling, grassy church grounds rises the massive granite edifice of St. Paul's. Julie pulls into the pitted driveway and comes to a halt under a large white sign that reads: Pine Street Inn St. Paul's Shelter.

By September 1986, St. Paul's, as the shelter was known, had been operating for eight months. It had opened the previous winter with a one-year lease from the Archdiocese of Boston, to sleep up to fifty women, seven nights a week. The church basement was open from five in the afternoon until eight the next morning. Dinner was served from five-thirty until seven, lights were out by nine, and the women were wakened in the morning at quarter of five and transported back to the Pine Street Inn in shifts until about seven-thirty. Like the Inn's main units, St. Paul's sponsored no daytime program.

Fourteen people were on the staff. Three of them, two counselors and a supervisor, worked the three-to-eleven evening shift, and two the eleven-to-seven. In addition, a regular "fill-in" person was budgeted to oversee the showers on the three-to-eleven shift. More often than not, fill-ins weren't available, and this task fell to one of the counselors. During the day, a two-person maintenance crew, members of

St. Paul's parish, changed the bedding, laundered all the night clothes, cleaned bathrooms and the kitchen, and vacuumed the floors.

One staff member was assigned to the three van runs from the Inn in the afternoon between four and six-thirty. Before that the evening shift held its daily meeting; restocked the shower area with towels, soap, shampoo, and other supplies; and set up the kitchen for dinner, putting out Styrofoam cups, paper plates, and eating utensils, filling and heating a large percolator of hot water, and setting out juices and cocoa mixes.

At the sound of Julie's honking, two people come running out of the cellar door. From the back seat they take the steam trays, cartons of milk, and the plastic bag full of bread that Julie has brought from the Inn, and disappear back inside.

Amanda takes her place in the line that has formed at the same door. New smells assail her, a blend of heating oil, dust, deodorant soap, and the slightly sweet incense that clings to the woodwork, stair rails, and walls. And sweat, not that of locker rooms but of stale perfume.

Ahead, she can see, the queue is straining through a tight vestibule, moving first a few steps right, then another few steps left, toward a well-lit room several feet ahead. A notice just inside the door announces in cheerful Magic Marker colors:

Welcome Ladies!

For the safety of all who stay or work here, please take note of the following rules:
— no weapons, bottles, or drugs in the building
— no loud or abusive language
— all guests must shower
— towels, nightgowns and shower shoes are not to leave the building.
For your safety, we request that all guests use the van runs that depart for Pine Street Inn at 4:30, 5:15, 6:30 and 7:30.

Thank you

Taped around the notice are pages from a wall calendar of Ansel Adams photographs, vistas of the Rockies, Yosemite, and Buddhist grave markers in Maui. As if they mattered, Amanda thinks. She still can't believe that she is here.

The line moves again. Soon she finds herself on the threshold of what appears to be the shower room. She expects to see, sitting at the small, Formica-topped table just inside the door, a familiar, large middle-aged woman with bright blond hair. Mona told her that Jackie is working here now. Amanda can visualize the tight blue jeans, running shoes, and oversized shirt. An untended, lit cigarette would be anchored in a plastic ashtray at the counselor's elbow. Across her lap would be draped some sewing project that she'd be working at as she checked people in, yards of colorful calico.

Now, as Amanda steps up, she hears herself saying, "I was told to ask for Jackie." The woman takes her in silently for a moment, then answers, "I'm Jackie."

No. Amanda shakes her head, clearing it. She's imagining things. Tears fill her eyes, but she manages to swallow them back. That was four years ago, when she'd walked into Pine Street after having recovered from her pneumonia at Harbor Light. Now an unfamiliar face is searching hers, encouraging. A pen is poised over the bed list, and the woman is saying, for a second time, "Your name?"

From his bedroom window, through the rain-laden dusk, Father Bill Francis has seen the Pine Street van pull up to the rear of the church. The shelter is important to him. If the problem of homelessness hasn't redirected his vocation, it has reinforced an emphasis on ministering to the poor that has grown more resolute each day he serves as pastor of St. Paul's.

St. Paul's has become one of the poorest parishes in the archdiocese. At this point Bill Francis is being threatened with the loss of Father Mike, his only assistant, because there aren't enough baptisms, marriages, and confessions being performed to justify two priests, and the parish isn't carrying its own meager operating costs. It hasn't for years. The sobering truth for the parish priest is that as a shelter his church is serving three times as many women as it does on Sunday mornings at the English-language mass. Fewer than twenty souls arrive these days for the eight-thirty.

The priest listens as, downstairs, eighty-nine-year-old Annie Sullivan, the housekeeper, makes her way from the dining room of the incongruously suburban clapboard rectory into the television room. P.D., the faithful Rhodesian ridgeback and greyhound mutt, lopes behind her. His initials stand for Personnel Director. When Father Bill had pleaded for an assistant early in his tenure at St. Paul's, a friend at Chancery had given him the dog, telling Bill that this "personnel director" was the best he could do. Father Mike had come later.

Both men were rank neophytes in Annie's eyes. The rectory's long-time housekeeper had arrived at Boston Harbor fifty-six years earlier on a boat from County Galway, Ireland. Annie still insists on doing some light housework to justify her room and board, but it is for her memory and her wit that Bill values her most.

It used to be, she'll still tell him, that she had to stop her Sunday morning chores by ten-thirty in order to dash across the lawn and get a seat for the eleven o'clock mass, in the upstairs *or* the downstairs church. And even then she sometimes had to stand.

Up through the late fifties, most of the women in this closely settled Irish and Italian neighborhood followed routines similar to Annie Sullivan's: rising early to get the dusting, sweeping, and wash out of the way before the markets opened at nine o'clock, devoting themselves to the cohesion and order of their small but beautiful patch of the world. Long before noon they were out trimming rose beds, sweeping front stoops, and strolling down the hill to Dudley Street to buy the night's pot roast.

Now Bill knows that Annie doesn't dare step out the front door even in daylight. He switches off his desk lamp and goes down to join her.

Bill Francis isn't the only one who has the fate of the parish uppermost in his mind. On the opposite edge of the church grounds, beyond the hard, bright arcs of its floodlights, Rita Brereton is hoping that she'll be able to sleep through the night. The only nun living in the old convent, she can hear through the floorboards the one-month-old infant crying again, and the soft voice of his seventeen-year-old mother, Juanita, trying to calm him.

Rita had persuaded Bill Francis to make the tiny basement apartment available to the young mother when she got out of the hospital. Juanita had nowhere else to go. The baby's father is a married man known throughout the largely Hispanic community, with a family of his own. Though motherhood has elevated Juanita's status in the community to that of a married woman, it has also conferred on her in many respects a false and tragic sense of security. The man isn't about to leave his legal wife. And Juanita's financial outlook couldn't be bleaker. The girl's welfare check doesn't even meet the meager rent that Bill and Rita are obliged to charge her. And except to love her baby, Juanita doesn't have any idea how to care for him.

Juanita wants to return to work as soon as she is able to, but Rita knows from experience that whatever salary she can command won't cover her child-care expenses. As Rita listens to the cries subside, she prays that Juanita won't, like so many of her peers, seek a way out of her dilemma by taking up with another man, having more babies, and sliding deeper into a state of unfulfillment and dependency. More than anything, Rita wants to help her see that this route isn't inevitable, that she has options.

At least for the moment, Juanita has a home, unlike the women across the street, who don't even have a room in which they can hold and comfort their loved ones. Rita hopes that tonight no one there will be foolhardy enough to try to make the trek from downtown on foot, as some women sometimes do, and that once indoors for the night, they won't throw a fit and decide to leave. She hopes, too, that the night won't bring any car break-ins, knife fights, or joy rides across the church grounds.

The psychology of hills isn't insignificant to these hopes. She knows that the violence below on Dudley usually stops short of the exposed and heavily patrolled hilltop. But there isn't a single home among the elegant old two-family Victorians on the circle of Half Moon, Robin Hood, and Lingard streets yoking the church that hasn't had its locks smashed and its basement windows broken. It is all a matter of what the drug market requires on a given night, a market that shifts so rapidly from hour to hour that even insiders don't know in advance how the night will play itself out, how many deals will be scored, and who might get killed in the process.

Rita sometimes tries to imagine what kind of a world will greet Juanita's son when he grows up, if he is lucky enough to survive that long. When she stops to consider the transformations witnessed by the older generation of parishioners, she realizes the futility of the exercise. For Margaret White, who lives two doors away, almost nothing remains of the neighborhood that she knew as a young girl.

St. Paul's was once one of the preeminent parishes in Boston, the envy of many an aspiring priest who saw in its exhaustive schedule of well-attended masses and social events a sure route to the attentive ears at Chancery, and even a key to influence in Boston's secular political circles.

The original St. Paul's was constructed in 1907 by a frugal and fanatically energetic community of Italian and Irish Americans. This was the golden era of Boston Catholicism, achieved by immigrants who were far enough removed from the boats to have stepped up into the middle class, but not yet so acculturated as to have rejected their ethnicity and moved to slab ranches and parochial schools in the suburbs.

From the beginning, St. Paul's had one of the most active social programs in the archdiocese. Pastor Joseph Anderson wrote to his bishop in 1908:

> You will have to excuse this hastily written letter, as I am going crazy over the charities and the Bazaar — However, everything is booming — Boston meetings with the ladies at the Somerset and the nun[s] yesterday at the Lenox were great successes. The indications are most favorable and encouraging. I have the Hibernians, Forresters and the Knights also stirred up and the rivalry to outdo each other is beginning already to manifest itself. Each will have an evening at the Bazaar.

The numerous societies, clans, and sodalities consumed the energies and talents of parishioners, who had few other outlets for entertainment. They also sustained church coffers. Women with surnames like Walsh, Mahoney, and Dacey directed the activities of the Married Ladies Sodality, the Young Ladies Sodality, and the Sunday school. The church had a Holy Name Society and sponsored field days, missions, novenas, breakfasts, and bazaars. It was the center of community life in the north Dorchester neighborhood, shepherded by a succession of energetic and committed priests whose own life experiences weren't far removed from those of their people. These priests settled personal disputes, found jobs for the unemployed men, forgave them their sins, and acted as middle men between the newly arrived foreign families and the confusing, often hostile, world beyond the parish boundaries.

In exchange, the church reaped benefits from the growing prosperity of its members. By 1918 the parish had 1,700 families, and by 1921 five masses were said each Sunday for the parish's 7,000 souls. The need for a new church had been obvious for several years, and by 1922 a three-year parish fund drive had raised $70,000 toward the costs of one. The downstairs church, begun and completed the same year, consumed $197,226. Twenty years later the debt was retired, a remarkable feat in Boston church history. Even more remarkable, in 1936 work began on the vast upper church, a towering structure of gray stone and brilliant stained glass, which in time would be filled with enough oak pews to seat several thousand.

The newly well-to-do clergy of St. Paul's, like their counterparts throughout the city, became skilled politicians with a significant impact on broader civic life. Father Anderson regularly attended political meetings downtown, advised elected officials, and in 1908, when the city charter was being amended, was invited to represent the interests of the church on a committee of the Boston Finance Committee. His successor, Father Cunningham, oversaw the acquisition of real estate (property being the prime tender of Church power in those years) abutting the church, to "protect us from undesirable owners, obtain for us sufficient land for school and convent and help to keep up the property of the neighborhood," as he explained to the diocesan secretary in 1937.

That same year, the upper church was formally finished and consecrated at a solemn high mass celebrated by Father Cunningham and attended by dozens of local church dignitaries.

Ten-year-old Margaret White sang in the choir that morning, high up in the balcony stall at the back of the church, overwhelmed with pride. To her, St. Paul's was "the most beautiful place on earth." From the age of four, she had wanted to live in its shadow. Now her hopes had been realized — her family had just moved to the parish where her aunt had lived for years. And for the next sixty-odd years, Margaret would be one of the parish's mainstays, occasionally its organist, and its staunchest supporter.

Margaret's family shared Father Cunningham's vision of the status of his church and the sunny future of its surrounding properties. Her youthful impression was that St. Paul's parish "seemed so different from other places that I'd seen. The people were much more tolerant, much more open. It was largely an Irish parish. There were some Italians and some Canadian people, Nova Scotians. But by and large it was Irish. It was a very stable neighborhood, rather thickly settled."

In the autumn of 1986, Margaret still could see the rectory from her parlor window. But gone now are the seamless days of prosperity, when St. Paul's was a populous neighborhood of professionals, office workers, clerks, and factory hands, who kept their children clean and their gardens trimmed.

"My roots are very deep here," she says. "Maybe I'm unusual, but I never thought of moving. I had a very strong commitment to the church here, and to the parish, and the people who remained who were my friends." Her voice is firm and proud in the preserved hush of rose chintz and mahogany in her parlor.

Momentous as it was for the young Margaret to be present at the dedication of what she and her friends have always called their "mini-cathedral," another event around the same time made just as profound an impression on her.

The Cifrino family were long-established parishioners by the time the Whites arrived. Two brothers owned the largest homes on Half Moon Street, across the street from each other and from the church. There they supported their large families and created a fortune in the grocery business. And there, in 1936, they entertained a personal friend, a cardinal from Italy, one of those lofty church eminences that Margaret and her friends had only read about and marveled at. The girls pressed up against the bushes surrounding the Cifrinos' gardens, hoping desperately to get a glimpse of the man who, as it happened, was soon to become pope.

"He was here!" Margaret still remembers. "Of course, at that time it was a big deal. He stayed across the street. So when he later became Pope Pius XII, we remembered, you can imagine!"

Margaret White became a schoolteacher. Her weeks were spent in a classroom north of Boston, where she instructed Catholic children in English, drama, and speech, but she looked forward to weekends when she could be home.

"The streets were very orderly," she recalls. "People went about their business. It was well structured, there was no commotion, no rowdiness. And there were no muggings.

"In those days, the priests were very active. They weren't social workers as they may be inclined to be today, but they would take an interest and try to find a man a job. There was always an active St. Vincent de Paul Society. They'd go out and investigate a family and see what the need would be. I'm sure many parishes had St. Vincent de Paul Societies, but sometimes you wonder if certain parishes would admit that they had any poor! Nothing was ever hidden here. There were people who had some means, and there were people — I wouldn't say this was a poor parish, but they were poor here. And it wasn't covered up. It was dealt with."

After World War II, many returning veterans moved to the suburbs. "These things were almost imperceptible at first, but yes, the neighborhood was changing," Margaret admits. The war followed too quickly on the heels of the Depression for many St. Paul's parishioners to be able to recover from the economic blow. When others began buying homes, they stayed behind.

For the next decade or so, the decline in the neighborhood was subtle.

"There didn't seem to be any difficulty at all about walking the streets, no fear at all. Until about 1964. And all of a sudden, everything seemed to happen. You wondered how you could make it from the church down to Magnolia Street alone. Because there were many muggings and house breaks and fires. We might have felt it was arson, but we couldn't prove it. Until this neighborhood — well, parts of it — looked like a bomb hit it."

Margaret still wonders why no one tried to stop the devastation that she witnessed day after day around her.

"The term they use now is red-lining. You couldn't get money to buy a house, for house repairs, because I believe they sort of red-lined the district and just wrote it off."

For a time in the late sixties and into the early seventies, the sky was bright with another fire every night.

"If you talk about shortage of houses, that's partly the reason, because whoever 'they' is, they let this go on. Nobody could stop it. You just wonder who was torching the city of Boston, and neighborhoods like this. It was terrifying."

Margaret marks Christmas Day 1964 as the turning point in the neighborhood's decline. Her elderly roommate, renowned as the neighborhood's baking wizard, had planned a day of visits to friends.

"She was always baking cookies and cakes and brownies and things for everybody," Margaret recalls. That afternoon she set off down Dudley Street, carrying a cake for a friend on nearby North Avenue. Snow swept down Dudley, curled into the vestibules of closed storefronts, and amassed in vacant lots. The streets were virtually deserted. She decided to wait for the bus rather than battle the elements. She was glad for its warmth when it arrived and rode the few blocks without incident. But later she was unable to remember what happened after she stepped off at the corner of North Avenue.

"Kids came up behind, gave her a smash, knocked her into the gutter, her things went sprawling, hat off. She made her way to her friend's house to call the police," Margaret says. It was the last time the woman ever traveled alone in her own neighborhood.

Six months later the pastor of St. Paul's tendered a more specific overview of his changing parish population in a memorandum to his superior at Chancery, requesting a third assistant priest.

"St. Paul's, Dorchester is fast becoming a mission territory," he wrote. Beyond the dwindling elderly stalwarts of the parish were the growing number of "indigent and uncooperative white Catholics." These, numbering several hundred at the time, were families "mostly on Public Welfare, many with school-age children. These are mostly non Church-goers and through indifference, liquor or invalid marriages have almost completely lost contact with the Church. With constant pressure and *personal* pleading from us they send their children spasmodically to religious instructions. — little cooperation, — no religious conversation at home, — high average of children who are backward both as to intelligence and discipline.

"Our parish," Father McElroy continued, "is 50% colored. — Only a handful of practicing adult Catholics among them." One of the most interesting observations in this memorandum was that "Ours is one of the few really integrated parishes in Boston."

In 1964 that meant black and white, not, as it was to become twenty years later, predominantly Puerto Rican and black, with a smattering of Cambodian, Laotian, and Indian families. Also, "integration" in 1964 was largely the result of the cheap housing available in the neighborhood. The interracial mesh was a fragile and volatile one. Father McElroy's memo continued, "It would take very little to alienate races or individuals. — Ours is a 'powder-keg area.' "

As events after 1965 showed, city and church leaders didn't take sufficient heed of the warning intended with these words.

St. Paul's never did get the parochial school Father Cunningham had envisioned, but in 1967 it did get its convent. Mary Cifrino left her house at 9 Half Moon Street to the parish in the hope that it would be used as a convent for the Sisters of the Blessed Sacrament for Indians and Colored People. A transfusion of fresh energy was desperately needed by the parish then, and Father McElroy's letter to Richard Cardinal Cushing regarding the gift hinted as much.

"I sincerely feel that this will not only be a life saver to this Parish," he wrote, "but that it will be one of the greatest steps taken by the church in this Diocese in the field of integration."

Sadly, it was a hope that never materialized as Father McElroy had wished. The sisters arrived, but less than a decade later, in 1975, only two nuns remained in the large, drafty house. These two moved to 16

Lingard, and the parish sold the Cifrino house to a Puerto Rican family for $14,500. The new owners of the property were foreclosed upon in short order. After three changes of ownership in ten years, the property had become a "drug house," where addicts bought and consumed their purchase, usually heroin.

In 1980 Margaret White and her friends watched their second Pope, John Paul II, sweep down a burnt-out and devastated Dudley Street in an open motorcade. For them, it was a moment of bitter irony.

"Oooohhh," Margaret says, shuddering even now. "Times have changed."

By 1975 St. Paul's parish was up for grabs, and Father William C. Francis wanted it. Ordained seventeen years and director of the Spanish Center across from the archdiocese's Cathedral of the Holy Cross (and, coincidentally, nephew of its founder, one of the most influential American Catholics in history, Cardinal Cushing), Bill Francis asked his uncle's successor, Humberto Cardinal Medeiros, to let him take over St. Paul's. The cardinal agreed: Bill Francis was the only priest who had even applied for the job.

Margaret White couldn't have been happier. Surely, Father's bloodlines, status, and avuncular style would return to the parish some of its lost patina and endow it with more favor from Chancery.

But Bill Francis's visions couldn't have been farther from Margaret White's. He had spent ten of his seventeen years as a priest in Peru, a member of the Missionary Society of St. James the Apostle. He had returned to Boston at the request of the archdiocese to run the Spanish Center. But Peru had transformed him.

"I'll never forget Cardinal Cushing saying to us, 'You go down there and you'll come back a better person, because you'll learn from those people,' " he says. "You did. You learned from them.

"A lot of priests, young priests, I find today, are very shy about going into the inner city, because you get banged around. Your car gets ripped off. Your house gets ripped off. You get ripped off. All you hear about are the problems.

"You *always* learn from these people. You always learn. And they put you to shame. They really put you to shame."

At the Spanish Center Bill Francis knew that he was performing an important task, administering programs for the archdiocese's fastest-growing population. But after a few years he felt that he was just putting in time. His twentieth anniversary was approaching, and time wasn't something to be wasted. He missed the immediacy of living with the poor, as he had in Peru. St. Paul's was a dying parish. That was where he wanted to be.

It didn't take long. What he'd been searching for quickly started to find him. On his first Christmas Eve in the russet clapboard rectory, he received a call from a woman he'd never met before. She told him that a very pregnant sixteen-year-old Hispanic woman was standing on the doorstep of a minister's house in nearby Upham's Corner in the freezing rain. She had no home. Neither she nor her eighteen-year-old husband and first child had anywhere to go. Could he put them up for the night?

Maria's contractions were well under way by the time Bill Francis gathered the family. He drove them to the hospital, had her admitted, escorted her down to delivery, and remained with her and her husband the whole time, translating every step of the way, so that Juan could witness the birth of his second child. When it was over, daylight was coming up, and Francis, drained but exhilarated, realized that it was time to prepare for the first mass of Christmas Day.

He decided to bring Juan and the older child home with him until he could find the young man some work. Mother and newborn would follow in several days. Finding work for an illegal alien required a number of irregularities, which Bill, in his brief time in the poor parish, was already prepared for. Using means similar to those of St. Paul's first priests, Bill eventually found Juan a custodial job in a hospital nearby, and shortly afterward he contacted a friend at the State Department, who legalized the arrangement. His ministry had begun.

In 1985 the Cifrino home went on the market again. Rita Brereton was at St. Paul's then, and she was to play a decisive role in the disposition of the Cifrino property — and of half the church as well.

Rita was a School Sister of Notre Dame. In 1980 she had returned from three years in the rural hill communities of Puerto Rico because she wanted to refocus her work and live among poor inner-city Hispanics. Before moving into the convent and into the life of St. Paul's, she worked for six months at a Boston family shelter, Renewal House.

Rita shares Bill Francis's sense of urgency with respect to the poor. "The ultimate altruism is 'love thyself,'" the thirty-nine-year-old nun is fond of saying. "And love thy neighbor as thyself. It's that simple. You cannot consider a society stable where there are people who have nothing, who are not functioning as humans."

Rita began spending her time much the way Bill Francis did, taking women to the hospital and helping them find work, child care, and financial support.

Their efforts were closer to what Father Anderson had done for his recently arrived European immigrants than they were to the activities of the staid, middle-class, doctrinally homogeneous church of the fifties. But Rita and Bill would have differed sharply with Father Anderson about their role in serving their parishioners. No longer did they view themselves as authority figures, as paternalistic guides, better educated and more knowledgeable about the best interests of the poor than the poor themselves. Gone for good at St. Paul's, it seemed, was the principle that the clergy knew best. It had been replaced by an attitude of humility, receptivity, and responsiveness to the needs of the parish's poorest members.

"The primary agenda of poor people, wherever you find them, is to be listened to," Rita says. "They'll say, 'I want you to respect me and to know that I know my situation. You listen to me, and I'll tell you what I want and I'll tell you what's the best way for me to do it.'

"When somebody says that to you, and you stick it through with them, you're lucky. They don't need me. But they are willing to allow me to be with them. That's when I become enriched. And in fact *they* become enriched because they know they don't need me. There's no illusion. They will continue to live and die without me, because the situation is beyond anybody. But people, individuals, can work together and help each other, and love each other and appreciate each other. And that's the conversion. That's the real change."

At first Rita and Bill devoted themselves to these principles by ministering to the overwhelming demands within their own parish. Then in 1982 they took in some of the city's homeless women.

When Rosie's Place was burned out of its South End location by arsonists, Bill Francis offered the use of the activities room behind St. Paul's basement chapel until the shelter could find a permanent new home. Rosie's stayed for a year, sleeping fourteen women each night behind the functioning chapel. Because the shelter and the chapel were divided merely by a wall, members of the parish had regular contact with the women. Rita and Bill began to see that serving the homeless was a natural extension of what they had already been doing. They began attending meetings about the homeless problem, and they joined discussion groups planning new services. They decided they wanted to open a shelter themselves in the space that Rosie's had occupied.

"For women," Bill says, "because there was nothing for women available."

But one of the few sources of funding available for shelters, the state's Fund for the Homeless, rejected their request. Bill and Rita concluded that either efforts to help the homeless were so uncoordinated that money wasn't being matched up with opportunities when they appeared, or homelessness was becoming a kind of social service fad, and the established interests in the field weren't eager to see newcomers get into the act. Disappointed, they decided to bide their time and see what developed.

They didn't have to wait long. One day in September 1985, Valerie Lanier, a friend of Rita's, knocked on Bill Francis's door. Valerie was director of the Paul Sullivan Housing Trust, a nascent program at the Pine Street Inn that was buying, renovating, and running lodging houses for small groups of homeless people. The trust already had three houses in operation and wanted a fourth.

"The Cifrino house is up for sale," Valerie told Bill, "and I'm going to get it."

As soon as Valerie had seen the house, she knew that she could transform it into a home for a dozen people. Bill called a community meeting at the church rectory for neighbors and parishioners to hear what Valerie had in mind and give them a chance to react.

The night of the meeting, Val and her boss, Richard Ring, were astonished to hear the neighbors greet the proposal with enthusiasm. Afterward Bill invited Rich to stay for a beer. The subject of shelters came up again, and Rita and Bill expressed their frustration at not having been able to get financial support to run one.

"Well, what kind of space do you have?" Ring asked. Rita immediately offered to show him. When Rita opened the basement door of St. Paul's and flicked on the lights, he was astounded. The Pine Street Inn's women's unit had been overcrowded for a long time. Every night thirty-five to fifty women slept on blankets on the floor of the lobby.

"I could put fifty beds in here!" he exclaimed. He rushed back to the dining room. "If we can have it, we'll move in December first," he told Bill Francis.

Two weeks later Ring was writing to the director of the state Shelter Resource Unit of the Welfare Department.

Dear Pat:
By a stroke of good fortune the Pine Street Inn has unexpectedly found itself in the position of creating 50 new shelter beds for homeless women

at St. Paul's Church in Dorchester. . . . The basement turned out to be clean, comfortable and spacious — much larger than I had antici-pated. The space is so ideal that Pine Street could run a 50 bed shelter there tonight if need be. What makes the arrangement so attractive is that beyond providing an excellent site, there is no community opposi-tion; the people in the neighborhood have already had experience with a shelter and actually want a shelter to be there.

Several weeks later Bill tested the waters at his Sunday masses. Peo-ple like Margaret White cautiously affirmed the idea. "Well," she said, months after the shelter had become a reality, "this isn't the kind of thing you go looking for, but you accept these things when they have to be. What I'm saying about this parish is that I think they do accept."

At the Spanish mass the reaction was just what Bill had expected. After he introduced the idea, one of the women in the congregation stood up in her pew.

"Everyone has the right to sleep with a roof over their head," she said from where she stood. "Why are you bothering us with these details? We've got to do it! And it has to be as comfortable as pos-sible!"

For the parishioners of St. Paul's, the shelter was an opportunity to open their doors to those needier than themselves. "They can't un-derstand why there should be a problem of homelessness," Bill says. "This is our house, and we have to open our house — that's their thinking."

Twenty-two women slept at St. Paul's Women's Shelter the night it opened, January 13, 1986.

For Richard Ring, St. Paul's was both a gift and a grand experi-ment. The Pine Street Inn had never run a satellite program before. No one was sure it would work, or how the women would feel about being moved such a distance every night, how the staff of fourteen would feel working so far away from the Inn's home base downtown, and how the St. Paul's community would respond to the shelter over the long run.

Ring signed a year's lease for $13,108, and the Inn paid another $12,397 to cover half the cost of a new boiler. It contracted to pay for three-quarters of the church's heating bill, two-thirds of the electrical costs, and all the gas and water bills. The Inn also took out adequate fire and liability insurance. It wasn't a cheap investment by any means.

But Rich Ring hoped that it would be a long-term one and that the lease would be renewed without any opposition for years to come.

By September of 1986, St. Paul's basement was filled nearly every night, and the life of the parish had been transformed. When the chapel was first turned over to the shelter, Bill worried that his Hispanic parishioners would miss the intimacy of the small chapel in the move to the upstairs church. He was sure that attendance would temporarily fall off. But just the opposite occurred: the congregation grew, to the point where they couldn't all fit downstairs if they tried.

"I view it as the Lord's way of kind of blessing the whole thing," he says. "As long as [the shelter] is here, we're going to see this parish growing. I really feel that. The parish now is much more alive. Much more alive."

On these fall evenings other worries press in on Bill Francis. Gentrification is beginning to affect even this benighted part of town. The Paul Sullivan Housing Trust paid $125,000 for the Cifrino home. Two weeks later, Valerie Lanier was offered $200,000 for it. Bill understands very well that gentrification will affect not only those in the parish who own homes, but those who don't as well. "Ten years from now, what is this area going to look like? If this single woman over here sells to yuppies. Someone else sells to yuppies. Some of these elderly people, they'll be forced into it. I don't blame them, if they can get the money. But if you get that kind of a crowd in here, what are they going to think about having a shelter next door?"

Amanda awakes to the five o'clock darkness and a woman's bass voice booming through the dorm. She lies still and stares up at the ceiling. No one has said a word to her yet. Last night, after her shower, she had immediately crawled into the bed assigned to her.

She looks at the rows of beds — seven down and eight across, with just a foot or two between them. Around her, forms stir on their cots. Some get up from the narrow pallets; others might be dead, they are so still. Women with gray hair and frail bodies stoop down to pick up their bags and place in them the wallets they have gripped all night under their pillows. They look ghostly in the half light.

Amanda rolls onto her side and regards the confessional at one end of the room. Here secrets have another meaning altogether now. Secrets are all you have. How you share them and horde them, and even invent some, determines how well you survive.

So many women with gray hair. Can it be that none of these women have anyone to care for them? She closes her eyes again, slightly queasy from the musty odors of confined sleep. She wants to keep this new reality, its coughs and hostilities and smells, its intrusions and its hopelessness, at bay. Inside, something is dying. Last night she'd felt the essential part of her collapse so far through the endless tunnel of herself that she wonders if maybe this time she will never come out again.

She is completely alone now. There is no Thomas or Nanna or Jane or Bill to come to her aid. There are no walls left in the entire world that can restrain what is happening to her. With the greatest effort, she struggles upright at the second wake-up call and swings her feet down to the floor. She dresses, pulling on a fresh pair of underpants, the same socks she wore the day before, and her sneakers. Then she stands and follows the smell of fresh cigarette smoke to the small door in the chapel's back wall.

It gives onto the dining room. At the half dozen rectangular folding tables there, a handful of women are already sitting, lost in silence and reverie, buried in a nicotine haze, trying to begin the day. They sip tea, bring cigarettes up to their lips, and pick at donated day-old pastries. Some of them spoon cold cereal. No one is speaking. Shrunk into themselves, they seem enveloped by the room itself. The tables, covered with white cloths, cut flowers in glass jars in the middle of each, don't fill even half the space.

A small cafeteria window on the left opens onto the kitchen area, just large enough for two people to work in comfortably. Inside a staff member is setting out packs of cereal.

Beyond the tables, four salvaged sofas squat in a crude semicircle facing a television atop a yellow plastic milk crate. Even the couches seem dwarfed by the space and stranded, like the few women who occupy them, the superfluity of broken-up living rooms. Some distance beyond them, the room finally ends in a darkened stage flanked by crimson velvet.

Amanda turns and studies the homey touches the staff have added to diminish the imposing void of the former meeting hall. The kitchen's makeshift plywood wall is papered with pieces of the women's own artwork. Accomplished abstractions have been taped up next to nervously crayoned scenes of the Holy Family, a drawing of a princess, and a sketch of Mickey Mouse. Amanda steps closer and studies the most striking piece among them, a pastel landscape of a house floating in the middle of what looks like the ocean. She scans a listing of the Friday night films rented from the library and shown after dinner: "A Star Is Born," "The Autobiography," and "Winnie the Pooh." Beneath this list is a roster of places throughout the city that offer free lunches. On the adjacent wall, by itself for emphasis, hangs an AIDS poster warning the women to engage in safe sex.

Her survey completed, Amanda wanders back to the room she woke up in. The place isn't without its humor. At both ends of the former chapel, the confessionals have been converted to broom closets, with toothpaste, tampons, and towels in place of kneelers. Over the door to the showers, gold gothic lettering recalls a former identity: St. Theresa's Reading Room. Only now, the few literary offerings — titles like *Temptation's Triumph* and *Savage Embrace* — are stashed atop the former main altar, its elaborate gold leaf tabernacle still intact.

Amanda sees something else, something that momentarily excites her, and she approaches the altar to take a second look. Off to one side of the main altar, in the alcove that originally housed a secondary shrine, sits a child's desk, Amanda-sized. She looks around to be sure she isn't being watched. Safe, she approaches it. On top rests a lamp, which works when she switches it on. A student chair is pushed into the knee hole. For an instant, as she contemplates the possibilities, the pangs of loneliness subside.

Behind her, weak light has begun to slant through the stained glass windows onto the tangled mass of sheets and impermanence. Another call from the deep-voiced night supervisor pulls her back to the present. Weary, she lines up for the van. Those who work in the day labor pools leave first. They'll spend the next eight hours standing in assembly lines, snapping lipsticks and blush-on compacts together for minimum wage. Others have regular jobs as parking lot attendants, security guards, or nursing home attendants. Then it is her turn to board the same van that brought her to this place the night before.

The morning is chilly and misty as the van retraces last night's route down the hill. The streets are empty. Once again Amanda is struck with the sense of reality receding — and now the first pangs of hunger. In the weeks leading up to her decision to come back, she'd stopped eating. She also hadn't slept much.

She refrains from joining in the early morning repartee. She doesn't want to talk to anyone. She just wants to shut down, keep to herself, and stay quiet. Mostly, that day and the next several days, she will cry.

Dropped off at the door of the Inn, she tells herself that the object is to get through. To survive the day.

It is only six in the morning, but she doesn't want to stick around. She shoulders her backpack and heads down Berkeley Street toward the river. In fifteen minutes, she has left the South End behind and passed into fashionable Back Bay. In her denims and wire-rimmed glasses, a youthful four foot ten inches tall, she blends easily with Boston's many students.

And, she thinks, beginning to trudge, if she doesn't, so what? For the past two years, she's been punching a cash register at Woolworth's, absolutely miserable out of her cotton-picking skull. Her landlady had begun bitching at her about this, that, and the other thing. Amanda slowly began to realize that she was getting no support from anyone, that she was going to have to tell the rest of the world to take their act and shove it up their asses.

More than anything this morning, she wants to drop out of sight, completely disappear. And then, out of view of the world, to take care of herself. She cuts through the Public Garden and makes her way down Charles Street to her destination, the Esplanade, along the banks of the Charles River. It is one of the most peaceful places she knows of, silver and private at daybreak like a dream that hasn't quite ended.

Out on the wooden piers, gulls perch and strut. She sits quietly for a while, taking in the scene. She doesn't have a real true friend left in the entire world. She's never been in this situation before. There has always been *one* person she could talk to, but not now. Reaching over, she opens her satchel. Pressing aside the rest of her possessions — a pair of slacks, three balls of socks, three pairs of underpants, four shirts, a sweater, and a radio — her fingers comb the bottom. She feels the mirror, toothbrush, and toothpaste. Then she comes to the fresh spiral notebook she packed in at the last moment.

The first time she was on the streets, she'd done a lot of writing. She'd figured it all out, everything that had gone wrong — at least, she thought so at the time. She'd filled two legal-sized notebooks in the form of letters to Jane and her mother. The second time she'd fled from home, in March of 1982, she had left the letters to Jane out on her bed where Jane could find them, and mailed the second set to her mother. Amanda had wanted to see how Jane and her mother would respond. But it hadn't worked out. Jane had refused to accept her suggestion that something had been wrong with the way they'd been brought up. From her mother Amanda had heard nothing. In the end, the letters disappeared. Amanda assumed that they were destroyed by their recipients, and she had nothing to show for her difficult struggles to come to terms with her past.

This time, she has decided that she will write for herself. She intends to keep a day-to-day diary of everything that happens to her while she is homeless. She fervently hopes that it will be the story of her recovery.

"I'm a very strong person," she tells herself as she looks out across the river. "But even strong people say, 'Wait a minute, I need somebody else to help me with this mess.' "

After Thomas died she'd tried to hang on as long as she could. But she always knew that if she had to, she could leave work, leave her room, and split. She could always go back to Pine Street, and find Jackie Pierce there to talk to.

She is ready. Ready to deal with stuff. Ready to say, "Okay, I'm gonna need help, I'm gonna need friends."

That evening she repeats the trip to Roxbury. Sitting at the check-in table at the head of the line into the showers is the woman she's been waiting to see again, after four long years. For the first time in weeks, she is happy.

"Finally!" she thinks. Jackie looks just as Amanda remembers her from Pine Street, large, warm, and motherly, with her pure blond hair, oversized blouse, jeans, and ubiquitous cigarette. It was Jackie who had gotten her settled into the rhythms of Pine Street in the summer of 1981 after Amanda had recovered from her bout of pneumonia. A counselor at Harbor Light had told her to ask for Jackie when she returned to the Inn, and she had. Though the two women had only exchanged occasional friendly words after their first meeting, Amanda found herself in the intervening four years remembering Jackie more vividly than any other person she'd met during those months on the street. She felt that they might have become friends if she'd given it a chance.

For a split second the veteran counselor doesn't recognize the woman in front of her as Amanda.

"Hi, Jackie, remember me?" Amanda helps her.

The counselor's brown eyes widen. "What are you doing back here?"

she cries. Then, recovering from her surprise, Jackie hugs her.

Later, at dinner, she comes into the dining room and quietly sits down beside Amanda.

"I'm sorry to see you back," she says softly. "Something must have happened. When you want to talk, just let me know."

"Thanks," Amanda says.

After a few minutes, Jackie says, "Come on, let me show you around."

She walks Amanda through the shelter routines, from shower room to dinner and beds. She explains where things are stored, how to get her nightgown and robe from the communal rack against the wall near the showers. She doesn't probe or push, for which Amanda is grateful.

The next morning when she sets off from the shelter again, she's in better spirits. It is important to know that someone cares and isn't going to rush her. She's not sure what she would have said if Jackie *had* pushed. Probably she'd just have erected a thicker wall around herself.

What is important now is to get the feel of the streets again, to plant herself firmly on the pavement, in the smells of early morning outside the Park Street subway station, at the Mug 'n Muffin, a favorite coffee shop among the shelter women, and at Brigham's, where she used to indulge in hot fudge sundaes with Nanna. She's been so tied up in knots lately, she's been unable to experience anything but her own anxiety, self-doubt, and pain.

"Don't rush into things," she tells herself as she turns off Beacon Street onto Charles, following her established route. "Take it one day at a time. One small step at a time. After all the garbage and shit you've been going through lately, take it easy. Relax for a bit. Go slow for a while."

One morning not long after this, on Charles Street, something catches her eye and she stops in her tracks. Ahead of her, a bundled figure lies curled in the doorway of an antique shop. It is still very early and there are few other pedestrians out. Amanda takes a few steps closer. The person wrapped in several blankets is as still as a stone, every muscle clenched into a defensive knot. Strands of gray hair escape from an opening in the soiled bedding. As Amanda watches, a frail, feminine hand reaches out to test the air. She draws a bit closer now, and notices for the first time several empty bottles scattered nearby.

"Morning," she calls, knowing enough not to approach too close, or make the woman feel trapped. Then, without waiting for an answer, she resumes her walk, moving slowly but purposefully by. She knows that she'll have to prove herself over time, convince this discovered soul that she has no motive other than friendship, that she doesn't want to call the police, or shoo her away, or rob her.

But the morning has been totally transformed. She decides, then and there, that she will return the next day. She'll come back every morning until the woman trusts her enough to answer. She'll keep an eye on her. And maybe, over time, they'll exchange a few words. Perhaps, gradually, Amanda will be able to help her.

The prospect lifts her spirits as she makes her way to the Esplanade. She opens her diary and makes a note about it. It feels good to think about someone other than herself.

There is Jackie to think about, too. Her father is dying. Amanda remembers what it's like, going to the hospital every day, not knowing what to expect from one hour to the next. But the biggest surprise of all in Amanda's return has been the news that Jackie has an infant daughter. It is a bit of a shock, really — Jackie is in her early forties and already has four teenagers. But she is obviously crazy about the baby. Amanda can't wait to see a photograph of her.

Amanda finds herself spending many hours going over all these things in her mind. But when she returns to the Inn at the end of the day to wait for the van, she is reminded of the naked facts of *her* situation. Then everything becomes a blur of confusion again. She withdraws into herself and begins to cry. Here she is, thirty-five years old, with no one to care about her, no home, no job, nothing.

ELEVEN

In from the Cold

WHEN PAUL SULLIVAN died suddenly on July 21, 1983, at the age of forty-eight, he was in Glacier National Park in Montana on a cross-country camping trip. He had been "on leave" from the Inn since the previous November under pressure from his staff, who had dubbed the open-ended sabbatical his first "vacation" in years. Richard Ring, who had deferred to Sullivan's determination to run the Inn fourteen years earlier, had now taken his place as Pine Street's acting executive director.

Ring was awakened at six that July morning at his Milton home by the phone call from Paul's distraught brother, Frank. The six-foot-tall, still fit former Naval Air Force ensign replaced the receiver in its cradle with trembling hands. For the next two hours Ring moved about the house in a daze. What numbed him wasn't the fact that Paul had died of a heart attack. Sullivan himself had expected that end to his frenetic and often self-extinguishing life. It was that he had died so far away from the world that meant everything to him, instead of on the floor of the Pine Street lobby, where Sullivan and everyone else had always assumed he would end his days.

Even though Paul was no longer actively running the operation, he remained its spiritual leader. Ring knew his death would rock the agency. And he realized, in those lonely first hours of July 21, that the Inn's future would be largely determined by how successful he, Richard Ring, was at preserving a sense of continuity in the management, the philosophy, and, perhaps most important, the tone of the Pine Street Inn.

It was time to call Frank Kelley.

In the modest rectory of St. Boniface at the tip of Quincy's Snug Harbor, a grief-stricken Kelley reflected on all that celebrity had taken out of Paul. More, obviously, than any of them had known. He thought, not without irony, that Paul had survived politically so well because he'd never embraced any of the numerous ideologies that had sprung up around the issue of homelessness. But that neutrality hadn't saved his life.

Before the day was over, thousands of phone calls were pouring into the switchboard at the Inn. People who had never even met Paul Sullivan face to face were phoning in disbelief. For years Paul had worried about becoming so much the personification of Boston's homeless that he would obscure the city's view of those he served. Although he unabashedly exploited his magnetism to garner the most money and publicity he could for the Inn, he didn't want to divert attention from where it was needed most, from the Inn's guests and its daily, often unglamorous, operation.

The early reactions to his death in almost every quarter of the city might have justified his fears. The enigmatic "saint" of Boston's homeless was the subject of an editorial in the *Boston Globe* the day after he died, and the mayor, Kevin H. White, issued a public statement of regret. Cardinal Medeiros ordered that Sullivan's funeral be held at the Cathedral of the Holy Cross, making the reformed alcoholic the first layman in memory to be so honored.

On the morning of July 25 some thirty clerics, including the cardinal, a monsignor, and a bishop, walked down the center aisle of the cathedral. The processional passed more than a thousand mourners, including the governor, Michael S. Dukakis, and his wife, Kitty, judges, legislators, members of the City Council, contenders in that year's crowded mayoral race, elderly South End neighbors, and hundreds of denizens of Boston's skid row.

One of those bearing the casket was seventy-year-old Gertrude, who with her husband had been saved by Paul Sullivan one winter morning in 1980. She still lived at the Inn, working six days a week at the women's shower, giving out nightgowns with tireless kindness. Gertrude couldn't believe that her young man was gone. Balancing the coffin on her shoulder close to the gray braids that encircled her head, she wept.

Throughout the cathedral, men and women cried openly. To one side of the altar, vocalists led by Ralph Hughes sang Sullivan's favorite hymns, "Ave Maria," "Panis Angelicus," and "Amazing Grace." Frank Kelley officiated at the mass, reading for the gospel his friend's favorite New Testament passage, Matthew 25:33–46: "Come, O blessed of my Father, inherit the kingdom prepared for you from the foundation of the world; for I was hungry and you gave me food, I was thirsty and you gave me drink, I was a stranger and you welcomed me, I was naked and you clothed me, I was sick and you visited me, I was in prison and you came to me. . . ."

In the deeply emotional moments of the close of the service, Cardinal Medeiros, dying of cancer, who'd struggled from his own sickbed to attend the mass, delivered a eulogy. Standing at the pulpit in his crimson robes, the cardinal said, "I was in conversation with Paul. Paul was a man of deep faith. I felt so honored, and so proud, when he called me 'my Father.' And I felt like his father. I felt so good inside to be the father of such a man. And so I come here to pay my humble, and profound, tribute to my son — perhaps my best son, in this city of Boston." Six weeks later the cardinal, too, was dead.

Over the next several weeks, some $45,000 came to the Inn, mostly in amounts of $5 and $10, from all over the country, along with handwritten, humble, letters of regret. The vast bulk of contributions were from elderly people on pensions who had never set foot inside the Inn but who had read about Sullivan's work or had seen the shelter featured on television at holiday time. Almost all apologized for how little they could afford to send along.

One note, which echoed the sentiment of many, conveyed just how potent a spiritual force Paul Sullivan had become. It said in part, "It [the funeral mass] reminded me so much of the tribute paid to our beloved Cardinal Cushing. They were two outstanding men who gave of themselves to help others."

Within a month Richard Ring was named executive director of the Pine Street Inn. In the Inn's next newsletter he commenced the task of binding his troops together. While expressing his commitment to upholding Paul Sullivan's agenda, he knew that changes in the scale and the dimensions of the Inn's operation were inevitable. With the $45,000 that had come in following Sullivan's death, for instance, he and the Pine Street board were planning to get involved in permanent housing for the homeless, establishing a subsidiary program, in the form of a trust, in Sullivan's name. Ring wrote:

Paul was a realist, and had fewer illusions than most about this type of work. His approach was simple, direct, pragmatic, and he was an astute observer of human nature. He knew that a person might "start over" over and over again. Yet, in welcoming and accepting each Guest, Paul knew that the person might one day succeed.

Paul accepted every opportunity to involve people with the Inn. Over the course of time, he probably made his way into half of the church basements in Greater Boston, spreading his message. To any civic organization that asked what it could do, Paul offered ideas, simple ideas. He would ask them to bring in old clothes, used bed linens or canned goods. He would ask people to consider forming a food group to serve supper to our Guests once a month. He stressed involvement and made people feel a part of the place.

One thing Rich Ring would never forget. On the morning of Paul's death, after informing his staff of the sad news, he had returned to his office and begun mechanically sorting through the day's mail, restless and divided in his heart between the past and the uncertain future. Halfway through the stack of bills, he came upon a postcard addressed to him from Glacier National Park. The postmark was July 20, just before Paul died. The message read: "I think we have found a bit of heaven."

If Paul Sullivan had one satisfaction in the final year of his life, it was to hear the state's governor-elect, Michael Dukakis, announce that homelessness would be his administration's top human services priority.

"Who would have believed it?" The governor's voice carried through the State House Senate chambers and via television into living rooms across six states that January day when he delivered his inaugural address. "Hunger in America in 1983 — hunger and homelessness in the most affluent nation on the face of the earth."

With his uncanny prescience, Sullivan might have divined that the Pine Street Inn, and services for the homeless all over the country, were on the verge of unprecedented expansion. But almost certainly, even in his wildest dreams, he couldn't have foretold the magnitude of what was to come.

That year, 1983, was a landmark for homeless policy in Massachusetts. The first one-night census in Boston and Cambridge, conducted by the United Way's United Community Planning Corporation and the Massachusetts Association for Mental Health early that winter, found 1,032 men and women staying in shelters. Interpolating from the respondents' estimates of how long they had been in shelters, the survey projected that 3,000 to 3,500 homeless people walked the streets of the two adjacent cities every year. The Massachusetts Coalition for the Homeless and other advocates immediately claimed that the census failed to reflect the "hidden" homeless, those who didn't use shelters. They argued that when the street population was taken into account, the total was much higher.[1]

What *was* known in Boston in the winter of 1983 was that the same three shelters were offering a hot meal and a cot to Boston's homeless in the old South End neighborhood where they'd begun a decade or more earlier and that they could no longer meet the growing demand alone. The Pine Street Inn, Rosie's Place, and Harbor Light had 411 beds, all told. Beyond the Pine Street Inn's move to larger quarters, nothing much had changed at any of them. Like many of their guests, the staffs remained committed to their marginal political and theological counterculture status and to operations that were, for the most part, impoverished and invisible: a human services underground.

The only other facility for the homeless in Boston was the Parker Street Shelter, located downtown near City Hall. Parker Street remained part of an unfinished dream, the centerpiece of a comprehensive case management program for the homeless mentally ill that had never developed. The program's designers had envisioned psychiatric referrals from the other shelters to Parker Street, one-on-one casework, rehabilitation centers, and ultimately, permanent residences for the deinstitutionalized mentally ill. None of this had materialized.

For a homeless person, the last and most expensive alternative to the streets in those days was the handful of welfare hotels. With few questions asked, these flophouses accepted their clients' monthly disability check in exchange for a few nights with a bottle out of the cold and the damp.

The homeless remained tethered to a cycle of foraging for food and begging for spare change during the day and taking refuge in the shelters at night. To receive general relief, the Welfare Department required one to have a permanent address. Medical care, job and housing referrals, facilities for storing clothing and belongings, and psychological counseling were, for all practical purposes, nonexistent. So were daytime drop-in centers where such services could have been offered, in settings of safety, warmth, and companionship, from eight in the morning till four in the afternoon, the often aimless hours when most of the shelters were closed.

In Boston, as in most state capitals and medium-sized cities across the country, the problem of displaced men and women had become increasingly visible and pressing by 1983. They were often unkempt, sometimes disoriented, and uniformly stranded. Even more disturbing, although few reliable studies existed to prove it, these homeless, it seemed, were not only being drawn to the big cities from elsewhere but were being produced by the cities themselves.

Despite the state's booming economy, the vaunted "Massachusetts Miracle," dramatic shifts in the *nature* of the economy were producing a new population of "mainstream poor," those who were unemployed (and, in many cases, soon homeless) as a result of market forces.

The city's job base changed greatly in the twenty years between 1960 and 1980. Boston had been a blue-collar town, its workers reliant on small manufacturing trades, mostly in the leather and textile industries. Unlike the heavily industrialized cities of Detroit, Chicago, and Cleveland, Boston didn't experience the crushing layoffs those cities suffered in the early seventies. All the same, its light industries were moving to the Sun Belt. By the mid-seventies, unemployment had risen to 12.5 percent, and the blue-collar base was being supplanted by a high-tech service economy fueled by the talents of young Harvard and MIT entrepreneurs who founded companies like Lotus, Digital, and MicroSoft.

In 1960 Boston's blue-collar families owned and lived primarily in multifamily homes of two to four units, often with relatives on other floors. As jobs left the city, and then court-ordered desegregation of the public schools began in 1974, many middle-class whites left Boston for the suburbs. What happened in Margaret White's parish of St. Paul's was occurring all over the city.

Virtually no new private housing was built in Boston during the seventies. Demand was low, and as a result rents were artificially depressed, rising less quickly than the rate of inflation. Indeed, the tenant lobby at the time was so weak that some 70,000 of the 100,000 units that had fallen under rent control in 1975 were actually decontrolled by 1983.

By 1985 the percentage of Boston's population living in rental units was higher (70 percent) than in any other U.S. city except New York. Given all these factors, it seems impossible that the city could have developed a critical housing shortage.

But the tenants of 1985 were a different population from those of the 1960s. They were older, with a much higher percentage of blacks and Hispanics and many more students. In all, it was a poorer group: Boston's poor had increased from 11 to almost 17 percent. The city's minority population had increased from less than 10 to 25 percent.

Also the housing was different. During the same twenty years, Boston had developed the third largest public housing system in the nation after Chicago and New York. And, as a percentage of the total housing stock, Boston's public housing, at 20 percent, was the highest of any U.S. city, including New York. In 1960 Boston had 14,000 city-run public housing units. By 1985 a total of 43,200 apartments were publicly funded.

Although these additional 29,000 units of public housing increased the city's housing supply, some 40,000 private units had been lost. In many instances, public housing had actually replaced privately owned properties. The process was euphemistically called urban renewal; the promise was higher quality and more plentiful affordable housing for the poor.

But the results were disastrous. First, the private property that did survive immediately began to inflate in value. By 1980 Boston's new high-tech economy had attracted some 57,000 newcomers to the total city population of 601,000. The number of households increased by 16,500 in the first half of the new decade. As members of the city's growth elite in financial, business services, and medical industries, the newcomers were earning impressive salaries. They wanted housing they could invest in. The average cost of a house in Boston increased from $82,600 in 1983 to $165,000 in 1986. Between 1980 and 1986, 15,909 new condominiums were created in Boston, most of them converted from rental apartments.

The resulting pressure on the private rental market became intense. In 1983 the median advertised rent in Boston (for units of all size) was $455; by 1987 it was $736. The percentage of Boston tenants paying more than 50 percent of their income for housing (for housing experts, a key indicator of shortages) was 11 percent in 1980. Five years later that figure had doubled.

Applications for apartments in public housing projects skyrocketed. The waiting list at BHA increased from 7,000 families in 1982 to 13,900 in 1986. And matters at the BHA were already chaotic: in 1981 the authority had been put into court receivership for incompetent management. Some 4,000 of its 18,000 units, almost 25 percent, were uninhabitable because of poor maintenance and neglect (repairs would cost from $75,000 to $100,000 *per unit*).

And, although the city had the nation's highest percentage of public housing, it had no control over most of it: more than half consisted of private developments subsidized by the federal Department of Housing and Urban Development (HUD). HUD had foreclosed on 4,000 of these and wanted to auction them to the highest bidder. As for the other 19,000 apartments, many of them were coming to the end of their twenty-year mortgages and were in horrific states of disrepair. According to the original agreement with the federal government, the developers would soon be free to rent or sell them at market rates.

If urban renewal inadvertently made private property more costly for families in a boom economy, its second impact in Boston may have been to increase the city's homeless population. Rooming houses in the South End — home for many single, elderly, and economically marginal residents — virtually disappeared, dropping from 25,000 units to 2,100 between 1960 and 1980. On a 1985 questionnaire, 20 percent of the Pine Street Inn's guests listed a South End lodging house as their last permanent address.

Any aspirations the city itself may have had to finance housing construction in 1983 were dampened by a bleak financial picture. A 1981 state referendum that had frozen real estate taxes at 2½ percent of property value dealt a severe blow to the city's budget (one-third of which came from real estate taxes). Thousands of public employees had been laid off, programs aborted, and schools closed to cut spending. If Boston was going to confront the problems of a shrinking supply of affordable housing in more than purely symbolic terms, it was going to need the help of the state and the federal government.

The lack of housing was not the only factor accounting for the growth in the shelter population. Of the 22,000 people discharged from state mental hospitals over the previous fifteen years, many had fallen through the system's cracks. And despite the Department of Mental Health's 1980 ruling that mental patients could not be discharged to shelters, many such people, too disconnected or alienated to sustain themselves in the apartments or rooms they were placed in, just walked away from them and into the Pine Street Inn.

Others, Vietnam veterans with delayed post-trauma stress syndrome, or untreated psychiatric or drug and alcohol addictions that had become unmanageable, in the years since their military discharge, had drifted into the shelters.

One group of homeless had never been institutionalized or evicted from their homes or fired from their jobs. In some respects the most troubling of all, this group had been cut off from deeper and less easily decipherable roots. Their mere presence suggested a disturbing breakdown of some essential glue in American society, a failure not just of large systems but of family and community to provide security, support, and a sense of belonging to all of its members.

Surveys of this population did not come until later, and when they did their findings were often disputed. However, with some consistency these guests, at shelters for single adults (those traveling without children, though many are parents), responded to questionnaires with the information that they were employed or employable (about 68 percent), had developed alcohol and drug problems (64 percent), and had chronic medical problems as a result of their substance abuse (about 50 percent). Only about a third of them were mentally ill, but fewer than half of those were receiving mental health services. About one-fifth were veterans. And most felt they would be capable of independent living if housing — and, in many cases, some social service supports — were available.

Boston faced a disproportionate share of the statewide homeless problem by 1983. It had the largest shelters, the greatest number of social service agencies and nonprofit and church groups interested in addressing the problem, and the most politically entrenched real estate community in the region. The city had, however, no more authority over welfare policy, HUD's public housing, or the state's mental health system than did the smallest hamlet in Massachusetts.

By tackling homelessness head on, Governor Dukakis intended to ameliorate these constraints — indeed, to eradicate homelessness throughout Massachusetts. His advisers would later admit that Dukakis saw in homelessness a problem that could be solved in the course of a single term if it were properly managed and structural solutions adequately funded. Even before Dukakis was sworn into office, the governor-elect's transition team had gathered an advisory committee composed of advocates, shelter directors, and cabinet office designees, to begin hammering out such a comprehensive solution. Overnight the human services underground became the policy-making elite. Homelessness in Massachusetts became official.

The advisory group, known as the Governor's Advisory Committee on Homelessness, grew to fifty-six members. It was actively chaired by the governor's wife, Kitty, and by the Catholic bishop of Worcester, Timothy Harrington. Inside the administration, the governor ordered every cabinet-level agency (Public Welfare, Mental Health, Elder Affairs, Veterans' Services, Communities and Development, and Administration and Finance) to establish a staff position specifically to represent the needs of the homeless in all agency policy making. This approach, rather than the creation of a separate agency on homelessness, was undertaken at least partly on the theory that homelessness was the result of past failures by these agencies to deal with family and individual problems before they turned into crises. These new advocate staffers in turn made up an interagency Planning Team on Homelessness that coordinated the agencies' efforts.

Meanwhile, the advisory committee had produced a four-part strategy for ending homelessness in Massachusetts: prevention, emergency services, supportive services, and stabilization. Prevention meant keeping families and individuals who were on the brink of losing their homes from doing so, primarily by providing them with financial assistance and tenant-landlord mediation. Homelessness, it was obvious, was much more costly and difficult to solve than were housing disputes and temporary cash flow crises.

Emergency services meant building more shelters, particularly for homeless families. It also meant "sheltering" families in welfare hotels and allowing them to stay there longer than the thirty days allowed under federal emergency assistance guidelines. In developing its statewide family shelter program, the advisory committee overwhelmingly opted to avoid the Pine Street model, calling instead for *small* (twenty to forty beds) community-based and community-managed programs.

Supportive services meant social workers, who could counsel homeless families in crisis and identify long-term counseling needs. It also meant providing the mentally ill with the case management, supported housing, and follow-up care that currently didn't exist. Stabilization, the fourth element in the strategy, was universally understood to mean permanent housing. The state needed to begin building more low-cost homes.

One of the great advantages that Massachusetts had in its assault on homelessness, thanks to the Massachusetts Coalition for the Homeless, was an extant infrastructure for community-based social services. Since its founding three years earlier, the coalition's aim had been to develop a broadly based membership that would be ready to provide services when a sympathetic executive was elected to office.

Their effort succeeded. Across the state the coalition could call on hundreds of committed private shelter providers, nonprofit organizations, and churches to work with the state in new grassroots programs. In Boston, whose sheer size, numbers, and vested interests made its problems unique, the Emergency Shelter Commission, the coordinating agency begun by City Councilor Ray Flynn, became the city's liaison to the advisory committee.

The second advantage Massachusetts had at this juncture was its ability to pay for new housing and social welfare programs. By the end of 1983 the state's balanced-budget mandate, thriving economy, and aggressive pursuit of tax revenues had resulted in budget surpluses. By 1984 the legislature was in the luxurious position of being able to consider *both* a surtax repeal that would return $300 million to the taxpayers and unprecedented appropriations for programs for the homeless.

The state was also financing its homeless programs with significant federal help. The federal Job Stimulus Bill of 1983 netted the state more than $36 million; all but $3 million, designated for housing rehabilitation and weatherizing, and another $2 million for maternity and early child health care, went into shelters and other homeless services.

The state legislature passed an omnibus homeless bill that fall. Chapter 450, as it was known, combined with a number of new state programs, began to attack homelessness in the four areas delineated by the Advisory Committee.

First, Chapter 450 provided funds for those threatened with eviction. The state expanded its emergency assistance program (50 percent federally reimbursed) to pay for up to ninety days' rent, heat, utilities, and a clothing allowance. If a family was evicted after that, the program would pay for the storage of furniture during the period of homelessness, as well as moving expenses up to $150 and, when the family found a new apartment, the first and last month's rent.

"Emergency Services" — shelters — became something of a boom industry in Massachusetts beginning in 1983. The Department of Public Welfare expanded the program of shelter construction begun under the previous administration. Targeted to homeless families, the program paid 75 percent of a shelter's first-year start-up costs and 50 percent of operations in subsequent years. The shelters were all to be owned or leased by local nonprofit agencies (in-kind services and donations would make up much of their balance of operating costs), and all capital costs would be borne either by them or others in the private sector.

Until enough family shelters were opened, families receiving Aid to Families with Dependent Children (AFDC) would continue to be put in welfare hotels. Chapter 450 suspended a previous sixty-day limit on emergency assistance funds spent on hotel rooms.

For individuals, the state in 1983 opened its first, and only, directly operated shelter, a 110-bed facility at Shattuck Public Health Hospital in Jamaica Plain. Shattuck also began a special respite unit for the homeless who needed postoperative or long-term bed rest.

Chapter 450 also required the state to provide social workers for families staying in shelters and hotels. It mandated a case management approach to the homeless mentally ill, covering not only the psychiatric but the social and economic needs of mentally ill individuals. The Department of Mental Health (DMH) created a Homeless Services Unit and in Boston funded an outreach team to link up homeless individuals on the street and in shelters to services at community mental health centers.

Finally, Chapter 450 struck the residential requirement for general relief (the state-funded welfare assistance program) and for food stamps. Homeless individuals, even those staying in shelters funded by the Welfare Department, were now eligible for monthly relief checks.

By the fall of 1986, Massachusetts' expenditure for emergency assistance had increased from $6.7 to $28.5 million in three years. An additional $8.3 million was being spent on fifty-two family shelters across the state.

An array of social services had been added, primarily in the family shelters. A housing services program worked with tenants and landlords to prevent evictions and encourage landlords to rent to low- and moderate-income tenants with rent subsidies. Programs designed to support especially fragile families while they made the transition from shelters to apartments were offered. Day programs had been created for preschool children and for single adults. Welfare-funded medical services were expanded. Mental health services, reorganized under the Homeless Services Unit, were beginning to develop a case management program.

In addition, the state had spent some $500 million on a variety of programs for low- and moderate-income housing, both construction and rehabilitation. (Low income was defined as $17,000 and moderate as $22,000.) It offered mortgage reductions and its own rental assistance certificates. A housing abandonment program sought to protect multifamily homes by providing maintenance funds to owners and tenants.

In 1986 Boston had nine shelters for homeless single adults (a total of 915 beds) and fifteen family shelters. It also had a new mayor. Ray Flynn came to office in 1984 on a populist plank that won him 65 percent of the vote. Flynn, the only city councilor to attend the public funeral for the city's deceased homeless, held on Boston Common in 1982 by the coalition, identified with the city's dispossessed. The son of a dock worker and a cleaning woman from South Boston, Flynn had been raised among people who just managed to scrape by. His early career as a probation officer had quickened his awareness of the complex social problems that beset the families of those who "drop out," including juvenile delinquents and young alcoholics. And his years on a city council hamstrung by a strong mayor whose constituency was drawn from among the city's wealthy strengthened Flynn's near-obsession with being the voice of the poor.

Flynn often rose at five to help serve breakfast at the Pine Street Inn. His brother, a Boston police officer, had volunteered there for years. On the Thanksgiving Day after his election to the mayor's office, Flynn spent so many hours in the shelters that he forgot his own dinner; he and his family ate with the hired help in the kitchen at one of Boston's venerable old hotels, the Parker House.

Before he was sworn into office, Flynn joined the U.S. Conference of Mayors' Task Force on Homelessness and Hunger. Within a year, he had become its chairman. At Boston's City Hall the plight of the homeless shifted overnight from an enthusiasm shared by a small coterie in the redevelopment authority to a major issue in the mayor's office.

For the first two years of Flynn's first term, the city spent about $6 million on providing capital grants, dispersing city-held property to shelters, setting up meals programs and medical services, and operating Long Island Shelter. Though the city depended on the state to finance the shelters and social and mental health services, Flynn helped in the ways he could, using his influence to ensure that licensing, fire inspections, and property acquisition proceeded quickly and easily for inexperienced shelter operators.

Boston received the lion's share of the state's "homeless prevention and stabilization" housing monies, much of which went to the city's middle class. In 1986 the state spent $35 million in Boston alone to reduce mortgage payments for moderate-income home buyers. Another $14 million subsidized construction projects in which one-fourth of the units were for low- or moderate-income households. More state money was used to bring public housing units into compliance with safety and building codes (in 1986, $21 million, and the year before, $23.5 million). A mortgage of $151 million, and capital grants totaling $40 million, went toward redeveloping the massive Columbia Point project into 1,282 units (only 400 of them, however, to be low-income).

But the new frontier in affordable housing was in public-private partnerships, and Boston was becoming a virtual laboratory for an idea that liberal housing experts had been dreaming about and refining since the early seventies. Joint public-private initiatives were hardly new to Massachusetts. Its high-tech industry was the offspring of many such marriages. Its universities, government, and medical research labs worked in tandem. And the network of nonprofit agencies across the state providing homeless services was, by everyone's account, far more effective than centralized state agencies. But housing — real estate development — was virgin territory for such ventures. It would take the mayor, merging necessity with an activist vision of the public sector's role in this area, to set the experiment in motion.

Flynn's challenge was to increase housing construction and to preserve the stock of affordable apartments on the private market. Rather than accomplish this through the centralized bureaucracy of the BRA and the BHA, he turned to nonprofit "development" groups, many of them born in the seventies as tenants' rights organizations protesting urban renewal. These Community Development Corporations (CDCs) would design, construct, and manage new low- and moderate-rate housing.

Instead of the massive, multi-unit projects of the sixties, the CDC-sponsored housing would be small structures of 25 to 116 units (rentals and limited-equity coops) within their immediate neighborhood.

Funding would be in the form of low-interest loans, foundation grants, state loans, and city tax abatements, rather than the cumbersome and, as the Flynn administration saw it, ineffective tenant voucher systems or landlord tax subsidies of previous housing programs.

A decentralized housing system, like the decentralized network of shelter providers, would, in this view, be able to meet the distinct needs of individual communities while minimizing the financial risks. One or two management failures wouldn't undermine an entire public housing system. And with major developers and state planners as consultants, failures would be kept to a minimum.

A major source of property for these new ventures was the 113 parcels of abandoned property in the city. Rather than sell these to the highest bidder, as had been done in the past, the city designated as developers the nonprofit groups whose proposals included low- and moderate-rate units.

This wasn't all. All commercial development in Boston became subject to the Flynn administration's "linkage" policy. Developers of projects of 100,000 square feet or more were required to contribute five dollars per square foot over a twelve-year period to a Neighborhood Housing Trust. The money was to go toward filling budget gaps in already subsidized housing projects. By 1986, $45 million had been raised in this way (amounting to revenues of $4.5 million annually). That year the terms of the policy became even more costly for developers: another dollar per square foot was added as part of a "jobs linkage" program for Boston's unemployed. And another linkage program was soon created: developers of prime downtown city-owned property were required to develop as well a parcel in a depressed area of the city.

Between 1980 and 1986, 8,600 new housing units were created in Boston, 17 percent of it affordable to low- and moderate-income residents.

The second part of Flynn's housing agenda was to preserve reasonable rents for the poor and elderly. A ban on the conversion to condominiums of units occupied by low-income, elderly, or handicapped low-income persons went into effect, and rents on such units were capped at the inflation rate of the Consumer Price Index. For all others, rent increases were virtually fixed at 12.5 percent a year.

Developers of condominiums were required to give tenants one year's notice before conversion, the right of first refusal, and, if the tenant moved during the notice period, $750 to $1,000 in moving expenses. (In spite of this, 4,661 deeds for condominium conversion were filed in 1986 — a record high.)

Finally, as HUD properties either fell delinquent or approached their twenty-year expiration dates, the Boston Housing Partnership, the city's largest public-private partnership — a state-funded consortium of state officials, academicians, bank presidents, and other members of the business community — helped CDCs acquire some of them.

In all this the federal government wasn't completely inactive; it spent $20 million on the Bromley Heath projects in Jamaica Plain and another $32 million on the Columbia Point redevelopment project. In 1981 the Reagan administration restructured HUD's public housing program. It reduced by more than two-thirds its expenditures for housing construction and maintenance, replacing that with a greatly expanded (and much cheaper) rental voucher program, designed to help low-income renters find apartments on the private market. With the vouchers, families paid no more than 30 percent of their income for rent in eligible apartments — apartments whose rents fell within federally established "fair market" limits. The BHA administered almost five thousand of these Section 8 vouchers; however, because true market rents in Boston were among the highest in the nation (and most suburbs in the metropolitan area had some form of exclusionary zoning that effectively eliminated low-income residents), the vouchers worked in only about half of all cases.

Paul Sullivan undoubtedly would have been both surprised and pleased by this groundswell of political activity. Surely all those millions of dollars were providing homes for those who wanted them and a decent shelter for those who for the time being could manage nothing more. The Pine Street Inn — still legally an independent, nonprofit agency administered by a private board and only 50 percent state funded — had become de facto a public institution, the city's largest and by far its most expensive shelter.

In 1979, the year before the Inn moved, it was receiving anywhere from $31,000 to $42,000 a month reimbursement from welfare ($2 per man per night), for an estimated annual budget of $420,000. In 1983 the state's contribution was $1,979,700, which paid for all staff salaries and half the Inn's operating costs; the other half was "funded" by in-kind contributions: sheets, pillowcases, blankets, and most of the food. By 1986 the state's contribution rose to $3.6 million, for 630 guests, on average, a night.

The Inn's paid staff had grown from 4 in 1969 to 130 full-time and 70 part-time employees in 1986. The floor counselors were now managed by 29 supervisors, who, in turn, were overseen by 6 administrators. Some 5,000 volunteers complemented the Inn's corps of paid employees every year, preparing meals and helping out on shifts. By 1986 the Inn boasted a mailing list of 30,000 volunteers and contributors. It also had a development office, and the following fall it hired a "director of advocacy" to handle its public relations and lobbying efforts. These staffs occupied separate offices in a building next door to the Inn, purchased for $800,000.

The Inn enjoyed broad public support. Its early reliance on volunteers had paid off in valuable political capital. Although Pine Street had come, increasingly, to resemble a large state institution in its size, administrative structure, and internal organization, it possessed one crucial asset that government bureaucracies didn't: a constituency. Despite its growth, the Inn continued to successfully nurture its image as a personal and caring place. Bostonians proudly displayed Pine Street Inn bumper stickers on their cars, sent their cast-off clothing to its bins, and in hundreds of small ways felt that they were an essential part of the operation. People felt good about "doing" for Pine Street, and the dividends for the Inn were incalculable.

In political circles its influence and will were secure. Without the Inn, what would Boston do about its homeless problem? For this reason alone, it seemed that at every major press conference on homelessness — by the mayor, the governor, or members of the Emergency Shelter Commission — Richard Ring shared the podium.

By 1986 the character of the staff had also changed tremendously. Members of what insiders knew as "the original family" remained in key administrative posts, but their hold on the Inn's policies and personality had loosened as a result of the swelling floor staff, whose numbers alone gave them considerable influence. These new floor counselors were very different in educational background and often in social class from the earlier generation. Most of them were under thirty and had college degrees from places like Dartmouth, Hampshire, and Brown. They had traveled extensively and brought to the Inn resumés that often included prior experience with the homeless in cities from Houston to Calcutta.

They also brought a new attitude. Though they might have professed contempt for the term, it was a new careerism: many were hoping to advance up the career ladder at the Inn and ultimately to run a shelter or a related program of their own. To old-timers, the goal of eliminating homelessness and shelters altogether seemed lost on many of these young people.

Despite a new era of political and fiscal support outside the Inn, these differences were beginning to create cleavages within concerning the Inn's mission. Should it continue to be the place of last resort for those who came to the door, asking no questions, expecting nothing of its guests, just providing a place to sleep and a hot meal? Or should it be something more, challenging and encouraging guests to improve their quality of life? Three psychiatric nurses from the Department of Mental Health already had been added to the clinic staff. Many staffers wanted to see more — more of exactly what Paul Sullivan had fought tooth and nail to keep out of his Inn: on-site rehabilitative programs; small, decentralized lodging houses; and professional drug, alcohol, and psychiatric counseling.

Frank Kelley, Sullivan's old friend, was now president of Pine Street's board. He, like Richard Ring, had mixed feelings about both the potential and the dangers of this dissent.

"Paul simply focused us on taking care of people who were homeless," Kelley says. "What has happened in this society is that homelessness has become the 'shelter' for a lot of different groups who have agendas for society — workfare, welfare, whatever. And I guess I don't entirely trust that, because they weren't there when it started." But even Kelley acknowledges that in 1986 it had become more difficult to maintain Sullivan's clear and simple vision of almost twenty years before.

▨▨▨▨▨▨▨▨▨▨

TWELVE

Starting Over

MONICA DONNER stands with her back to the lobby of the Pine Street women's unit and looks into the courtyard, walled off from the road and enclosed by a ten-foot-high wrought iron fence. Many of its redwood benches, shaded by beech and plane trees, are occupied by last night's guests. It is the first of October 1986 and still early. The sultry day promises to be one of the last of Indian summer. Monica, glancing at the sky, hopes that the rain will hold off until evening: in half an hour her women will clear out for the day.

Past the privacy wall at the far end of the courtyard runs Harrison Avenue at its bleakest: abandoned lots, warehouses, and housing projects. Behind Monica, dominating most of the Inn's 70,000 square feet and five floors is the men's unit, which sleeps anywhere from seven to ten times as many men every night as the women's unit does with its fifty beds.

Flanking one side of the garden is the Inn's garbage drop. Industrial disposal bins, often filled to the brim, press against the fence. Along the other side runs the driveway that serves as the approach to the men's entrance, one hundred yards in from the street. The ongoing social exchanges between men in the driveway and women in the courtyard, and the fact that a number of the women have boyfriends or husbands who regularly sleep next door (and others earn their keep by engaging in various forms of sex with male guests on the periphery of the property), at times makes the physical segregation within the building seem bureaucratic and artificial.

But only at times. Monica has been at Pine Street only a year and a half, but it hasn't taken her nearly that long to understand that most

of the women in her care, taking advantage of the early-morning security inside the courtyard to straighten out their belongings, read
the newspaper, or just rest, want nothing to do with the Pine Street
men — or with any men. Most have been abused by men for years or
have been abandoned by the man they loved at a time of critical need.
Many have been maltreated by staff at mental institutions, and almost
all of them, beneath even the toughest and most aggressive façades,
are terrified of the violence of men. The women's unit is the one place
where they can be safe for a few hours.

Monica is the seven-to-three shift supervisor. Her forty-seven years
are worn mildly on her gentle, accessible face and pale blue eyes and
in her frank, understated manner. A Sister of St. Joseph for almost
twenty-five years, she's spent the last fifteen living and working in the
inner city. She loves the city. She loves city people, the city's freshness
and energy. Like most of the sisters in her order — the largest female
order in the Boston area — she spent most of those years as a teacher.
Her last assignment was as an art and English teacher at Cathedral
High School, less than a tenth of a mile down Harrison Avenue from
the Pine Street Inn.

But proximity wasn't what first exposed her to homelessness. Monica had to go around the world to find the Pine Street Inn. As a parochial school teacher, she found that one hundred and fifty students,
seven periods a day, along with the endless meetings and weekend
obligations attendant on the job, eventually took their toll.

"I just got jaded," she says. "There was no way to get out of it except
to quit."

In June of 1984 she did just that. She had been granted a sabbatical
leave and decided that she needed to get as far away from Western
civilization as possible in order to find spiritual renewal. She spent the
next nine months in India and Nepal, three of them practicing Buddhist meditation. In the end the journey didn't disappoint her.

"You just want to be of service to people who are really in need,"
she concluded about the future direction of her work. "There's plenty
of people to help most of the folks. So if you're going to give your
life, and work for nothing, and all that stuff, why not give it in places
where nobody else wants to work?"

What Monica, a white Irish American from South Boston, traveled
around the world to learn, Sandy Jones, a women's unit shift supervisor at the Inn, had absorbed growing up poor and black and female
in the Roxbury section of Boston. She never knew her father. At sev-

enteen she'd married a heroin addict; shortly afterward she was the mother of two children. But she had little time and emotional energy for them. She spent her nights sitting up to make sure her husband didn't inject so much heroin into his veins that he'd go into convulsions. Exhausted, she struggled through the daylight hours trying to hide from the fact that he was routinely stealing to support his $250-a-day habit. Then he went to federal prison for selling drugs to an agent.

Sandy got help. At the age of twenty-one, she was divorced and took a job as a nurse at Boston City Hospital to support her children. Then in 1973, Paul Sullivan hired her to work at the Inn after she got off her shift at the hospital. It had been with reluctance that she had agreed, when the Inn relocated, to work in the new women's unit.

In the spring of 1985, she had just been promoted to director of the unit. She was a few weeks away from a much-needed vacation and looking for counselors to fill in during her absence. One afternoon, a short, deeply tanned woman came through the door. Monica was wearing an embroidered Indian blouse, a print skirt, and wire-rimmed glasses.

Despite the profound differences between the two women in background and experience, Sandy immediately liked the nun who'd just walked through her door.

"I don't know if I'm going to be good or not," Monica confessed to her that day. "I've never really been around homeless people."

Sandy responded with the quick empathy that is her special gift. "Well, I think you really have to care. And I think you have to give a little bit of each: a little bit of what they want and a little bit of what they need. When you mix that together, I think you get just the right recipe."

As the third director of the women's unit in six years, Sandy was keenly aware of the sometimes sensitive position of her small program in the much larger operation of the Inn. For starters, it was a young program. Until 1980 the Inn had functioned as an institution solely for men, and its public image and institutional ethos still reflected this. Sandy knew that many people in the city still didn't know the Inn served women, and many had no understanding of the unique problems encountered on the streets by homeless women. She also knew that within the Inn there were those who thought the women's unit was pampered and far too genteel, that it held its guests to higher standards of comportment and self-control than did the men's unit.

These critics cited as evidence the higher staff-to-guest ratio (men's unit shifts had 5 counselors for 350 to 600 men; the women's unit, 3 for 50 women), and the fact that drunken behavior, commonly accepted on the men's side, was often cause in the women's unit for throwing a guest out and prohibiting her from returning for a period of time, usually three weeks.

Sandy understood these attitudes. When she had first come to the unit, she had found her own expectations severely challenged.

"What I was looking for was alcoholic women," she recalls. "Women we could help. I'd taken some courses, and I was looking to help women get on their feet. That's all I knew. As far as knowing that they were mentally sick people, I didn't know. It took me a year, or a year and a half, before I really settled down with them. I was nervous. I didn't know what to expect. And I didn't know what I was expected to do for them."

The early months precipitated in Sandy a soul-searching that led in time to a transformation in her assumptions about what homeless women need and respond to.

"I'll tell you what I did. I came in here, and I began to know them just as women. Never mind all the other stuff. Never mind whether I could help them or not. Just understand them as women. And once I started to do that, started treating them just like I treat myself, or anyone else I knew, then I began to be able to help them."

At the time, Pine Street was the only shelter that didn't limit the number of consecutive nights a woman could stay (the smaller women's shelters resorted to limits as the only fair way to give everyone a chance at a warm bed). As a result, the women's unit staff at one point or another saw virtually every woman who used the city's shelters.

Sandy's experience taught her that women used shelters for different reasons than men, that they needed a different atmosphere, and responded to different forms of help. She came to understand that they were seeking safety more than anything else. Many had been through the mental health system, and after being released from state hospitals in the mid-seventies, had been simply forgotten.

"We don't know what they've been through. Those women come here and they do well. Any time that they can stand in line, get up and have their breakfast, follow the routine here — that's pretty tough for some people. The part that we're helping them with here — understanding them, letting them be themselves — no one has ever done."

Some women in the unit were not mentally ill. They were poor;

they were young runaways; some were drug addicts. Sandy saw women older than her own mother and women whose newborns were taken away from them in the first hours of life because they did not have a permanent address. She soon realized that the often impenetrable silence or anger of the women masked the scar tissue of countless wounds, of neglect, abuse, and loss: psychic injuries that no single cure, no alcohol rehabilitation course, could possibly heal.

From the viewpoint of critics, it may have seemed as if her counselors weren't accomplishing much. But with the limited resources she had available — she couldn't afford special programs or separate units for pregnant homeless women, for instance — she was trying to do the one thing she considered fundamental: to earn the trust of the women who came to the shelter.

Sandy saw in Monica Donner the qualities necessary for this task, and it was only a matter of weeks before she asked Monica to take her old place as shift supervisor. For the most part Monica agrees with Sandy on the needs and capabilities of the homeless women who stay at the Inn. Much as they might want to, neither woman shares the assumption of many homeless advocates that their primary job is to get the women out of the shelter and into affordable housing and that this will solve the homeless problem. To the contrary, they believe that a lot of the women they see simply can't make it on their own.

"Not everybody can have an apartment just because they don't have a home," Monica, over time, has come to think.

New staff and outsiders, however, often expect this to be the case. People are so eager to embrace a solution, to "will" homeless people into it, that they will do almost anything in the name of helping them toward that narrowly focused goal. In the process, Monica believes, they overlook the needs and the dignity of the individual.

She calls it "do-goodism." And she knows what it is because she, too, in the beginning, did her share of patronizing, prodding, and pushing.

"Jane Burke," she recalls. "That was one lady I pushed. I don't know whether I pushed right or not because she says two different things to me now. She says, 'I would never have made it through this winter if I weren't in an apartment.' And another, right up front, you know, 'I'm better when I'm around a lot of people. I really get lonely when I'm by myself.' She loves it [her apartment]. Watches TV until three o'clock in the morning, never gets up, never leaves. But she's kind of depressed now. She's very proud of herself with her apartment. But it's a mess. I don't know. Are we doing these people a favor? We wrestle with that."

Monica's years in a religious order have given her a finely honed sensitivity to some of the dynamics underlying charity work. She knows that often the underbelly of altruism is unconscious pride that one is better off, or has the answers, or can solve the problem. Too often those on the receiving end are forced by the hidden terms of altruism into the game of pleasing the care givers, conforming to their solutions, making them believe that their cures are the right ones.

"We've been in it so long that we know that you do no good if you do everything for people. We've already been the saviors of the world," Monica says, referring to her experience of religious orders. "So we know you're only saving yourself when you do that. You're making yourself feel good. So people say, 'Aren't you wonderful? You do all these nice things.' "

It is more difficult but, Sandy and Monica believe, more sound, morally and practically, to help the women achieve their unique potential as individuals. No single solution will work for all homeless women. Monica tries to wait for the appropriate solution to reveal itself, for the initiative to come from the individual woman. Her job, she feels, is to recognize and encourage the change when it begins, not to push women into the superficial trappings of "normalcy." She tries to help prepare those who can take advantage of whatever opportunities exist for them and to be available to them. Once the women have taken steps to achieving greater self-esteem, a financial base, or greater autonomy, she becomes part of a support system that will be there in moments of loneliness as well as celebration.

"When people show that spark that I'm looking for, I'm willing to help them. The more I can just toss the ball back to them, make it easy for them, facilitate it, tell them, why don't you try this? the better. Maybe they didn't think of all their options. But you have to treat them like they're adults! That's the respect that we need to show people. That they're adults. And that they can do for themselves."

This morning, as Monica spots Amanda Daley sitting by herself on a bench in the courtyard, she is worried about the tiny, emaciated woman who has been withdrawn and tearful since she arrived two weeks earlier. Monica knows that Amanda has been staying at St. Paul's, but there hasn't been any mention of her in its log book, so Monica doesn't have any way of knowing if any counselor over there has talked to her.

The only woman Amanda has spoken to is another guest, a Native American woman named Genevieve. Burdened by periodic psychosis, Genevieve, a beautiful woman with high cheekbones and flashing, almost black eyes, has a husband and two children in New Hampshire. For several weeks now she has been completely stable after having received treatment at Boston State Hospital.

On Amanda's second afternoon at the Inn, Monica saw her go up to Genevieve, take a seat next to her on the bench, and begin to talk. They seemed to hit it off immediately, exchanging small talk and impressions of the other guests. For several days they were both too shy to ask the other's name. By now, however, Genevieve sits next to Amanda almost every morning before the lobby clears out, and again in the afternoons while they wait for the St. Paul's van. All the same, the budding friendship seems to have its limits. The two women don't leave the Inn together in the morning. Even if Genevieve becomes Amanda's street companion and a closer friend than she appears to be at this point, she won't be able to meet the many needs Amanda has brought to Pine Street.

Monica walks over to her.

"Amanda," she begins gently, "you know, there are things available to get you back on your feet. Are you interested in the Homeless Welfare Program?"

Amanda hears her, but she doesn't respond.

"If you want," Monica goes on, "you can even sign up for a training program to work with computers."

At this, Amanda lifts her head. "Monica," she tells the nun. "I don't know what I want to do right now."

Monica nods. She doesn't pursue the issue — she's gotten her message across. Now it is up to Amanda. She returns to the building.

Once she is out of sight, Amanda turns back to Genevieve and is about to pick up the conversation that was interrupted by Monica's approach. But Genevieve cuts her off.

"Go in there and explain to her what's going on."

Amanda mulls her friend's unexpected adamancy. She isn't sure she is ready. She's scared. But maybe Genevieve is right. Collecting her thoughts, she stands and makes her way back into the lobby in search of Monica.

Minutes later she finds herself alone in the small office off the lobby. She starts, trying to be brief and calm as she gives the patient counselor an overview of what she's been through in the past five years. Monica sits quietly and listens. But part of the way through, Amanda starts to cry, and then she isn't sure what she is saying, or whether it has any coherence, or if it makes any sense.

Forty-five minutes later, she is finished.

"You're a strong person," Monica remarks.

"Oh yeah." Amanda's sobs are renewed at this. "I'm a strong person. But even strong people up to a point say, wait a minute, why is all this shit going on?"

Monica gently presses her again about looking into welfare, explaining that Amanda is eligible for a monthly check and food stamps. This state policy is new since Amanda was last on the streets.

"Why don't you go down to the Homeless Welfare and get everything started on that?" Monica feels that Amanda needs to start taking some positive steps for herself. She looks up as a volunteer named Marsha comes in, and asks her to accompany Amanda downtown for moral support.

"Sure," Marsha replies. And Amanda agrees.

The late morning finds Amanda and Marsha emerging from the Park Street subway station into the bustle at the tip of Boston Common. Flower vendors, helium balloon merchants, the usual panoply of newspaper hawkers, Hare Krishnas, jugglers, and street musicians mill around them. Not far away the recently regilded dome of the State House glints at the crest of Beacon Hill.

The two women trudge up Tremont Street toward the imposing crescent-shaped plaza opposite City Hall. They pass the Old Granary Burying Ground where Paul Revere and Sam Adams are buried. They swing wide of the doors at the busy Parker House hotel and continue along Cambridge Street. From one side rises the world of the city's court system — Suffolk Superior Court, the Supreme Judicial Court, the Court of Appeals and Municipal Court — and from the other, the world of power — City Hall and the JFK Federal Building. The vast high-rises seem to close in on the human world below, blocking out the sun. They are overwhelming, with all of their windows and myriad offices.

In fact, Amanda and Marsha are lost. Hurrying, harried business people — lawyers, government employees, politicians — stride past them in both directions. The two women stand in the middle of the sidewalk, buffeted by the pedestrian flow, unable to decide what to do. No one stops to offer them help, and they are too intimidated to ask.

Suddenly Amanda turns and recognizes, two blocks away and coming toward them, a man who stays at Pine Street. Marsha sees him at the same time and waves with relief.

"You look lost." He limps over. He is in his late thirties, wearing jeans and a dirty work shirt. "Where to?"

They tell him.

"Come on," he says, and reverses his direction. He escorts them two blocks, then ducks down a back street, coming to the entrance of a small brick building at 43 Hawkins Street. The Overseers of the Public Welfare Building, built in 1924, is now almost entirely obscured by the modern concrete towers around it.

Inside, the lobby is fronted by offices with clouded glass partitions. Benches, many occupied by unemployed men, line the large open area. In the middle, elevated in a small information booth, sits a firm-jawed matron. Marsha walks up to her and explains what they are there for.

"Are you homeless?" The jaws open and snap shut around the question, unnecessarily loud.

Amanda is glad she hasn't come alone.

"No," Marsha replies evenly.

Amanda steps up.

"I am," she whispers.

The woman directs them into the office of an intake worker, who tells Amanda that in order to receive her check, she needs a social security card.

With that, Amanda and Marsha are again outdoors in the maze of government office buildings, this time looking for the Social Security Administration Building. They turn away from the high rises and walk down to the fringe of parking lots, bars, and restaurants on Merrimac Street just outside the Faneuil Hall Marketplace.

This is the last place Amanda expected to find herself today. She is momentarily stunned by the coincidence. Several days ago Jackie's father died. Ever since Amanda has been back at the Inn, her counselor's grief has brought back so many memories of her own of the final days with Thomas. Though she hasn't known how to express it to Jackie, she's felt a special connection to her loss. This morning, she read in the obituary papers while sitting in the courtyard, is the funeral, and it is being handled by the Joseph A. Langone Funeral Home, less than a block from where she is now standing. At this very moment, she realizes, Jackie is sitting inside Langone's, comforting her mother and surrounded by her children and her husband. Amanda can hardly believe it. She was meant to pass by here, it seems, and contribute her support, however silently, to her friend.

Amanda approaches the funeral limousines waiting by the curb, their little black flags flapping from the antennas. It is a far cry from Thomas's last journey, his ashes sent without fanfare to a Rhode Island graveyard. She tiptoes up and peers into the parlor. It is possible to make out figures, but only indistinctly, as in a dream. Silently she conveys her feelings through the glass. Then she turns away, telling Marsha that she couldn't see much of anything through the dim. The two continue on, but for the rest of the morning, her heart is with Jackie.

By the end of their rounds, Amanda has a temporary social security card as well as an officially stamped copy of her birth certificate. And starting today, she'll be getting $41.05 a month from welfare, plus food stamps.

She and Marsha stop for a cup of coffee, then return to Pine Street, where they part company. Amanda wants to walk a bit. She strolls the extra two blocks down Washington Street to Harbor Light, where so many lifetimes ago she met Thomas. Perhaps today it is appropriate, she thinks, to stop in for lunch.

The women's unit lobby is still quiet later in the afternoon when Amanda returns. Joan Norton, the psychiatric nurse, is arriving. Amanda watches her let herself into the clinic. Joan does referral work, making sure that the acute mentally ill guests get services at community mental health centers or, where necessary, sending them to psychiatric hospitals for evaluation or commitment.

Joan's job, and that of her counterparts at three of the city's largest shelters, began the previous March when the Department of Mental Health, in a delayed response to Chapter 450, reorganized its Boston services to implement the "continuity of care" concept originally designed in 1980 by Parker Street's first director, Carol Bower Johnson, and others. This was no accident: in 1985 Johnson had been appointed to the newly created position of coordinator of homeless services for the DMH.

In reorganizing, the department did away with the city's six autonomous community mental health "catchment areas." A single administrative and fiscal unit, Metropolitan Boston Mental Health Services,
was now administered by a single director, reporting directly to the
commissioner of mental health. The director oversaw seven departments: the six community mental health centers (CMHCs) and the
city-wide Homeless Services Unit.

Homeless Services ran the Parker Street Shelter, which by 1986 had
115 beds in three separate locations. In addition, a six-member outreach team had conducted a study of the shelter system to assess the
mental health needs of the homeless. In 1985, partly as a result of
their findings, four psychiatric clinicians, including Joan, were funded
to work directly in the shelters with guests. Joan's job was intended to
complete the circuit of service, from shelter to special psychiatric shelter and long-term counseling at the CMHCs, envisioned by the original planners of Parker Street.

At the same time the Massachusetts Mental Health Center, one of
the city's CMHCs, secured a grant from the National Institute of Mental
Health for a six-bed special inpatient diagnostic unit for homeless
people. The number of beds soon increased to ten. Mass. Mental now
also provides overnight and weekend consultative services to the shelters by phone, to cover emergencies when the psychiatric nurses
aren't available.

This arrangement of services is unique to Boston. The rest of Massachusetts uses a case management system through local CMHCs. But
the numbers of homeless mentally ill in Boston were seen as too great
for such an approach.

On paper the system works in the following way: shelter psych nurses
like Joan evaluate mentally ill guests and refer them to the outreach
team, which reports to Homeless Services. The staff there try to connect the individual with a therapist at a local community mental health
center. Joan relays this information to the guests, and the outreach
team helps to see that people get to their appointments.

Emergency, involuntary hospitalization is a major component of the
system. Hospitalizing their mentally ill guests is one of the most stressful tasks for shelter workers. It is usually initiated when a guest becomes uncontrollable. The procedure, called "pink papering," for the
color of the emergency form, is the sole vehicle by which the shelter
staff can impel psychiatric intervention against a guest's wishes. According to the stringent commitment laws, created in the mid-1960s

as part of deinstitutionalization, a guest has to be either acutely suicidal or acutely homicidal to be committed involuntarily. In the fall of
1986 the Massachusetts legislature, which has responsibility for any
changes in the commitment law, didn't consider as acutely suicidal the
behavior of someone who went barefoot in the winter, didn't eat, and
was prey to brutal beatings, robbery, and sexual assault — as many of
the homeless guests Joan saw every day were.

Pink papering is at best a Band-Aid. It often takes from one to
three hours to obtain, via ambulance, a commitment form from the
outreach team psychiatrist, fill it out, and return it for authorization.
All the while the guest may be attempting to kill himself or another
guest. At any given time only six to ten homeless people in Boston
can be pink papered to Mass. Mental Health's special unit. When these
beds are full, emergency cases can in theory be admitted to one of the
CMHCs, but in reality these facilities are already so drastically overcrowded that often the shelter's only recourse is to turn the guest out
doors.

If a pink papering goes through, a guest is sent to one of the homeless diagnostic beds for ten days and is given a psychiatric exam, a
CAT scan, and a physical. By law a person can be hospitalized involuntarily for only ten days unless a medical team determines that longer-
term hospitalization is necessary, in which case court approval is required. Unless this is granted (and provided there is a "permanent"
bed available) the patient has to be released. If, however, upon admission, the patient agrees to be hospitalized voluntarily, the maximum number of days he can be detained for observation is reduced
to three, and many homeless mentally ill who have been through this
revolving door choose voluntary commitment in order to be released
sooner.

Voluntary treatment takes two forms. The individual can go to one
of the other five CMHCs or be placed in Parker Street.

The psych nurses and shelter staffs believe that the system needs
much fine tuning. Too many of those who need long-term psychiatric
care do not choose treatment once they are hospitalized. Many choose
voluntary committal, check themselves out after three days, and return to the Inn. As a result, Joan sees the same mentally ill people
return night after night, their condition unchanged or worse. It is
virtually impossible to track them.

They are highly resistant to psychiatrists and to the analytic process
and often fail to keep therapy appointments. Mental health profes-

sionals often don't want to deal with them, and the guests know it. As
one clinician candidly confessed to a study team researching psychiatric services for the homeless in 1983, "As a clinician, you don't know
how to deal with these people. There's nothing we can offer them.
They have to tell us what they want. There's no gratification in working with them. They're smelly and retractive. We're not trained to
deal with these problems."[1]

Joan can't blame the guests for any of this. She has gone with them
for outpatient services at some of the most prestigious medical centers
in Boston. "We were shunted from place to place to place to place,"
she says. "I shared the frustration of trying to get services. I could
understand why they're resistant to getting into the system."

The system continues to back up like a bad traffic jam because of
the almost total lack of permanent "supported housing." Boston lags
behind every other community in the state in creating housing for the
deinstitutionalized mentally ill (known as Chapter 689 housing, the
fund that paid for Pine Street's relocation). In the fall of 1986, when
one homeless woman was ready to go into a supported residential
setting, there was no place for her. By the time a place was available,
she had withdrawn again in disappointment, mistrust, and anger.

"The person has to be ready and the bed has to be there," Joan
says. "Timing is everything. And often, it doesn't work out. The person is begging to go, and there is no place to put them, or there is a
place and they are saying, 'I'm not going anywhere. I'm fine and dandy
the way I am.' "

This means that the shelter psych nurses find themselves doing one-
on-one counseling in addition to all their other duties. Joan's caseload
is massive: she and the other psych nurse at Pine Street have to be
available to some six hundred guests on a daily, informal basis.

Divorced and in her fifties, Joan is calm, direct, and honest. Before
coming to Pine Street in 1985, she worked at McLean Hospital in a
pilot after-care program. She also ran a transitional group for patients who were about to leave the hospital for group homes and independent living. At Pine Street she faced the fact that most of the
guests had had very unhappy experiences in the mental health system
to which she had devoted her career.

Amanda's experience with therapy had been traumatic, in the case
of Catholic Charities, and disappointing one other time after that,
when she went to a mental health clinic. Instead of listening to her,
they kept talking at her, telling her to keep her job, try and stick it

out. Now, as she sits in the quiet of the empty lobby, she believes she's found more caring than she ever had in the "real world."

She doesn't know whether to laugh or to blush when she remembers her first conversation with Joan Norton. She was aware of Joan from the very first, both at St. Paul's, where Joan came every Tuesday night for dinner, and in the Inn's lobby. Joan's style is informal. The guests know she is a psych nurse, but she never makes a big deal about it, knowing that many would refuse to say anything to her if they felt she was trying to counsel them.

But if her professional style was informal, her wardrobe, Amanda thought, needed a little toning down. She always wore dresses, pantyhose, and heels, never anything casual. It was intimidating. Amanda suspected that nobody had told her it would be better to dress casually.

One Tuesday night, after a pleasant chat with Joan over dinner, Amanda was sitting on her bed. As Joan moved through the room, stopping here and there at beds to say hello to people, Amanda thought, Here's your big chance. Not since her days with Thomas had she felt such an urge to assert herself.

"Joan," she called out, "can I talk to you for a minute?"

Joan came over and sat down.

"Don't get me wrong or anything," Amanda proceeded, "but have you ever thought about wearing blue-jean skirts and jogging shoes?"

Behind Joan, Amanda could see Genevieve on the next bed bury her face in her hands and begin to moan.

Amanda blundered on. "It would make me feel more comfortable when it comes to talking to you."

"Well, thank you very much," Joan said.

Later, after she'd left, Amanda thought, "Any lady who can sit there on a bed and listen to that, is something."

Now, as Amanda waits for the lobby to fill up with women seeking a bed for the night, Joan comes out of the clinic door and walks over to sit down next to her. Amanda is pleased.

"I hear from Monica Donner that you're having some problems."

Joan suspects that Amanda has been suffering from a personality disorder for years, one that is intensified during bouts of depression.

Amanda nods.

"Would you like some help?"

Amanda jumps at the chance. Joan sets up an appointment for them to talk the next day.

THIRTEEN

Again

AT NIGHT, in the alley entryway to the Pine Street Inn, shadows and whispers and long, slow stares crowd along the periphery. Occasionally laughter veers in, coming from one of the figures who materialize out of the blackness beyond, but otherwise the silence is so heavy that its specters try to avoid breaking it. Only the insane speak without being spoken to, mumbling incessant litanies or crying out in fitful spasms. Around them a dozen or more cigarette butts flare, then die. A speech with no words; a waiting without appearing to; needing, without wanting to.

It is a week into October, and twenty-four-year-old J.T. Lenoch is in the alley tonight too. He braces a laced black army boot against the running board of the Inn's red Chevy van, leans in, and grasps the handles of the enormous soup-filled thermos inside against the floor of the vehicle, testing its weight for reassurance. He paces a few feet, stops, grinds his heel into the silty driveway.

This restless nervousness is a feeling he's not used to. None of them knows what is going to happen out there tonight — not Bill Holmes, who'll be driving, not Chris Black, who'll be on board. Not even Rich Ring, who's been around since Creation. J.T. lights up a Camel, runs his fingers through his unkempt sandy hair, and frowns. What they are about to do has never been done in Boston. They are going to go out into the streets to find the street folks who don't come to the Inn. The van crew will have soup and sandwiches to offer them, as well as a trunkful of sweaters and blankets to improve their prospects for warmth.

The winter before, the city had sent a van out on the coldest nights, rounding people up and running them out to Long Island or down to the intake shelter at City Hospital. But this will be entirely different. J.T. stretches his lanky legs, thrusts his hands into his hip pockets, arches his back, and practices one more time.

"Hi, I'm J.T. We're going to be starting this new thing where we're going to be out, such and such a time. We got some soup. You guys want some? You want some cigarettes?"

He laughs and shakes his head. He sounds like a real moron.

Last winter on February 16 a street alcoholic named Walter Gonzalves froze to death in the doorway of the St. Cloud, an abandoned residential hotel only three blocks from the Inn. Walter had slept at night inside the boarded-up structure for years undisturbed, until renovations had begun to turn it into condominiums. His death made the front page of the next morning's *Boston Globe*. The following day the paper's Metro section featured prominently a report that at least four people had tried to get Walter to go to the Pine Street Inn the night he perished. By the time Gonzalves was buried six days later, he had become something of a *cause célèbre*, representing that painful enigma, the street dweller who refuses to go to a shelter.

Just weeks before, another Boston institution, a homeless man known as Jimmy the Broom, had burned to death in a fire that he'd set to keep himself warm in the drafty depths of a downtown parking garage. Like Gonzalves, James Woods had refused to stay at shelters.

Those who reflected on Jimmy and Walter realized that no kind of assistance existed that the two men might have accepted — and that might, in the end, have enabled them to survive. In a changing city landscape — with fewer and fewer out-of-the-way places for such people to hide from the cold, and a dwindling number of small grocers and merchants on whose generosity people like Jimmy and Walter had once relied — a mobile outreach service was needed to offer food, clothing, and the rudiments of warmth during the coldest weather.

The street deaths in the winter of 1986 stimulated the idea for a rescue van. As the concept evolved at the Pine Street Inn, the van would have a roving all-night team of people experienced in working with shelter guests. The team would circulate throughout the city, stopping to offer street people soup, sandwiches, and, if necessary, transportation to the emergency room. More important, they could prevent accidental deaths like Walter's and Jimmy's by "rescuing" people from inclement weather and bringing them back to the Inn.

The Pine Street Inn Rescue Van was funded by the Department of Public Welfare for a six-month trial period, from October 8, 1986, through April 15, 1987, at a cost of $45,000. Four van workers were recruited from the staff of the men's unit. After consulting with out-reach teams in other cities that operated similar programs, the van team consulted with the real experts, their guests. They attempted to chart a map of the city's secret, provisional havens, dwelling places that were often no larger than the shape of a man. Night after night their goal would be to establish some sense of connection and trust with the most marginal members of the diverse populace known as the homeless.

J.T., the youngest member of the team, had worked as a floor counselor since coming to the Inn eight months earlier. Raised in Iowa and in Madison, Wisconsin, J.T. was one of nine children in a close-knit farm family, where tolerance and interactive skills were requisites to survival. The idea of being part of the van team had excited him from the moment he'd heard about it. He likened the outreach con-cept to learning to walk again — he'd have to discover new ways of relating to homeless people without the security and unspoken ground rules of the Inn to make it easier.

As nine o'clock approaches, the team is ready to go. Bill hurries out the door and hops behind the wheel. The van backs onto Harrison Avenue and noses quickly through the South End. It is an Indian summer evening, and people are lingering on their stoops later than usual tonight. At Mass. Avenue the van turns right, heading for the Back Bay. They pass Symphony Hall and enter the city's student quarter. Northeastern University, the New England Conservatory of music, and Berklee College of Music are all within a block of Sym-phony Hall. Not far away, Boston University sprawls between Ken-more Square and the Charles River. The quiet leisure of the South End, with its black families and young white couples, gives way here to the pulse and display of an outdoor disco. Tonight young people in fluorescent sweat pants or punk black, with variegated hues of hair, idle on the lawn in front of the Christian Science Church or walk on the curb. The mood along this strip is one of youthful confidence and brazen nonconformity. All at once J.T., riding shotgun, thrusts a finger out the window toward the crowd and says quietly to Bill, "There."

Standing on the corner, a man and a woman observe the bohemian tide with amusement. She is in her thirties, J.T. guesses. Her dirty feet are bare on the hazardous pavement. She is wearing only a pair of soiled cutoffs and a cotton T-shirt. Her bleached hair is matted on either side of an approximate, and dark, center part. Ribbons of razor scars run from elbow to wrist. Her face, too, is scarred and swollen with alcohol. But — she senses him watching her and looks up — her eyes are intelligent, watchful. And when she laughs, which she does now, the electricity she transmits almost makes up for the absence of front teeth. Her laughter makes her lovely.

Her companion is tall, square-jawed, and intense. His concentrated gaze doesn't waver, J.T. discovers, after he has stepped out of the van and introduced himself.

"Hi, I'm J.T. We're starting this new thing . . ."

For a split second J.T. searches the sky. "These guys must think I'm crazy," he tells himself. "Or from some Christian group, or Catholic Workers."

"I'm Traveler. And this is Wendy."

Behind him Bill calls out from the driver's seat. He knows Wendy — they go way back. J.T. feels relief flow through him.

"Hey," Wendy calls back, her voice spirited and raspy.

J.T. is sure that Wendy and Traveler are finding this rather humorous, but he can tell their laughter isn't ridicule. Everything seems a little unreal to them, from the giddy but safe footing of love.

"You want some coffee?" J.T. asks.

"Mmm, no. No thanks." Traveler waves the offer away. "You got any cigarettes?"

Beside him, Wendy is a hundred volts of laughter, and as J.T. reaches back in the van, feeling for the carton of Camels, he relaxes. It's going to work, he feels. The night's first encounter is a good omen.

Greyhound had brought her north as soon as St. Pete's let her go. Wendy had rolled into Boston in the summer of 1980 on borrowed cash, borrowed blue jeans, a carton of cigarettes, and $25 in borrowed bills. She returned to the familiar back streets behind the bus station and the Combat Zone with the same old yearning, a slew of new hustles, and a desire to bury her dead.

She had busted wide open the terms of probation intended to keep her straight. Which wasn't such a big deal, she decided. She shouldn't have been charged in the first place. *She* was the one who'd been beaten

up. Was it any wonder she had no respect for the criminal justice
system in this country?

But her ramble northward was about much more than laws and
history. It was about faith — or, more precisely, the loss of it. At some
point, in some jail cell or uncomfortable bed in a detox ward, she'd
lost faith in Papa's idea that an invisible hand would guide her through
pain and out the other side into seasons of pleasure.

She had begun a journal, and in the first entry she recorded the
moment when she'd lost her faith.

Do I Care?

I doubt that I can call this a short story or essay. Nor can I expect
anyone to understand this brief account of one of the many steps toward
my self destruction. Someday I hope to write down the alpha and maybe
the possible omega of it all. Until then, here is the following. Papa told
me a long time ago that life was a circle. And at intervals we had to go
through certain experiences. He said that even though at one interval
the experience or event may be painful, the next could be quite pleasant.

But Pop didn't know that the majority of the stops within my circle
would be extremely painful and fill me with bitterness. Sure, I've had
some good happy times and experiences; but very far and few in between.

My life had always been in shambles since birth. But the cocoon like
world in which I lived, started to crumble at an alarming rate with Papa's death and my divorce from Benjamin. Coincidentally both occurred in the same month. I felt that everything and everyone I loved
or touched would always disappear from my life eventually. I used to
lay in bed at night, often wishing it had been Benjamin who died and
not Pop. It seemed so unfair. A monster lives, and a gentle sensitive
man dies. But what will be, will be, I guess. And the future definitely
wasn't shown for me to see.

I *do* believe life is a circle, and when finally completed comes to only
one end. Death. But little did Papa ever realize that I would jump out've
my particular circle, and try to live in a unique sort of sphere. Even
though deep down I knew that *my* way was doomed, I'm not sure if I
cared or not. That was almost ten years ago and so much more has
happened since. Too much. I should say. I've seen and done things that
many people two and three times older than myself never could fathom.
Or ever believe. Maybe, someday, I'll be able to tell of the past ten years
of horrendous hell and self torture. . . . I have continued to live in
my own destructive and defeated fashion. But do I really care? Tell me.
Do I?

That summer of 1980, Wendy decided she was a free agent, a fugitive from every system that had ever held her. She thought about

this as she trudged away from the grimy Greyhound station, down Arlington Street. She glanced toward the H. J.'s, where seven years earlier, too wide-eyed and innocent to understand, she'd been set up by a pimp. She supposed that being a fugitive meant she was dangerous. It meant that she was anonymous, or ought to be. And that was fine by her.

Her route took her into the South End, where she headed for the park in front of the Church of All Nations. Like Williams Park in St. Pete's, Edgar Helms's church had reverted to a haven for tramps and street folk. Hot in her jeans and leather shoes, Wendy found a place under a tree and lit up a smoke.

Across the way she could see a small circle of men checking her out. Eventually one of them broke away from his buddies and came toward her. He introduced himself as David Lee.

"I was asking who's that Indian broad over there," he said to her.

Twenty-two years her senior, he could have been her father. And he was a Micmac, a member of her father's very tribe.

"What tribe you from?" he asked her.

"Arapaho."

"Never heard of 'em."

She crushed her cigarette under her toe. "Don't feel bad," she told him. "I don't even want to hear about it myself."

He grinned.

"Would you like a drink?"

Okay, she thought. He's not handsome, but he treats me like a lady.

"Sure." She got to her feet. "What Indian doesn't?"

Less than an hour off the bus and into her new life, she'd met the man she'd been looking for, the man she thought she could stay with. And she did, for three years.

She was a good squaw, rustling bedding out of nothing on those frosty autumn nights beneath the highway ramp off Albany Street. Attuned to the exquisitely liberating possibilities that lay in giving herself over to the influence of her quarter-breed blood, Wendy took an Indian name, Suktiliana (Little River) and exchanged tribal marriage vows with her man. She entered into that ancient nomadic culture as deeply and as passionately as she was able to, adopting its roots, its legends, and its history as her own.

She became, in short, an urban Indian. She panhandled, she learned to make tomahawks out of flint from the nearby Blue Hills, and she spent the coldest nights of a full year curled in a tightly wrapped envelope of wool, uncomplaining, high up in the crawlspace above the roofing shop where David occasionally worked with his uncle.

And she drank. One night, she got so drunk that she wandered into the path of an oncoming car. Struck and nearly killed, she wound up in a heavy cast and crutches, her leg held together with pins where the bone had been cracked. She got so drunk that she fought — the encounters cost her her front teeth. And she got so drunk one night, according to shelter lore, that she beat up a man with no arms or legs and stole his wallet.

For this last act of gratuitous violence she was barred from the Pine Street Inn indefinitely. After that she had nowhere to go when David got drunk and mean, except to fall into a snowbank or a culvert somewhere and hope for swift oblivion. That first winter in Boston toughened her more than anything in Florida had.

Then in February, with spring just around the corner, she contracted pneumonia. She and David decided that it was time to get in off the streets. Options were limited. Their only recourse, as David saw it, was the sofa bed in the living room of his mother's one-bedroom apartment in a subsidized housing project for the elderly in Mattapan.

It wasn't long before the streets began to look very good again to Wendy. David's mother was incapacitated as the result of a stroke. Wendy, fresh out of the hospital and still fairly immobile herself, did the housework, food shopping, and the cooking, using money from her welfare check and food stamps. But Mrs. Lee did not approve of Wendy and didn't hesitate to tell her so.

"You must be the biggest lush ever was," Mrs. Lee said to her one day.

"Have you ever taken one look at your son?"

"Well, he sobers up once in a while." Then, after a pause, she mused, "I just don't understand it. He had such a beautiful wife, and three lovely children."

"Alice," Wendy reminded her, "they have been divorced for years!"

To Wendy's relief, the arrangement came to an end when David's nephew escaped from Deer Island prison, and Mrs. Lee insisted that he be allowed to stay with them. Before long, every unit in the elderly complex had been burglarized. A police search uncovered a stockpile of goods in the nephew's closet. Mrs. Lee was evicted.

For another two years the pair shifted on the streets, under the eaves at construction sites, wherever they could find a warm, dry place.

But in time something basic altered between Wendy and David. He had taught her so much that she was grateful for; in a sense, he had given her the life that her father never did or could. But in three years, the acid of frustration, fear, and resentment had eaten away at the tenderness of their relationship. It seemed to happen every time. She'd start out taking care of another emotionally needy person. Together they would end up victims of each other's rage. Drunk, they would abuse each other verbally, claw, strike, bite. There was too much jealous insecurity, too much dependence. In the end it came down to which one of them was physically stronger, and Wendy invariably was the loser.

In the summer of 1983 she got herself sober and went down to stay with her mother, who by this time, with Henry Fayre, had resettled in Mississippi. She remained for three months. Then David wrote to her, enclosing a bus ticket. She came back, but it was over. In December of 1983 she divorced him.

Frankie Flower caught her on the rebound. A red-headed leprechaun of an Irishman who lived upstairs from a tavern on South Broadway, Frankie wanted to be Wendy's daddy. He wanted to play house. And so she tried to be his good girl. Still sober, she got an office job, came home on time, and kept him happy in all the usual ways. But underneath it all, a voice kept telling her that she was twenty-eight years old and washed up. Married three times (she always included Vinnie), divorced twice, widowed once.

One morning in the fall of 1984, with this vision of the void that her life had become, Wendy came to in another treatment center, this one in rural Tennessee. It was a desperate return to the familiar, a last gesture of hope when all else had failed. She'd gone home to Granny, who returned to Tennessee for part of every harvest, a ritual return in preparation for the final rendering.

This time, Wendy had free-fallen until she came to what seemed a starting point and a sanctuary. Her room, the silence of the ward's hallways, and the farmland seen from every window reminded her of the chronic disease hospital where she'd spent so many lonely months as an eleven-year-old. Those recollections restored her to an unexpected inner peace, and on its strength she began to do something that she hadn't done in years. She started writing poetry.

Many of the poems she composed from her hospital bed during

that stay would remain in her head unrecorded, but memorized for future recitation. A few she wrote down. They became a record of her feelings from the time she snapped and left Frankie Flower and Boston, to the limits of her faith that fall in recovery. The first was entitled "A Winter Sorrow."

> As she steps wearily off the bus,
> The winter winds hit her face;
> Work was long today a little much;
> So she hurried down the dark streets to her place.
>
> Entering her room the warmth comforts,
> Putting the coffee pot on she lights a cigarette;
> The loneliness increases the pain;
> But she doesn't allow any tears yet.
>
> She feels the love so desperately needed,
>   will *never* come her way;
> And she wonders continuously how she'll get
>   through another day.
> Can she keep on facing people who have another
>   life to share?
> Can she keep on putting up a front, and
>   *not* show her despair?
>
> She's unable to forget her past nor the pain,
> Realizing that life could never be the same.
> The radio's sad tunes can be heard drifting through her
>   door,
> But little does anyone know she is
>   *no* more.

Two weeks later she described her struggle to remain where she was:

Laying here in the hospital, I've had plenty of time to think and remember. But most of my memories I would gladly like to forget. Even though it was alcohol that got me into the hospital, I sure could go for a big jug of white port wine. At least if I had some booze, I'd be able to drink myself into oblivion and have no pain or haunting memories to torment me.

I'm like a fish out've water being in Tennessee. Waking up each morning to the sounds of roosters crowing, chickens clucking, and hogs grunting. Country life can be confining and a person really has no privacy. Everyone seems to know what you do or don't do.

The loneliness I feel is so overwhelming, it's as if I'm being suffocated. I've no friends here, and I'm very uncomfortable around most of my relatives. People have been nice to me, but I still feel like a sideshow freak. After all, this is the sticks, and you certainly don't find drunks hanging around the street corners here as you do in Boston. The only reason I've been sober for two weeks is because this town of Cory is in a dry county; plus I have no funds to purchase any liquor from a bootlegger.

I miss Boston, the anonymity, the subway, and especially Francis. I belong in a city instead of the boondocks; after all I'm really a street person at heart. Sure it's rough out there in that concrete jungle; and of course the so-called normal, upstanding citizens regard us street people as human garbage. But I know far more loving and caring people who exist on the streets. We each carry the same burden of guilt, anguish, and extreme loneliness. But even as a crowd, our own personal turmoils and inner struggles eat at us with every breath we take. Most of all, we share the sad knowledge of our slow suicide from alcoholism.

The peace of the country soon became the ground for open conflict. Wendy wanted to go back to Boston, but for once, Granny didn't want to let her go. She'd paid Wendy's bus fare out, she argued, and she felt that she had a right to exert her will in her granddaughter's best interest. Wendy's uncle stepped in and convinced his mother that any effort to control her would end in disaster.

I feel like everything and everyone is closing in on me. Worst of all I can't think of a way to escape. Being pulled in so many different directions at the same time is breaking me down. All I want to do is run and hide. It's impossible for me to answer to everyone's demands. Most of all I'm unable to answer my own. My emotions have been stretched to the limit. Is there no end? . . .

I believe my father would understand what I'm going through. At least he hasn't already tried and condemned me like everyone else. I'm probably more like him than my brothers. They've no use for me or our father, nor I for them.

It was almost winter in Boston when she returned. Alone, she ferreted out a safe, dry spot underneath a ramp at the end of a protected alley. In time she made a nice little apartment for herself there, a double-bed mattress on top of heavy packing crates, quilts, lots of reading material, and privacy. She knew everything she needed to about taking care of herself. And with Jake, who lived in his own place farther down the alley, coming by every now and then to check on her, she had all the company she desired.

Now, as she stands on a street corner on a balmy Boston night with Traveler, that seems a long time ago. She can't even remember how she met him. She just wanted someone strong, who wouldn't depend on her too much. Sometimes they talk about getting married. But if Traveler's the smartest s.o.b. on the streets of Boston, he's also the meanest, so she knows that she'll never do it. Whatever else she's messed up in her life, she's gone out of her way to be a good squaw, and she knows that Traveler wouldn't even give her the chance.

By week's end the rescue van crew has discovered a thriving world that until now they've known only from rumors, their own wanderings, and the rare newspaper photo: the subway tunnels and fire escapes that are home every night to those clever enough and desperate enough to escape detection by the subway police and private security guards; the cardboard shelters that go up and come down with the sun alongside the most powerful financial institutions in the city; the loading docks under which the dirt is often warmer than pavement and provides, for maybe three hours at a stretch, the most extended and uninterrupted rest that denizens of this world can get before danger or detection drives them away.

The crew has made the acquaintance of 204 men and 36 women they've never seen before. They've distributed countless Styrofoam cups of soup and inched their way between the dumpsters down narrow public alleys for hours in the middle of the night. In the course of their travels, they've begun to name the alleys and abandoned weed lots where they find the inhabitants of this underground world. One of the primary habitats, an alley that runs the length of the Back Bay between Boylston and Newbury streets, has become Rat Alley. A decrepit parking lot in the South End is known to the folks who sleep there every night as the Rubber Rodeo, and next door to it is Camp Fire Park, an overgrown lot where in warm weather the drifters set up a nightly barbecue. After a week it has become manifest that the preliminary staffing estimates for the van were conservative at best. It is a grueling job.

Holly Ellison has been on duty a few nights now. A low-key young woman with close-cropped sandy hair and serious hazel eyes, Holly graduated from Boston College in 1985 and immediately took a job as a floor counselor at the Inn. She found herself overwhelmed, not by the homeless people who milled past her in the lobby, but by the power that she and her fellow shelter workers wielded over them. Hers was the power, almost literally, of life and death: to throw people outdoors for the night, to enforce curfews for some and make exceptions for others. She'd been dismayed by the shelter's politically motivated decision in the spring of 1986 to close the lobby to "overflow" guests once the weather got warm. In the past, extras and late arrivals had been allowed to sleep on the lobby's benches and floor. But now the Pine Street administrators wanted to pressure the state into providing another large shelter facility.

"Every night we had to ask fifty or sixty men to leave the building and walk down the alley. It was incredibly frustrating," she says.

Holly came to feel that she needed to work in a more equitable relationship with the homeless, and the van seemed to provide the framework that would make this possible. On the street the homeless could choose whether or not they wanted her help.

"This was their turf," Holly reasoned. And within a few short nights, she felt that she'd chosen wisely. "Right away, it felt good for us to reverse that power dynamic."

Two more fill-ins soon joined the team in response to the demanding realities of the job. Both were attracted to the job for reasons similar to Holly's and J. T.'s. Peter Hurley was a veteran of the old Pine Street. A gentle and soft-spoken man of thirty-eight, Hurley became the crew's senior statesman. One of a handful of old-timers who'd remained floor counselors rather than seek promotion to administrative posts, Hurley had witnessed the Inn's growth, the increasing crowds and restrictiveness, and he was burned out. The van offered an opportunity to return to an earlier, more flexible ethos.

Michael Malone was a relative newcomer. When he first arrived at Holy Cross College, he was a scholarship student planning to teach high school Latin and Greek in Chicago. But instead, when he graduated in 1980, he moved to Boston and joined the city's Little Brothers of the Poor program. Little Brothers provide friendship and mixed-age community living for elderly adults in several American cities and abroad. At Little Brothers, Michael became deeply committed to the value of continuity: once a worker adopted an older friend, he or she made a commitment to maintain that relationship for the remainder of the elder person's life.

When Michael arrived at the Inn in 1983 as a fill-in staffer in the men's shower area, he was struck by the total *lack* of continuity in the lives of the homeless and in the shelter system as it was set up. He saw that guests who developed a genuine relationship with a counselor and were helped to find apartments and jobs often needed the counselor's emotional support even more after leaving the shelter. He saw that many guests developed a profound emotional dependence on the shelter. It became the only source of stability in their lives, one they were loathe to give up for a theoretical and lonely autonomy.

For Michael, the opportunity to work one on one with street people outside of the Inn's packed lobbies was irresistible. It would give him the freedom to develop a few deep relationships rather than hundreds of superficial ones.

These complementary motives and philosophies bound the van crew together and made them a bit like rebels with a cause inside the shelter organization. They dressed like the people they met on the street and began to live by their clock, sleeping during the day and riding the empty streets at night. Most important, they accepted as their first principle that they weren't out on the streets to convert anyone to a preference for shelters, but instead to offer what help they could, and to respect the terms of those who asked for it.

They began to establish a nightly rhythm, knowing where to stop when and how long to stay before they wore out their welcome. But they hadn't begun to discover all there is to know about the streets, not by a long shot.

One night, having finished their rounds earlier than usual, Chris slows the van to a crawl along a side street at the foot of Back Bay, while he and J.T. try to decide where to head next. J.T. thinks he hears music coming from the dead end of Rat Alley, midway down the block. They pull up to the curb there and peer down. Shadows, dumpsters, and trucks choke the short delivery area, but now, without a doubt, the sound of easy listening is rising from the depths of the alley.

After searching the dim for several minutes, J.T. nudges Chris. Partly obscured by the bulky vehicles, on an apron of asphalt about halfway in, a middle-aged man with salt and pepper hair is reclining on a lawn chair, reading a magazine and listening to his radio as if he were sprawled in the comfort of a suburban backyard.

He looks up at them and waves.

"This is wild," J.T. whispers to Chris. They decide to investigate.

The man stands as they approach and comes forward, extending his hand with a gentle, proprietary air.

"I'm Jake. What can I do for you?"

The pair introduce themselves. It seems that Jake already knows about them. In fact, Jake seems to know about a lot. He tosses his head toward the back, deeper into the alley, and informs them that he has a few guys staying with him.

J.T. and Chris follow with their eyes. All they can see, except for a rusty five-story-high fire escape, is a rubbish-strewn alcove like so many others that punctuate the alleys in this part of town, where they often find people curled up for the night. But Jake, like a gregarious host, encourages them to explore. Then he goes back to his magazine.

Curious, they oblige. Ahead, the back wall of the alcove meets the side walls of the two abutting brick buildings. It looks like that's all there is. They are about to give up and return to the van when Chris suddenly makes out an opening. In the far right corner, a dark flap of some heavy material serves as an entryway in what now appears to be not a solid wall at all but a massive sheet of mesh-reinforced dry wall that hides yet another space within. The two go up and push back the "door" of wallboard. What they encounter defies description.

Inside, in a space about fifteen by twenty-five feet, below a ceiling that has been painted black and decorated with crudely spray-painted silver stars, two men sit among an assortment of comfortable easy chairs, beds covered with patchwork quilts, wooden side tables, and bookcases full of poetry, philosophy, and accounting texts. They are watching a rerun of "The Honeymooners" on a television set that rests atop a cable spool coffee table. In one corner stands a refrigerator, and beside it, on a wooden shelf, a hot plate, toaster oven, and microwave. J.T. realizes that he is no longer standing on pavement but on vintage rugs.

Jake has sidled in behind them and is grinning. His companions get up at the intrusion and both introduce themselves as Jake, too. Without any challenge from the speechless van team, Jake One proceeds to tell the story of how they came to be here, surviving comfortably off the refuse of the neighborhood, undetected and undisturbed for years now.

He and the red-haired Jake, whose real name, Chris and J.T. learn, is William, had both been thrown out of the old Pine Street Inn one cold, rainy night seven years earlier, for rowdy drunkenness. The buddies had made their way down to the subway grates at the corner of Marlborough Street and Massachusetts Avenue, two blocks from the Charles River, to spend the remaining hours before daylight. It wasn't the first time they'd been shown the door. These veterans of the streets, both in their fifties at the time, knew where to go.

But the next morning they were awakened by a resident of the building at the corner dumping his garbage directly on their heads.

They decided, no more. No more standing in lines for food or for beds. No more waking up and going to bed on someone else's time-table. No more being treated like human refuse. They'd find a place of their own if it was the last thing they did.

They believe that someone must have been looking out for them that morning. In less than an hour they had strolled into this alley. Jake noticed an opening at the top of what was then a solid wall of reinforced wallboard. There was a space behind it; that much was clear. The question was, what?

With William's assistance, he hoisted himself up and dropped be-hind, landing on his feet. He discovered that he'd fallen into a dry room, into which was wafting warmth from an air duct off the adja-cent building.

"All that was here was concrete and four mice," he tells J.T. and Chris.

The two men broke a door into the wallboard wall. Then they roamed the neighborhood alleys, dragging home dishes and reading material, appliances and canned goods, that residents had tossed in their dumpsters. Painstakingly, they made a home for themselves.

Before the bottle redemption bill went into effect in 1983, they had earned their cash in what they call the "slave market," the day labor pools. Now they take in the small amount of money they need by collecting bottles and cans, redeeming the nickel deposits at local li-quor stores, usually in an even trade, spare tin for pint bottles of Cos-sack vodka. One Christmas the art gallery on one side of them gave them a sleeping bag. They allow the two to tap off their electricity. The guys at the fire station on the other side, Engine Company 33, let them use their water hose.

The urban bungalow, Jake One proudly informs J.T. and Chris, has become a way station for anyone who needs a place for the night, a safe harbor of comfort and civility in an otherwise unmitigated cli-matic and social cold.

Now all three men stop talking. Jake One politely nods farewell as he pulls up a red vinyl kitchen chair, straddles it backward, and turns his attention to the tube. "Nightline" has come on, and they want to watch it.

Henceforth the three Jakes' hideaway is known to the van crew as the Penthouse. It becomes one of the regular stops on the overnight tour of duty. One night not long after they first discover it, J.T. and Holly find themselves unexpectedly dropping in on a party there. The guest of honor is none other than Wendy.

"Just for the hell of it," she tells J.T. and Holly, laughing. "Because we needed one."

She is in high spirits. "My own little apartment was just down the way there," she points to the MBTA ramp at the dead end of the alley. "Me and Jake go way back."

J.T. and Holly dispense their sandwiches and soup and prepare to leave the revelers to their celebration, when the Jakes announce that they want to make a donation to the Pine Street Inn. Jake One dips inside the bungalow and emerges holding a large plastic bag. Holly opens it and peers inside. She laughs.

"Thanks, guys."

In the van she passes it to J.T. The sack is full of prescription eye glasses. It was anyone's guess where they'd found them.

◪◪◪◪◪◪◪◪◪◪

FOURTEEN

One Day at a Time

SHORTLY AFTER SEVEN A.M., when the women's unit change-of-shift meeting breaks up, Monica Donner sets out the daily worksheet. Duties are distributed informally. Someone needs to open the cramped clothing room and regulate traffic there so that congestion is minimized, and nobody dallies too long or takes more than the day's change of clothes, the official allotment. Later in the morning someone else has to restock the "cage" and number the night's bed list.

The cage is the nerve center of the unit. Located just inside the lobby's front door, it resembles a warden's post or an observation deck in a state mental hospital. Secured behind a heavy metal mesh screen, an attendant dispenses bed numbers to the women who line up here at four every afternoon. Each woman's name is logged next to the bed number she's given, and whatever valuables she wishes locked up for the night — usually small bills, loose change, and food stamps — are tucked into a small manila envelope and stored in a drawer in the cage until morning.

The bed list is the only record of a guest's stay that the Inn maintains. No identification is required to get a bed, and the women often use aliases. First-time guests, if they are noticed, and if a staff person has time, are asked to fill out a data card, giving their name, age, date of birth, and next of kin to be notified in case of emergency. But these cards are confidential, and information about known guests' whereabouts is rarely given out.

The cage also maintains a small supply of toothbrushes, soap, toothpaste samples, tampons, and sanitary pads. On the narrow window ledge that lets in a bit of natural light sit two cookie tins full of spools of colored thread and stray buttons (but no needles), a statue of the Virgin with a rosary wrapped around her feet, and a shoe box filled with Tylenol, Robitussin, several of the older guests' medications, and stacks of small medicine cups for administering them. A second ledge has been taken over by a beautifully wrapped birthday present for one of the guests from one of her children. For weeks she has refused to open it, but the staff is keeping it there just in case she changes her mind.

What little mail the women receive is sorted and filed in an alphabetized accordion folder stored in the cage. A list of those for whom mail is currently being held is posted on the lobby bulletin board and updated every few days. Finally, a frequently exhausted supply of shopping bags with handles is kept in the cage for anyone who wants one.

The remaining formal staff responsibilities on the seven-to-three shift are two. If any guest needs to go to the hospital, a staffer rides along on the Inn's morning van run to the local hospitals so that the woman feels comfortable in the vehicle, which is usually also transporting a few men. And someone fetches lunch from the kitchen (usually a cup of soup, a piece of bread, and cookies or pastries) for the few guests permitted to stay inside in good weather.

The first hour of the day shift is the busiest. On benches the women are putting on nail polish, reading their horoscopes, smoking cigarettes, or staring into space. No matter how hard the staff tries, with fresh flowers on the windowsills and seasonal decorations on the walls, the lobby never transcends its resemblance to the waiting room of a train station. Scuffed brick-red floor tiles meet concrete walls painted a faded yellow. The low ceilings and narrow windows almost completely occlude the daylight. Divided roughly in half by several structural beams and a metal rail, the lobby was obviously designed to accommodate two separate functions — dining and waiting — in a very constricted space. By the autumn of 1986 the concept has long been obviated by the suffocating overcrowding. Every available bench and bit of floor space is used during the morning and late afternoon peak hours.

From outside, guests enter the sitting area, which consists of six wooden benches arranged in two rows of three at right angles. A dark green metal desk occupies the corner of this section by the barrier rails. From three to seven every afternoon, a staff member sits at the desk and tries to keep order, calling out names on the St. Paul's list when the van arrives out back, and hustling the women who are sleeping at the Inn to the second floor for their showers. Late at night, after the women have gone to bed and the lights have been lowered, a solitary staffer often reads under the glow of the ancient fluorescent lamp, half listening for late-night arrivals or dorm emergencies upstairs.

The back portion of the lobby is taken up by six small picnic tables and benches, all bolted to the floor, with a cafeteria-style serving area to the right. Directly opposite are two doors, one to the nurse's clinic, the other to the clinic director's office. Opening on the third, rear, wall is the clothing room.

Fifty small metal lockers line almost every inch of the lobby's remaining wall space. They rent for a dollar a month and have a five-to-six-month waiting list. There is a bathroom with three toilets, three basins, and mirrors. A pay phone is mounted just inside the front door.

It is almost 7:45 when Ned opens the clothing room and begins calling in the women, one bench at a time. Monica pulls a clipboard off the wall and walks out to the lobby.

"Anyone going to the hospital this morning?"

Obscured by heavy clothing and banks of overstuffed bags are the crutches, casts, and bandaged limbs that bespeak the disastrous consequences of street life to the women's health. Feet and legs, swollen from the miles of walking each day, commonly develop ulcerated sores. With no place to wash cuts or blisters or change dressings, homeless women frequently have to cope with infections. Frostbite, scabies, and lice are almost universal. The lobby, like other crowded places where the women feel safe congregating, is not a healthy place. During the cold months it sounds like a TB ward, there is so much coughing. Cancer and gynecological problems, also not uncommon, are crippling on the street. And all of these health problems are compounded by the exhaustion, malnutrition, stress, and alienation that beset the women as a daily matter of course.

Generally fearful of hospitals and waiting rooms, they neglect themselves. In the past they've been looked upon by the medical profession as lepers. For their part, emergency room staffers grow impatient with the failure of the women to follow treatment plans or take their medicines. The Inn's hospital van is an effort to bridge the gulf of suspicion and fear that divides guests and medical personnel. The driver and a women's unit staffer accompany the guests into the emergency room and alert nurses to their presence before leaving.

But the unit nurse's clinic still does the lion's share of breaking down barriers to decent health care for the women. It is a small but bright room with informational posters taped up on the walls and medical supplies in evidence everywhere. Open from 2:45 to 8 P.M. each day, it is staffed by two nurses who perform basic first aid, relying on the rudiments of emergency room equipment: sterile dressings, topical ointments, bacteriostatic soaps, thermometers, stethoscopes, and over-the-counter medications to get rid of lice and scabies. The nurses clean and dress wounds, soak ulcerated feet, and dispense many round of antacids and Tylenol. They also do routine follow-up checks on problems that, neglected, can lead to more serious complications. They remove sutures, check casts, and dispense plastic bags for keeping casts dry in cold, wet weather. They administer eye drops, test blood pressure, and run urine checks for diabetics.

Joan Norton works out of the clinic, as does a public health nurse who administers TB tests. Twice a week the guests can see a three-member traveling health care team that includes a doctor. This enables them to receive gynecological exams, medical prescriptions, and diagnostic lab tests.

The team, one of three in Boston, is funded by the Robert Wood Johnson Foundation and the state's Department of Public Welfare, part of a nationwide project known as Health Care for the Homeless. The three teams travel to the city's shelters and daytime drop-in centers. Twice a week they perform lab work at a clinic they operate at Boston City Hospital. And they run a twenty-bed respite unit at Shattuck Hospital, where homeless people can recover from surgery, fractures, and long-term ailments.

The fact that the nurse's clinic sees anywhere from twenty-five to thirty-five women every night more than justifies its existence. However, even the best shelter health-care system can't prevent tragedies. Just the week before, Joanne Turner, a spunky sixty-five-year-old black woman, a favorite among the staff, was discovered to have a gangrenous foot when she prepared to take her shower. Doctors at the hospital said they would have to operate. Joanne, who is delusional and goes by three different names, wanted no part of it. Not a single family member could be found to sign a surgery waiver. Finally and, for the shelter staff, painfully, the hospital had to go to court to get permission to amputate the diseased limb. Though saved from fatal infection, Joanne will no longer be able to walk the streets alone or protect herself from assault. She has become completely dependent on the shelter.

By 1986 a new threat had entered the picture: AIDS. Twenty-one homeless people in Boston were diagnosed as having AIDS by late that year. AIDS information posters had been put up all over the Inn. The clinic was dispensing free condoms, and the counselors talked to women about safe sex whenever the subject came up. However, twenty of the twenty-one diagnosed cases had been intravenous drug users. The Inn had no drug prevention or treatment program of any kind, and it wasn't actively connected to drug treatment programs or halfway houses in the community.

Monica looks back into the lobby. How could anyone describe the tedium of the hours spent there on the hard wooden benches, or the acrid air from which no number of floor moppings will eliminate the stench of endless cigarettes. The faces, impassive, heavy-lidded, stare at the talk show blasting from a television in one corner of the room. Only newcomers and crazies speak or move. The rest, awake or sleeping, sit slumped across several seats. They read paperbacks, or remove possessions from their purses and put them back again. There is no place here for privacy, except a place within, if it still exists. No room for growth amid the torpor and the apathy. It is no longer shocking that Polly breaks into erratic, high-pitched screams for her baby boy of sixty years ago or that Helene refuses to change her vomit-covered clothes before being driven over to Boston Detox.

There is a danger in seeing most of this behavior as some form of mental illness. Monica knows that the logical extension of her position — that a woman's motivation for change has to come from within — would condemn most of the women to vegetating in shelters indefinitely unless some external event — marriage, a family member's intervention, or a financial windfall — alters their circumstances. These possibilities are slim at best: many of these women have been sitting in this lobby since it opened six years ago.

But Monica isn't dealing with a logical universe, and she has only a finite number of hours in the day to try and make a dent in the problem. One day at a time. After the women have cleared out at eight-thirty, she will spend the rest of her morning trying to help those who she feels can make it. Today Hope is going to sign up for welfare, and Janice has an appointment at the Brae Lynn apartments downtown.

By nine-thirty the lobby is almost empty, and there is a lull in the activity. Monica is off somewhere in the administrative reaches of the building. This leaves Ned and the shift's other staffer, Linda, to move the stragglers out the door. Once they do, the unit will be fairly tranquil until noon, when one of them will get soup for those women who are staying through the day, and Monica will drive anyone else who's around across town to the Women's Lunch Place.

Ned is leaning against the cage with a copy of the "Free Meal Guide to Downtown Boston" in his hand. Willa, a very thin and uncommunicative middle-aged black woman, had handed it to him on her way out the door. It is covered with her scrawl. He opens it and reads: "See no evil, do no evil!! Is not predjudice But deaf, Dumb & Blind to Niggers only Female Sex Code I.SIG C.G.W. '1987.' " He shakes his head and wanders into the office, where Linda, back from the hospital run, is reviewing the previous shift's log notes. He holds out the flyer for her to read.

The only obvious thing about Willa's ramblings is the unalloyed pain that they express. Linda, like Ned, just shakes her head. She is frustrated enough this morning; Willa's note only fortifies her sense of futility.

When Linda arrived at 6:45 this morning, she discovered that Roberta, a lame homeless woman in her sixties, had been barred. For several weeks Roberta had been claiming that she needed to stay in the lobby all day because she couldn't navigate on her swollen leg and crutches. Several counselors began to feel that Roberta was taking advantage of their sympathy. She was demanding, a drain on the staff, and was doing nothing to help herself. They decided to try a pink papering, hoping that a medical team would order her to be hospitalized.

Linda had argued that they ought to let her stay. Yes, Roberta could be maddeningly infantile and whiny, like many sick elderly people, and yes, it would have been better if she hadn't left the suburban psychiatric hospital where she'd been staying, but all these points had become moot when she arrived at the door of the shelter. In any case Boston City Hospital informed the staff that Roberta wasn't commit-

table under a pink papering. She certainly wasn't endangering anyone else, and since she was staying in the shelter, she wasn't a danger
to herself.

When Linda arrived at work this morning, she learned that Roberta
had been barred under a "placement barring." The rationale was that
being prohibited from returning to the shelter would put her in a
better position to be pink papered. She'd been condemned to the streets
with absolutely no guarantee that she would be committed to a psychiatric ward.

This sort of decision making at the unchecked discretion of staff
dismays Linda. It erodes her belief that the Inn is the open and truly
charitable institution that it purports to be to the outside world. Even
if it *is* the city's largest and most powerful shelter, the Inn isn't really
open to all. It can exact its own cruelties, in the name of good. She
knows that almost everyone on the floor staff feels this tension at one
time or another.

Ned sympathizes. A pianist by training, he began working at the
Inn to support himself while he was a student, aspiring to a career as
an accompanist to vocalists who work in Boston. Though he's left the
Inn several times in the past several years, he's found it hard to stay
away for good. He knows that staff sometime make decisions like this
one because it seems better to do something than to let a guest vegetate one more day. It also meets the staffers' need to believe that they
are doing something useful, forcing individuals, if need be, to make
"progress." The biggest reason for burnout among staff, in his years
of experience, is their feeling that they are merely acting as attendants, custodians.

Linda diverts him from these thoughts now by pointing to a log
note from last night. He leans over and reads: "Janet Small — rumor
amongst the guests is that Janet was shot today by her boyfriend in
Blackstone Park. She's supposedly at BCH." His eye travels down the
page: "Confirmed."

Ned turns on his heel and heads into the cage. He'd intended to
update the mail list, but now he is too depressed to do anything. Dis-
piritedly, he leafs through the contents of the accordion folder. There
are never any personal letters. It's as if all the women have ceased to
exist except as patients at hospitals and clients of the state. He pulls
out doctor's bills, hospital bills, overdue library notices, social security
checks. Never a postcard or a handwritten note. Every envelope is

computer-addressed. The women are completely institutionalized. And because they only become more and more so, he thinks sadly, institutions like Pine Street thrive.

From the other room Linda hears him shout, "I'm bored with poverty!"

"I don't blame you."

Ned looks up, startled. The voice has come from right in front of him, and it is the voice of Hope de Graf Tillotson Powers. Shocking pink and yellow nylon strings wrap the waist of her violet raincoat. She is smiling her upper-crust smile.

Hope has just returned from Brazil, she says. The airlines have lost her luggage. She is expecting it to be delivered this afternoon. In the meantime she is to be taken to sign up for welfare. She tells him all this evenly, then pauses and smiles.

Ned has forgotten. Quickly he enlists a volunteer, Sheila, who's just walked through the door. Minutes later Sheila and Hope are boarding the elevated Orange Line train down the block at Washington Street. En route to the Park Street station, Hope chats amiably and intelligently, attracting the attention of other passengers. A tall, slender Yankee with wispy, graying blond hair and sapphire blue eyes, Hope, with her slight derangements, her colorful nylon waist strings, and her tennis shoes, could easily be one of Boston's loftier eccentric dowagers. She is, even at fifty-five, Sheila gauges, a strikingly beautiful woman.

"I know you're married," Hope says to Sheila, woman to woman. "But don't go anywhere alone. People will think you don't have any friends. That was my big mistake. After the divorce I used to go to Symphony alone."

Hope tells Sheila how, many years earlier, in a wealthy Boston suburb, she had eloped with her first love, much against her parents' wishes. The parents may have been right. When her husband was diagnosed several years later as manic depressive, he turned to alcohol, and Hope was reduced to begging money from her parents. They never let her forget her foolishness, giving her just enough to get by on.

Hope persevered. She bore two children and followed her husband, pursuing job after failed job, to California. By then, Hope recounts, her mother, a servant, and her wealthy aunt had left the country to live in Rio. For a time they tried to convince her to move down too. Her remaining relative in the States, a brother who was a Harvard-trained anthropologist then teaching at the University of Texas, died. Hope began to take office jobs, including one at Cal Tech, because she and her husband needed the money and because she needed something to keep her from losing her mind.

Finally she divorced the man she'd given up her family for and got an apartment. One weekend she let her children use the apartment while she was away. When she returned, the gas and electricity had been shut off, and all the food in the refrigerator was spoiled. Hope just collected her things and left.

The disintegration of her life accelerated over the next two years. She moved into another apartment, and from there to a lodging house. Eventually she returned to Boston and sought shelter at Pine Street.

She concludes her tale ruefully. "That's the rub. I never knew who loved me and who didn't."

By now they have emerged from the subway at Park Street. They cross Tremont and make their way to the Homeless Welfare Office, where they are quickly ushered into a partitioned office. A plump, kind-faced young caseworker, who tells Hope her name is Nancy, motions the two women to chairs on the other side of her metal desk. Hope takes a swift, discreet look at the unadorned walls around Nancy, gives Sheila a secret smile, then looks down at the paperwork weighing in the caseworker's hands. She looks like a child who's just been admonished.

"You want this to be in the name of Tillotson?" the caseworker asks as she begins to fill in Hope's name and vital statistics at the top of a printed form.

"Well, I don't know what the rules are." Hope leans forward earnestly. "I was told by an attorney that to change your name costs two hundred dollars. I was married before. I don't know if I can be Powers or Tillotson.

"It was given to me at birth." She turns to Sheila. "They called me Hope deGraf Tillotson. My mother's name was Mrs. Katherine Tillotson. Mine was Mrs. Hope deGraf Tillotson Powers."

"So," the caseworker patiently resumes, "for the records, the name is Powers?"

"Yes. Social security and everything else . . ."

"Were you born in Boston?"

"Yes. I have . . ." She fumbles in her bag but comes out with nothing.

"Do you have a photo ID?"

"I have a Massachusetts nondriver's license somewhere."

"We're going to give you a photo ID, Hope, so you can cash your checks."

"I lost my ID."

"No, they're going to give you one."

"I have my bank card," she offers. Then, in an aside to Sheila, "At that time, I had all my credentials."

"You don't have any money in the bank right now, do you?"

"I may, or I may not," Hope answers truthfully. "My aunt was sending money to that account, and they might reopen it. I've got to get a lawyer and go there."

"Yeah," the caseworker urges her, gently but firmly. "You should find out how much you have in that account."

"Well, I asked her for enough for an apartment, you know. Just to get me on my feet. My plan is to find a place and then look for a job.

"Yesterday I wanted to see if I'd gotten anything. Or just out of curiosity. To see if I was still a person or something," she laughs. "A man let me in with his bank card, believe it or not, and I put mine in a machine and it came back twice. It said, 'damaged.'" Inside the bank, a teller had informed her that the account was closed.

The caseworker tells Hope that the Welfare Department will pay her first month's rent and security if she is able to find a place to live.

"And the limit would be?" Hope asks.

"There's no limit," the young woman says. "You'd have to make sure you could afford it, after the first month. Right now, your welfare for the month is $82.10. If you get an apartment, it goes up to $283.90. So, say, you find a place for $280. That's great. You'll be able to pay out of your Welfare check. If you find a place for $350, you'll have to keep in mind that you'll have to make up the difference."

"And," Hope muses, "I have to consider whether an employer will hire me."

"Right." The caseworker hands her food stamp vouchers and then gently leads her back to the waiting room and over to a small cubicle where the ID photo equipment is located. Hope sits for her portrait, smiling and holding her chin down slightly in a Lauren Bacall pose.

It is over. She has passed muster, all without pain, confusion, or embarrassment. Effusively thanking the young woman for all her help, Hope marshals every available ounce of inbred good will and exclaims in a burst of heartfelt emotion, "I find that attractive men like fat women best."

Back on Harrison Avenue, the only remaining referral work this morning is to help Janice find an apartment. After nine months in the shelter, her state of mind is abysmal. Once a sweet-faced, creamy-complexioned woman from South Boston, the mother of five grown children, Janice looks bitter now, her once ready smile hardened into indurate grimness. She is too ashamed to ask any of her children for help, or even to reveal to them where she is staying. All day long she sits in the corner of one of the lobby's benches, a neat cardigan buttoned at her throat, still looking every bit the secretary she was for nearly all her working life.

Janice's relationship to Pine Street is special, and tragic. For years, she says, she was one of its receptionists. In the old building, Janice says, she worked right alongside Paul Sullivan, answering the telephone, screening his calls, and trying, whenever possible, to manage the questions herself rather than burden him. During her hours on duty the whole operation relied on her quiet competence.

Then she moved on to other jobs, until the year before this, when she was hospitalized for major stomach surgery. Divorced for years, she'd left her job and had entrusted her accounts and financial affairs to a niece while she was in the hospital. In Janice's absence the young woman charged hundreds of dollars worth of clothing and accessories, then realized, too late, that she would never be able to cover her purchases with real money. By the time Janice was released from the hospital, still weak and unable to fend for herself, her financial affairs were in chaos, virtually beyond repair. She had no job and she'd lost her savings and her apartment. Her only income was a supplementary social security (SSI) check. Janet was one of many homeless women who hadn't benefited from Chapter 450 programs. She had "fallen out" — of her home and her job — without her needs being recognized by those in a position to help. Because she was not on the street with her children, and not seriously mentally ill, Janice could in reality benefit from Chapter 450 only in that she was now eligible for general relief. But the meager check didn't substantially alter her position.

The women's unit has many women like Janice, good, simple women who have worked all their lives and are alone now — single, divorced, or out of touch with their children. It never occurred to these women that in old age their word wouldn't be enough to convince officials that they had been good tenants, good employees, good citizens. It never occured to them that if they didn't horde their receipts and rent checks, they would someday find themselves in poverty, no longer known by neighbors, and having to endure the humiliation of admitting that they had no *proof* of having been stable, responsible human beings.

And this morning, it will happen to Janice all over again, as it does every time she goes into an apartment manager's office looking for a place to live: the polite contempt, the veiled condemnation.

The manager's office of the high-rise apartment complex downtown is pleasant. Glass walls on two sides look into the lobby. Sitting forward on her chair, her hands already slightly moist, gripping the purse perched on her knees, Janice watches a young mother pushing a baby carriage onto the elevator and thinks she could be happy here. The woman behind the office desk has introduced herself as Sister Someone — Janice has already forgotten. The apartments are managed by the Catholic Archdiocese. Now the nun's questions begin.

What was her last address?

She's forgotten.

What was the landlord's name?

She's forgotten.

Then the landlord won't be a suitable reference. Does she have rent checks to prove that she lived there? That might help.

No. Janice tries to explain, again, that she made her checks out to the woman with whom she was living. The other woman had found the apartment in the first place, which is why Janice doesn't remember the landlord's name. But as a result she doesn't have any telephone or utility bills, either.

Why had she moved so frequently?

Before her operation, she had lived in a dangerous neighborhood. The drug activity was frightening to her. Then, one day, her apartment was broken into by young kids, and Janice discovered that her roommate's son was part of the drug ring that was responsible. She felt that she couldn't call the police or press charges because it would only have hurt her relationship with her friend. Her only option was to leave. But how can she explain all this to the sister?

The phone number of her next of kin?

Her children don't know where she is. Her uncle is very old now, and ill. If he has a phone, she can't remember the number.

Sister is sympathetic, but she can't make special exceptions for everyone who comes into her serene, plant-filled office. She informs Janice that she can't be terribly optimistic: she is two hundredth on the waiting list.

Helene inches herself down the sloping tiled corridor off the Emergency Room at City Hospital toward Room Five. She doesn't want to be here. Her body is trembling. She is covered in a cold sweat. She leans against Linda, stopping every foot or so to catch her breath or try to stay the waves of nausea that seize her purged stomach, causing her to double over in pain. She dreads Room Five more than any place on earth.

The sign on the door reads: "Boston City Hospital Drug and Alcohol Triage." At the desk sits Sal LaMarca, assistant coordinator and rehabilitation counselor. He looks up and recognizes Helene. A knowing smile plays briefly across his face.

"Well, hello, Mrs. Stamp."

Helene is a loyal customer at Room Five, one of the regulars.

"Why don't you have a seat down the hall, and we'll get to you in a minute."

Helene isn't someone the system rushes for. If she's been here before, she'll be here again. Most of them are. Thirty-three percent of the people who use the state-funded detox facility account for seventy percent of all admissions. A revolving door.

On paper the detox and halfway-house system looks adequate, if not exemplary. Boston has six fifteen-bed alcohol detox units (there's a total of twelve in the eastern part of the state), available for people who walk into Room Five ready to get sober. They are transported to one of these units when a bed becomes available. There they shower and are given pajamas and a pair of slippers to wear for the duration of their stay. Their clothes are stored in lockers in the rooms. Nurses, on duty twenty-four hours a day, administer Librium (doses vary; the average is 75 milligrams the first day, 50 the second) and check vital signs every two to three hours. Dilantin is administered if a patient goes into withdrawal seizures (a "loading dose" of 1,000 milligrams, then 300 milligrams three times a day on succeeding days). Meals are served three times a day.

After five days, if the patient has withdrawn from the physical effects of addiction, he or she is encouraged into one of the publicly funded twenty-day rehab facilities, then into a six-month halfway house, and finally into a three-quarter-way house, before returning to independent living in mainstream society.

In reality the recovery rate in this, the only system that exists for homeless alcoholics, is abysmal. The vast majority of clients return to the streets after their five days in detox and return to Room Five countless times.

Now Helene will sit in the cramped, dark waiting room down the hall for an unpredictable period of time, perhaps for hours. She will stare at the blood-stained floor, breathe in the overwhelming stench of vomit, and share the filthy wooden bench with the terrifyingly drunk men who will come in during the course of the day. One is already there, curled up in a fetal position on the bench. She will have to take the metal folding chair.

By law Helene must be given a bed, even if the unofficial female quota of twenty percent has been filled. In fact, she may or may not get a bed today. She may end up back at Pine Street. She doesn't know, and she won't know until it happens. So she sits and shakes and waits.

FIFTEEN

☑☑☑☑☑☑☑☑☑☑

The First Song

EARLIER IN THE MORNING Amanda had made her by now customary way to the banks of the Charles. In the chill morning air of Halloween, few gulls flashed across the river's sage surface. The sailboats have long since been removed for the winter. Alone, even in the hand-me-down yellow ski jacket that once belonged to one of Jackie's kids, Amanda shudders. She has been thinking about her mother. Renata is dead.

There was no warning. One day in January 1985, a mere five months after Thomas died, her father called Jane out of the blue and told her that Renata was sick. The next day she was gone. When Amanda heard the news, the first thing that came into her mind was the song the Munchkins sang in *The Wizard of Oz* over the body of the Wicked Witch of the West.

"Ding Dong, the witch is dead," she kept thinking. The tune refused to go away. She started singing it out loud, and soon she couldn't stop. She didn't cry, she didn't feel bad. I'm *glad* the bitch is dead, she told herself.

At the end of the horrible summer of 1978, when her mother and father had intruded upon their Brighton house, they had returned to Sharon. Jack found work again, though at what no one seemed to know. Whatever it was, it didn't meet the mortgage payments. The couple lived in the house that Jack had never completely finished building, without electricity or heat, cooking on the hibachi on the floor.

When a young neighbor down the street learned that the bank was going to foreclose on them, he offered to buy the house at a favorable price, and Jack Daley agreed. At that point the Daleys essentially abandoned their house and all their belongings. They left furniture, bicycles, books, and even crystal glassware behind. It appeared to the new owner that they had simply locked the door on their past life and walked away from it — as Amanda, in time, would do too.

For extended periods over the next several years, neither Amanda nor Jane knew their parents' whereabouts. All they had was a post office box number to which they could address letters. From their best efforts to track them, the daughters surmised that the couple must have moved several times but managed to stay roughly in the same vicinity.

Jack and Renata finally surfaced again, setting up housekeeping just a mile from their former home in a one-room shack that listed by the side of a busily traveled, but sparsely populated route. To the best of anyone's knowledge, the shack had last been occupied by a vagrant, who used to hop the freight trains south when the weather got too cold. The shack had no heat and only cold running water. Its rotting sills and clapboard siding had all but peeled away from the joists. The only repair that Jack and Renata Daley undertook was to coat the exterior with several gallons of bright red enamel paint. After this was done, Renata cut off all contact with the outside world.

No one knows what happened inside those lacquered red walls over the next several years. During that time Amanda saw her mother on only three occasions: at the funerals of two of her grandparents, and at Jane and Bill's wedding in 1983. They had little to say to each other at those events.

The few former neighbors who knew where the couple was living surmised that they sustained themselves on provisions bought at the twenty-four-hour convenience store just down the busy thorough-fare. The only time Renata left the shack was to make regular trips to the town library, three miles away. She never spoke to anyone on these missions. She would walk into the reading room, check out several dozen books, and bring them back when she was finished with them, usually the next week. The library staff used to joke that they'd soon run out of new material for her.

And then, just a few years past sixty, she was dead.

Not only had Jack failed to take out the health insurance that might have covered her medical care while she lived, but he didn't have the life insurance to pay for a casket and a burial plot when she died. He did the only thing he could think of — he went down to the American Legion and begged the money from his drinking buddies.

At the funeral the few friends who showed up, shaken, asked what had happened. Jack told them that Renata had been bedridden for two months, unable most of that time to pass water. One day as Jack was going out, she asked him to help her with the bedpan. He did, and she fell off. Then, Jack told the friends, "She quit. She just gave up."

A suicide? some of them wondered.

"It was suicide to live the way they did all their lives," concluded one neighbor.

"It should have been me," Jack tearily confided to one of their friends from the Museum School days. "She taught me everything I know."

The friend later mused, "You know, I'm inclined to think that it's true. To draw, one learns to see. There was that relation between two artists that was very close."

Nanna was at the funeral, smiling pleasantly and chatting with those around her, as if, one witness observed, she were at a social gathering. Afterward she sent thank-you notes to the people who attended.

Amanda didn't receive a note because she didn't go. She was working at Woolworth's, and the funeral was scheduled for the week of inventory. Amanda wanted to win the customer service award that year. And all she could hear over and over in her head was the Munchkins' jubilant song above the body of the dead witch.

She made her decision. "Fuck the rest of the family," she said. "I'm not going to that bitch's funeral."

It seems to her now, as she watches several fat gray pigeons peck at the pavement, that she's been looking for a mother all her life. It began early, in grade school, with Mrs. Baker, the gym teacher. Then in high school it was Sue, the field hockey coach. There had been Sister Mary Moore. And the mother of one of the other girls. After high school, it was Anna at the Mission Church, then Mary at the Protective. But all of these moms had had something wrong with them. Two of them had died of cancer, one of a heart attack.

The week before, she had described her own mother to Joan Norton. She heard herself portray a mother who had been sick all the time, and weak. A mother who had failed to protect her, who had

stood by during all her father's beatings and drunken rages, overwhelmed by circumstances too powerful for her to counteract. A mother
who had collapsed of a nervous breakdown from which she never
recovered.

Joan hypothesized that Amanda's mother had suffered a serious
postpartum depression after Amanda was born and had never been
treated for it. In those days the social and psychological impact on
women of giving birth didn't receive much attention. At best, a new
mother's depression and mood swings were ignored; at worst, they
became the butt of demeaning jokes. Renata Daley would have had
few resources to turn to for help. Joan explained to Amanda that
severe depression over time *can* lead to periods of psychosis, as appears to have been the case for her mother.

After her mother died, Jane went to the shack and found a large
cardboard box filled with letters that Renata had apparently intended
to send to her daughters, but never had. With them were copies of
the superficial, chatty letters she did send, plus all of the letters the
girls had ever sent her.

For Amanda, the whole truth of her mother's history still remains
shrouded in mystery. The bizarre babbling, the voices, the stalking
around the house naked in front of her children. No one had ever
bothered to explain to her what *had* happened to her mother. Not her
father, not Nanna. Perhaps they couldn't deal with it either and had
decided to ignore it, or make excuses for it, until it was too late.

The last time Amanda had seen her father was several months after
the funeral.

"Papa," she'd screamed at him in a moment of agitation, "the part
that scares me is the fact that Mama was just as nutty as some of the
women are down at Pine Street. The only difference was that she had
a roof over her head."

By then, she'd put two and two together in her mind. Something
had been wrong.

"Jane," she'd say, "Mama killed herself! She starved herself to death.
Something was wrong!"

But Jane refused to listen to such talk. Even Nanna failed her. For
Nanna the story had ended. "Oh, poor Renata died," she would say,
and that was it. For the first time in her life, Amanda saw her grandmother as failing her, incapable, at this critical juncture, of genuine
emotional expression.

But a little warning light had gone off inside. Amanda began doing some genealogical research, and she concluded that every single generation on both sides of her family, going back many years, had had some incidence of mental illness. Every single generation.

Amanda was beginning to realize that what had happened to her mother could very well happen to her. She knew she had to find a way to prevent the one death she was capable of preventing: her own. At some point that year, as she contemplated returning to Pine Street, she said to herself, "If I have a choice in the matter of how my life ends, I'm going to do it. Even if I have to start at the advanced age of thirty-five, I'm going to do it."

It is almost time for lunch. Amanda collects her things and sets out across the footbridge into the busy city streets, to wend her way toward the Women's Lunch Place. This is where she meets up with Genevieve every day now. After lunch they go off together for the rest of the afternoon, sitting and chatting in the park or strolling to Woolworth's downtown. They return to the Inn when it is time to sign up for the St. Paul's van.

The Women's Lunch Place is located in the basement of the Church of the Covenant, just a block from the Public Garden and the Ritz-Carlton Hotel. For most of the street women it is the first choice of lunch programs since it is one of only two (out of sixteen) that cater exclusively to women. The Lunch Place runs on a shoestring, the inspiration of a Mount Holyoke College graduate and ardent feminist named Jane Alexander, who resolutely refuses to compromise on the privacy that her drop-in center affords the women. She doesn't let psychologists, social workers, academics, or members of the media inside the door, convinced that hers is thus the only place in the city where hard-core or severely traumatized street women can feel safe.

Amanda thinks Jane has done an outstanding job in creating a simple but comfortable space, with calico tablecloths and flowers, tasteful posters, and an atmosphere of calm. Of course, you have to like quiche. If you don't, well . . . She likes quiche. But she knows that if she ever gets off the streets again, she won't want to look at another slice of quiche for ten years.

Genevieve is waiting for her at one of the tables. Amanda greets her, drops her knapsack and pulls out the chair across from her friend. Lunch isn't quite ready yet, Genevieve tells her. In the kitchen, Amanda can see, a number of staff members are banging away. Jane's mongrel dog wanders comfortably among the guests.

This is an entire world, Amanda thinks to herself, complete. The city's hidden map of soup kitchens, shelters, and homeless hangouts, and the people she is meeting — all her needs are being met. She has food, clothing, shelter, and more real friendship than she ever knew on "the outside." If she needs medical help, it is here. All the emotions are here as well. Men die on the streets, and women give birth in out-of-the-way abandoned tenements.

Back in 1981, when she first ran away to Pine Street, she didn't bother to maintain ties with former co-workers, acquaintances, or family. How could they understand a world at once so different from, yet so similar to, their own — more similar than they probably want to realize. This time there are few ties left for her, but she has no intention of keeping them anyway.

She can understand why some of the women at Pine Street have been there forever, and will probably stay. You don't have to work or worry about where your next meal is coming from. If you act decently, they'll always let you in. And no one will push you to get out. It beats punching a cash register every day, going home to a cheap apartment in a lousy neighborhood to spend night after night completely alone, staring at the television or being beaten up by some guy.

Amanda is glad she came back. "You're following exactly the same pattern everybody else follows when they've had a childhood like yours," Joan has told her. "You're doing everything perfectly normally."

Here people don't judge her. To the contrary, they encourage her. For instance, her diary. Here at the Lunch Place she would sit alone at a table and write about the previous day's events and her morning's thoughts along the Esplanade. Often she would add to these when she got back to the Inn at the end of the afternoon and was waiting for the St. Paul's van. She never once had to invest in a pen. At least once a week she found one that had been dropped on the pavement.

She was encouraged in her diary writing by Joan and Jackie, to the point that an old ambition of hers, to become a writer, had been rekindled. At the Women's Lunch Place, Jane even went to the trouble of setting up a writing corner with a small table and a typewriter for women who wanted to use it.

Then, in early October, someone had swiped her notebook. She was sitting in the lobby late one afternoon and decided to write down everything that she'd done on October first, the day she signed up for welfare. It had been an important day. But when she looked, she couldn't find it. That was several weeks ago now, and though she's bought another notebook, she still hasn't written in it. Her heart is no longer in keeping a day-to-day diary. She hasn't decided what to do with the notebook.

She is glad that she and Genevieve are solid now. Gen has proved to be a sensible, down-to-earth companion with far more practical experience than Amanda has managed to accrue over the years. Genevieve has a worldliness about her, the mellowing effects of marriage, motherhood, and running a household, that helps to keep the ups and downs of shelter life in perspective. And although she sometimes gets annoyed at Gen's passivity in certain situations, Amanda has come to rely on her common sense.

The most notable problem they have had was over Buff. As far as Amanda is concerned, Buff is a domineering woman with a lot of problems that she isn't dealing with. Part of the way she avoids them is by befriending women she can order around and cling to. Buff has been on the streets for years. She doesn't spend her nights at Pine Street because she's been barred there so often. Usually she finds a bed at Rosie's or one of the smaller shelters, or stays on the streets.

When Amanda arrived at Pine Street, Genevieve was Buff's most constant companion. This lapse in her new friend's judgment Amanda found impossible to understand. Buff, seeing Amanda as a threat, started pressuring Genevieve to move into an apartment with her. The tensions mounted. Amanda thought living with Buff would be terrible for Genevieve and told her so. She knew Buff and her tricks, she told Gen. Furthermore, she thought, Gen should have had more common sense than to get hooked up with Buff to begin with. Amanda wanted Genevieve to drop Buff, but Buff wasn't to be gotten rid of easily.

Genevieve, no doubt baffled and ambivalent about Amanda's demands, never told Buff about them, hoping, perhaps, that Buff would cease to be an issue once Amanda realized that Gen could maintain friendships with both women. After all, there was hardly a graceful way to say, "I'm going to drop you as a friend because I don't think you're suitable." But in Amanda's mind, at least, the shift in alliances was a *fait accompli*. She and Genevieve were becoming exclusive best friends.

Buff hadn't seen it that way. She continued to show up at the Church of the Covenant every day to be with Genevieve. And every day Amanda was furious that Buff couldn't leave Gen alone. Buff was constantly bothering them, a nuisance. It was clear to Amanda that Buff was trying to get Gen back in her fold so that Amanda couldn't be friends with her.

Then two weeks ago on Saturday, the showdown occurred. Buff arrived at the Lunch Place as usual, found Genevieve, and took a seat beside her. Buff was angry that day. She meant business.

"You're impinging on my right to talk to Gen," Buff said accusingly to Amanda.

"Genevieve doesn't want to talk to you," Amanda yelled back, matching her indignation. And she delivered the most wounding salvo she could think of: "Because you stink!"

Buff was silent for a long moment. Such a remark was off limits in this population. Worse, it was probably true. Buff narrowed her eyes and hissed at Amanda, "Why don't you go back to Sharon and grow up?"

"Buff, I already went through that experience once," she retorted. "And I wouldn't care to repeat it."

Amanda looked at Genevieve, who was equally shocked. But Gen didn't reprimand her. She just stood up and gathered her things together, almost as if she needed to get away not just from Buff and her pain, but from Amanda's stinging words. Amanda followed her.

Outside, Genevieve started trudging toward Pine Street. Still she said nothing to criticize Amanda for what had just taken place. She let Amanda walk alongside her. When they reached the Premier Diner, just around the corner from the Inn, she suggested that the two of them stop in for coffee. It was her way, Amanda realized, of declaring her loyalty in the wake of the ugliness. Eagerly, Amanda assented. They were friends now, and if the prized bond had cost them both a bitter moment, that didn't weaken it. To the contrary, nothing, not even Buff Walen, would come between them now.

They haven't seen Buff since that day. But Amanda has heard through the grapevine, not without satisfaction, that Buff still walks up to people at Rosie's and says, "I've been ordered by Genevieve to take a shower."

No, Amanda thinks to herself, coming back to the present, there is no reason for her to move out of the world of the streets — not yet, anyway. Not until having a home can be a positive experience. She realizes that this concept is next to impossible to convey to someone on the outside, someone with a home looking out on those without.

Then an idea dawns on her. She gets up from the table and takes her knapsack over to the writing desk. Opening her notebook, she smoothes down the first page and writes the sentence that has just come into her mind.

"Boston, we are your street people, your homeless."

She stops for a brief moment, reads it over, and adds a second line. "We are your father, your husband, your mother, your wife, your son, your daughter, your run-away teen-ager."

Again she stops and reads. She likes it.

> We are the drug addict, the alcoholic; we have gone through programs of rehabilitation time after time; gone through the pain and frustration of trying to straighten ourselfs out, only to end up homeless! After a while, we too give up and said, "to HELL with it all." Why try to help ourselves only to end up back on the streets, back in the shelters, back in the dope scene, back in the saloons again! It is an endless cycle, a frustrating cycle, to be repeated over and over again!

The thoughts just seem to be flowing with a will of their own.

> We are human beings, with pride, with feelings, with dignity.
> We all share a common problem. We are all "HOMELESS!"
> All we want is a room with four walls; two windows; a floor; a ceiling; and a door with a lock on it, and a key that fits that lock!
> THIS IS ALL WE WANT BOSTON!
> Some place to call our own, some place to call HOME!
> Think about the men and women who have come to regard Pine Street; St. Paul's; Rosie's Place; Harbor Lights; Sancta Maria, Shattuck; and Long Island, as "Home Sweet Home!"
> Think about the men and women who do not get a bed to sleep in at night because all of the beds in all of the shelters are taken for the night! They get to spend the night walking around the city trying to stay out of trouble; trying to stay alive during the winter; hoping to see another day; wondering if today will be like yesterday; wondering if they will still be homeless!
> Ah! Yes! Boston! We are your forgotten, neglected, Homeless society!
> We are your STREET PEOPLE! BOSTON!

She puts down the pen. She is finished. She's never written this way before. When she allows herself to read it through, it is just what she wants to say, and there is more where it came from. She can't wait to show Jackie.

At this thought she bends down to her knapsack, fumbles inside, and finally brings up her wallet. Where photographs would usually be, it is empty. She has destroyed or lost every photograph of her family that she ever had. But she pulls out a smudged square of newsprint, flattens it on her knee, places it beside her own writing, and reads it once more. It is Jackie's father's obituary.

After meditating on the notice for several minutes, she carefully closes her notebook and returns to Genevieve. Lunch is broccoli quiche. The two women eat silently for a few minutes. When they are almost finished, Amanda turns to her friend and tells her, "I've made a decision."

Jackie walks in right on time that afternoon, ready to take the first van run to St. Paul's. Amanda is ready, too, and as soon as the night shift attendant starts calling off names, Amanda is up and running after Jackie, down the back corridor and out the door as fast as her legs can carry her. The sprint takes her breath away.

"Jackie!" She seizes the few remaining seconds that they will have alone. "Will you be my counselor while I'm here?"

The older women turns, looks at her, and smiles. "Sure," she says.

SIXTEEN

The Art of Letting Go

As she does every night now when she comes into the dorm, Amanda observes the fish, which are doing just fine. The two elegantly finned giant goldfish drift toward one another in the twilit tank to one side of the altar. There used to be three, but one was stewed a while back when a guest, thinking that the fish must be cold, raised the thermostat as high as it would go.

Several weeks have passed since Amanda accosted Jackie outside the van, and they haven't had another private conversation since. This is how she wants it. She feels much better just having taken the first step. She intends to move slowly.

And this partly explains why she likes to be among the first to arrive at St. Paul's every night. The pace is still leisurely then. The first women in are able to take their time, drop their bags on their beds, and rest before heading to the nightgown rack and then into the showers.

A few early arrivals usually monopolize the two bathroom sinks, scrubbing out the day's socks and underwear in order to give them optimal drying time on the radiators overnight. Next to the counselor who sits monitoring the showers and giving out bed numbers as the women come in rests a plastic bin freshly restocked every night with sample tampons, sanitary pads, shampoo, soap, conditioner, and mini-deodorant rolls. Occasionally packages of cheap plastic hairbands or gold-tone barrettes are donated by local companies. When the counselor isn't looking, a few women will try to snatch something — a bar of soap, a sample. There is no street value in these items; it is just being able to take something, anything free, that matters. The rest of the women relax and smoke. They talk. The shower room is perhaps the one congregate experience of the day where everyone sets aside their defenses, lets go, and becomes themselves.

Genevieve didn't ride over with Amanda tonight. She won't be coming until later. Yesterday she had a cervical biopsy and she is getting the results of it now. Amanda takes an unoccupied chair in the shower room. She's not ready to bathe yet; she just feels like listening to take her mind off her worry that her friend might have cancer.

Julie is on duty tonight. Wearing surgical gloves, she is checking the women's scalps for lice. Amanda reaches for the bed list. Besides the usual aliases, someone has registered under "I like to have sex with sheep." Another as "Marilyn Not Available." The staff accommodates these whims. And there is still the possibility that "Easy Pain" will show up before the night is out.

Often, now, when Jackie is up here, Amanda will return after dinner and sit with her until it's time to go to bed. It isn't conversation she wants, just the comfort of physical proximity. Simply knowing that Jackie is there, and that some connection has been made, has given her a feeling of confidence.

Amanda gets up and wanders down to the dining room. The other thing that's kept her going has been the dinner group. The group had been evolving before Amanda arrived, and she quickly chose a seat at their table each night. They are five women who, although they go their separate ways during the day, routinely come together for the evening meal. They share the day's events, trade street gossip, and comment on the news as it appears on the television that's turned on midway through dinner. Their table creates a small center of energy and laughter in what would otherwise be a depressingly silent dinner hour, for almost every other woman makes a point of sitting alone at an unoccupied table or, when sharing a table is inevitable, of seating herself as far as possible from another guest to avoid conversation.

Dinner tonight is chili, one of the staples, heavily spiced and heavy on beans. The dinners aren't bad: chicken, veal, Salisbury steak. And lots of breads. The very worst they can expect is sandwiches and soup. Fruit comes in about once a week. Salads are a rarer commodity. But there is no end to the desserts. Slightly mashed cakes, pies, cases of cookies, and day-old doughnuts. All of the women complain about putting on weight and about the high-sugar diet that keeps them at low energy and subject to wild mood swings throughout the day.

Now the other members of the group begin to float in, fresh from the showers. Lucky sits and empties the contents of her purse at the other end of the table. Amanda watches oranges, batteries, and a leftover eggplant parmesan pressed between slices of bread emerge as Lucky searches for her Winston Lights and her lighter.

In many respects, Lucky, a petite Wampanoag Indian, is the most intelligent and quick-witted of the group. Her jet-black hair is always perfectly coifed in a French twist. She dresses in tailored pantsuits and well-fitting shoes, and she speaks in a fluid, mellow voice that always conveys perfect dignity and authority.

Lucky tells of being a twin, born on a Cape Cod reservation not far from the Kennedy compound in Hyannis. Her mother died in childbirth, along with her twin brother. As a result, Lucky was raised alone by her grandmother, who implanted in her imagination forever the conviction that the circumstances of her birth had destined her to become "something special." From her grandmother she learned how to raise and work with flowers, ride horses bareback, and swim naked in the ice-cold ocean waters. She married at thirteen and bore two children, who in turn have had many children of their own.

But her grandmother's prediction eluded her. One New Year's Eve after his shift ended, her husband, a police officer, was on his way home to take her out dancing when he was shot dead at point-blank range by an eleven-year-old he was trying to prevent from breaking into a car.

"So you see, honey," she'd say to Amanda whenever the subject came up, "that's why I don't like the holidays."

Now Lucky lives in the shelters and leads a quiet existence, going out to day labor jobs and maintaining a low-level drinking habit.

Behind her comes Alice, who sits down with a plateful of food that will never put a pound on her rail-thin frame, no matter how much she eats.

"Boy, am I tired." Alice rests her head against her arm and immediately forgets about her plate. When Alice is tired, her backwoods Arkansas accent is so thick that she becomes almost unintelligible. Alice has an ineffable sweetness about her. Sometimes she brings an embroidery project home from work to keep her hands busy in the evenings. Yet in spite of Alice's ready laugh, Amanda knows, there is much pain in her life. As far as Amanda can see, Alice's husband has completely ruined any chance she might have had for happiness. He is a chronic alcoholic who lives in the Pine Street men's unit. For seventeen years Alice has allowed him to follow her, sponge off her earnings, hang outside her places of work, and be such a nuisance that she is constantly getting fired because of him. Time and again they have traveled from one state to another, one job to the next, one shelter to the next.

But she loves him, and she believes he'll fall apart without her. So she stays, though by now married life for Alice consists of a one-night stand once a month at a roadside motel that she pays for out of her hard-won earnings.

Colette Richards is the last of her friends to make it to the table. She comes billowing over, a plate of chili held ahead of her vast, three-hundred-pound frame. Colette never speaks above a rasping, almost incomprehensible whisper. She loves to draw, and comes alive whenever one of the staff pulls out the few art supplies that are stacked in a corner by the kitchen. Then Colette becomes completely immersed, creating drawings of primitive figures, animals, and trees, calling counselors over to see her work, exuberant in a way she seems to express only through her eyes, which gleam fiercely.

Amanda learned from Genevieve that Colette was abused by her husband for many years. She tolerated it until the day she came home and discovered him abusing their daughter. She rushed to stop him, and in the ensuing beating, he stepped on her throat and crushed her vocal chords.

Genevieve and Amanda complete the group.

Julie has come down from the showers to get something to eat, and she joins them.

"So are you going down to the Cape to see your boyfriend this weekend, Lucky?" she asks.

Lucky laughs. "You bet!"

Lucky takes the Plymouth-Brockton bus to Cape Cod every weekend, and every Monday night she comes back full of tales about riding horseback in the open country. Lucky swears she is forty, but she is probably closer to fifty-five. Tonight her back hurts from standing all day at the cosmetic factory where she works. She starts to complain about her aches and pains, but Julie cuts her off.

"When you get on the horse, they all go away," she teases.

"Both horses," Lucky quips back, "if you'll pardon the expression!"

Amanda laughs and feels herself begin to relax.

Tonight massive bunches of flowers stand in buckets on a table near the kitchen door. They've come in from one of the local flower markets late in the day. Julie points them out to Lucky, and instantly Lucky, wearing a bathrobe that is far too long for her, is on her feet, examining them. With able hands, she begins to separate the flowers.

"We need vases, Julie dear," she calls back over her shoulder. "And newspaper. I don't want to get the tablecloths wet."

Julie obliges. She goes into the kitchen and emerges with a half-dozen jars, enough for almost all the tables.

"This baby's breath is lovely, really lovely," Lucky muses, handling it deftly. With expert fingers she begins to cut the stalks of the carnations and mums, placing them in the jars and surrounding them with coronas of baby's breath, keeping up a steady banter with anyone who passes by.

Soon her first floral arrangement is completed. Amanda thinks it could easily win a ribbon in a flower show, and as Lucky brings it to the middle of the room, holding it in front of her to display it to the group, Amanda tells her so.

With mock majesty, Lucky sweeps the train of her long tattered robe behind her. Holding the arrangement above her head, she smiles and slides down into a deep curtsy of acknowledgment. The room breaks into applause.

After the group disbands for the evening, Amanda remains in the dining room thinking about Jackie.

The unusual thing about Jackie as a figure in Amanda's life is her normalcy. She's been married, she has kids. She's not dealing with any major problems in her life. She is just a very nice, normal, motherly, warm, caring woman with lots of love to give. With Jackie it's there for the asking.

When she came back to the shelter, Amanda felt, it was easy to pick up their friendship again and dust it off. Even in little ways, the way Jackie keeps tabs on how well she's doing on gaining weight, for instance, or reminds her to dress warmly, Jackie lets her know that she cares.

Jackie is the oldest member of the staff by a good twenty years, a long-time Pine Streeter who goes back to the days of Paul Sullivan. The depth of her combined personal and institutional experience gives her an unmatched authority with the women. Conversational and highly practical, profane and frank, Jackie talks and smokes and stitches in the shower room exactly as she does in her own kitchen.

Jackie is a woman's woman, fluent in children and men and sex and custody rights. She treats the women in her care as if they are all in it together, as equals, because she basically believes that they are.

Jackie knows that motherhood, love, and loss don't discriminate among class or advantage, and that even homeless women — perhaps especially — need to be reminded of the ways in which their mothers and grandmothers created *their* domestic worlds and how they too might, if they had the opportunities to do so. With unconscious ease she tries to make that world real to the women in her conversation.

"You won't believe what my daughter did this morning." She'll begin griping, comparing notes, or offering advice, drawing her auditors out, probing, as she would with a friend, sometimes asking their advice.

Or she'll laugh in her smoky voice, amused at herself. "Shit," she'll bark, "I'll never get this needlework done in time. It looks like a piece of garbage. Jesus!"

By her own estimate, she can be bossy and nosy and bitchy; she doesn't take any ragtime, and she can spot a fake a mile away. But it is perhaps her ability to suspend judgment and simply listen that draws so many of the women to her.

Now Jordan Green wanders in, the first off the van of women that Rosie's Place sends over every night after their beds are filled up.

"I was raped again," Jordan confides to Jackie. She sits down on a folding chair. Jordan, a frequent guest at St. Paul's, is mildly retarded. "My father raped me. My sister's boyfriend raped me. And then, I was — You know the Northampton T stop? The sub shop there? Well, he grabbed my mouth. In the alley there.

"It's not fair, me retarded, handicapped, and all." She pushes a handful of papers at Jackie. "I had to arrange an adoption, see?"

Jackie looks them over. They are papers for the abortion Jordan underwent the day before at Boston City Hospital. This is the sort of thing that gets to Jackie. Her philosophy about homeless women is entirely different from Monica Donner's. When rape and abuse, discrimination and poverty are *the* recurring realities for the women who come through the door, she doesn't believe in just waiting for the spark of motivation to appear.

"These women are not going to show a ray of hope unless it's pulled out of them," she says. "They've been hurt so many times. They're not going to come in here all enthusiastic, and say, 'Here, I'm here! Gimme money! Gimme a job!' They're not going to do that! They're withdrawn. You need to really probe, and find out what you can do for them. It may not be housing. It may not be a job. But there may be something."

Jackie tries to just listen.

"Another thing I always let them know is that I'm not comfortable saying to a woman who could be my mother's age, 'You've got to go to bed. You've got to take a shower.' Unfortunately, we run a large shelter, and the only way you can possibly run it effectively is by having rules. Like the nine o'clock bedtime. I let them know it's because you have to get up so early in the morning, and we can't leave the TV running when there are other people who get up and work. I want them to know that they're human beings, as far as I'm concerned. It's very hard. It's very hard on the women."

Hope de Graf Tillotson Powers is among the late-arriving guests. Tonight she is wearing gray slacks and a costly-looking brown cashmere sweater. But more notable, to Jackie's seasoned eye, is her air of fragile melancholy. Hope holds herself cautiously, as if she's afraid that something inside may break.

Collapsing heavily on one of the vacant chairs, she remarks to Jackie, "I love your loafers." Then she sighs. "I've been thinking about going back to loafers myself. So feminine on a woman's foot. Tell me, where do you prefer to buy yours?"

Jackie mentions a well-known shoe store chain, and Hope, beginning to get her emotional bearings again, moves on to other topics. She's making an effort, trying to keep her smile. She had her tuberculosis test this afternoon, she tells Jackie. Then she pauses to admire Jackie's complexion.

"I don't wear any makeup," she allows. "But I bought some purple lipstick and polish today." She extends the tips of her tinted digits and muses, "Just to do something outrageous."

Jackie can see: Hope's nails radiate a hideous iridescent violet.

"In this life, you have to amuse yourself," Hope asserts as she admires her handiwork. "I think it's a characteristic of Bostonians, don't you? To be slightly outrageous?"

Jackie is somewhat preoccupied for a moment, trying to figure out the piecing design on a panel of the baby quilt she is stitching, while she hears Hope begin to reminisce about the days when she used to patronize jazz clubs.

"My favorite time to hear sets used to be around midnight." Her chin rests against the heel of her hand, braced on the chair's writing surface, as she says dreamily, "The players were always relaxed then, and playing to an almost empty house. It was when they were at their best. I loved it." A far-away expression has entered her eyes.

Jackie looks up and smiles sadly. She tries to imagine all that Hope has lost. She thinks about Jordan, who's just gone through an abortion without even knowing it.

In the course of Jackie's reflections, Genevieve has managed to drift right past her and into the dorm without having been seen. Amanda, who has been mentally holding her breath in the dining room, waiting to see her friend's face, spots her and waves.

Genevieve floats in and sits down, but says nothing. Amanda can feel a knot forming in the pit of her stomach. Gen's eyes, burning, are turned inward. As Amanda watches, a strange light seems to go out in them. Then she just looks dull and dazed. She lifts her head and gazes at Amanda as if only just realizing she is there.

"Oh. Hi, Mandie."

Seeing Genevieve enter the room, Tracy has come over. A mean-spirited young woman who claims to have graduated from Wellesley College and who sells newspapers on street corners, she sits down and studies Genevieve for several minutes. Then in a loud voice she says, "Genevieve, you're getting so fat around your middle."

Genevieve answers, almost in a whisper, "I know."

"Are you using Librium?" Tracy is still almost yelling.

"Well, I am, but what does that have to do with it?"

It is obvious to Amanda that Tracy has some cruelty in mind, but she can't see a way to prevent it.

"Sodium," Tracy replies conclusively. "I don't take it anymore, because the sodium breaks down and forces me to retain fluids."

Genevieve doesn't answer.

"But, Genevieve," she wheedles, "it's just around your middle. Your arms are thin, and your legs are thin. It's almost as if you have a tumor in your middle somewhere."

Amanda pushes away from the table and runs out of the room. After trying the showers, she finds Jackie in the dim office, smoking and writing a note in the log by the soft light of the desk lamp.

"I've come to turn in my valuables." Amanda says. She begins to pull out her bills, change, and food stamps. Jackie obliges. She slides them into one of the usual small manila envelopes and records the amount on a small ticket. Then she passes it over to Amanda, who has remained standing beside the desk, to sign. The counselor tucks the envelope into the huge safe behind her. Too heavy to move, a leftover from the days when the office was the church sacristy, the safe now holds buttons, threads, the night's valuables, stacks of old memos, scarves, and plastic medicine cups.

Amanda had made no motion to withdraw, and now Jackie watches her expectantly.

Falteringly, she begins. "Can I talk to you?"

Amanda is afraid she will cry. She doesn't want to.

"Sure." Jackie motions. "Have a seat."

She puts her arms around Amanda and lets her know that everything is okay. With these words of encouragement, for the next hour Amanda tells her about her life, everything she can think of — about her father, about the dirt pile, about growing up in Sharon, about running away from home, the days and nights with Thomas, her mother's suicide, the closeness she'd felt to Nanna, and the sudden distance.

Jackie just listens. Long before this, she had begun formulating a plan for Amanda. She doesn't believe that the shelter was Amanda's only option, as it is for many of the women who are there. But it is the one she chose. From the beginning Jackie has tried to show Amanda that she is interested in the fact that Amanda came back and that she wants to help her get out, so there won't be another repeat performance.

Jackie knows that Amanda's sharing her grief and her feelings, as she is now, is a necessary first step if Jackie is really going to be able to help her. She's heard far worse tales than the one Amanda is pouring out. But she knows that Amanda needs desperately to talk to someone, that she craves attention and affection, perhaps insatiably. Jackie knows, too, that she has to be careful not to foster too much dependence. But that problem can be dealt with down the road. Right now Amanda needs affirmation and mothering.

Gently the counselor urges, "Why don't you go to bed now? We'll talk again tomorrow night."

Amanda nods, says goodnight and leaves the office. She feels that she has found what she's been looking for. She's taken a step closer to home. In bed, she lies for several minutes trying to fall asleep, but it is useless. She is too alert. She sits up. In the darkness she reaches into her knapsack and feels for her notebook. She pulls it out and tiptoes over to the altar, sits down at the desk, and remains there in the dark for what seems a long time. Then she turns on the lamp, opens the book, and begins to write.

> Here are you at the Pine Street Inn, homeless, asking yourself, over and over again, "What am I doing here? Why is this happening to me? What did I do wrong, to end up here, of all places?" . . . You sit there, on a bench, sharing it with three or four other women, staring at other women as they walk by, sit down, only to get up again. You meet one counselor after another, in rapid succession.
>
> After a while, though, you can't even remember whose name goes with which face. The images become blurry after awhile.
>
> You desperately want to sit there and cry very hard. You force yourself to hold your tears back, to wait until later.
>
> Your stubborn Irish pride will not allow you to let the counselors, or, the other women know that you are scared stiff, you want to cry, that you are upset about what is going on in your life. . . .
>
> Finally you get to the point where you can walk up to her, one night, and say, "Could I talk to you for a minute, please?" So she will sit down with you where ever you feel comfortable. She will light up a cigarette and wait for you to start to talk. She will listen to you intently, listening to what you are saying, asking an occasional question, or, making an occasional comment. And all the time, her warm, friendly, brown eyes are watching your face intently, seeing the pain in your eyes, the expressions and emotions that all say, "I need a Friend," as they fly across your face.
>
> While you are talking to her, every once in a great while, you look down at your hands, or, at the wall, until you regain your composure, steady your voice, until you can speak normally again.
>
> She knows, now, without being told, that you are finally ready and willing to trust her. That you want her as a FRIEND.

Now, across the altar, she can see the glow of the fish tank, whose occupants continue to drift back and forth in their contained and exposed beauty. Sometimes they meet each other, but more often they pass in the murk of perpetual night.

Amanda is ready to go to bed. Somewhere in the room someone is screaming in her sleep. Someone else is crying. Somewhere two women are making love, and the strangers who are holding one another briefly against a violent and loveless world will soon be cast back into the separate state of neediness that they all share. The darkness prevails and grows silent.

SEVENTEEN

Trust and Friendship

NOVEMBER HAS SLIPPED quietly into December, and, much to her amazement, Amanda is almost happy. Genevieve's scare about cancer turned out to be just that. At least for now everything is benign.

The two friends still spend every afternoon together, but the focus of Amanda's life has shifted. Seeing Jackie has become the high point of her day. The duration and intensity of her conversations with the counselor have dropped off since that first long one and several heart-to-hearts during November, late at night in the office when she went in with her valuables, but Jackie has become her mental and emotional fixed point. If she's going to make it through this experience, and she believes now that she will, it will be because of this special woman.

As she moves through her days, she makes a mental note of every incident that happens to her, even the least significant, to tell Jackie about when she returns at night to St. Paul's. Sometimes she stops at the shower room when Jackie works that detail. Sometimes they talk over dinner. Amanda doesn't get much time with her — ten minutes here and there. But it isn't the quantity that matters. Jackie genuinely seems to care. If Amanda has a disagreement with another woman, if she needs advice on how to handle a sticky situation with Genevieve, she turns to Jackie. When Jackie gives her advice, she follows it to the letter.

By now her days are fairly prescribed. When she isn't worrying about getting to the Lunch Place at a certain time, she is figuring out the best route to Woolworth's by way of Welfare.

Amanda now has her own bed at the shelter and wears the same nightgown every night. Bed 50, tucked away in the farthest corner of the room, matters to her more than any other physical aspect of her circumstances. Once or twice in the beginning, she'd had to take a bed in the middle of the room, and she hadn't slept all night. Lost in the crowd, with less than two feet between her and the next person, she'd felt too vulnerable. Having the same bed to return to every night matters. From bed 50 she can keep her eye on the shower room door, the office door, and the dining room door, as well as on all the other beds, all at the same time.

One chilly, rainy afternoon not long ago, she'd come into the dorm, dropped her things, and trudged off in wet sneakers to find Jackie, who was sitting in the dining room warming herself with a cup of tea. She sat down, and the two of them talked until Jackie had to go start the showers.

"Oh," the counselor casually remarked on her way out. "There's a nightgown for you downstairs. Small. It doesn't have 'St. Paul's' written on the back of it."

Amanda ran out to the rack and flipped through the hanging gowns. She found several brand-new ones that didn't have any marks on them. From these she chose one with full sleeves, a ruffled hem, and blue flowers spilling all over it in a delicate ribbon design. It was more splendid than any Christmas present she had ever been given. She loved it.

Running into the showers, she held it up.

"Yep," Jackie said. "That's the one."

Amanda dropped into the nearest stall and put it on over her clothes. Emerging, she waited to see Jackie's expression of satisfaction, then rushed over and gave her a hug.

"Thank you!" she said. "Very much!"

Every night now at lights out Amanda finds Jackie, to give her a goodnight kiss before going off to bed.

Amanda has written six essays in the month since she composed her first one. All of them are about homelessness. She's described what it feels like to wait in line, to approach a counselor. She's tried to put into words the raw pain of the first hours in a shelter for homeless people.

These days, when she isn't writing, she is observing the environment around her, watching other homeless people on the streets, collecting ideas for new pieces. The hours and days have begun to speed by in this way. Some afternoons there isn't even enough time to curl up on one of the benches and finish her observation notes before the van arrives.

The child's desk on the altar has become almost her exclusive domain. After dinner, if Jackie is busy, she'll sit down, flick on the light, and open her notebook. When she is writing, she doesn't associate with the other guests. Her writing sets her apart. What matters to her is the staff's reactions, comments, and encouragement to her writing.

On Thanksgiving Day, just a few weeks back, when a reporter from the *Boston Herald* came to the Inn to cover the parade of city and church officials who traditionally put in an appearance on that day, she'd handed him a copy of what she considered her best piece thus far. She'd composed it on the Esplanade the Sunday morning before Thanksgiving. It was entitled "Street Life."

> We, who stay at the Pine Street Inn, end our days, by lining up for beds.
>
> At 4:00 p.m., everyone is on the edge of their seats. When one of the counselors calls out "St. Paul's!" there is a mad rush to be one of the first eight people in line for the first van shuttle run to St. Paul's. When you get on that first van run you get a bigger selection of nightgowns, pajamas, and bathrobes, to pick from, your favorite thongs are still in the bucket. You take a quiet shower, eat a peaceful and relaxing dinner, and then spend the rest of the evening, resting.
>
> Sometimes, usually on a Saturday or Sunday evening, either Jackie or Julie, sometimes, both of them, will bring their quilting projects to the table and work on them while they are talking to us all. Sometimes I join in the conversation, or read, or I'll write. It helps me to forget about the fact that I am homeless.
>
> Think back to the last time you made a new friend. Think about everything you have in common with each other. You live in the same city. You might even work in the same company, work in the same department, and have the same boss. That person can be an acquaintance, or, be a real friend. If you don't like that person, you don't have to continue the relationship.
>
> Try making friends with another woman in a shelter. You are both homeless. Chances are pretty good, one of you comes from another city and state. You come from different walks of life. Since you are new to shelter life, and don't know any better, you make friends with the first woman who comes up to you, and says "Hi!" You later find out, the hard way, that she was using you. She didn't want to be friends with you. She has problems. She doesn't want to deal with those problems, either.
>
> And chances are, unless you are very lucky, you will get hurt, badly,

a couple more times, before you find a true friend. In the mean time, you will be in a very vulnerable position. You will end up being more cautious about getting to know, making, and being friends with another woman.

There is a homeless welfare program set up for the men and women who stay in the shelters, or survive on the streets. The client gets $82.10 a month. That gets split into two checks, $41.05 per check, every two weeks. We get medicaid to pay for any doctor or hospital bills in case we need medical attention. For those of us who qualify, there are food stamps to supplement the diet we get fed staying in the shelters, or, living on the streets.

You have no idea how important that check makes us feel. It's a check! It's got our name on it! We can go in a bank and cash it. We can spend that money in any way we want. The money belongs to us. We can go to the movies on a rainy day. We can go into a restaurant, sit down, and get waited on, like normal people.

You have absolutely no idea how much better a homeless person feels about themselves when they can pull their wallet out of their back pocket, look inside it, and see a couple of bills in it, especially when that wallet has been empty for a very long time.

For those of us who want to work, there are companies who hire us for day labor. It helps get your mind off the fact that you are homeless, for a while. We get paid $25.00 a day. They ask a person what kind of work he or she prefers. Then they drive us to all the companies that are looking for help.

If you like working for a company and they have openings, all you do is fill out an application: the agency gives you a reference, and you start working for the company on a full time basis. Then after you've saved a few pay checks, you can get a room some place and get out of the shelters.

The counselors, the men and women who deal with us on a day to day basis never get any recognition from any one, including us.

We dump our fears, worries, and sorrows on them. We scream and swear at them. We are rude to them. We refuse to listen to them knowing all along they are right and we are wrong. We yell at them, and they listen to us, knowing we need to let off steam, hoping we will not take out our frustrations on another guest.

These men and women don't give up on us very easily. No matter how often we feel like giving up, they are there, giving us encouragement. If it's needed, we may even get a good, hard kick on the butt, in the figurative sense.

They try to help one of us, only to have that man or woman turn on them and reject them. But the counselor will still respect the homeless person's pride and dignity, back off, and give that person some space. But if, at some point in the future, that person needs vital help immediately, that counselor will be there too, pitching in, helping in every way he or she can, until that person is okay again.

There they are, five days a week, two days off for their weekend, talking to us, listening to us, being kind to us, and caring about us.

Ladies and Gentlemen, Take a Well-Earned Bow!

By now, of course, I can almost hear you saying to yourself, "That doesn't sound too bad at all. No wonder I keep seeing the same bums, the same ladies with those paper bags year in and year out. No wonder they don't feel like doing anything. They don't have to work, buy food, clothes, and they don't have to pay rent, either! Hey, that's some life they've got."

Well, I'd like to see you come down to Pine Street some time or other and look at us here in our surroundings.

Today is a special day. Even more special than Thanksgiving, when she got up the nerve to give that reporter a piece of her work. Today she has finished a piece intended for one pair of eyes only. From her corner, she can hear the showers running. With the exception of Beatrice, who always lies down on her bed as soon as she comes in, Amanda is alone in the room.

She tells herself, "It's now or never."

She goes into the dining room and finds Jackie paging through a quilting book.

"Have you got a minute?" she asks, pulling up the chair beside her. Quickly she slides an envelope out from between the covers of her notebook and hands it to Jackie.

"Here."

With a quizzical expression, Jackie opens it. At that very minute the phone in the kitchen starts to ring.

"Damn," Jackie curses. But she doesn't get up. She is busily reading.

"Shit!" After several more rings, when no one in the office has picked it up, she swears again. But she doesn't stop reading.

Amanda doesn't dare look her in the face. Her head bowed, staring at her hands, she just keeps thinking about the woman sitting in front of her, who has so much love, just for the asking. The pages she has just given Jackie express all that Amanda feels for her.

The homeless woman is a guest at the shelter; she has to tolerate the presence of 49 other women, all of whom stay at the shelter with her; she has to follow directions given to her by 4 or 5 counselors at various times during the day or night; she can sit in the shelter all day, or, she can walk the streets; she has no real freedom; no privacy; no space; she has to line up to get a bed to sleep in at night.

Under those conditions, try getting to know, like, and begin to trust a counselor who works in the shelter you are staying at.

Once you have found a counselor to talk to, confide in, and trust, you have to be very, very patient.

She has 49 other women, all of them with their own individual problems, other than just you, to talk to, listen to, and keep an eye on.

When I came back to the shelters in September I was in very bad shape, physically, mentally, and emotionally. I had no confidence in myself. I really sincerely believed that no one else in this entire world cared about me at all.

There you were, a familiar face, in the middle of all these new, strange, and confusing surroundings of St. Paul's shelter.

There you were, someone I knew a little, someone I had been able to trust completely, in the past, a long time ago.

You could tell I was hurting badly inside.

You wanted to tell me that everything would turn out okay after a while.

You wanted to tell me that I was wrong thinking that no one else in this entire world cared about me at all.

First, though, you gently started to tear down the barrier I had erected around myself, to put distance between me, the rest of the world, the people in it, to protect myself from being hurt again.

First, you had to gently break through the shell I had locked myself in, along with the hurt, anger, pain, and frustration that I was keeping bottled up inside myself.

You kept telling me, over and over again, that you cared.

You were the only counselor in the shelter I wanted to have anything to do with; the only one I felt I could trust even a little bit, even though I still wasn't ready to confide in you, just yet.

You know that . . . and I knew that.

I trust you completely.

Now you know why!

December 5, 1986

Amanda sees the pages come to rest on her friend's lap. She looks up. Jackie reaches for her hand.

"Thanks," she says, squeezing it. There are tears in her eyes. She's smiling from ear to ear. Amanda smiles back. Then she pulls her hand away. She looks down at the floor again, gathering the nerve to ask Jackie something she's never asked anyone before.

"Jackie," she begins.

The counselor cocks her head, intent.

"Can I ask you a big favor?"

"Sure!" Her voice is expectant.

Amanda takes a deep breath.

"Can I call you Mom?"

Jackie smiles. She leans over and draws Amanda into an embrace.

"Sure." She holds the small woman close to her. "If it makes you feel better."

It does. It means that finally, at the age of thirty-five, Amanda has a place in the world.

As Jackie holds her, this homeless woman who is less than ten years younger than she is, she knows that she needs to go slowly. She has let Amanda talk about what's been bothering her. And recently she's begun to let her know, gently, that she can't stay in the shelter indefinitely — that, if she stays, things are going to get worse for her. In small ways Jackie has started to make Amanda understand that she is different from most of the women here, that she has a little more to work with. Shelter life is not a pretty life. It is not a good life. She is conscious of having to set standards for Amanda where Amanda doesn't now have them for herself. She is willing to do this, for as long as it helps. She knows that the road she'll have to walk with Amanda is still a very long one.

◪◪◪◪◪◪◪◪◪◪

EIGHTEEN

The Women's Group

TONIGHT IS WOMEN'S GROUP, St. Paul's only regularly scheduled "program." Every Tuesday evening, from seven-thirty to nine, the women are invited to gather on the sofas and discuss a topic that Jackie and Julie come up with during the week. Joan Norton always tries to attend, driving out from Pine Street for dinner and staying afterward for the discussion.

At dinner, in her customary seat at the head of the group's table, Lucky soaks up baked beans with a hard roll. At the other end Amanda sits in stony, determined silence.

"It was awful," Alice is drawling. "I worked my fingers to the bone! I was so doggone tired, I went and got me a candy bar."

On a normal night her friends would laugh at this. Alice's complaints are an art form, her way of amusing those who don't have bosses to be beleaguered by.

Tonight no one laughs. Amanda isn't speaking to Lucky, but no one knows why.

She's pissed off. That's all, really. But it's enough. A few days before, Lucky had snubbed her. She had come into the dining room for dinner wearing her sunglasses. The staff knows by now that when Lucky shades her eyes, it is to retain her dignity. When she has been drinking and crying, her eyes get red, and Lucky knows that her sadness brings the others down. The glasses are an effort to protect them, and herself. December is a hard time of year for her. But Amanda took it personally.

Tonight before dinner, she noticed Lucky sitting on her bed, crying.

Jackie went over to her, and Amanda overheard her telling Jackie that she, Amanda, wasn't talking to her.

Now, at the end of the table, Amanda thinks smugly that when she ignores somebody, she doesn't say anything to her, she doesn't look at her, she doesn't have anything to do with her. And she knows that nothing gets a person's goat quicker. An irrational feeling of vengeance has welled up in her and fixed itself on Lucky. And, since Jackie hasn't said anything to her about it, she doesn't intend to change her attitude a whit.

Outside in the parking lot on this cold December night, Joan has just arrived behind the last van run of the evening. Patti Jones and Eileen Heller, two young lesbians, are staggering toward the shelter door. They are high as kites, probably on cocaine, their drug of choice. Celia Bell, a plodding, seriously depressed young black woman, shuffles behind them. She still looks as suicidal as she did three weeks ago when, after she threatened to kill herself, Julie found a package of razor blades in her purse.

Joan waits in her car until the women are inside. She is feeling the months of work, the late hours, the overwhelming caseload, and the lack of real treatment options for her mentally ill homeless men and women. She is very tired. She wonders if, for all her efforts to prevent staff burnout, she isn't becoming a victim of it herself. With a caseload of 630, and only one other psychiatric nurse to share it, she is on call almost all of the time. Wearily, she gets out of her car and heads for the door.

Julie looks up from the log note she is writing.

"Whew." Joan lands on a cushioned chair and lets her feet splay out in front of her, before she gets up the energy to unwrap her scarf. "It's cold out there."

"You look beat."

It is Jackie who speaks. When she came in, Joan didn't see her tucked into a corner at the desk.

"Yeah," Joan nods. "I am."

"We thought we'd talk about relationships tonight," Julie says. "Relationships with others in the shelters, with people outside the shelter —"

"Men?" Joan asks.

"Well, we talked about sexual relationships last week. Men and women — lovers in general. If they want to bring it up again, that's okay." She adds, "We did, by the way, urge them to take advantage of the free condoms at the clinic."

"Good." Joan nods.

"But we thought we'd talk about some of the difficulties in making friends in the shelter. Negotiating differences, trying to keep the tension levels down." She pauses. "Christmas is a hard time of year."

The phone rings and Jackie picks it up. Joan listens as Jackie talks to a woman whose husband just threatened to kill her, then left the house. The woman is terrified. She needs shelter for herself and her child — tonight. Jackie hangs up, dials a nearby family shelter, tells them the story, then calls the woman back and informs her that the police will be there to get her and she should be ready as soon as possible. The woman is still weeping, frantic, but grateful.

It isn't always this easy. Sometimes the police come to St. Paul's with women and children who have no place to go. Some nights an exhausted child will sit wide awake in St. Paul's office until well after eleven while Jackie tries to find a place for the child and her mother to stay. On rare occasions, if she can find two beds next to each other in the dorm, she'll let them spend the night even though it's not officially allowed.

"Joan," Julie looks up. "I noticed that Patti and Eileen just came in, and I wonder if at some point soon we shouldn't have a session on drug abuse. A lot of the younger women are coming in here night after night absolutely off the wall. None of us are trained to deal with it. When they come in screaming like hyenas, then start these jagging fits, I don't have a clue about who to call, or where the drug treatment programs for women are."

Unfortunately, Joan says, there aren't a lot of programs. In the entire Boston area, the state funds just one detox program, with twenty beds, maximum, for female drug addicts — scandalously inadequate.

Julie remarks that she doesn't even know how best to approach the women about getting some help.

"That's the hardest part," Jackie agrees.

"Especially" — Julie picks up on the remark — "because the philosophy here has always been that we're not supposed to intervene, or proselytize about the guests' substance abuse. I see that as such a throwback to Paul Sullivan's time. He was dealing with alcoholics. It's different now. Some of these women are just slowly killing themselves on drugs."

"But we don't want to scare these women off, either," Jackie inter-
jects. "If they don't feel that they can come here without getting a
heavy lecture, where *can* they go? Because you *know* they won't come
here anymore."

Julie agrees. "It's a real bitch."

In the dining room Celia has just pulled a fresh stick of pepperoni
sausage out of the pocket of her sweatshirt. With a switch blade she
saws off generous chunks and offers Amanda a piece.

"I got it at work," she tells her.

"Where's that?"

"The Marriott. I work under the banquet chef. He's a real prick. I
hate him." She laughs. "The feeling's mutual."

Out of the corner of her eye, Amanda watches Patti getting herself
some dinner. Patti's hair is cropped in a punk crew cut. Even indoors
she almost never bothers to remove her leather jacket. Tall and hefty,
a hooker in the Combat Zone, she is always on a diet. She is a good-
hearted, messed-up kid, Amanda thinks, who's just gone through a
lousy abortion, and she isn't even twenty years old.

Celia, leaning on her elbow against the table, tells Amanda proudly,
"I just spent $600 that I'd been saving for an apartment on Christmas
presents for my boyfriend!"

She feels so good about what she's done that Amanda doesn't have
the heart to start talking about bad judgment. Celia enumerates what
she's bought, a compact disc player, a sweater, Amanda can't keep
track of it all. Finally Celia herself loses interest in her bounty and
decides that she wants to clean the fish tank.

Now Amanda is alone at the table again, reading her notebook.
Hope Powers, just arrived, sits down beside her.

"May I borrow your pen, please?"

Amanda hands her a ballpoint. She watches Hope date a letter written in black fountain pen ink.

"It's not very professional looking, is it?" Hope examines the unmatched inks. "But I guess it goes with the stationery" — a tattersall
check design in burgundy and cream on pale blue.

"It's nice," Amanda tells her.

"I thought so."

Hope is wearing bright blue eye shadow that extends all the way up
to her eyebrows. She's still admiring the paper.

"It's Mary Quant," she elaborates. "She designs fabric. You can only
buy a small amount at a time, but I like to buy distinctive things. They

make a statement. I think a person has to have style. And in order to have a style, you have to be consistent." She laughs. "This is quite philosophical. But I prefer it to Plato — or Play-doh." She laughs again.

"Did you study philosophy?"

"Only as an adult," Hope answers. "At an evening college. These were older people — a church group — and I quivered with fear." She pauses. "Now, after all the fear and pain and terror I've been through, nothing makes me quiver. I'm glad I'm here. I have no fear. I'd like to think that people as they age learn to quiver less, without the pain. I'd like to get a job with people my age and see if they've learned to quiver less. People with money — " Again she pauses. "But I find that people with money are often very afraid."

"Okay, ladies!" Jackie has come into the dining room carrying a large baby food jar in one hand and a poster-sized piece of white tag board in the other. "Any last offerings?"

To encourage participation and avoid individual embarrassment, Jackie and Julie have come up with a method for running the Women's Group. Everyone is invited to write a question or a comment related to the evening's topic, anonymously, on a piece of paper. The questions are then collected in a jar. Jackie and Julie alternate reading them aloud, one by one, inviting reactions and comments from anyone who wishes to speak. There is only one rule: no one is allowed to criticize another woman's viewpoint. If someone disagrees, she can make her point without putting the speaker down after hearing her out.

Julie turns off the television, which elicits complaints from the women who don't want to be involved. Jackie meanwhile walks from table to table, passing the jar, urging people to stay ("You've got a lot to contribute") and moving those who are willing into the circle of sofas so that they can begin.

She leans the tag board against the TV. On it in bold black Magic Marker is written RELATIONSHIPS IN THE SHELTER. As ideas are presented, Julie will write them beneath the title. Later she will tack the sheet up by the cafeteria window, where the women can ponder it and contribute to it for the rest of the week.

Now Jackie sits in the middle of the sofa that faces the dining area, ruefully noting that again tonight they've managed to interest only a dozen women — the same group as usual. Well, she hopes, perhaps the others will get something out of it just listening on the sidelines. Who knows? Maybe some of them will join in next time.

She watches Amanda come in with her latest project, a white pull-over she's knitting for herself, and circle behind the arc of sofas until she reaches the one that Jackie is perching on. Julie is already cross-legged on the floor in the middle of the semicircle, waiting to begin.

In her customary seat, discreetly detached from the proceedings at one of the long dining tables behind the sofas, Joan wonders how much of the discussion will actually address the subject tonight. Joan herself never speaks at Women's Group. She feels that it is important for her to be unobtrusive since many guests retreat in distrust at the mere mention of psychologists. But tonight, she suspects, a lot of the women will be uncomfortable talking about something so personal and immediate in front of the others.

Failed relationships of one sort and another have plagued most of these women for years, if not their whole lives. It is one of the reasons they are in the shelter to begin with. There is literally no one left for them. In a shelter they are thrown together randomly, having little in common, reliant on a facility that couldn't be less conducive to building a positive self-image. They must fend for themselves from morning until night, then return to a scene of bedlam, tension, and despair, where there may not be enough beds to go around or places to sit down while they eat. On top of all this, burdened by their private sorrows and their loneliness, what kind of relationships can they possibly form in the shelters?

The miracle is that they do at all. Many, it is true, are friendships of convenience: a companion at lunch. Yet within the more stable group of the half-dozen homeless women who make up the live-in staff, Joan has seen relationships of remarkable depth, maturity, and endurance form. This has led her to believe that the shelters could help women — in important ways — to bond together and develop peer groups and friendships that will not only make the period of homelessness more endurable, but will survive and provide the foundation for a life beyond the shelters.

Most shelters, as they currently exist, don't foster relationships. The majority of the guests keep to themselves and don't converse with anyone. What little interaction takes place seems to conform to a few patterns with conflicting objectives. Cliques form around lifestyle and shared interests. The young women tend to stay together. There is a small group of lesbians, a group of older women who drink together, and a drug-consuming set.

Some women maintain cordial relations with all of their fellow guests without forming close ties to any of them. Most of these identify more strongly with the lives they led before becoming homeless. Yet in spite, or perhaps because, of this, they find it important to sustain around themselves an environment of civility and mutual respect. And some women use the shelter setting, and the relationships they form here, to work out unresolved personal issues that they've brought with them. Joan is beginning to see this in Amanda's behavior. And possibly in Bonnie's.

A forceful, articulate young black woman, Bonnie, has begun to speak while Joan has been ruminating. Tonight Bonnie wants to talk about racism. Her intelligence often intimidates the other women. Julie knows that she has to tread lightly.

Bonnie recounts the ordeals her white boyfriend had to endure. Just before she came to the shelter, he was beaten up several times by black men who were jealous of him, she says. Racism brutalized her childhood. The only black child in an all-white Boston parochial school, she was routinely singled out and punished for any wrongdoing when the teacher couldn't find the real culprit. As she talks, she becomes more and more agitated. Julie tries to get her to think about how her early experiences have affected her shelter relationships.

"Well, look at all of you!" Bonnie cries angrily. "The whole staff is white. How can you, as a white woman, understand my experience of racism?"

At this, the other black women shift quietly in their chairs.

"You're right, Bonnie," Julie answers quietly. "It's something I struggle with. Just like I'm sure there are women here who can't understand my experience as a Jew. It's something we all need to be sensitive to."

Bonnie doesn't respond.

"Do you experience racism inside the shelter?" Julie probes. "And if you do, what can we do about it?"

Some of the other women speak up. If racial slurs are made, should they try and settle it between themselves or take it to the counselors? The staff stresses that the women hold the keys to resolving interpersonal conflict in their own hands. It is an ideal that isn't always realized, they know too well. But wherever possible, they try not to intervene.

Amanda listens. Bonnie, she feels, has unconsciously started looking at the shelter as a home that "owes" her as much sensitivity and uncritical support as she might expect in a real home. Shelters encourage this kind of dependency, Amanda believes, by giving people beds, food, clothing, even friendship. A lot of the women, as a result, don't try to leave. She understands; if it weren't for Jackie, she probably wouldn't be trying either.

The first time she was on the street, Amanda didn't know what she wanted or how to use the system. But now she feels light years away from that confusion, especially now that she has a special relationship to Jackie, and in a very real sense, she feels detached from what the others are going through.

She looks at the women around the room. In a shelter, she thinks, you're dealing with alcoholics, drug addicts, people who should be in institutions, people who are more or less capable of doing things for themselves, provided someone gives them a good solid kick in the butt. Then you've got the people who are just there. You can't possibly expect to accomplish the same results with all of them. But she believes that the staff shouldn't cater to demands like Bonnie's. She is always complaining about the shelter not doing enough about this or that need of hers. If they listen to her, they'll only feed her dependency. In the final analysis, it's up to each woman to walk up to somebody and say, hey, I need help.

Lucky excuses herself quietly and makes her way out of the room. Joan looks after her, thinks about pursuing her, then changes her mind. When she turns back to the group, she sees Amanda observing her. There is a slight smile on her face.

Soon it is time for lights out. As the staff make their way back to the office, Julie spots Lucky sitting in the dark just inside the back door, smoking. She is still wearing her sunglasses.

"You seem bummed out, Lucky." Julie sits down in the chair next to her.

"I'm just sick of the shelter. I can't take it no more."

She crushes her cigarette, stands and takes several paces, then sits down again and stares fixedly ahead.

"Do you want to talk?" Julie asks.

"Won't do no good."

Lucky continues to sit, staring into the darkness, frozen in grief.

After lights out, the staff gather quietly in the office, shutting the heavy oak door that separates them from the sleeping area, so their light won't disturb the women. Always, one or two of the guests can't sleep. They'll sit up in easy chairs by the altar and read under a very dim floor lamp, or pace nervously in the shower room. In the middle of the night they will come knocking timidly at the office door in search of Tylenol and company.

The long narrow office runs behind the altar. Stained glass images of saints, lambs, and thorn-encircled hearts still fill the windows. The twin closets originally used for vestments now house life-sized statues of the Virgin, the mature Jesus, and St. Paul. The trio, decked out in clothing room castoffs — hand-knit scarfs and alpine caps — are the creative contribution of night supervisor Bob Barrett, a reminder that even here at St. Paul's, it is necessary to laugh at oneself and the world.

When everyone is reasonably settled this evening, Bob pulls out a copy of a recent night's bed list and says quietly, "Okay." [1]

The rest of the staff lean in, across a desk or over his shoulder, studying the names. Every several weeks the staff have an information session, sharing with each other what they know about each woman. Bob instigated the sessions because he felt that some regular mutual reinforcement was needed to supplement the spontaneous discussions about the women that take place nearly every night. What those discussions lack is any clear sense of what the staff's counseling expectations should be, or whether they should have any expectations. The Inn has no training program for staff, no established policy about what services or basic psychological supports they should be providing their guests, and no record of whatever counseling efforts are made. The lack of guidelines threatens to undermine the staff's commitment, sense of effectiveness, and belief in the merits of what they are trying to do. These sessions, helping to focus the groups's goals, are essential.

"She's new," Jackie is saying now about one of the first names on the list. "And I feel there's some sexual abuse in her childhood. She's not new to Pine Street. She's been here before, but she's an inpatient at Lindemann."

Joan nods, listening. Lindemann, one of the psychiatric hospitals that accept the homeless, is home base for the Homeless Outreach Team.

"But she was inpatient on a voluntary," Jackie goes on. The staff knows all too well what this means: the hospital has no legal authority to come to the shelter and retrieve their patient or require that she return to treatment. "Their answer to me when I called," Jackie says, "was 'Well, the group knows she's staying at Pine Street.' " Jackie is angry. "And because she's not forcibly committed, there's not a damn thing they can do about it. So I got her in here, and I was probing. Twice she said to me, 'My parents are divorced.' That came out of the clear blue sky. She doesn't know where her mother is. But her dad, she said, he was a bad father. So I kind of picked up something happened. Then she said it hurt too much to talk about it."

Julie wants to make sure she knows who the woman is, so Jackie describes her. The group decides that for now Jackie should continue to work with her, to try to persuade her to return to the hospital when she feels ready to do so.

In the beginning Bob had been anxious about how well he would work with Jackie. A graduate of Dartmouth College, he'd worked with homeless men in Houston and in the men's unit at Pine Street, but he'd never worked with homeless women before taking on the job of shift supervisor at St. Paul's. Jackie, on the other hand, has been at the Inn since the day the first woman walked through the door. And she is old enough, almost, to be his mother.

But he quickly realized that his fears were unfounded. Jackie was supportive, encouraging, insightful, and spirited. Really, he thinks, she is invaluable. Jackie is more skilled than any of them in reaching out and making contact with the guests, getting them to open up. She is a good role model for Julie. She knows how to approach the women with psychiatric problems. And she is a walking encyclopedia of the homeless women in Boston, carrying more information in her head than the Inn keeps on all its data cards, which contain only what he calls basic "prisoner of war" information. Many times, when they think they are seeing a new guest, Jackie will say, "Nope, she was here four years ago. Her brother dropped her off."

Another new name comes up.

"She doesn't want to give any information," Julie says. "She said she doesn't want a counselor to sign a data card or she'll walk out the door."

"Okay," Bob answers, "give her time."

He's recently had the same experience. A newcomer had said to him, "You know, I'm only here because this is an emergency shelter, and I really don't care to answer any questions." He backed off. Occasionally a woman would use the shelter for just a night or two and then disappear. But Lisa continued to show up for several weeks after putting him off. Whenever he asked her how she was doing, she told him she was waiting for a retroactive paycheck and that she'd be gone from St. Paul's by the weekend. He's decided that if she is back next Monday, he'll push her a little.

Bob believes that the staff ought to have expectations for each guest that are realistically geared to her individual needs and capacities. No two women are alike. When Sally Mattes comes in every night, drunk and verbally abusive, she sits by herself. No one bothers her, and the other women don't seem to be adversely affected by her. It is impossible to intervene in her drinking because she drinks after she gets off work and before she comes to Pine Street. This is Sally's pattern and the staff knows it. But Bob isn't so sure they'd tolerate the same from anyone else.

However, this standard of individualized expectations is nearly impossible to maintain, primarily because so few of the women distinguish themselves in any way or communicate their needs.

What happens to them? he constantly asks himself. Their names never get in the log because it records only behavior that's unusual for that person. Ironically, he sees the system encouraging women to behave in attention-getting and inappropriate ways just to be noticed. The shelter sends a double message. The "good guest" is the one who doesn't cause any trouble. As a result she is also the one who gets no attention. The "difficult guest" is unpredictable, possibly mentally ill. She is the guest whose illness is "interesting," the guest who puts demands on the staff. She is the woman likely to receive the most attention, because solving crises helps the staff feel that they are doing something.

"It's like, if I deal with this crisis, there will be some resolution, and it will make me feel good," says Bob.

Julie agrees. A recent graduate of Hampshire College, she came to work with the homeless after a series of office jobs and stints as a freelance writer had left her feeling unfulfilled. She started working in a local soup kitchen and has been with homeless people ever since. "I think the young 'heroics' get more validity by being the crisis-intervention person. I needed a lot of stimulation when I first came. Breaking up a fight or being able to arbitrate between people gave me a boost, made me feel like I was doing more for the women."

All of these factors have contributed to the review process that is going on now. Bob wants to address the passive, depressed woman who just keeps coming back, as well as the more aggressively assertive woman.

"The most painful thing for me," Julie says, "is feeling like, not only do we sometimes not help people, but we sometimes debilitate people. I really see that the shelter has made some people worse, much worse than when they first came to us."

She presses her point. "I think we're talking about our most lucid people. Usually the more lucid ones are the less interested in getting counseling because they're still autonomous enough to say, 'I want to do this by myself. I don't want to become part of this population.' There are people in here who seem pretty lucid who we've never had a conversation with. We can't get them to interact. Maybe some of it is psychosis. But I think more of it is self-preservation: 'As long as I don't interact with these counselors, or anybody in the population, I won't be barred, I won't be hassled, and nobody will get into my business. And I'll get out of here.'"

Unfortunately, this tactic often doesn't work. Shelter living seems only to aggravate the low self-esteem most of the women have when they arrive, and for those with established failure syndromes, the stress can activate them, tragically.

"It's a situation in which people feel inclined toward failure over and over again. It becomes so ingrained that their leaning toward failure seems a better option than trying to get out."

Before she came to the shelter, Julie believed that all most homeless women required was an affordable apartment.

"I thought that there would be two different types of people," she says. "One would be the classic street woman, who's delusional and debilitated and overwhelmed and probably terminal. I would service her by being a friend, or by being a listening companion, by keeping her fed. The other type of woman would be the recently victimized, in crisis. And I thought that those women would really leave. I really thought that there were many people who were here strictly because of housing displacement. It was my hope that that was the case, because it would seem that that would be easier.

"But it's not the case. I'm starting to feel that the majority of our population is mentally ill. There's no way around that. Now I'm not saying that mental illness is one clear-cut thing. But I think everybody here comes in from a situation where low self-esteem and crisis in their lives have provoked a self-debilitating experience. They no longer feel they can come to people for help, or that they can pick themselves up.

"I never realized that such a subtle craziness could exist. I had no idea that people could appear lucid to you for months and months and months, and then suddenly you find out that they think they're receiving telepathic messages through the television and that they've thought so for years. Or that there could be people who complained and hated the shelter and talked about it as if they wanted desperately to get out, and never made even the slightest attempt to pursue a way out. They don't seem to be in crisis about the fact that they're here every night. A lot of them have kids in foster care. They have a whole life established around their homelessness. But they're not looking through apartment ads every night, and they're not trying to upgrade their situation. It's an assumed normalcy. Well, that's mental illness to me."

It is difficult in this situation for staff to gauge how much "help" to offer, or what kind.

"At times I wish we had a much more active role with the guests," Bob says. "And then I question, is that for the guests' benefit, or is that for staff's own fulfillment? At other times, I think it requires a lot of discipline to be satisfied that you're just providing a safe place where people can relax and chat. Just *these* relationships take a long time to develop, and that should keep you going. That is really hard to be satisfied with. You don't see results. It's not concrete."

St. Paul's offers no pregnancy counseling, no drug and alcohol counseling, no job training or housing information. And if such information were made available, how many women would use it? Would they start to feel so pressured that the basic premise of St. Paul's — to offer them safety and privacy — would be violated? Would they stop coming?

But now Bob realizes that he is missing a new discussion that the others have taken up. Jackie has lowered her voice almost to a whisper so as not to be heard outside the room. She is talking about Amanda. Jackie's beginning to have a problem.

"I feel that I really need to set some limits." She turns to Joan.

Amanda has been at the shelter almost three months, not an unusually long time in relation to the other guests. She has reestablished a sense of security here and, by extension, has greater security about life in general. But now she is moving beyond that and seems eager to achieve a kind of mastery in the shelter — to "graduate" from the rank of guest to something more authoritative, while not surrendering the strong self-image as a homeless woman she's developed through her writing.

"She was coming into the showers every night, and I put a stop to that," she said. "It was just suffocating. Now she's started writing me these notes, pretty much telling me how to run things. 'I don't think you should allow this.' Or, 'This morning, Kate spoke to someone about moving their coffee cup.' And she names names, like a supervisor would. 'I don't think Genevieve's eating properly. Genevieve's not taking her medication.' Most of the notes come on Saturday morning about what happened Thursday and Friday on my days off, and how things should be changed."

In light of the notes, the tiff with Lucky has taken on greater importance. Maybe Amanda is striving for a favored status and is beginning to express a new self-confidence in ways that are destructive to the more vulnerable women here.

Joan ponders this for a minute.

"When I first approached her," Joan recalls, "she was very happy for the contact with someone, because at that point she had very little. She was doing a lot of crying and was obviously upset. She was alone. I can't remember exactly how long it had been since she'd lost her boyfriend. That was clearly the first issue she talked about."

Jackie is surprised. "It's really strange, because all the talks I had with her, there was never a whole lot of talk about Tom. There were evenings where we did talk about Tom, but I honestly thought of that more as a brother-sister relationship. I never once heard her say, 'I really loved him. I really miss him.'"

"Well," Joan says, "I think *that,* and the mother's death, combined with her anger, was another terrible loss that left her with so many unresolved issues."

Jackie suggests that by taking a position of authority in the shelter, Amanda may be trying to repeat the positive shelter experience she had with Tom.

"That's a good point," Joan says. "In the shelter, there is a feeling of connectedness within that she didn't have outside." She pauses.

"If she is using Thomas as a role model for behavior in the shelter, then her role model would say, 'You try to improve the lot of others, but you also become a leader and get yourself into a better situation.

And you try and let people know what it's like to be homeless.' Which she's done with her writing."

Jackie agrees. Instead of resolving the past issues that drove her to the shelter, Amanda is beginning to create an identity for herself in the setting of the shelter. It may strengthen her now, but Jackie worries that if Amanda's identity becomes so invested in being a homeless woman, she won't be able to leave.

Joan interrupts her thoughts. "I have a sense that she's a fairly bright woman. And that if the conflict were removed, she could reach her potential and do very well. But she's stuck. Which is interesting, because she's mirroring her mother's life without having had the constraints that her mother had — except the psychological ones."

The group digests the discussion silently for several minutes. "I hope she can get into long-term." Joan means long-term therapy. "Not with someone like me, who can only do Band-Aid stuff in the shelter, but somebody who could really be with her over the long haul."

No matter how much you think you know about homelessness, Jackie reflects, the women always surprise you. You have to be ready for that, even open to it, if you are going to help them grow. She was unprepared for the power issues that are now surfacing with Amanda, and she needs to adjust her course a bit.

She remembers that once early on, Amanda had come to her, concerned because she thought Genevieve had stopped taking her Librium. In retrospect, Jackie realizes, her response was the right one. She'd said to her, "Amanda, Genevieve is a grown woman. And if Genevieve chooses not to take her meds, that is her decision."

Henceforth she needs to more clearly delineate the role of counselor and that of guest with Amanda and not allow her to imagine that she is going to start making decisions for St. Paul's.

Jackie doesn't have to wait long to confront Amanda. One night, when she enters the office to jot a note in the log, she discovers Amanda, uninvited, seated in Bob's chair, leafing through a magazine that someone had left on the desk.

A warning light goes off in Jackie's mind, but she waits to see what is up. Immediately, Amanda broaches the topic. What does Jackie think about her doing some counseling work with the other women?

Jackie takes a deep breath and sits down. She explains to Amanda that she doesn't think it is necessary for her to counsel other women. That's what the staff is here for, she says.

Amanda tells her that there is a new woman who looks very uncomfortable. She thinks that by befriending her, she'll be able to help her.

"Sure," Jackie agrees. "That's fine, as long as that's all you're doing." But as far as Amanda setting the rules, Jackie says, that is not up to her to do.

Amanda understands. She kisses her mom goodnight and goes to bed.

Jackie sighs, enters her note, and heads back to the kitchen to make herself a cup of tea. Against the wall, among the stacks of donated cookies and empty cartons, a piece of tag board leans forgotten. "Relationships in the Shelters," it reads. The rest is blank.

NINETEEN

Links

HOOPS OF GOLD garland the miniature artificial Christmas tree that has taken over the Inn's lobby desk, and mounds of metallic-flecked tissue wrap the base in a wonderland imitation of snow. On the benches nearby, heavy overcoats and layers of sweaters pack the women more tightly together. Some are forced to sit on their bags, others on the floor.

While a few short fuses and fragile temperaments were to be expected on the rainy autumn days leading into the holidays, by Christmas week the unremitting cold and gray skies have generalized an atmosphere of barely contained upset. An explosive, brooding intensity greets startled visitors who come to the door with bags of donated food, clothing, and wrapped articles.

One evening just before dinner, Hope de Graf Tillotson Powers sits off by herself, unable to make the effort to go over to St. Paul's. She hasn't removed the blue gingham scarf and the cashmere coat that have protected her from the cold all day. From her motley assemblage, purple tube socks, wet sneakers, and violet-tipped fingernails protrude.

Sensing Hope's profound sadness, Carol, a relatively new staffer, sits down beside her.

"What did you do today?" she asks, trying to draw Hope out.

"I cried." Hope doesn't turn toward her. After a few minutes, she continues. "My caseworker, who I like, is going away, and I'm going to have to work with someone else." Her voice starts to break. "I don't want to cry. I don't want to be weak."

Carol reaches an arm around her shoulder.

"Weak is one problem I don't think you have, my dear," she says.

"Tell my caseworker that."

Hope extends one of her hands and looks at her nails. "I've tried to file my nails square so that they'll be good for typewriting," she tells Carol. "Or something."

She falls silent again.

"Hope, do you want to talk?" Carol prods.

"Won't do any good."

Carol stays beside her nevertheless. Sometimes, she's learned, companionship matters more than words. And now Hope is speaking again, in a faraway voice, not exactly to Carol, but to someone Carol might once have been.

"I have to get a room," she is saying. "That would be just a start. I'll take the first thing I can find. Just to have something. I should be able to find one. And then any job, just to get me going . . . I'd want something with a tub. I suppose I could fix something up in my room. A sitz bath, is that what they're called? . . . Then you can get into the tub all nice and clean and . . . ," her eyes grow misty, "dream your dreams about the man who went away . . ."

Silent tears begin to course down her cheeks, and she makes no effort to stop them. She describes for Carol the beauty of Rio de Janeiro, its fountains and cathedral, its forests and the dark heart of the Amazon. It is there that she lived at her mother's house for a long period before becoming homeless. There she fell in love. But she refuses to emigrate.

"And because I wouldn't sell out, I'm relegated to a rat-infested closet," she weeps. "That's what it's come to. How's that for patriotism?"

Across the room, dinner has begun. Hope gathers herself and struggles to stand, ruefully remarking as she does, "I said I didn't want to talk, and here I have."

Carol remains seated. "It wasn't too painful, was it?" she asks softly.

"Yes." Hope wheels around. "It was."

The Pine Street lobby has grown so cramped that Amanda has to wait until she gets to St. Paul's to work on her journal. The sweater she's knitting is finished except for the collar, and she'll need a quieter setting than the lobby in which to pick up and count the neckline stitches. So she just sits. These days the van can't come soon enough.

But St. Paul's is hardly a refuge. A pronounced change has come over the group. Colette, the group's artist, has announced that she is leaving. She's accepted a proposal of marriage from Danny, a street person who hangs around the Combat Zone. Privately, her friends are appalled. They see Danny as simply a mooch, after Colette's check. He gives her a measly thirty dollars of it and drinks the rest. He treats her like dirt, but she is head over heels in love with him, so the women keep their thoughts to themselves.

A more direct impact on Amanda's life is that Genevieve has gotten a job. For several weeks now, she has been departing every morning on the earliest van in order to get to the parking lot where she is a security guard. It is cold outdoor work, but she likes the people, and her supervisor has promised her a desk job as soon as one becomes available.

Without Genevieve, the days have become much longer for Amanda. She still walks down to the river and wanders the streets in the afternoons. But now she doesn't have anyone with whom to share the hours at the Lunch Place, or the wintry afternoon streets, or the endless wait in the lobby for the van to arrive. Before, the two of them used to trade wry asides about the people around them and the events of the day, but now Amanda has few conversations with anyone except the overburdened staff at the Inn.

When Genevieve returns at the end of the day in her handsome uniform, she is tired. Genevieve tries to minimize the new difference between them, but the job is beginning to change her life. She is making new friends and is less interested in the trivial disputes and happenings of the shelter. She's gotten an attractive haircut. And with her first paycheck, she went out and bought herself a beautiful pearl ring.

Lucky has begun to talk about applying for a room at a lodging house. Even Alice, whenever the subject comes up now, says that she plans to look for an apartment, in spite of her husband, after the New Year.

An unfocused restlessness has crept into Amanda's day. She finds herself asking the same questions over and over again: "Why is it I had to come back to the streets, to the shelters, for help? Why is it I couldn't get that kind of help from a counselor in an agency on the outside?"

For months, across the street from St. Paul's, Sister Rita Brereton has watched the former convent slowly take on new life under the sure

hand of her friend Valerie Lanier. After Val had succeeded in buying
the former Cifrino house for the Paul Sullivan Housing Trust the
previous spring, she'd jumped right in, hiring contractors to rewire,
paint, finish the basement to make additional rooms, and install bathroom and laundry facilities.

"Half Moon," as the house is being referred to throughout the Pine
Street Inn, is scheduled to open March 1, 1987. The fourth lodging
house that the trust has opened in the city, it will be home for six men
and five women who are currently homeless. Now Valerie needs to
find its future residents.

As director of the Inn's youngest and boldest program, Val Lanier
is in a position to make things happen in housing for homeless people. And she is one of the only people in the city of Boston who is
doing so.

By December of 1986, three years after Governor Michael Dukakis
identified homelessness as his administration's primary human service issue, and three years after Mayor Ray Flynn became chairman
of the U.S. Mayors' Task Force on Homelessness and Hunger, only
five lodging houses had been opened for homeless people: one by
Rosie's Place, one a private transitional program for women, and three
by the Pine Street Inn's Paul Sullivan Housing Trust. No one else has
ventured to foster small stable communities of people who have little
more in common than the fact that they haven't had homes for years.

Val is the woman to take such a risk. In 1974, at the age of twenty-
three, she arrived in Boston with $900 in the bank to take a full-time
job for which she wasn't going to receive any salary. The job was at
Rosie's Place. In a year, she had become its director.

The first St. Patrick's Day that Rosie's was in business, Val remembers, she was making celery soup when Paul Sullivan came through
the door. Celery soup was a big deal at Rosie's. Once a week Val received a donation of two cases of celery from the farmer's market.
Celery became the nutritional anchor in the otherwise uncertain meal
program.

"What are you making?" Sullivan asked her.

"Tomorrow's dinner," she told him.

"What?!"

"It's green isn't it," she parried.

Paul was incredulous. "Don't you know how to make a boiled dinner?"

"Meat on a weekday?" she rejoined. "We don't have the money."

The next morning there was a knock on the door. Sullivan stood on the steps with the makings for a boiled dinner.

"You know," she confessed with a laugh, "I really don't know how to make a boiled dinner."

He walked past her into the kitchen with the provisions. "Fine. I'll teach you how." That afternoon, he cooked dinner for twenty-five women.

"There was a lot of that kind of support. If it wasn't for Paul, I don't know what I'd know about the business," Val recalls.

But it soon became apparent to Val that shelters couldn't do enough on their own, even those whose staff actively tried to find people apartments. She wanted to create housing. In 1981 she left Rosie's Place and began a program known as Open Door Housing, creating homes for homeless women and families. Open Door managed to renovate one triple-decker, for one family and eight women, but the organization folded shortly after that because Val couldn't interest private foundations or banks in funding permanent housing for the homeless. It was a valuable, if painful, lesson for her.

Val then accepted an appointment by Kevin White as the first commissioner of the city's newly established Emergency Shelter Commission, a post she held for a year and a half, during which the city, still responding to overflow conditions at the major shelters, just added more shelter beds to its inventory. When the Pine Street Inn offered her another chance to run a housing program for the homeless, she leapt at it.

Now, three years later, with three houses open and another on the way, Val is beginning to believe that the Paul Sullivan Housing Trust program will fly. She promised the board of directors that the first four houses would be traditional lodging houses, not rehabilitative programs. (This was to safeguard the houses financially; had the Inn decided to stop at just four houses, or even to get out of the business, the four original experiments would stand a much better chance of surviving than they would if elaborate supportive services personnel were required for residents.)

Each building is purchased with private money: donations and foundation grants. The costs of renovation (ranging from $11,500 to $27,000 per unit) are paid for by a combination of private contributions and a state fund for lodging house rehabilitation. Staff salaries and management costs are carried by the Inn. Furnishings, blankets, and linen are all supplied by the trust; many of the items are donated to the Inn. In each house the public rooms — parlors and dining rooms — contain easy chairs, sofas, and television sets. Each bedroom has a bed, bureau, desk, and lamp.

Residents of the three houses are tenants, not "patients," or "guests." Mixed in age, sex, and race, they contribute 25 percent of their income (wages, welfare, or social security) toward their rent. The rest is paid by the state through a voucher program administered by the Boston Housing Authority. The residents can, if they choose to, remain in the house for the rest of their lives.

Each house has a manager. These managers, it is expected, unlike the managers of the old rooming houses, will do more than fix toilets and hand out keys. They will be available to tenants for practical advice and conversation and will help ensure the stability of the house community. The live-in managers work twenty-four hours a week in exchange for free room and board and a salary of about $8.50 an hour.

Val is excited about Half Moon. The house means a great deal to her personally. It was Val who phoned Father Bill Francis on his first Christmas Eve at St. Paul's and asked him to take a homeless family into his rectory for the night. Since then, they've become close friends. Bill has been keenly enthusiastic about the lodging house. In fact, she hopes to name it the William C. Francis House after him, as a lasting gesture of affection and respect.

Across the street at the shelter, there is much excitement over the prospect of Half Moon. The staff assume that several of their women will be eligible for residency there. Also, they view with enthusiasm the opportunities that proximity offers in the situation: the women who move into Half Moon can come back to the shelter for dinner from time to time, providing hope and a sense of possibility for the women who remain.

The tenant coordinator at the trust, Daryl Melke, has asked the staff to nominate women they think are good candidates for housing. Some of the questions she wants them to consider include:

Can she take care of herself? Does she keep herself neat, care for her property, Pine Street's property?

What is her interest level? How does she engage with the world? How does she handle her daily activities? Can she enjoy herself?

What is her ability to relate to others? How does she deal with anger and anxiety? How does she deal with other guests, with counselors?

How is she limited? What is her physical ability, her psychic ability? Is she functional with medication, without medication?

For Jackie, Julie, and Bob, the responsibility they've been entrusted with is daunting. A cursory review of their regular guests immediately nets a list of women most likely to succeed in housing. Yet this very immediacy highlights painfully for them the old issues of how rewards are doled out in the shelter system. There are probably many women they might nominate if they only knew more about them. But because they've never spoken up, these women are likely to be passed over now. Suddenly the staff is aware of how much power they've been given over other people's futures.

For several nights after lights out, they meet and discuss various candidates. The next day, if the candidate's desire for housing isn't known, the staff make some quiet inquiries. Several of the women approached aren't interested in this sort of congregate living. But most of those nominated are eager to hear more. The staff's list includes Genevieve, Amanda, Lucky, and Alice. They pass it along to Daryl Melke.

Amanda is seated on a molded plastic chair in the somewhat cramped confines of the women's unit clinic. With her are Genevieve, Lucky, and Alice. It is ten-thirty on a Friday morning. Standing in front of them, introducing herself, is Daryl Melke.

Daryl is informal but professional. She outlines the living arrangements at the new house. Everyone is to have her own room. The kitchen facilities are shared; so are the baths. She explains how the rents are assessed, the role of the resident manager, and the basic philosophy of the house: everyone is on her own to get jobs and maintain her social life as best suits her individual needs.

Amanda is nervous. She knows that she, like the three other women, is being sized up and that the list of candidates is a long one. She wants desperately to make a good impression. She dressed carefully this morning in a fresh shirt and jeans. She tries to look as attentive as possible. The house sounds better than any living situation she's ever had. She likes the connection that exists between the trust and the Inn. She likes the fact that the house manager used to be a counselor at Pine Street. She thinks that she could get along with Daryl

Melke. And best of all, she realizes that she could move into housing without ending her relationship with her mom, who would be just a stone's throw away every night.

Part way through the meeting, Lucky excuses herself and quietly leaves. She isn't interested in group living if it requires sharing kitchen space and baths. She's had bad experiences with such arrangements in the past. People leave food to rot, and steal from each other. One person's sense of hygiene is rarely another's. When she finds housing this time, it is going to be an apartment that she won't have to share.

For her part, Amanda emerges from the meeting elated and hopeful. Over the next several days, she begins to reflect on how her situation has changed in ways that make leaving the shelter suddenly seem right. Little has altered outwardly, she realizes. She still doesn't have a job; she hasn't progressed through any measurable steps of rehabilitation. In her talks with Joan, neither of them has ever discussed housing as the goal toward which her short-term therapy is supposed to be directing her. But she knows she is ready.

A number of factors seem to have converged to make the idea of returning to an apartment feasible. Later, in her journal, she will repeatedly point to the importance of encouragement. Without that, she probably wouldn't be thinking of moving so soon. Equally, if not more, important is the connection between the lodging house and the people she's come to trust in the shelter. She will be able to stay in touch, not only with Jackie and Joan but also with her peers, the members of the dinner group, and other guests who, even when they got under her skin, provided a ready companionship she'd never known in the outside world. She won't have to leave any of this security behind her if she's chosen for Half Moon.

But another subtle factor has laid the foundation necessary for her new confidence to take hold. For three months Amanda has been released from the chronic feelings of low self-esteem and failure that have always beset her efforts to make it in the world. On the streets she wins the battle against failure by refusing to fight any longer on the world's terms. Walking away from the standards of mainstream society, more or less admitting defeat, has freed her to explore herself in an environment in which anything is possible *except* failure. The sensitive offers of help from Jackie, Monica, and Joan soon after she arrived helped her to avoid withdrawing into the isolation that makes the shelter a hell for some of the women, one from which they'll never escape. Amanda knew from the beginning that there was nowhere lower for her to fall to; by the same token, there was nowhere to go but up. She's found people to talk to, people who have encouraged her. Anxiety has slowly given way to a new sense of self-worth. The streets, and her writing about them, have given daily life an immediacy and emotional significance that it hasn't had before. Being open to the present has meant being open to possibility. This is a new freedom and flexibility for her.

When others began to talk about moving into the lodging house, she found herself caught up in the excitement of what seemed the best of all possible worlds: an extension of the shelter, with its continuing connections to the people who care about her, combined with the benefits of privacy, autonomy, and freedom of movement. Perhaps, she thinks, it will even prove to be the threshold to a new life: as a writer, maybe as a student, as a self-possessed, whole person.

▧▧▧▧▧▧▧▧▧▧

TWENTY

Simple Gifts

THE DINING ROOM at St. Paul's has been transformed. The tables, cloaked in bright red, are overhung with twisted streamers and leggy pompoms. Medieval carols float through the cavernous hall, emanating from Bob's tape player in the kitchen. The lights have been subdued, and in the far reaches of the room by the stage, tables are piled high with colored paper, popcorn, glitter, yarn, and old fabric, which Jackie is now picking through.

"Okay, everybody," Jackie greets them. "We need your imaginations!" She takes a seat and dives in, beginning to work an elfin form out of a loose skein of red yarn.

Colette Richards, ecstatic, approaches and surveys the jars of poster paint and sheets of white posterboard, momentarily too dazzled to do more than clasp her hands. The other women are more tentative, unsure whether to lend themselves to activities that border too closely on private worlds of memory, love, and pain. There is little precedent here for taking such risks; to work together, laughing and sharing, is, with the rare exception of Women's Group, a foreign venture in the shelter. The younger women, especially, begin to guffaw shyly and tease Bob and Julie about getting involved in something so corny. It brings to mind for them all the horrible junior high school classes where the claims of individuality demanded that you refuse to go along. Bob isn't concerned. Neither is Jackie or Julie. If nothing else, they know that the dinner group will be enthusiastic.

Now Patti swaggers in, wearing her omnipresent leather jacket. She takes one look at the decorations and bursts into tears. Ashamed and unstrung, she rushes to a dark corner and flings herself into a chair, sobbing uncontrollably. The room goes dead.

After a minute or two, Bob gently approaches her. "I can't stand this any longer," she sobs. "I can't take the shelter anymore. I'm going to kill myself!"

Celia and Eileen, the two young women she spends time with on the streets, sit down beside her. They start to cry too. A look of concern passes between Julie and Bob. Jackie looks up from her elf, then down again, determinedly, for the sake of the other women.

"I don't want to be here!" Patti is screaming. "I want to get the hell out of here!"

Bob gets a plate of supper and takes it to the end of the unadorned table where Patti, no longer crying, sits, numbed. Choosing a seat as far from her as possible, he begins to eat without a word. Julie returns to the dinner group and tries to draw them back into the mood the staff has spent the afternoon trying so hard to establish.

It doesn't take long. The tubes of glitter, the spools of thread, balls of yarn, popcorn and cranberries, tin foil and tissue paper, waiting for hands to shape them, temporarily erode the dismal circumstances of their present life. They are, after all, the materials of memory, however long neglected; emblems of the years when handling yarn or threading a needle in the name of creativity was simply part of a universe taken for granted.

Conversation remains muted by the music, but a sense of bashful adventure slowly takes hold, a sense that there isn't really too much to lose by setting to work on the cotton salvages and colored paper. A few women get up and cross the room to the table where Jackie is working. Protesting that they don't know how to make ornaments, they pull up chairs, and soon they are stringing popcorn or winding yarn into rough rag-doll forms.

Before long, the concentrated energy at the table attracts more participants. The women start to piece together expressions of themselves — some whimsical, others zany and rebellious — calling up techniques that after years of disuse they find surprisingly serviceable. There is much improvisation: sharing tricks for making angels from Styrofoam balls, and baskets from paper. Bob has convinced a calmed Patti to stay, and now begins to work intently at a square of tag board, pulling various colors of yarn through it to create a continuous rainbow around the words he's lettered in the center: A Home Is Shelter; A Shelter Is Not a Home.

Finished, he gets up and goes into the kitchen, puts on a Glenn Miller tape, and turns up the volume. Meanwhile, unnoticed, Patti approaches one end of the table. She cuts a large and well-proportioned star out of the white foamcore board, applies rubber cement to its surface and carefully begins to dust glitter, red, green, silver, and gold, on each of four points. Amanda, glancing up from the sundae she is eating, is stirred by the unguarded expression on her young friend's face. Oblivious to her surroundings, Patti is completely absorbed in what she is doing. At this moment, however, she catches Amanda studying her and smiles sheepishly.

"What do you think I ought to put on the top point?" she asks.

"Patti, that's beautiful!"

"Aw, shucks," she jokes.

"Why not mix them?" Amanda suggests.

Patti agrees, and when she is finished, the women decide by acclaim that the star deserves the place of honor at the top of the tree.

At this the evening's entertainment arrives. Men and women, about a dozen in all, wander in, in torn blue jeans and mismatched shirts and sweaters, looking not very different from the women who watch them expectantly from the tables. Some are little more than teenagers, others have gray hair. They carry tambourines, flutes, and guitars like a group of traveling minstrels.

The group calls itself The Whammers & The Jammers. Its members lead very separate daily lives, earning marginal livings in offices, at day labor, on the streets. The only thing they have in common, besides the love of music, is that each of them is handicapped. The keyboard player, blind, earns his living playing to lunch-hour crowds on a street corner at Downtown Crossing. A number of the mentally retarded vocalists work in sheltered workshops. The Whammers & The Jammers perform wherever they are invited, for free, making gifts of their reggae, spirituals, popular tunes, and old-fashioned folk songs.

The ornaments are soon abandoned to hand clapping and sing-alongs. The tree is draped, willy nilly, with the night's productions, the lights strung, and the unthreaded popcorn consumed. Too soon the party is over, and the women are in bed. In the dining room, warmth lingers in the recently quit sofas, mangled piles of unused fabric scraps and spilled glue, the general dishevelment of a good time.

Long after it grows quiet, Patti decides that there is nothing more she can add to the winged clothespin angel she has spent the past two hours laboriously constructing out of calico, cotton gauze, and remnant yarn. She walks up to the tree, gingerly holds one of the few remaining bare boughs, and fixes the fragile spirit to its stem, then turns in for the night.

Wrapped packages almost block the entry to the office on Christmas Eve. The presents were delivered in large plastic bags earlier in the day, the labor of hundreds of church groups converging on the donations department that morning. Today the women who use the shelters will receive gifts almost everywhere they go. Most of them will be arriving at St. Paul's after having been to the Rosie's Place party, where gifts are distributed at lunch time and exchanged between friends.

Before the women come, Julie wants to individualize the packages instead of simply distributing them randomly, irrespective of size or the recipient's personality, as is so often done. For an hour and a half she painstakingly removes the labels affixed to the wrapping paper that describe the contents. She compares the items with a recent bed list and tries to match each gift to a guest. Many of the gifts are items suggested to church groups by the Inn's volunteer office: scarves, gloves, knit hats, nightgowns, slippers, and packages of toiletries — washcloths, soap, brushes, and combs. Occasionally a group will send a few luxury packages — cosmetics or a whole skirt and sweater outfit — but by and large, when the women sit down after dinner around the tree at St. Paul's, they'll be opening their second or third hat or pair of gloves of the day. As she pulls off label after label from such items, Julie reflects sadly on the many things you can't give a homeless woman. What they really need doesn't come in a box with reindeer all over it.

Upstairs Father Bill Francis begins to celebrate the Nativity Mass with a small cluster of parishioners. A handful of women from the shelter, coats pulled tight over their nightgowns, slide into pews at the back of the church, as far as possible from the glare of the altar lights. After several hymns, Father Francis reads from Isaiah:

> Thou hast multiplied the nation, and not increased the joy: they joy before thee according to the joy in harvest, and as men rejoice when they divide the spoil . . .

For unto us a child is born, unto us a son is given: and the government shall be upon his shoulder: and his name shall be called Wonderful, Counsellor, The mighty God, The everlasting Father, the Prince of Peace.

A volunteer has accompanied the women from the shelter, and as the collection basket approaches, she feels something being slipped into her hand. One of the women, having noticed that she left her purse downstairs, to save her from embarrassment is giving her a dollar bill for the collection.

Christmas Mass ended, the women downstairs gather around the tree and open their packages. Amanda receives gloves and a scarf.

"My third today." She laughs.

For Tracy, there is a sweater that is far too small. Patti opens a package of cosmetics that she immediately gives to Hope. Only Lucky receives something that fits: a skirt and jacket. She'll put the ensemble in her locker for a day when the clothing room has nothing for her. There are piles of wrapping to dispose of. And then Christmas is over.

The year 1986 closed with no word about the lodging house. Two weeks after the meeting in the clinic, Amanda met Daryl Melke for a one-to-one interview. Going into it, she decided that she was going to lay all of her cards right out on the table. As she had with Monica Donner and Jackie and Joan Norton, Amanda reviewed her life path for Daryl Melke.

"I told her the whole damn mess," she says later. "That way she knows where I'm coming from." If Amanda learned one thing this time on the street, it was that disclosure helped her overcome her fears before they overcame her.

TWENTY-ONE

Elsewhere

THEY HAD DRAGGED a Christmas tree into the Penthouse, propped it in a bucket, and cadged a few strings of lights from up and down the alley. But just as quickly, they dragged it out again and left it to rest against the side of a dumpster, one of many tinsel-weathered ferns between the fire station and the Common. Prudence had carried the day; Jake, gauging the overtaxed ganglia of cords that fed off his single electrical outlet, called it a fire hazard. He wasn't about to sacrifice survival for sentiment.

Sentiment, however, is not so easily rebuffed. As New Year's Eve approaches, the Jakes put in their supplies as the city becomes charged with anticipation that will blossom into the nightlong street festival known to Bostonians as First Night. On December 31, hundreds of thousands of party-goers in the streets around them will revel until well past midnight, entertained by more than a thousand street performers and magicians, by opera, laser shows, and face painters. They'll be barked at by street-corner sausage vendors and by people pushing flower carts. They will improvise parties in every free wedge of space, and the evening will culminate with an extravagant fireworks display over the harbor while the Boston Pops plays Handel's Water Music Suite.

Hunkered down in their cave in the middle of this boisterous mass of humanity, the three Jakes sit with their vodka. The television set is on, and they are waiting to watch the illuminated ball descend in Times Square to the strains of Guy Lombardo playing "Auld Lang Syne" for what is purported to be the very last time.

Not far away, at the bottom of the subway steps by the Prudential Center, Traveler and Wendy have been celebrating on their own. It hasn't been a good week. The icy temperatures have hit them hard. So has the booze. They watch the crowds crush upward from the platforms below, hurrying toward the street, and panhandle half-heartedly. Neither has the will or the energy tonight.

Traveler is getting querulous. Wendy is dimly aware that he has veered into anger over something; she doesn't know what. She tries to humor him. But she's thinking to herself, with a certain degree of familiar dread, "Don't push me, Traveler."

For the rescue van, it's going to be a crazy shift. The prospect of trying to get through the crowds to their regular folks is almost too daunting to contemplate. But the crew realize that the street people will be wary enough, and smart enough, to find hiding places until the revelers disperse. Early in the evening's shift, they decide, they'll check a few of the more public places on the fringe of the action — the back of the library, the Common — then they'll restrict their tour to the outlying areas, the financial district and the area around Mass. General, where the party won't go.

Their instincts prove correct: the street folks know how to take care of themselves when their otherwise overlooked habitats are invaded. J.T. and Holly find them holed up in garages, curled under highway ramps, and huddled by dumpsters downtown, waiting out the night.

At ten minutes to midnight the van heads into the Back Bay, arriving at the Penthouse door just in time to be offered chairs. The countdown won't be long. Jake has adjusted the TV to get the best possible reception. Holly notices that the place has been cleaned up for the occasion. There is plenty of booze. Their host offers them a drink, but they decline.

The alley outside becomes quiet and empty as the crowds head down to the harbor. Those in the Penthouse are all leaning toward the tube, watching the glittering orb, symbol for millions of everything that's ending and everything that's about to begin. As it slowly drops, their voices chant in unison, "Five, four, three . . . ," and then the Penthouse resounds with a roar, cheering, "One!"

With not much more in the world than each other, the friends hoot, laugh, and embrace. It is 1987.

Traveler has broken a bottle against the tiles and is holding a jagged portion of it by the neck, high up over her. Wendy cowers, but there's nowhere to go. Paralyzed by anticipatory fear and the sickening certainty of pain, she watches the glass descend. Down it comes, ruthless, determined. It rips into her leg — once, twice. She screams. Her body contorts involuntarily. The glass has cut clear to the bone.

TWENTY-TWO

Big Winner

IT IS SCANT CONSOLATION that the holidays, with their pressures for cheer, are over. Amanda walks the lonely streets of New Year's Day aimlessly, feeling a sadness she can't account for. Nothing is open. Even the remains of First Night parties have vanished, thanks to the efficiency of the city's cleaning crews.

"What you have been seeking is close at hand," her horoscope read this morning. "With patience you emerge a 'big winner.'" She feels curiously deflated.

Soon enough, like any other, this day is over. Back at St. Paul's, Amanda picks at her dinner. Before it is eight o'clock, she is curled up in her bed. She turns her face to the wall and starts to cry.

How long she remains in that position she doesn't know. Someone has come over and is sitting down on the edge of her bed. Without even seeing who it is, Amanda turns and flings her arms around the comforting presence, sobbing. "I'm scared shit!"

Her whole body shakes. Haltingly, she tries to explain. She is beginning to doubt that she is ready to move out. She is afraid of the isolation again, of the distance from Jackie.

"I'll be going from sleeping with fifty other women to being alone in my own room." She sobs. "The thing is, I don't know where my relationship with Jackie's going to go. The only relationship we've ever had has been a counselor-client relationship."

The volunteer, who has noticed her anguished silence and stopped, now manages to calm her. Amanda leans back against her pillow. Subdued, she confesses that she is terrified that her life will revert to its former sterility and hopelessness. Things are suddenly moving too fast. She feels trapped, afraid on the one hand of losing an opportunity and on the other of moving out before she is ready to stand on her own two feet.

Later, in the office, after Amanda has fallen asleep, the staff discusses Amanda's need to move on. They are unanimous on this point.

Then Jackie speaks up.

"You know," she says, "we encourage the women to get close to us, to open up. But if they get too dependent, we need to almost push them away. It's not good for them. What if, tomorrow, we're not here for them? How do you handle this, Bob?"

Bob nods and shrugs. He understands, but he has no answer.

The trauma of transition remains a taboo subject among many advocates for the homeless. They don't want to see the pressing need for housing diluted by arguments, so easily distorted, that many currently in shelters aren't emotionally prepared to move into homes of their own. They worry — to some extent understandably — that this concept, popularized, will result in a stalemate in housing programs for the homeless.

However, helping homeless people to cope with the difficulties of transition is the most crucial link in the fragile chain that will connect many to stable homes and ensure that they remain in them. Fortunately for the guests at the Pine Street Inn, transition is not a new issue for Val Lanier at the Paul Sullivan Housing Trust.

"For some, the first three months is the critical time," she says. "For others, it's after the first year. It's almost like there's too much stability. We're facing that now with some people — where do I go from here? — thinking that it was going to give them all the answers, and us knowing that it was just the beginning for some of them. And maybe they're not wanting to make that next step, yet young enough that they're going to have to. They're somewhere on the step: either leaving the lodging house and going to somewhere good, or leaving the house and going back to a shelter."

Valerie also knows that traditional lodging houses, like Half Moon, are just the beginning of the diversity of housing options needed for the homeless. Val wants to create lodging houses for women who need twenty-four-hour-a-day supervision, a house for alcoholics, and one for AIDS victims.

"For some there's a step before, and for some there's a step after," she maintains. "There are those who need transitional [assistance] — six months to two years — who really need the daily help of shopping, learning how to clean again, and wash themselves, proper behavior. There are those who are using the lodging house now, in a very positive sense, as a stepping stone to go somewhere else.

"When I was first at Rosie's Place, I thought as long as you got the majority of the women into a house, you'd be fine. It's not true. There are a lot of reasons besides poverty, alcoholism, and institutional living that make people homeless. And there are a lot of things that alcohol, institutional living, and poverty do to people *besides* make them homeless.

"I'm just starting to understand that a roof isn't enough. Good management isn't enough. There are a lot of other issues. Being poor makes people become paranoid, makes them crazy. Craziness sometimes makes people poor. Craziness also sometimes makes them hit the bottle. There are so many things interrelated that just having the house and giving them money and having them work there isn't enough. There are a lot of other problems to deal with."

Val is in agreement with Julie about the damage that shelters, in and of themselves, can inflict.

"Shelters take people backward. You've begun the backward process until you can get back into a lodging house. And then you may need support services you never needed before you became homeless. I don't want to face that. No one in the shelter world wants to face that. And anyone who's an advocate for the homeless doesn't want to admit it. You just don't want to, because there's a sense of hopelessness to admit that in all the good work that shelters do, we still take them backward."

Valerie speaks for all who began working with the homeless more than a decade ago, years before the Coalition for the Homeless and national lobby groups began establishing a homeless political agenda. "A lot more is demanded of us now. The governor, the mayor, are saying, what's the solution? You people have been working on this so long, give us the answer. We say here, we try. We do not have all the answers. We are a small part of the solution for some people, and we try to do it well. We don't always do it well. We care a lot."

TWENTY-THREE

Not Exactly Paris

THE DRIVE OVER the final mountain on this early evening in January is the drive from the present into something so old and sweet and bitter all at once that Wendy tilts her head back and swallows another gulp of the warm dry air.

Where she is going, slumped low in the passenger seat of her step-father's small blue compact, the Trailways that blows through each dawn at 5:20 doesn't even make a flag stop anymore. A town of dust, one filling pump, one coin phone, one newspaper box, and a pharmacy and a sandwich shop that compete for pride of place: New Free-dom Drugs and the ditto Family Restaurant.

Behind her spreads the outskirts of Brody, Mississippi, raised on cotton and the doctrines of John Wesley, and undisturbed in those leanings up to twenty years ago. Since then Brody has grown up, with the considerable assistance of a vast army base and a nonunion labor force that has won the hearts of a handsome number of northern high-tech suitors. Their rose marble and black glass lodgings now dominate the downtown peak where just a short time ago steeples and bells held sway.

Still, the outlying areas haven't changed. Shabby winter greens bank the highway. The car passes weathered shacks with crudely painted ads for pony rides, a dehydrated water slide park, and the Showcase Lounge, a dim cinderblock casbah, that night featuring Playgirl cen-terfolds. Beyond the last concrete superette, the car labors up the mountain and passes the looming white crucifix planted like a marker at the edge of civilization before coasting south into the desolate valley on the other side. Henry Fayre, at the wheel, looks straight ahead.

Two weeks earlier Wendy was sitting on a pile of newsprint in one of the alcoves along Rat Alley with her quart of wine and her cigarettes, almost emptied of life. She'd watched the rats, fatter than she was, crawl all over her on their way to the garbage. She was wasted at thirty-one. Nowhere to go. She ate in a week what a normal person ate in a day, and most of it came from the garbage. The thought of Vinnie, dead at her age, may have crossed her mind as she watched icicles bleed between the charred sections of brick and trickle close to the wall her face leaned against, or felt the itchy pain of the multiple stitches in her leg. If she stuck around much longer waiting for Traveler to come back, she'd be dead soon, too.

She's not sure exactly what happened after that. She remembers this last morbidly realistic assessment of her circumstances, and then coming to in John's room in Plymouth with a bottle of contraband Valium within easy reach and a body on the verge of giving out. John was an old street chum who'd gone straight. He'd bailed her out a number of times between different men, and she'd always ended up splitting on him. Now he'd saved her life. But as she stared at the pills and felt the clean sheets brush against her skin, she remembered nothing about it. Probably, she thought, he'd discovered her shortly after her drunken epiphany, half dead against the base of a dumpster.

Every four hours for the next two weeks, she popped another pill. She couldn't keep food down, and she couldn't stand noise. She'd been drinking around the clock for months, and she didn't know anything. She subsisted on downers until she was sober enough to pick up the phone and call Granny.

In a matter of hours a deal was struck between the old lady and Wendy's mother in Mississippi. John drove her south in his sixteenwheeler, en route to California. When he dropped her at the Trailways station in downtown Brody, he gave her a hard hug and wished her luck, and that was when she got scared. But by then it was too late.

Her stepfather didn't say much after she slid in beside him in the front seat, and as the valley opens in front of them, she is grateful to him for bringing her to the last place on earth where she will be taken in and allowed to sleep on a mattress again and given one more chance.

After another ten featureless miles of flat, yellow earth, they come to three whitewashed cinderblock bunkers: one a Chevron station, another a car dealership, and the third left for broke, a family restaurant in more optimistic times. They turn right onto a dirt road and pull up outside a swamp-brown trailer. Henry kills the engine. With effort, frail and still shaky, Wendy gets out. She takes a few steps across the gravel, then squints up at the door where she thinks she sees her mother standing.

Molly hasn't set eyes on her daughter in four years. She stares at the almost toothless, hobbling, and haggard woman standing in front of her and bursts into tears.

That night, after Wendy has gone to sleep, Molly hangs onto the cord of the wall telephone like a woman who is drowning. Beside herself, she's dialed the Help Hotline in Brody, sure this time that her daughter is going to die. This Wendy bears no resemblance to the lovely teenager whose eight-by-ten graduation color portrait still smiles shyly from a gold frame on Molly's bedroom bureau. Her skin now is as pale and lifeless as cold dough. Molly doesn't want to imagine what diseases she's picked up in the last four years. She clutches the telephone receiver, stifling her sobs in fistfuls of tissue, and listens for the third straight hour to the man on the other end of the line telling her to be patient, give Wendy a few weeks, decent food, and rest, and she'll begin to look like a human being again.

Molly remembers the first time Wendy scared her, just before she went down to Florida during high school. Molly had finally saved enough money to put a tombstone on her baby boy's grave in Michigan and had gone there alone to perform her private ritual of restitution. While she was in Michigan, she got a call. Wendy had gone crazy. It had taken five police officers to subdue her and get her to a hospital, all because she'd had too much to drink.

That is exactly half her daughter's lifetime ago now, Molly thinks. How many times since has she begged judges to help her by committing Wendy to a psychiatric hospital? And that bizarre Indian marriage she'd gotten into. Now it is Molly who is thinking about killing herself.

By March Wendy can almost count the number of times she's left her bedroom, much less gone past the front screen door. But she hasn't touched a drink, the longest stretch of sobriety she's had since she was eighteen.

The morning for her is waking up and looking out at the highway from one set of windows; from the other she sees identical trailers planted on tiny lots wrapped in chain link, distinguished only by a folding chair on the gravel, a sparse zinnia or carrot garden in front of the cars.

Once or twice, in the beginning, she went outside after breakfast. At the end of the short gravel driveway, past the gray mailbox and the few other trailers, stretch uncultivated fields backed by shaggy trees. If she turns left, a dirt road takes her past buckling white-washed shacks with crates full of old television sets and damaged appliances sagging on the grass behind signs that read DO NOT ENTER KEEP OUT.

Never any voices. Never any children.

Past these, there is nothing but wide fields of winter rye, all for sale and no one buying. She would stare at the flat land caught in by hills so distant they might be mythical, feel the sun coming up along her back and hear the haunting, ever-present cry of the roosters, and know that there would never be enough trees to shade her from August when it came. Standing there on the outskirts of this nowhere town, it occurred to her that there was very possibly no place on earth farther from where she had once expected to be at this point in her life, no place farther from Paris.

In the living room on these early spring days she watches her mother work on quilts, smoke, and drink coffee until Henry returns for dinner. She can flop down on one of the two easy chairs and let the drone of the television wash over her. Or she can walk the five feet to the refrigerator and pour herself a glass of Pepsi. Another five steps will take her to the end of the trailer, if she wants to use the washer and dryer. She takes two showers every day just to relieve the tedium.

She has to give her mother credit. Molly has done her best to make the place feel like home. A couple of Papa's better oil paintings hang from the paneled walls, between little knickknack shelves weighed down with pictures of her brothers and their kids. All the end tables have doilies on them, as they always did up north in Massachusetts, anchored by plastic floral arrangements and ubiquitous ashtrays. Molly has even managed to find several attractive throw rugs to mask the mustard wall-to-wall indoor-outdoor carpet. She's hung baskets in the avocado green dinette and a cutting board above the two-burner electric range.

It had taken Molly clear through February to persuade Wendy to cut and dye her hair. Now Wendy's glad she did. Molly also shelled out for a pair of glasses, so Wendy can actually see her sunny chestnut curls when she looks in the mirror.

They talk, the two of them. Wendy tells stories about Traveler. She tells Molly that he was the worst of the lot, the toughest and the meanest. But he was also the smartest. Molly nods as she pushes her needle through yet another square on her quilt. It's like it was with Papa, Molly muses. Wendy gravitated to him because he was intelligent. In so many ways, that has been her downfall; she can't accept simple people, many people — Molly, certainly, among them.

Molly asks her daughter how a woman lives on the street. She is genuinely interested. Where did she go to the bathroom? How did she eat? How did she keep clean?

Wendy answers patiently. It feels good to talk about the world she knows so well, better than any other. On Sundays, she tells her mother, they drink aftershave on the streets of Boston. Aftershave and mouthwash. She tells Molly about the shelters. They're pits, she says, awful places. She was kicked out of every one of them. She laughs. She occasionally badmouths some of the counselors at the shelters.

Why does she get such an attitude about people who try and help her? Molly wonders. It is such a mystery to her, the way Wendy uses people and manipulates them, then turns on them with contempt. Where did all her anger and self-hatred come from? What did Molly do wrong as a mother? But Molly keeps these thoughts to herself. For the past three months, she feels like she's been walking on eggs.

At the other end of the living room are the two bedrooms, which share a common wall. After she and her mother have exhausted their conversation, Wendy spends most of every day in her room. She reads on her bed and listens to tapes on the tape deck her stepfather bought her soon after she arrived. She's also discovered that she still loves coloring books. It is a good afternoon when she can sit for hours listening to Patsy Cline through the headphones and pushing stubs of crayon around the printed images without getting blue.

John, her rescuer, writes from Boston. He tells her he knows how hard it is to do what she's doing. Stick to it, he writes. Be patient. You'll be glad in the end.

One Saturday afternoon Wendy's brother Jacob comes up from Georgia to visit. They sit on the sofa in the living room and talk for

four hours. Other members of the family come in and out of her life
in these months, uncles and aunts, nieces, cousins. Molly hopes that
they, who know Wendy's crazy-quilt past, can bridge the gap she feels
between her life on the streets up north and in this southern town of
a thousand strangers. But the talks and family visits are about all Wendy
feels up to. After they're over, she retreats to her bedroom.

On the other side of the closed door, Molly sews and does the laundry and makes grocery lists and worries. Besides Wendy, she's looking
after two of her grandchildren. The oldest, Tommy, who is twelve,
adores his aunt Wendy. He tries so hard to please her. When the
mobile library comes to town once a week, he borrows books for her.
He buys her crayons and whatever coloring books she hasn't already
gotten at the dry goods store. But Wendy seems to need to keep her
distance. Whenever anyone, even Molly, tries to hug or cuddle her,
she winces.

"Don't touch me," she'll snap.

She's edgy, tense. Molly can't count the number of times she's told
her, "Go out and meet some people. There are lots of nice young
people here."

But Wendy answers, "They're too ignorant. I have nothing in common with them."

Her sobriety is an act of will so intense, so concentrated, and yet so
directionless that it frightens Molly. What are Wendy's goals? What
does she see for herself beyond sobriety? Wendy wants nothing to
do with the people around her. She wants only the world of her
books.

Not for the first time, Molly begins to sense that the life she thinks
of as "normal" is too dull and uninspiring to hold Wendy for long.
Perhaps she's been in that other world of bravado and fantasy and
danger for so long that she feels like herself only when she doesn't
belong anywhere else. When she is different. It is as if Wendy is protecting, even nurturing, some inviolable pact with that life even now,
Molly thinks, not knowing where it will lead but knowing and clinging
to it nonetheless.

But Wendy's sense of alienation in New Freedom couldn't be more
profound.

Over the mountain in Brody, where the newspapers come from
every day, life flows on a current of cotillions and Friends of the Library lectures on Dostoevsky. Deviled eggs and cheese balls are served

at teas and wedding showers, with local girls playing background music on baby grand pianos, given to them on their sixteenth birthdays. Roxanne Pulitzer's book tour will be front-page news here. Debby Boone takes "love offerings" at the local shopping malls, and the daily religion page runs headlines like "Study Shows Religion Makes Life Happier." On Sunday morning the townspeople pour out of countless churches, the women wearing silk dresses, matching shoes and handbags, rabbit fur stoles, and hats with veils on them. Wendy hasn't been inside a church in years and has no intention of starting now.

Life in the valley proves to be a pale imitation of Brody's city customs. She has seen what is out there. Occasionally in the afternoons, when she agrees to go into town with her mother, they drive across the highway and roll slowly up a short incline and then down again to Bob's turquoise aluminum-sided store, the only place in town to buy clothes and, when shipments arrive, red plastic loafers, china dogs, garden hoses, pine oil cleaner, and anniversary clocks.

Or they browse through the greeting cards in the drug store, pick up a jar of Nivea cream and a coloring book. Sometimes they end their outing at the Family Restaurant. Carefully pulling open the torn screen door, they spot a vacant vinyl booth and settle in. Emily brings them iced teas without waiting to be asked, sweet, with lots of ice, and tall spoons. When the jukebox is working, it grinds out country and western all day long and well into the evening, until Emily has rolled up the last fork and knife into the last paper napkin on the orange cafeteria tray for the next day's business.

Not infrequently, as Wendy and Molly drive through town, they pass other women in faded cotton skirts or jeans, sweeping their front porches. Sometimes Wendy sees a woman about her age, sitting with a young child on cinderblock steps outside of her trailer home, watching her husband on a tractor, sweat running down his shirtless back, struggling to stir up soil and hope from the stones in the small plot they've undoubtedly bought on credit.

Nothing could be farther from everything she's ever known, or anything she can imagine for herself. She returns to the trailer and crawls back under the covers, tunes in to Patsy Cline, and waits for dinner. Afterward she'll step out onto the gravel and smoke a cigarette, watching the mountains turn blue, backlit by the sun. She waits until the fields and shacks and worksheds have grown hazy in the twilight, and the red clover has deepened and flamed before the sun

finally dies. Then in the darkness she thinks about the boys back north
and wonders what has become of them.

If Wendy had had what, for her, would have seemed the dubious
opportunity to return to the Horizon Hospital program in St. Petersburg instead of to her mother's place, she would have learned that
the leading views about alcohol addiction had changed dramatically
since she'd been there in 1980. Not only was the problem of addiction
now understood with greater sophistication, so was the treatment.

After 1980 the staff of the private facility bought out the management and introduced a broader range of treatment approaches with
the underlying philosophy that the *whole* person and not just the "addict" needed to be treated.

What they and other pathbreakers began to conclude was that alcohol per se was not the disease — as so many states had argued stren-
uously fifteen years earlier, in the nation's first successful efforts at
decriminalization. The disease was *addiction,* and it could take many
forms. Drugs, alcohol, work, even pathological relationships were now
being seen as expressions of the same underlying complex of emotional need and low self-esteem.

These days at Horizon Hospital, Andy Siegel, a staff counselor, registered nurse, and recovering "cocaine jet-setter," as he describes himself, conducts recovery program workshops. He also tries to extend
the new understanding of the problem on the part of alcohol treatment professionals by giving visitors' tours and attending conferences
whenever he can.

"Okay, people recognize that alcoholism is a disease," he says. "The
field today says *no. Addiction* is the disease; alcohol is one of many
substances. By labeling alcoholism a disease, we're doing a disservice,
actually."

Bad public policy, he explains, has resulted from faulty perceptions. For instance, the many states that decriminalized drunkenness
with the argument that alcoholism was a disease have separate laws
dealing with drug offenders. By law, alcoholics could be involuntarily
committed to a detox facility by the police or, with a court hearing, by
social service agencies and family members.

With respect to drug addicts, law enforcement remains aimed exclusively at arresting traffickers. Treatment is virtually nonexistent.
Andy points out that regardless of what one believes about the effec-

tiveness of involuntarily committing a person for addiction treatment, this double standard means that there has been no pressure to establish detox programs for drug addicts. Even states with reasonably adequate alcohol treatment facilities are an embarrassment when it comes to providing decent drug detoxification, which is becoming a more critical issue in the era of AIDS.[1]

Another disservice, Siegel says, is in the quality and effectiveness of treatment. Up through the early eighties, alcoholism was treated according to what is known as the behavioral model. The behaviorists still dominate most public and private treatment facilities. Simply put, the behaviorist approach says that you cure addiction by changing the basic behaviors that lead a person to drink. You reinforce the new learned behaviors with a new set of friends, a support system (like AA), and a new lifestyle. "One day at a time," the Alcoholics Anonymous motto, warns, among other things, of the need for the alcoholic to keep watch daily for the reemergence of old negative behavior patterns.

More recent thinking in the field is that although behavioral psychology may be an essential tool for recovery from addiction, it is not the only one. Increasingly, experts are arguing that addiction is a very common response to having become "stuck" developmentally because of childhood abuse, neglect, insufficient nurturance, or a number of other emotionally damaging early traumas. Whatever the cause, these early formative experiences create in addictive personalities two fairly constant phenomena: low self-esteem and an inability to trust others and establish real intimacy. In searching for ways to get out from under these crippling emotional weaknesses, addicts become hooked on whatever frees them from feelings of inadequacy: intoxication, money, success. At the same time they become obsessed with controlling their environment and the people around them as much as possible.

In an effort to address the deeper issues at the root of addiction, hospitals like Horizon are now adding to the behavioral approach an array of psychoanalytic techniques aimed at helping people get back to their "stuck" points and working through them. Horizon Hospital uses therapeutic communities — groups of patients who help make decisions about the group's activities — intensive individual counseling, biofeedback, assertiveness training, values clarification, and psychodrama and movement groups, among many other methods.

Andy Siegel doesn't have to know Wendy personally to be all too familiar with her behavior when he hears about it second hand.

"So she is in relapse." He nods his head. "If you don't make any friends, if you don't do anything, then you're not really changing. You're going to go back to it. It doesn't matter if the person's working or not. Returning to mainstream society's not the idea. If you're an addict, you need to be with other recovering people, or you won't be in recovery.

"Relapse is a progression that starts with isolation, with loneliness, with making excuses for not going to [AA] meetings, with changing your eating patterns, sleeping patterns. Your emotional instability will come back. There are thirty-nine signs, the *last* of which is picking up the drug or the drink," he says.

The addict's loneliness, he says, isn't so much situational; it isn't just the sense of having nothing in common with others or of identifying with street life. It is the continued inability to "break the intimacy barrier" with others. Siegel himself lived on the streets and has treated many hundreds of others who have as well. To those who argue that street alcoholics don't get sober because the emotional cost of losing their drinking buddies and their lifestyle is too high a price to pay, Siegel has a different answer.

"One of the things that I've observed is that there seems to be a real factor of laziness, lethargy. The street people I've had, every one of them had some type of abuse as a child," he says. "Usually sexual abuse. The laziness is often a reaction to that. 'I'm worthless anyway; it was my fault that it happened.'

"The other thing is that it's a lifestyle that really prohibits much intimacy. You don't sit around and have philosophical discussions, you don't let people in too deep. That is a problem with survivors of abuse. They need to learn how to be intimate. Wendy stopped drinking, but she didn't learn anything about intimacy. That would be pretty overwhelming. You want to go back to something where you can at least have people around."

"When do you think you'll be ready to go back to work?" Wendy's stepfather asks her one evening.

"I'm ready."

It is her attempt at survival. She's not allergic to work. But her sudden willingness is less an urge to rejoin the laboring class than it is a desperate effort to keep herself preoccupied and sane. Henry Fayre comes through, lining up a job for her not far from where he works.

Each morning at six-thirty she leaves the trailer with her stepfather and pulls onto the highway. By seven she will be seated in a production line over a computer board. She works alongside other women at a common table, plugging little circuit chips onto the panels that make up the guts of the nation's pay phones. The small elements are picked up and fastened on by hand. The work requires fine hand-eye coordination. For this she earns $4.10 an hour, not including overtime. A good enough obsession for now.

Wendy is one of three hundred employees at Bitex, the major employer in the area. When it is time for her break, she opens her purse and takes out the book she carries with her. At lunch she reads again. The other women, mostly from the town and most, like Wendy, with high school degrees, pass the tedious hours keeping up a steady patter of chat and gossip. Wendy never participates.

"The stupidity!" she says when she walks through the door of the trailer every night.

"I'm a good worker," she storms. "My first day on the job, I put out over two hundred boards. These girls have been there two years, and they get pissed!"

Maybe you should try and make a few friends, Molly suggests.

"I don't like to talk when I'm working," Wendy snaps. "I can't help it. It's just the way I am. I'm sorry. I'm hyper. It's not that I'm trying to be rude. I'm just trying to do my job."

"Talk at lunch, then." Molly pursues the point.

"They're all talking about their kids and their husbands and what color curtains they are going to get for this room," Wendy answers. "What do I have? What can I talk about? How many years I slept in different doorways? I'm *afraid* to open up."

She makes a point of wearing long-sleeved blouses to cover the slash marks that ride up and down her arms.

It will come, her mother tells her, in time. Once you've made a friend, all that will come out naturally at the right time.

"But they're so stupid! So stupid! They've got no sensitivity," she storms. "If I reduce myself to reading Harlequin romances I might as well be two years old again! Jesus, I'm sorry. I just hate stupidity."

Molly goes back to her dinner preparations. There's no use arguing.

At the end of April, Wendy orders luggage from a mail-order catalog.

"Are you planning on leaving?" Molly asks.

"No."

Now in the mornings, on the half-hour drive to the plant, as she watches the view of meadows and farmland yield to lakes, she savors the quiet, smokes her last cigarette until her midmorning break, and begins to talk to her stepfather about how much she misses the boys in Boston. They had a camaraderie that she'll never find down here. She's glad she's sober. But how long can you live without real companionship? she wants to know.

TWENTY-FOUR

Out of the Shadows

ON VALENTINE'S DAY Amanda gives Sandy Jones a letter of appreciation that she wants put in Jackie's file. The act has a stamp of finality about it. It is formalizing her gratitude, but it is also a way of saying goodbye. Amanda knows in her heart of hearts that she's exhausted the resources of the shelter.

"I can't really go any further," she tells herself. What she doesn't know is how to reach beyond the confines of this world and make the long hours and endless days of waiting more than just that. In many ways, she has never known how to take the steps necessary to initiate change and growth in her life.

January has dragged into February, wet, gray, and stagnant, and still no word about moving. Half Moon, originally scheduled to be finished by March 1, is progressing more slowly than expected.

Amanda has become involved in an informal work program at St. Paul's, washing supper dishes for two dollars an hour. In early February she took her first earnings and opened a savings account at the Bank of Boston. Last week she got an official photo ID at the Registry of Motor Vehicles.

But she is becoming restless and dispirited. Joan Norton resigned in early January. Genevieve has been promoted to a desk job and is completely unavailable.

And so Amanda daydreams, anticipating what it will be like to be on her own again, starting over, having her own set of keys, to a door that only she can lock and unlock. She fantasizes about taking Jackie out for dinner with Genevieve, all dressed up in stockings and dresses, just the three of them. She'll get a phone. She'll be free to invite people over any time she wants. Daydreams make the waiting bearable. They also intensify the frustration she feels with her life.

She has grown increasingly sensitive to the shortcomings of those around her. The environment is beginning to get on her nerves, as are most of the people in it. When Genevieve stops taking her meds for a few days and has a fight with her therapist, Amanda begins to wonder how much she trusts her. And she is still angry with her sister, Jane, about so many things. Soon nothing is right.

Jackie watches this change with concern. Amanda is backsliding. She hopes the move won't be delayed much longer. One night Amanda comes into the shower room to discuss yet another incident that occurred in Jackie's absence over the weekend.

"Amanda," Jackie says to her abruptly, "you're spending too damned much time worrying about everybody else's problems. You're to go tomorrow morning and find a job."

The display windows of Morgie's, the retail store of Morgan Memorial/Goodwill Industries, on Berkeley Street in the South End, remind Amanda of Woolworth's, with their matchless collage of the rummaged and the remaindered, polyester shirtwaists and picnic baskets. Amanda takes a deep breath, pushes through the heavy glass doors, scans the racks of clothing, purses, table lamps, and toy trucks, and soon finds herself seated at an umbrella table that is missing its umbrella, filling out an application form with long-forgotten facts about herself. A kind woman wearing a pale pink sweater and a black skirt with large white daisies on it takes the form and reads it over.

"Okay," she tells Amanda, "you're all set now." They are short of help, Amanda is told. Come back tomorrow.

She does go back and, as she joyously announces to Jackie later that night in the showers, she has a job.

Every morning now she leaves Pine Street with Alice, who works nearby. They stop for breakfast at Billy's, a greasy spoon with a handful of linoleum-topped tables and generous cheese omelets before separating for the day. Once she arrives at Morgie's, Amanda goes directly to her department, women's clothing. Items there are tagged, counted, and inventoried two mornings a week. If she is efficient and gets this done early, she has the afternoon to neaten things up and put everything back where it belongs after customers riffle through and try things on. From Tuesday through Friday new clothes come into the department every day. She has to tag them, hang them up, and keep things straight.

She soon discovers a small alcove in the corner just past her department, called the Book Nook. Quiet and safe, it has the feel of a small used book library. An older man appears to run it, shelving books and straightening up all day long. Amanda starts to spend her free time there, talking to the man and offering to help. Soon she is arriving early so that she can do some work in the Book Nook herself before she begins her assigned duties.

Amanda has a phone call. It is April Fool's Day and, by coincidence, her day off. As she is summoned, she knows that the call is rife with possibility. She crosses the women's unit lobby and steps inside the office. Monica is seated at one of the desks, doing some paperwork. Something's up. With a clammy hand, she lifts the receiver.

An instant later she drops it on the desk. "I'm in housing!" she screams, throwing her fists in the air.

"I'm in housing!"

Monica looks up and smiles. Sandy Jones comes to the door.

"We all knew." Sandy grins. "Congratulations."

She ought not to believe it. It's too good to be true. A room she's never laid eyes on before, in a building she's never been in, is about to become hers.

She runs into the lobby and embraces the first person she encounters. She is going home again. And the best news of all is that Genevieve is moving in right across the hall.

Then she stops. She looks at the yellow walls and the wooden benches, and everything falls into confusion briefly. What is she doing? She loves this place in a way. Here she has been loved.

Feelings of exaltation and doubt struggle within her for several confused moments. She feels numb. Then the rush of all that must be done floods her doubt in a wave of giddy busyness. She has to get her belongings together quickly. How is she going to get everything over there? Who is going to get in touch with Genevieve at work? When will she have a chance to say goodbye to Jackie?

It doesn't take long. The few things she's been storing in one of the lockers since February fit easily into a few garbage bags. Now she wants to see her new room. Right now.

The turn-of-the-century brownstones are not distinguished in any way. They are handsome, serene, and gracious, tucked behind wrought iron fences. This is the Beacon Street lodging house, which happened to have two vacancies just as Jackie was beginning to believe that, construction delays notwithstanding, Amanda shouldn't wait any longer for a room in Half Moon.

Amanda steps out of the car and surveys the building with satisfaction. It will be hard to feel isolated on this heavily traveled section of Beacon, with its Oriental rug dealers, family markets, a beauty salon, and an ice cream parlor almost right across the street, and a villagelike commercial square just up the hill in Brookline. The rest of the neighborhood is made up of university students and professors, well-to-do professionals, and elderly Jewish residents.

Amanda heads for the door. No one is expecting her. She is asked to wait in the manager's office while Jerry, the woman who will help her line up social services once she moves in, wrestles with what to do with her now. The previous occupant of Amanda's room, it seems, has been hospitalized, but her effects remain. Jerry decides to worry about these logistical problems later. An eager and not-to-be-disappointed woman, whose spirits are swiftly sinking, is rooted in front of her.

Jerry tells Amanda to follow her, and they pass through an elegant Victorian parlor and a dining room, climb a flight of carpeted stairs, and come to a stop on the second-floor landing. Jerry opens a cardboard shoe box full of keys. A feeling of quiet comfort permeates the house at this hour. Four bedrooms and a common bathroom open onto this hallway. Some of them, Jerry tells Amanda as she looks for her key, have fireplaces. Everywhere, Amanda observes, the wainscoting has been freshly finished, the ornate ceiling moldings painted china white, and the mauve hallways hung with attractive museum-quality prints.

After several attempts, Jerry succeeds in locating the right key. Amanda pushes open the door and enters. It feels as natural to her as if she'd been doing it for years. The room is perfect, not too big and not too small. She walks its length, about twelve feet, across pebble-gray carpeting, and comes to the single window overlooking, through white sheers, a parking lot at the rear of the building. Then she turns around and surveys the room. There is just enough width to walk between the single bed against one wall and the blond dresser opposite. She examines the matching desk and the bed table. She opens the closet door. She tries the light; it renders the off-white walls sunny with a warm, early evening glow. She is suddenly overwhelmed by an unexpected, heady pride.

"Well, folks" — she turns to Jerry who is waiting at the door — "this is home sweet home!"

Then, stepping back into the hallway, she gingerly closes the door behind her. She is ready to return to Pine Street.

It is nearly two o'clock that afternoon when she takes a seat on one of the benches in the lobby. For months, she and Genevieve have planned this moment. Their first night in housing was to be celebrated with a steak dinner, complete with garlic bread, salad, wine, and dessert. But that is the last thing she can imagine now. More than anything in the world, she wants to go back to St. Paul's for one last dinner.

It won't be goodbye. Bob and Jackie have said she can visit St. Paul's whenever she wants. Just this morning Monica and Sandy assured her that any time she feels like it, she should stop by the Inn and say hello. They are part of her support system. She needs them.

And now, if everything goes as it is supposed to, there will be more supports. Jerry will be essential to making this happen. She'll find Amanda a therapist to take over where Joan Norton left off, and she'll get her into an Adult Children of Alcoholics group.

Amanda wonders what her new therapist will be like. She hopes whoever it is will have some experience in dealing with homeless people, because she knows beyond a shadow of a doubt that homelessness isn't something a person leaves behind. Homelessness changes you forever. And any counselor who tries to overlook it as a merely incidental "phase" in her life, relatively unimportant in relation to deeper, longer-standing problems, will fail her. She *is* homeless. She's not prepared to part with that identity quickly or easily.

In the office Monica Donner has other matters on her mind. She has just received a message from one of the federally subsidized elderly apartment buildings that Janice, the elderly woman who lost her savings to her niece's indulgences, has been accepted for an apartment. But a second message follows: Janice had to be rejected after the management ran a credit check on her store charges and discovered one of the unpaid bills her niece ran up when Janice was in the hospital.

Now Monica is on the phone with them. "Just because she owes Jordan Marsh, you mean to tell me this woman can't have an apartment?"

Sandy is standing next to her.

"You see," she muses out loud, "this is how they throw barriers up

between the women and housing. But they're a private company, so
there's nothing you can do."

Monica hangs up and just shakes her head. She can't look at Sandy
for a minute. She can't speak.

Amanda and Genevieve make the last trip that evening by van together. At St. Paul's the dining room is in chaos: a nearby family shelter is visiting for dinner. Youngsters, on foot and on scooters, grasp-
ing balloons, are chasing one another around the room.

Amanda and Genevieve eat hastily. Then they circulate, hugging
friends goodbye. To some they have already become unreal: they are
getting out. To others their good fortune is too painful to acknowledge. And to still others, the loss of their presence among the regulars
hurts too much to share their happiness. No one knows when they
will see each other again.

Soon Amanda has said fairwell to all but one person. She heads for
the office. Jackie is sorting through plastic bags full of donated clothing. Don't start crying, Amanda tells herself.

Jackie turns and looks at her. "Amanda!"

For the first time, both the counselor and her young friend are at a
loss for words. Jackie reaches out and takes Amanda into her arms.

"Now, I want you to eat well," she instructs Amanda. "And take
care of yourself. And don't get into trouble." Amanda clings to her
without saying a word, and then, with a nod, she lets go.

A few minutes later the shelter sign and the vaulting tower of St.
Paul's disappear behind the receding hilltop out the back window of
the cab. Amanda watches them vanish, and then with a catch in her
voice turns to Genevieve. "We've earned this."

"Yes," her friend replies. "But we didn't earn what we had to go
through to get here, Amanda."

When Amanda lets herself into her room that night, she doesn't
unpack. The only thing she does before she gets into bed is place her
notebook on the night table next to her and reach into her knapsack
for the photograph someone took at the Inn's Christmas party. She
props this against her notebook, slides under the covers, and studies
it before turning out the light. In the photo Amanda, wearing her
hand-me-down ski jacket and staring into the camera, is standing next
to Jackie. Jackie is beaming proudly at her baby daughter, Moira, in
her arms. But despite Moira's wide-eyed gaze, it is on the child's hand

that Amanda's eye always comes to rest. Just before the shutter clicked, Amanda had reached up gently and, like a sister, clasped Moira's hand.

Five o'clock continues to be her wake-up hour, alarm or no. She showers, dresses, and is down on the street at the trolley stop by seven, waiting for the fifteen-minute ride to work. She can't imagine what she'd have done if she'd moved into housing without a job. She is convinced that the loneliness and purposelessness would have sent her back to the streets in less than a month.

Even with the job, most days, she makes time to stop at the Inn on the way to work, on the excuse that she still needs to use the clothing room. She has no wardrobe of her own. But once she gets there, the pleasure of seeing her old friends is often blunted. She quickly senses the resentment of the women who have been in the shelter much longer than she was and are still waiting.

"Well, look, ladies," she thinks defensively, "if you had gotten off your asses and done everything I did, you wouldn't still be here."

But she knows she could never have done it without the encouragement and the will of the staff behind her. And the truth is, the job doesn't begin to fill the void that exists in her life now that she's left St. Paul's.

Soon after she moved in, she found a typed memo from Jerry under her door. It was efficient but detached, giving her names and addresses of local mental health centers and the hours when Jerry was available to talk to residents. Amanda was shattered. For days she was so upset about it she could talk about nothing else.

"All of a sudden, I get these notes from people I do not know, do not trust, and don't have any idea of where they're coming from. I don't know where the Brookline Mental Health Center is. I don't know who works there. I don't know nothing from a hole in the wall. I mean, and this lady's supposed to be my support system?"

She is alarmed that Jerry expects *her* to call Brookline Mental Health and make her own appointment. But on top of this, she is angry that after writing the memo, Jerry went off on vacation for a week. The first four days in the house, Amanda didn't speak to a soul except Genevieve. That Saturday night she called Jackie from a pay phone and they talked briefly. But now she is overwhelmed by feelings of abandonment.

She and Genevieve have begun to quarrel. The Saturday night of the first weekend, Genevieve invited a man to stay over with her. Amanda, who'd hoped to spend her Sunday off with Genevieve, was furious. By the second week they aren't speaking.

Amanda's days now consist of work and little else. She starts the morning at Morgie's by putting books in the Book Nook. She is proud of the progress she's made in the little room, set apart from the rest of the store by thin plywood walls. She feels at home in the miniature library. Then she deals with the clothes. She has completely reorganized the children's merchandise, putting sweaters on one rack, shorts on another rack, skirts on another, with the satisfaction of knowing that her supervisor approves.

By the time she gets home, some nights not before six-thirty or seven, she is tired. She drops her knapsack on her bed, makes her way back downstairs, and, still in her coat, fixes a cup of coffee. Then she remounts the stairs and relaxes for about an hour before heading across the street to the small grocery to get herself some already-prepared food to eat. The last time she cooked for herself was in 1974. Her old rooming houses hadn't allowed cooking, so she'd routinely gone out to eat or had brought cold cuts back to her room with her.

This lodging house has no organized evening social activities. And because she doesn't know how to get one, she still doesn't have a phone. Every other place she's lived either already had one or provided a pay phone. So she spends her evenings alone, propped up against her pillows, eating individual fruit pies and take-out coffee and staring at the second-hand television she bought on her first day off. She is lonely.

The next weekend is Easter. Already Genevieve has decorated her room with curtains, a pale pastel quilt, and wall posters. She's gotten a telephone and reestablished contact with old friends. She's taken the time to send thank-you notes to the staff at the shelter for their help. Now, to celebrate, she plans a full Easter dinner. She's invited Buff over for the occasion, and she asks Amanda to join them.

Amanda refuses. By now she's convinced that Genevieve just used her to get into housing. That Easter Sunday, while the sounds of the festive dinner can be heard throughout the house, Amanda spends the day locked in her room, putting together a jigsaw puzzle.

On the last Tuesday in April, Julie is sitting by the phone at St. Paul's and picks it up when it rings. It is Amanda, calling from work. She'd like to come over for dinner and attend the Women's Group. She wants someone to talk to.

There is a long pause on the line. Julie struggles. For one thing, Jackie is out sick. For another, the guests don't need the demoralization of having Amanda come in, dominate the discussion to meet her own needs, and then walk out the door again. And last, Amanda shouldn't be relying on the shelter for her social life.

"I'm sorry, Amanda," Julie says at last. "I just don't think that would be appropriate. It's not a suitable forum for you anymore."

Amanda can't believe it. She tries to think of something that will change Julie's mind.

"I was given to understand by Jackie and Bob that I'd be welcome to go back there any time."

"I'm sorry," says Julie. "It doesn't apply."

Stung and rejected, Amanda hangs up.

All of a sudden I'm not good enough to go over there and have dinner, she thinks. I can go back to Pine Street and talk to people there, but I can't go back to St. Paul's and eat dinner and talk to the women?

The next day she calls Brookline Mental Health. But the conversation proves a disaster.

"The person on the other end of the phone wasn't very business-like," she says later. "Another phone call came in. She goes, 'Oh, shit.' "

Amanda recoiled.

"You don't do things like that when you're dealing with the general public on the phone," she says, "I don't care who you are." The receptionist came back on the line and told her that on Wednesdays, today, there was a general group meeting. She would have to be evaluated and fill out an application. Fees were on a sliding scale, from five to seventy-five dollars per fifty-minute session.

After she hangs up and has a chance to react, Amanda decides to see if Joan Norton is willing to work with her again.

Nearly a month has passed since she left St. Paul's, and she hasn't called Jackie since the first Saturday night she was in her new home. Another month drags by. No one hears from Amanda. Then one sunny morning in early June, she marches into the Pine Street Inn's women's unit and announces, "I'm quitting my job."

The news elicits stunned silence.

"There's too much happy bullshit going on there," she says. "Woolworth's was nothing compared to this!"

First, she tells Sandy, the people at work tell her they are happy with her performance. Then they say they aren't. Four different people seem to have a hand in overseeing her, and all of them think they are her boss. She doesn't want to discuss it. She feels overwhelmed. She just wants to leave.

Jackie, recuperating at home from a staph infection that developed from a leg injury earlier in the winter, has been kept informed of Amanda's progress by staffers who have talked to Amanda when she's stopped by on her way to work. Now, when Jackie hears of this latest development, she isn't surprised. At a certain level, she feels, Amanda is pitted in an internal battle between the desire for independence and the longing to return to the nurturing environment of the shelter. Part of her unconsciously wants to fail, Jackie believes. Precisely for this reason, she feels that the last thing Amanda needs now is for Jackie to rush to her assistance and reinforce her dependency by helping to resolve the struggle. Jackie can only look on from a distance and hope for the best.

Somehow, miraculously, Amanda decides not to tender her notice that day. Instead she goes home, curls up with the Cabbage Patch doll and the stuffed dog she bought at Morgie's, and turns on the television.

The next morning she returns to work. For the next few weeks she continues to stop at the Inn every morning. Once or twice she invites friends there to visit her at work. Alice sometimes meets her for lunch. The world of St. Paul's isn't going to completely disappear on her, she learns.

She begins to decorate her room. At Morgie's she finds a set of small porcelain milk bottles and miniature castiron pots and pans like those in the dollhouse that her mother kept in the kitchen at home. She begins a collection of tiny china animals, which she arranges with painstaking care, first on her dresser and then, when the groupings have grown too large, on a low bookshelf that she buys for the purpose. For her bed she collects oversized stuffed animals.

She still carries one of the old-fashioned composition notebooks in her knapsack. Over coffee at breakfast and at lunch time, she begins to record her impressions of her workplace, its personalities, and the relationships she is developing with her peers. When there are quiet moments on the floor, she drops by her supervisor's office and that of *her* boss, showing them her writing.

Jackie returns to work at the Inn, and one day toward the end of June, Amanda decides to stop by and see her. With excitement and an element of dread, she enters the lobby. At that very moment Jackie comes around the corner wearing a pair of tan slacks and a large, colorful cotton shirt.

"Hi!" she calls out.

The two women embrace. Then they sit down and talk. The time passes quickly. Jackie remarks with concern that it looks like Amanda is losing weight again. Amanda describes her job. But as they talk, Amanda knows that things can't be the same as they once were. She'll continue to call Jackie from time to time, and she'll always feel close to her. But the shelter isn't her world anymore. Her support system, her circle of friends, her life, have grown beyond it. Jackie is no longer her mom. From now on she will be her friend.

The lodging house is just blocks from Amanda's old studio apartment. Now on her days off she ventures up to the old familiar streets. Here and there people start to remember her. At the Beacon Market one night, the sales clerk looks up as she is totaling Amanda's purchases.

"Hey," she exclaims. "How are you? I haven't seen you in a long time. You look great!"

At McDonald's, she is served by a girl whose sister had worked with her at Woolworth's. The next time Amanda stops in, the girl comes over to her table and tells her, "Oh, by the way, Agnes says hello."

Then one warm summer evening, as she is strolling down the hill toward home, the sweet, heavy odor of flowering trees evoking in her a rare feeling of serenity, a man approaches, frantic. He is flourishing a gun. He raises it to his temple and fires. Toy caps pop in the summer air. He fires again and again, passing her in a state of frenzy.

At the intersection Amanda calmly flags a passing squad car. The officer pulls over and listens to her story. After thanking her for the tip, he recognizes her.

"So, you're okay again," he says. "Welcome back!"

TWENTY-FIVE

Again

HOLLY SLIDES the last aluminum tub full of wrapped sandwiches into the van and yanks the door shut. The July night looks clear and mild. She and J.T. will be on until the sun comes up, passing out coffee and sandwiches, offering quiet conversation, transportation, and some connection to those who won't, for any number of reasons, go to a shelter.

Now she starts the engine and slowly wheels out. J.T., in the passenger seat, checks the supply of cigarettes they have to dispense and feels to makes sure he has the magnetic card that will get them into the automatic teller machines where some of their clientele take refuge. Then the two friends settle into the desultory conversation that carries them through the early hours of the night, when the work is slow. They swap tales about bad winters spent in other parts of the country. Some nights they talk about their dogs or their hometowns. Or they complain about their roommates. If one of them has taken a night off, they catch each other up on the street folks. It is a long and relatively lonely shift, especially on Sunday nights, with only a temperamental two-way radio connecting them to the Inn and civilization.

They've recently run into Traveler for the first time in months. He was down by the railroad yards reciting Robert Frost's "Stopping by Woods" when they came upon him. He told them that Wendy was sober and living in Mississippi and was never coming back. He himself had just returned from thirty days at Bridgewater. He'd been arrested for trespassing, up at the White Hen Pantry. He grinned, bemused by his own existence.

Sometimes as Holly and J.T. track the street people, they try to figure out what certain patterns of migration and relationship mean and what effect they have on those who remain behind. When Wendy left, the whole character of the loose-knit group she hung with changed. It was as if their glue had gone. They still travel the streets together, but a certain vitality has vanished.

By now Holly knows the streets and hiding places of this hidden world as well as anyone. And she knows at least a piece of nearly every person's story. She knows now that to live on the street is to live in fear — of other street people, of young punks, and of AIDS. And that many things become easy, even necessary — lying and stealing, for instance — when you're scared.

As she turns out of the South End onto Dartmouth Street and heads for the Back Bay, she reflects on how the original idea of "rescue" has been modified with the past winter's experience.

"Maybe we have saved lives," she says later. "We can't really know 'what if' — what if you hadn't brought somebody in on a cold night? But the van never really turned into the dramatic sort of rescue thing that Pine Street maybe thought it would. The public image is that we're trying to get people inside," she acknowledges. "That isn't the mission as perceived out here."

The team sees itself simply reestablishing connection where traditional approaches have obviously failed. Most of the people she will see tonight (probably forty-two out of fifty will be men) will be glad for the coffee and the company, but they won't ask for a ride to the Inn.

Women have their own reasons for not wanting to use the shelters. While the men want to avoid being rolled or finding themselves in the middle of a fight in the shelters, most of the women who stay out on the streets say it isn't worth their while to go inside. Some have been barred for being too loud or too drunk, and attempts to bring them in have resulted in their being turned out again before the night is over. So now Holly accepts their refusals without trying to dissuade them. Others are afraid of the congestion or don't want to be parted from their few possessions for the night. Many dislike being condescended to, treated like children. They feel what Holly describes as "a real disdain for the rigidity and rules of the shelter environment." Or they simply don't want to be labeled as either homeless or mentally ill. They don't want to be trapped.

These women find their own means of survival outdoors. But to call it a choice is hardly accurate; it is, rather, the lesser of two evils.

They hide. Under bushes in the city parks, when the weather permits, in entryways on Beacon Hill. After the rest of the city has gone to sleep and the trains have stopped, their shapes appear in doorways near subway steps, in the alcoves of automatic teller machines. Almost every night, the team can count on seeing a handful of these women somewhere in the shadows, no matter how cold it is.

Midnight finds the two van workers cruising toward Copley Square. They keep to a snail's pace in order to peer into the doorways between the Chinese restaurants and the bars and bookshops along the west side of the commercial street. But it is still too early. No one has settled in yet.

Holly suggests that they stop for takeout coffee. As they travel the last sleepy block before the square's untempered noontime of neon, Holly leans forward over the wheel and whispers incredulously to J.T., "Well, look who's here!"

Down on the pavement in front of them, a pack of mechanical rats is running in a circle. Woolly and gray, their black rubber tails flogging them for comic effect, they travel an orbit of futile flight and pursuit, while the metal butterflies piercing their sides unwind maniacally, like clocks running backward.

Wendy has come back. Tonight she's as high as she's ever been, on Listerine. The air is sultry and calm, she's reunited with Traveler, and the only thing wrong with the world is the blue laws.

The rats are amusing. She laughs. The funniest moment is when one of them collides with one of the little plastic toilets that are rolling on wheels toward the gutter, their seats flipping up and down, preposterous in Hong Kong hues. Then Traveler, grinning fixedly, with wet eyes, descends on the creature and with large hands revs it up again.

Now, as Holly watches from the van, Wendy gathers one in each hand and rises up on her knees. As the rodents' wheels whir and tails flail, she thrusts them at passing pedestrians.

"Would you like a pet rat?" She giggles.

A couple has paused, fascinated.

"See my pet?" She holds him up to her cheek. "His name is Rufus." And she lets out a hoarse laugh.

Wendy had known all along that she'd come back. She just hadn't planned on returning so soon.

One day in May she'd found her nephew Tommy fumbling with her tape deck in the living room.

"What the hell are you doing?" she shrieked at him. Startled, he fled from the machine and crouched in a corner of the room, staring at her fearfully.

"What I could tell you about the circumstances of your birth!" she screamed.

She knew that he adored her. She couldn't help herself; she just lost it. Swearing, calling him a little bastard — and worse, no doubt. She couldn't remember. Yelling in that horrible voice that terrified even grown men with its ferocity. From deep inside the restrained tension of months exploded. The dog happened by, and she kicked him, sending him yelping toward the kitchen in shocked pain.

Molly, on hearing it, rushed out to her. Too well versed in the crescendo of her daughter's violence, she acted instinctively. She slapped Wendy, hard, across the face.

That did it. Wendy gave her two weeks' notice at the factory, packed her tape deck and her gut buster, filled her mail-order suitcases, and was out of there.

"Wendy, you know it's that first sip you take that's going to get you," Henry Fayre said, as he ferried her over the mountain and out of the valley for what she hoped was forever.

Back in the trailer Molly began to gather up everything that Wendy had left behind, every reminder of her own failed hopes, and prepared to burn them. She would think about Wendy every night. She would pray for her. But Molly was now ready to admit that the daughter she had known had died twelve years ago.

"I know you're capable," Henry continued as they coasted down the other side of the mountain, into the compass of the crucifix. "You've got the ability. Do what's right."

"Don't go back to the same environment," he entreated as he said goodbye, "the same crowd."

Wendy had boarded many buses to Boston in her life. She'd said a million goodbyes. Once more she watched the red Georgia clay grow loamy and umber with the Carolinas, scanned the sky as it grayed into smokestacks and derricks, then softened over the Atlantic as they rolled through Rhode Island. She was as free and alone as a crow again, as a little river, Suktiliana.

*

She hadn't meant to get drunk. She'd gone straight to the Milner Hotel, put cash down on a room, dropped her things, and headed for Rat Alley. Sure enough, she wasn't disappointed. The boys were hanging out there, trying to beat the heat. Traveler, Troy, and Duff looked up and couldn't believe their eyes. She looked good, in a skirt and nylons, lipstick and Maybelline. She flashed a hundred greenbacks and grinned.

"The drinks are on me, fellas."

In minutes the old turf opened wide for her. Sitting high on a stool in a dive just outside Kenmore Square, she was where she'd often been before, in just the kind of place to forget the long struggle and the long season of loneliness. The reek of sweat and spilled beer swelled in the afternoon heat. After sitting stone sober for a full hour and meditating on the moment that was dawning, almost ordained, before her, Wendy turned to Troy. "Order me a draft beer," she said.

Now Holly pulls up on the brake and leaps out.

"Hey, Wendy!" She stretches out a hand and squats down to curb level.

Wendy cracks a broad grin, scatters a few rats, hooks a forearm around Holly's neck, and pulls her in for a quick embrace.

"Hey!" She's as tickled as a kid at the beach.

"When did you get back?" Holly stays crouched and keeps her voice low. It is her style to be as confidential and as respectful of personal space as she can be in circumstances that otherwise permit little of it.

Above them curious pedestrians pause, expecting something to happen, then grow bored and move on.

"I was sober for seven months!" Wendy is boasting.

"See, Holly." Traveler cuts in. "We've gotten married."

"No kidding?"

"No. No kidding." Traveler is suddenly somber as an undertaker, his hair, wet with perspiration, hanging in his eyes. "We got these rings, see. I talked this jeweler downtown into bringing the price down. We got 'em both for fifty bucks."

Holly glances at Wendy, who's only half listening to Traveler. She's started cadging change off passers-by. Hard as it is for Holly to believe, Wendy seems to feel secure with him. Is it possible that she's erased all memory of last winter's violence?

Holly suddenly has a vivid flashback to the last time she saw Wendy.

It was a freezing January night. She had approached the little shelter directly across the alley from the Penthouse where Wendy and Traveler occasionally slept. This time Wendy was alone, standing in the doorway stark naked, raving like a lunatic. She didn't even realize that Holly and J.T. were there.

Traveler is pulling a copy of Wendy's birth certificate out of his satchel. "I'm keeping all her papers," he tells Holly.

No one knows much about Traveler. He comes and goes, never staying at the Inn. You never see him twice in the same place. In his late thirties, he could sound as sharp as a razor, recounting his years at Rutgers, and then, in an abrupt about-face, boast that he's spent the past eighteen years drinking a case of beer a day and hitchhiking across the country and back. Traveler is the most ruggedly and stubbornly individualistic street person they've run across.

Wendy cuts in on Holly's thoughts. "He takes care of me," she says. "I'm not responsible enough."

Holly is sure now that Wendy hasn't forgotten anything about Traveler. She doesn't fully understand the dynamics of this relationship, but it has to be partly that Wendy needs someone to support her when she's at her worst, someone to make her self-destructive nature seem relatively normal. Alone, maybe she would feel too bad about herself.

"How've you been?" she asks Wendy.

"I was earning $17.50 an hour overtime," she says proudly. "Making circuit boards for pay phones in Mississippi. I'm an electronics technician." She leans back and laughs heartily. "Then I broke out. I couldn't take it down there. You know what I mean, Holly? One week it took me to blow a thousand bucks when I got back here. Buyin' booze."

"You people should carry forty gallons of wine in that van." Traveler picks up one of his favorite themes.

Now Holly notices fresh blood at the back of Wendy's head.

"What's this?" She leans over and gently prods through the mat of hair.

"Oh, nothin'," Wendy answers. "I just fell."

Holly knows she is lying.

"You want to go down to the hospital and have it checked out?"

"No." Wendy inches closer to Traveler. "I'll be okay."

Holly knows better than to argue.

"Anything else we can bring you if we're back this way later to-night?"

"Yeah," Wendy says. "I need a new pair of jeans if you've got them."

"Okay, we'll see what we can do."

Now a look of panic comes into Wendy's eyes. "Traveler!" She grips his arm. "Don't let me go into the horrors again, Traveler!" She closes her eyes and shudders. It is the most frightening thing she knows. *The darkness.*

"Oh, Traveler," she wails. "They put me in the blue room and they strapped me down. Don't let me go into the blue horrors!"

"I won't, Wendy." In his steadiest voice, Traveler tries to soothe her. He gropes in the pouchy reaches of the green army knapsack at his feet for something that will amuse her. But all he finds is the half-empty jar of Ragu spaghetti sauce and the chewed stick of Cracker Barrel cheese they fished out of a dumpster earlier. And an electric alarm clock. He briefly considers this last item, holding its cord in front of his face. A useless, thoughtless rip-off. And they don't even have a spoon for the Ragu. They haven't eaten in hours now. In fact, he realizes, they haven't eaten all day.

He takes the sandwiches Holly is proffering, gratefully.

Later, around two or three A.M., when the heat has ebbed and there are no more diversions on Boylston, Wendy and Traveler will retire to their alley bomb shelter. It isn't far — just four blocks up toward Mass. Avenue, past Lord & Taylor, Brodney's antiques, the Sunoco station, the Pru, and an Archer Kent, then into a recess of shadow and fire escapes.

By day, trucks go in and out of this alley almost ceaselessly, delivering picture frames and pet food to the service entrances of stores, and construction materials for the subway renovation going on at the far end. But by night, except for the Penthouse across the way, it is completely deserted and still.

The usual rats abound, but here they aren't as plentiful or fattened on the greasy discarded entrees left to putrefy in alleys behind the restaurants on these hot summer nights. And the subway trains rumble underneath, but in the larger scheme of life on the streets, their bomb shelter is still one of the best places on earth to come home to.

When Wendy and Traveler arrive, they sit outside awhile before turning in. The Penthouse still stands, but much the worse for wear, since last winter. Younger guys have started to come through, guys

Jake One doesn't know, some of them on drugs. They try to take the place over, and sometimes they rip Jake off.

His health isn't good. He is an old man, sixty-four now. Before Wendy left, he'd begun complaining of stomach cramps. In March, while she was away, the doctors at City Hospital discovered bleeding ulcers and admitted him. True to form, he went AWOL, leaving against medical advice the next day.

Then in April his breathing started to degenerate badly. His frail body trembled each time he inhaled. He was ashen and listless, and totally defenseless against the hordes of newcomers who began to drag extra mattresses into the Penthouse and get into noisy scuffles almost every night. Eventually it got so bad that Jake couldn't even sleep in his own home anymore. He would take refuge in the little bomb shelter across the way or outside, exposed to the cold, on one of the upper landings of the fire escape.

When he could no longer stand up, he was admitted to the hospital with a deflated lung. Weakened, he stayed put for a few days. But he got so worried about the Penthouse that one morning at four he slipped out of the ward and disappeared from the corridors of the hospital. On foot, and barely shielded from the cold, he made his way back to the alley.

Two days later he was readmitted, exhausted and sick, this time to the respite unit at Shattuck Hospital, established especially for uninsured street people. But after three weeks of roofs and regulations, he wanted nothing so badly as his own way in the world again. And so Jake had come home. Just like Wendy.

She extinguishes her last butt on the concrete and heads to the bomb shelter. The bomb shelter is an above-ground cinderblock cave constructed on a slightly elevated slab that runs the width of one of the buildings. Its dimensions are roughly four feet on each side. Three cement steps lead up to a dwarf wooden door that in summer closes out wind and in winter closes out nothing, not rain, cold, or snow. But for now the dark interior, padded with dense layers of old blankets, cast-off clothing, a few odd shoes, and a stuffed brown gorilla named Henry, is quiet, dry, and obscure. Traveler is inside, already out cold. They'll be safe here until Danny's liquor store opens five hours from now.

Promptly at eight, six mornings a week, Jimmy Salino unlocks the heavy glass door to his shop, flips the "closed" sign over, and checks the neon Budweiser clock that hangs in the window surrounded by a collage of pretty-girl beer promos. He sticks everything up. What the hell? It's all free.

Recent years have brought new neighbors to this block near Symphony Hall — mostly Thai and Japanese restaurants — but Danny's hasn't changed a whit. It still displays beef jerky and a canister of pretzels on its linoleum counter, lots of busty blondes pushing foamy ales, and plenty of Gallo, Almaden, and portable fifths of nearly every brand name of potable available. The clients aren't fussy so much as what Jimmy might call financially straitened — poor black alkies, street folks, music students. Jimmy has been around as long as jazz, and he hassles nobody. Street talk has it that he sells on credit to regulars.

True to her word the night before, Wendy is there first thing in the morning, sick and tired, cursing Traveler, who's at a used bookstore, ripping off some sci-fi and a set of Carlos Castaneda for the afternoon's read.

Now, as she points to the vodka and throws down her hard-won earnings, she can't remember how many times she threw up last night. Bad, bad, bad. Something is getting lost in these days and weeks with Traveler, and she knows it. Only she doesn't know what to do about it. All her brave talk doesn't mean shit. As she pushes her way out of Danny's, she runs smack into Traveler. They head for the park, where Wendy spends the mornings when the weather is sunny and warm.

The Back Bay Fens meander through hundreds of acres of changing, often surprisingly wild, topography from the Charles River, around the Museum of Fine Arts, and out to the city's westernmost limit. Designed by Frederick Law Olmsted, the architect of New York City's Central Park, the Fens are far less formal than the Public Garden and more rangy than the Esplanade along the Charles. So little of it is tended that Wendy can forget temporarily that she is in the middle of a city. She likes this, especially when she wants to meditate or read.

Emerging from her alley, she has only to amble two blocks to enter the park at one of its wilder parts, just opposite the Massachusetts Historical Society, where the land slopes steeply down into a gully of very dense, tall pampas grass. After lunch on hot afternoons some of the other street people sleep down there. Wendy prefers to lean against a tree at the top of the rise and take in the breezes that feed the length of the park and sweep across her face in the shade.

Many mornings Traveler accompanies her. If he's still out when she

wakes up, she gets up and noses into Auditorium station, where she's
likely to find Buddy, one of the group. He's game for anything. They'll
stop at Danny's, get their drink, then stroll along the edge of the park
as far as the twin green ponds, which are obscured from street traffic
by dense hedges of evergreen and forsythia.

This section of the park is well maintained and more domesticated
than the meads. Wendy likes the clean, open feeling here, the war
monument, walks, and gaslights, and the flowering crabapple trees
and rose bushes. She and Buddy usually find a place under a tree by
one of the ponds, where they won't be hassled by the mounted police
who patrol this section. Hidden by the bushes, she washes. Then they
share a bottle and amuse themselves watching neighborhood residents walk their dogs or push their babies or sunbathe at lunch hour.
Museum-goers venture in tentatively; they've heard or read about the
hazards of the park, the gay cruising that goes on at the other end,
the drug dealing.

At lunch time the pair retrace their steps to the ridge above the
gully, where the gang gathers to wait for the canteen that serves a
midday meal to the street people in the downtown area.

Wendy sees the same faces she left seven months ago, and she is
glad for that. One-armed Rockadock, who lost his other limb to na-
palm in Vietnam. Sweet Black Bill, who never says boo. Troy, hooked
on heroin, broken, like Rockadock, by the killing fields. She had especially missed Indian Pete, a mean-tongued, soft-hearted soul brother.
Pete is someone she can relate to. Like her, he is short. Like her, he's
always gotten the short end of life's stick. And there's Buddy, never
all there but, as Traveler likes to complain, always around.

Traveler had made her first days and nights back happy ones. But
he's started knocking her around again. Today he is already obnox-
iously drunk as they settle beneath a tree to wait for the canteen.

"I'm gonna kill you today, Traveler," Pete sleepily threatens from
his half-prone position on the grass. "Today is the day that I'm going
to cut you for good."

Traveler ignores him. He leans over to Wendy for a kiss. She slugs
him away.

"I'm a fighter," she warns him, pointing her finger. "But I only fight
when I have to, if somebody gets in my face." Then she knees him in
the groin.

Warned, Traveler settles back with his book. The hostility evaporates. And as they wait for the canteen, Traveler begins to entertain them, reading aloud from the *Rubáiyát*.

> And if the Wine you drink, the Lip you press,
> End in the Nothing all Things end in — Yes —
>   Then fancy while Thou art, Thou art but what
> Thou shalt be — Nothing — Thou shalt not be less.

Wendy closes her eyes and listens. The other day he ripped off a volume of Elizabeth Barrett Browning for her. She waits for him to recite from it, as she knows he will soon. She wishes that the days of happiness could have been for always. Tears well beneath her eyelids as she hears him start her favorite sonnet.

> I lift my heavy heart up solemnly,
> As once Electra her sepulchral urn,
> And, looking in thine eyes, I overturn
> The ashes at thy feet — Behold & see
> What a great heap of grief lay hid in me,
> And how the red wild sparkles dimly burn
> Through the ashen greyness. If thy foot in scorn
> Could tread them out in darkness utterly,
> It might be well perhaps — But if instead
> Thou wait beside me for the wind to blow
> The grey dust up . . . those laurels on thine head,
> O my beloved, will not shield thee so,
> That none of all the fires shall scorch & shred
> The hair beneath! — stand farther off then! — Go —

Getting beaten wasn't what she came back for, she thinks. Sure, they can always come up with a lark, as they have these past few weeks, trying to see how many bottles of steak sauce they could rip off from the char-pit restaurants along Boylston. It made for laughs and something to talk about back in the alley late at night when, without such stupid adventures, they might look at their own lives and begin to fight.

It was a sad and crazy-making paradox. Street guys were the only ones she could relate to, but they always ended up destroying the very freedom that drew them to her. In the end they forced her to flee. Up to now she's never blamed Traveler. Never peached on him publicly. She takes her knocks, she's loyal. But he's beginning to drag on her freedom. For the first time since she's been back, she feels herself wanting to pull away from him. The word "abuse" has crept into her consciousness. She pushes it back, refuses to accept it. But it just goes underground and makes her feel heavy and depressed.

It's the booze, she reflects, saddened. It destroys everything.

"Here they come!" Buddy breaks the mood.

"Morning!"

Matt, a compact man, disembarks from the squat silver canteen. He lifts the rear storage area to grab six meals, packed in TV dinner trays and covered by waxed white cardboard. They are the same meals the canteen's parent organization, the Kit Clark Senior House, serves to housebound seniors through its Meals on Wheels program. As a result they are better balanced and more nourishing than anything else the group is likely to obtain: entrées like Salisbury steak with peas and mashed potatoes or fried chicken and cole slaw, with little plastic tubs of chocolate pudding or raspberry jello and pint cartons of milk.

Now Wendy sees Jamie, a vivacious student nurse at Mass. General's Institute of Health Professions and co-coordinator of the lunch project. Jamie has hopped out from her side of the truck and come around to say hello.

"How're ya doing today?" she asks.

Wendy shrugs. She's not being coy. She knows that Jamie and Ellen, the other student nurse who coordinates the job, have taken a genuine liking to her. But Jamie and Ellen can be too concerned about her; they try and talk her into going to the ER, or into detox, when it's the last thing she wants to do.

Jamie is studying her face.

"So-so," Wendy answers finally. "You know."

"Everything okay?"

She nods, then lowers her voice. "Jamie, can you do me a favor?"

"I can try. What is it?"

"I've lost my Dilantin prescription."

Jamie nods. Dilantin is an antiseizure medication often prescribed for epileptics and for alcoholics undergoing detoxification to prevent the worst effects of withdrawal. Wendy claims she is epileptic and has told Jamie that she's gotten Dilantin from the doctors at City Hospital, but Jamie's never seen her with the pills. She can't prescribe any drugs herself, and the canteen performs only basic first aid on the street. The only thing Jamie can do is offer to take Wendy back down to

City. That's an option Wendy wants to avoid at all costs when she's drinking.

Matt, finished handing out lunches, wants to push on. It's important for the day crew to stay on schedule, much more so than at night, when there's no traffic to contend with. At midday, on the steps of the library and in the Public Garden, literally hundreds of people are waiting for them. Matt doesn't like to be late.

"See what you can do," Wendy whispers, pleading. "Thanks, Jamie. I appreciate it."

Maybe it's the heat, she's thinking. Or maybe Traveler's rough-housing. She doesn't know what it is, but she's not feeling too good. Shaky, a bandanna across her brow to keep her unkempt hair out of her face, she gropes her way back to the tree, where her friends are picking through their lunch. She reaches down in the grass for the vodka. Maybe all she needs is a good drink.

If it's hot after lunch they stay in the park a while longer. If it's mild, they drift down to the library and panhandle for the rest of the afternoon.

She isn't able to eat much, and as they stagger the five blocks downtown, flouting the Fahrenheit, she sticks close to Traveler's side, listening and nodding as he decides what books he's going to borrow, or palm, from the library today.

But to herself Wendy is thinking, not only is Jamie going to show up tomorrow empty-handed, but she's out of the Phenobarbitol that she's been secretly downing at sixty milligrams a day to augment the booze. Easy street is over. She feels black and drifty and dizzy. She squints ahead. They're almost at the library. When they stop, she's got to sit down.

Something is using her head as a drum. A piercing noise is about to split her skull in two. She tries to raise her hands to stop it, but gentle hands, sheathed in white, a medical jacket, dissuade her. Wendy realizes that she is lying on her side in a moving ambulance. She has no idea where she is, doesn't even know her name. She is racking her brain, trying to think of a name.

The nurse tells her now that they are heading for Massachusetts General Hospital. Her forehead is sweaty, her mouth, around the plastic airway they've pressed into her throat, is dry. Her tongue is still swollen. She feels like shit. It's begun, the hall of horrors. She wants to die.

In the daze of returning consciousness, her first thought is that it must have been a grand mal. No two seizures were ever the same. Sometimes she got the little dots of light before it happened, sometimes she just felt funny, as she had earlier today. It is always terrifying. Her greatest fear is that one day she'll go into a seizure from which she never emerges. When she said that she needed to sit down, she meant it. All she remembers is seeing little flashes of light, then feeling her body hit the pavement. After that, she lost it all.

The vehicle pulls into a parking space. She is jostled into an ambulatory bed and wheeled out onto the blacktop, then through several sets of humming automatic doors. Bodies pass by in blue and white, bearing the odor of antiseptic. Someone removes the airway from her throat.

But now she stiffens. She is in deep trouble. They've started securing her hands and feet.

She screams hoarsely. "Kill me! Kill me right now! Take a gun and kill me!"

With all the strength she has left, she tries to wrench herself out of the restraints. Her body is bathed in sweat. She doesn't want to vomit. That's what she fears, later that night, when she starts to get booze-sick and no one is around — choking on her own vomit. It has happened to countless street buddies.

"Don't torture me, for Crissake! I'm an alcoholic. Don't tie me down on my back!"

But her outburst has just the reverse of its intended effect.

The next ten hours are brutal ones. She passes in and out of consciousness in the cold ward, coming to and hearing the sounds of footsteps magnified hideously, the whispers of the night shift distorted into nails scraping on chalkboards. For most of the hours of darkness she is still trying to figure out where she is, what emergency room, in what city. She is trying to remember her name. Then she drifts off.

Long after daylight has bruised her eyelids again, she hears someone approaching. Her brain is a live beehive. She wants to get out of here. It is seven o'clock, she's told. The restraints are unfastened. She resists her desire to strike the nurse, accepts the Dilantin prescription, and heads for the door. She hates them. She hates her own weakness. She pushes past the last glass barrier between herself and the city, and swears. She's completely dehydrated and sick as a dog.

Across the street, resting his weight on one hip, Buddy is grinning. He's been waiting for her there for two hours. After all she's been through, he tells her, he thought she deserved a present. He pulls cash and change from his jeans.

Wendy laughs.

"Fuckin' A," she swears, and the pair link arms and head into the nearest liquor store for her quart of consolation.

Stemming isn't the easiest way to keep body and soul together.

Wendy is barefoot on the steps in front of the library, playing the comedic drunk. It is eighty degrees and August dry. Several of her pals are on the other side of the building doing the same.

Most of those who pass by look at her with disgust. They have money, but they're not about to give her any. She'd be cheating them somehow. If she wants to eat, she can work for it the way they do. The women are the worst. The looks she takes from some of them are enough to make her want to die.

What they don't appreciate is that stemming *is* work. Hard work. Just like whoring, farming, waitressing, office work, housekeeping, running a laundry, or raising kids. She knows, she's done them all. But no paycheck in the world can buy companionship. It's only on the streets that she's found love. And screw these women, she thinks, she's not going to try to justify her existence to them, total strangers. What do they want, a sign around her neck that reads: *I'm a Wife Too?* Or *I Can Type 70 Words a Minute?*

"Hey, mister." She dances on blackened feet, in cutoff jeans and a faded T-shirt, a purple bandanna tied Apache-style around her head. "Can you spare a quarter for cigarettes?"

"Thank you. Thanks, buddy."

She moves a few steps.

"Hey, darlin', help me out, will ya? You gotta quarter?"

She's in her own world, laughing at the urban carnival coursing by, absorbed by its own importance. She keeps up a commentary that's sometimes intelligible, sometimes not, and in the process manages to cadge enough change for the day, though her act leaves her totally depleted.

Each day is different. Some afternoons she gets lucky and lands a few bills. But in the warm weather, it's mostly spare change. It can take a whole day to earn the twenty to thirty dollars she needs.

"It all depends," she says. "It really all depends. It's easier in the winter, because people tend to feel more sympathetic in the cold weather. 'Here, get something warm.' "

While she does the work to support the two of them, Traveler perches on a marble step around the corner, reading Freud's *Outline of Psycho-analysis*. From time to time he looks up, anticipating the canteen or suddenly aware of Wendy's voice above the crowd.

"You know," he boasts to anyone willing to listen, "Wendy is a brilliant woman. You name it, she knows about it. Schumann, Beethoven, Nietzsche, Freud, Dostoevsky. Ask her anything about them — anything. Go ahead, ask her. She's brilliant."

But her man's words are lost to her on the other side of the limestone building, in the heat. "Hey, lady, do you have any spare change? Spare change?"

Within two hours on this Saturday afternoon, Wendy will have collected thirty dollars. She has no debts with any of the guys for cigarettes or a portion of a bottle, so she'll hand the take over to Traveler, who will buy the jug of wine.

Sometimes Traveler stems with her. But it is the nature of their division of labor that though he's never far away while she works, he handles the other end of things: ripping off articles when they need them and, when necessary, taking the rap for it, a night or two in jail.

"Poor Traveler." Wendy laughs. Traveler has crossed Boylston on his way to the liquor store and she is sitting on the library steps to rest. "He stole two boxes of Tampax for me. He goes into the Store 24, grabs the two boxes — I tell him exactly what kind to get, the slenders. He got caught! The manager's trying to stop him, right? He goes, 'Fuck you! My old lady's got her period!' "

She laughs. "Can you imagine going in front of the judge for that?"

"The first day I was with Traveler," she recalls, "I stemmed him a pint of vodka and a can of soda and a pack of cigarettes. Naturally, his brand. He just expected it."

The agreement they've made today is that Traveler will convey the cheap jug of port wine, their weekend's booze supply, down through the back alleys to the bomb shelter. Wendy will meet him there several hours from now. In the meantime she'll go fishing.

Fishing brings out the best in Wendy. It is one activity that she delights in and undertakes willingly on these hot summer evenings. It is an act of tresspass, the most dangerous, lucrative, and amusing of all of her work.

Wendy does her fishing at the $500 million hotel and shopping mall complex known as Copley Place. This glass and travertine city-within-a-city of jewels, Italian papers, hand-dipped chocolates, and French lingerie replaced nine and a half acres of tenements and highway in 1980. Copley Place is Boston's Trump Tower, a commercial centerpiece for designer boutiques, a temple to conspicuous consumption, with almost two thousand hotel rooms, six bars, fourteen restaurants, and more than one hundred shops.

And by no means least to the days and nights of Wendy, a twenty-five-foot-high waterfall that cascades into shallow pools lined with black tiles and banked by fresh ferns and white flowers. Its surface is populated by lily pads; its depths by the wishful pennies of shoppers. And on afternoons like this one, by Wendy's feet.

Wendy waits outside the glass-enclosed lobby until the security guards have disappeared from view. Then she rushes in, dodges behind the frothy plumes, and wades in without ceremony. She's donned a pair of dirty sneakers for the job. Scooping madly along the tiled floor, she gathers up coins. The trick, always, is to escape before the guards come back.

This evening she's busily filling her pockets when she feels someone try to grab her from behind. Instinctively she grabs back. She manages to get his tie and pulls. With a jerk, his walkie-talkie goes into the drink.

Now I've had it, Wendy thinks. The wet soles of her sneakers slam on the marble floor and she dives through the revolving door, the silver she's collected spilling out of her pockets as she runs into the middle of traffic, dodging headlights and horns. The guard is close behind. She can hear his panting and profanities.

I'm not ripping anyone off, she tells herself. If people are stupid enough to throw their money away, I'm going to pick it up. They're making a wish. I'm making my wish come true.

But there is no place to go. The guard has the advantage: he's wearing dry shoes. Then it occurs to her to jump over the short wall into the depressed courtyard that fronts the august Trinity Church. She knows the nooks and crannies of that square better than almost anyone. She drops down and crouches. She can hear the guard above her running back and forth, then all is quiet. Maybe, she thinks, he's given up. Cautiously, she scouts the periphery of the square. He is nowhere to be seen. She stands. She got away this time.

As she starts back to the alley, scot free, to tell Traveler what happened, her antic is easy to laugh about. Such amusements keep her going. She remembers just a few days earlier the luck they'd had in happening upon those cases of wine at one of the loading docks behind the Westin Hotel. For a wedding, they concluded. As no one was guarding them, Traveler and Pete seized the opportunity. They hoisted fourteen bottles and carried them around the corner to the back of the library, and they all had a good drunk for a few hours, until a pair of cops moved them along.

For every bad thing that happens, a good thing always comes along, she thinks. The days are strung together by such encounters, held intact by a certain rhythm, of anticipation, adventure, disappointment, bickering, and the long, soft, sad buzz of the booze.

She stops and squints. Ahead of her at the corner two black priests are holding out tambourines, soliciting passers-by. She's seen this pair before. She is sure they are sham. "Hey," she confronts them, walking up. "I know you're sham. Gimme some money."

One of them looks her over. She's wearing the same faded pink top she's had on for days. Her legs are bare, white scars blistered against a deepening tan from days in the sun. She means business, and he knows it. Silently, his eye canny and fixed, he proffers the tambourine. She fills her fist, leaves some for him, then turns and walks on. At the next side street, she swerves and runs a block, just in case, to lose him. Then she slows to a walk and starts laughing to herself. She hates shams.

At the alley she hooks a left and soon enough comes upon Traveler.

"What's wrong?" She drops down beside him and removes her sopping wet sneakers. She can see he is desolate.

They've been ripped off. Someone found their stash and made off with it. A whole jug. Now they'll have to put up with Listerine again.

She stamps her foot. "Fuck!"

She's angry at whoever has taken the jug — and she has her suspicions, as always. But she's angry at Traveler, too. Why does she have to look after everything? She can't do it all — earn the money, make a fool of herself going through all those hassles, *and* protect their stash.

She can see that he feels miserable, but that's not good enough. She makes snake eyes, narrow and hard.

"Goddamit, Traveler," she says. "Fuck."

After a minute she tells him, "Gimme a smoke."

He lights a Marlboro off the tip of his and hands it to her. She's not even sure she wants to tell him about the guard now.

On a good night Traveler would know how to make the best of such adversity. They'd have a good time. On a bad night, he'll wallow in self-pity until he's downright ugly, then beat the living daylights out of her. She sidles closer to him, reaches her arm around his thick shoulder, and gives him a consoling kiss.

The next night, the van bounces over the potholes in the alley and jerks to a halt several yards from where Wendy and Traveler sit.

"Evening." Holly leans out the window in greeting.

They hold up a bottle with a wide-necked top, its contents sloshing.

"Someone stole our jug." Wendy's voice is thick with alcohol. Holly alights and observes that Wendy is partially hidden in the far corner of the stoop, reclining in a soiled green blanket twisted around her legs.

"I wish you people would carry wine with you," Traveler says. "If a person's going into withdrawal, they really need a drink. You could be saving someone's life."

"Here." Wendy shoves the sloppy bottle under Holly's nose. It is so horrible that Holly recoils. Wendy laughs. They've mixed Listerine with Gatorade and added sliced oranges, lemons, limes, and crushed ice — a make-do version of the wine cooler they'd planned before they were ripped off.

Holly realizes that Wendy isn't coming forward as she usually does, but instead is hanging back in the shadows. She bends down, braces a hand on her knee, and looks in.

There is blood on Wendy's forehead.

"Wendy, you don't look too good," Holly says.

"It's nothing. I fell down the stairs at Auditorium."

Traveler intercedes. "Holly, she really needs to go to the hospital."

"I do not, Traveler. You stay out of this."

Gingerly, Holly reaches out and brushes the hair from the wound. "It looks nasty, Wendy. You sure you shouldn't have it looked at?"

"No, I'm okay. I'll go in the morning."

It makes Holly deeply sad. She realizes that the difficulties in this relationship are only compounded by the fact that the two are on the streets, and so incredibly dependent on each other. The problems of merging and of identity are multiplied tenfold out here. Traveler is at once Wendy's protector and her terrorizer.

"We could just take you down and bring you right back," Holly coaxes. She knows that part of Wendy's fear is that Traveler will get more violent and retaliatory when she returns.

"No, I'll go tomorrow," she promises. "After we go to Danny's. We're there at eight o'clock sharp. Soon as the door opens. We never miss post time, unless we're too sick to move." Then she laughs.

"Traveler!"

It is several weeks later, and she's got his forearm in her grip like a vise.

"What is it, Wendy?"

She rolls onto her side and begins to drive her heels into the dirt, the effort propelling the rest of her, head first, in an agonized spin that is arrested only when Traveler flings his weight on top of her.

"I'm here, Wendy."

Saliva dribbles out of her loose lips, down her cheek and onto the dirt. She thrashes briefly, then falls still. Traveler waits. For several seconds he doesn't move. Then, seeing that the seizure is over, he gingerly lifts himself up on his hands and knees over her, looking for a sign of consciousness.

It is close to noon at the midpoint of August, and once more they're in the park. The horrors, Traveler thinks, have begun.

But now Wendy opens her eyes. She is logy. She wipes the mucus off her face with the back of her hand. She lifts herself up on one arm and shakes her head, as if to free it of something.

"Sorry we're late!" Almost two hours later Jamie comes upon the pair. Wendy seems subdued, but she brightens when she hears Jamie's voice.

"I'm sick, Jamie," Wendy says. "I need to go to the hospital."

"What's wrong?"

"I just need to go. Call the Indian Council and tell them you're taking me to Mass. General."

"What?"

"The number is 598-0927. Ask for Jon."

Jamie spots a pay phone across the street. She does what Wendy instructs without waiting for an explanation. Somewhat brokenly, she

tries to explain to the woman on the other end of the line that Wendy
wants her notified.

"What tribe is she?" the woman asks.

Jamie has no idea.

"You better find out," the woman advises. "I don't recognize her."

Jamie returns to the edge of the park.

"Arapaho," Wendy answers. She drops cross-legged onto the sidewalk where she was standing a minute earlier and begins to chant in
a language Jamie has never heard before. She looks at Matt. Together, they lift Wendy, reeking of vomit and urine, into the front
seat of the canteen and drive as fast as they can to the hospital, where
Matt drops the two women and continues on his rounds.

In the ensuing half hour Jamie completely forgets about the Indian
Council. She walks Wendy into the busy waiting room. They register,
find two seats next to each other, and sit down to wait for a doctor.

Wendy turns to Jamie, suddenly sober.

"How could a battered woman be hit like this and still love the man?"

Jamie is taken aback. She wonders if Wendy's antics in the park
weren't a ruse to get away from Traveler. Wendy begins to speak
freely about herself as a battered woman. She knows, she tells Jamie,
why she puts up with it. It's because she hates herself. Because she
feels victimized. Because, at a certain level, she thinks she deserves it.
And she puts up with it, she knows, because she wants love so badly.

Jamie doesn't know what to say. After so many frustrating attempts
on her part to talk to Wendy about the violence that's been rained on
her, she's astounded by this candor — encouraged and confused by it
at the same time. All along Jamie has assumed that Wendy needs and
relishes the Maid Marian role she plays to Traveler's Robin Hood and
his Merry Men. She hasn't denigrated this. The need to be rescued
runs deep in many women. And Jamie has known that going to detox
would, for Wendy, be the first step *away* from having these needs met.
For this reason, she's never pushed. But now, she wonders, if Wendy
has understood the dynamics of her own abuse all along, why has she
put up with it?

But she quickly reminds herself that this phenomenon isn't unique
to Wendy. She's interviewed many women on the streets as part of
her outreach work. Abuse is one subject she always probes, always
with results.

"It's just so much a part of their life," she says later, "that it doesn't occur to them to verbalize it. Every single one of the women I inter-viewed had been abused, fairly young."

"Why don't you leave him?" Jamie asks Wendy now.

Wendy shrugs. "I love the man."

Jamie ponders this. Clearly, Wendy is disappointed in her solution. It's too stark. Maybe she should have tried a different tack. Or maybe the exchange has been too frank for comfort.

Jamie places a hand on her arm.

"I feel really sick," Wendy whines. "Why isn't somebody coming to help me?"

"Wendy, there are a lot of people here who are sick."

"You're right." She becomes repentant. "I have to think of other people. I know other people feel worse than I do. But I'm really sick. I've been beaten up!"

Jamie remembers Wendy's recent chanting in the park. She is mov-ing into full dramatic force again and enjoying her effect on the room. Jamie begins to wonder if she did the right thing bringing her here.

"I'm an epileptic!"

"You're fine."

"If somebody doesn't see me soon, I'm going to have a fit, I know I will."

"You're not going to have a fit. Calm down. Sit there, and you'll be fine."

"I know I'm going to have a seizure. I know it. I know it! I can feel it! Someone come quick!"

Jamie is at the end of her rope. Standing, she approaches a doctor who is loitering by the nurse's station.

"This woman says she's going to have a seizure," she tells him. "You're a doctor. I'm leaving."

It is late by the time Holly reaches the bomb shelter through a driving rain almost a week later. From behind the leaky gray door, Wendy's voice responds to her knock. Holly waits for her to open it. As soon as she sees Wendy's face, Holly realizes she is alone. She looks miser-able.

Holly brings her a cup of coffee the way she likes it, with lots of sugar, and sits down beside her on one of the steps. Wendy tells her that she hasn't seen Traveler for several nights. He has taken off for New York City.

It seems to make Wendy feel better to talk. For a long time Holly just listens, until it sounds like Wendy is nearing the end of her litany of condemnation.

"He never did anything to support me," she is saying. "It takes a lot out of you, supporting yourself. I'm not talking about whoring. I'm talking about stemming. It's emotionally draining.

"So" — with an unimpeachable air of finality, she announces the end of an era — "I fired him."

◪◪◪◪◪◪◪◪◪◪

TWENTY-SIX

Songs from the Alley

WENDY SHIVERS on a sliver of ledge, backed into the shadows. She needs to get the dancing out of her head and go to sleep so she can get to court first thing the next morning, because she is in love.

He's a baby — four years and one month younger than her. She giggles. His name is Kurt, he's Irish ruddy and, except for a full fox-red beard and muscular arms, he's so thin that he seems to cave in in all the soft spots. But he counteracts the look of hunger with a fine, offhand stance and eager brown eyes, and a heart that seems to flow like raw honey whenever he looks at her. And for all this she has a bottle of Listerine to thank.

She offered him a swig and he asked her to dance one night out on the pavement near Copley Square. To be precise, he asked Traveler's permission to ask her to dance.

"What are you asking him for," she barked. "He doesn't own me."

"Well then?"

"I don't dance." Suddenly shy, she drew back, ashamed of her legs.

"Sure you do!"

And that was it.

No music. Just dancing. Dancing, and charisma.

Two weeks later the dancing hasn't stopped. Not inside. Only he is in jail now, and has been for three days, while she's trapped outside in the swelter of a dead-end alley, half frantic trying to figure out how to get to him.

Friday night they were stemming out on Boylston, later than usual. He was by the curb, his palm out to slow cruisers. She, in her cutoffs and jersey, stayed close to the door of the Archer Kent, hoping to catch on a sympathetic crest those who were just about to pocket fresh change as they emerged.

One of the many questions that has tormented her since then is why they let themselves be separated as much as fifteen feet to begin with. For one thing, they could hardly keep their hands off each other. For another, it didn't make street sense. It left them too vulnerable, unable to come to each other's defense if one of them started to get hassled. She'd been careless. She knew the ropes far better than he; he was a pup. She should have known better.

But that was the last thing on her mind Friday night, when she suddenly felt someone rudely squeezing one of her breasts. She wheeled and shoved her assailant, who'd just come out of the drug store.

"Hey, buddy," she yelled, raising her fist to strike. "You touched the wrong tit tonight."

Out of the corner of her eye, she saw Kurt rush. Then she was felled. The stranger had beat her to the punch. From the pavement, the side of her head smarting badly, she heard scuffling. Then Kurt lunged and brought the man down. Slugging sounds filled the stilled air. The man cried out. Then all she could hear were horrible, repetitive jabs.

And then the whining, and the lights. The crack of hard leather and apparatus: handcuffs and two-way radios. They were being shoved into the back of a cruiser and wheeled over to Station D. She couldn't believe it. What about the guy who molested her? Was he going to get away scot free?

Station D is an old three-story brick and granite presence in the South End, erected in an era when even precinct stations were embellished with wrought iron grates and gaslights. It is wedged almost cozily on the corner of a block of brownstones, still a neighborhood station, with none of the cold defensiveness of the more modern, fortresslike stations nor the impersonal weariness of headquarters, just four blocks away.

The veterans at Station D remember the old days of the Tombs as if they were yesterday. It was at Station D that Pine Street's regulars used to line up to get their bed tickets every afternoon. As a result, at Station D more than anywhere else in the city, the general contours of a couple like Kurt and Wendy are familiar. More than that, they are known to the point that individual variations have ceased to exist; only the pattern to which they conform with such unerring precision, like fossils or fingerprints, surfaces and assumes the feel of a sufficient reality — enough, anyway, to get business done.

They were separated at the desk. Wendy watched her lover being jostled down to booking, where he was charged with assault and battery with a shod foot and put into one of the holding cells until they were ready to take him down to a permanent bunk. From there he remained visible to her.

The screws confiscated everything the two of them had, including a satchel containing her Maxi Thins. She needed them.

"They're mine!" she'd screamed after the arresting officer.

Kurt, in his cage, sprang to his feet and grabbed the bars.

"Jesus Christ, give my old lady her bag!" he yelled after the officer.

He loved her, that was obvious.

She started to cry. And as he was taken into the bowels of the building, she drifted into the street and headed back to the alley. Not a mite of justice. Station D is the worst, she thought. They don't even give you water. Nothing. Suffer!

She cried herself to sleep for a few hours and, when she woke the next morning, made her way to the corner pay phones. She used every voice she could think of with the officer on duty. She enlisted the boys, had them at pay phones all day, and the next day, and the next. They plagued the desk officers in three different precincts, trying every alias they could think of, to get a lead on the time of Kurt's arraignment Monday morning. They all struck out.

"Hey," she holds forth whenever any of them stop by the bomb shelter to give her any news, or to hear any. "These are *my* breasts! If I want a man to touch them, I'll choose the man who touches them. It's my body!"

Brave words, but they don't keep the fear or the aching at bay. Three nights alone. Three nights of knowing that he must be in agony. And all because of her.

Well, there's one thing that no legal system can take away from her. And that is the courage, respect, and love he'd demonstrated on that unlucky night when some jerk tried to cut in on their dream. She isn't about to let anyone ruin the best thing that has happened to her in years. If he hadn't won her with his slow foxtrot down under the neon moonlight, he had won her now, lock, stock, and barrel. She had to try and get some sleep. She owed it to him to meet him where they would be dancing still — in her dreams.

*

J.T. Lenoch, by now a veteran member of the rescue team, finds himself on one of the surface roads that wind along the wharves down by the harbor. It isn't a route he's used to taking, and the nocturnal summer downpour isn't making navigation any easier. He peers through the rain with expert eyes, trying to see if any groups of homeless men have formed makeshift shelters in the low, damp parks or on the backsides of the buildings that face the financial district. Rain has been falling heavily for hours now, and the storm drains are boiling with the runoff from surrounding streets.

He is about to head back to town when he spots a lumpish mass on a bench alongside an almost completely submerged field. He pulls up, crushes his cigarette, pulls his hood up over his head, and dives into the storm.

Ten minutes later, when he returns to the van, water is running off every surface. He dries his hands on his jeans and puts the van in motion again, shaking his head.

Once into traffic, he unclips the two-way radio and signals Michael Malone at the Pine Street desk.

"What's up?"

"I've just seen Traveler," he says.

"Oh yeah?" Michael's voice rasps back.

"You know this other woman Karen we've been hearing about?"

"Yeah."

"I've just seen her. They're down on India Street. Both really fucked up big time. He could hardly talk or see straight."

"Oh boy. What about her?"

"She was under a blanket, and just groaned. Blonde, I think. 'His old lady,' he called her."

"No shit?"

J.T. chuckles and clicks once more.

"See ya."

In morning's misty sunlight the delivery trucks look like steaming animals. Specters glide in and out of the shadows, calling to one another in muffled voices. The rain that fell in the night maintains a hold on the city even now, hours after it has stopped.

When Wendy looks up, she doesn't believe what she's seeing and turns back again to straighten her cave. But Kurt continues coming toward her, smiling, a free man.

That morning he'd arrived at the courtroom handcuffed, he said, and was ushered through the prisoner's pen to the defense table. Only then did he realize that he was alone. The other guy hadn't shown.

His court-appointed attorney came up to him and shook hands. He was a rumpled guy who didn't seem to give a damn about his job. They sat down, and the assistant district attorney took over the show. And a show it was, a seedy, low-life diversion for the smattering of court buffs on hand, old men with nothing better to do than hang around and listen in.

The DA told the judge that the "victim" had lost four teeth in the scuffle. He described at length the brutality of the attack.

No mention of Wendy.

"Aren't you going to say anything?" Kurt turned to his court-appointed attorney. But the rumpled man just shrugged.

"Your honor," the assistant DA turned to the judge. "The victim is a personal friend of mine."

Kurt's tale ends there. Then he just stares, gaunt and withdrawn, at the concrete wall.

"I'd hate to meet his other friends," Wendy tries to joke. But it doesn't change the way he feels. When it comes down to it, all they have is each other.

Night after night they lie in each other's arms, looking out the open door of the bomb shelter at the backsides of dumpsters and occasionally a slice of the Milky Way. They talk about their lives. Kurt was beaten and abused by his grandmother. He's lived in more states than she has, goes by twelve different aliases, and loves mushroom pizza.

There is a sweetness about him that takes her all the way back to Sean, her high school sweetheart, and the lost sweetness in herself. If life truly is a dance, she thinks, with Kurt she can be free to make her own moves to its music.

At first Kurt stayed at Pine Street and was bused out to the usual day labor jobs — roofing, construction, or painting — every day returning, spent, to line up for a bed and a shower. Off and on he'd succeed in picking up regular work, mostly at restaurants and bars. He was a natural for such jobs, an attractive, fit-looking young man with patient, lively eyes. He was well spoken, kind, and self-effacing. His attributes made it easy for employers to take him on and sorry to see him go, despite the heavy absenteeism that usually preceded his departure. At some point the alcohol always kicked in and got out of control. His sick-day excuses wore thin, and eventually he'd "walk" rather than be fired.

But he's never gone on welfare. It is a matter of pride that he's never taken a dollar of relief. As a result, the labor pool is a vital source of income for him.

"I'm realistic," Wendy would tell him in the beginning. "Why don't you go back to the shelter? Somebody's got to have a little common sense in their head. This is no place for you. I've got so many years out here it's like second nature to me. I've dealt with this for too long."

He would answer, "I want to get to know you better."

But by late summer this has changed. Now she begs him to stay with her night and day. Traveler has returned and is hanging around all their old haunts, trying to win her back.

Kurt needs little encouragement. In the last weeks of summer, he drops out of the labor pools and spends his days on the street. His income dwindles, but for the time being, he's happy.

The rest of the boys — Buddy, Troy, and Pete — have no choice. They have to accept him, and they know it. But he's green, a pup. Where was he last winter? In Florida, that's where. They doubt he could stand up to most of them in a fight. But the worst of it is not knowing Kurt's long-term intentions for Wendy. The boys feel a possessiveness, which they prefer to think of as protectiveness, toward their old Wendy. They aren't sure they like the idea of this outsider coming in and taking her away. They don't want her to leave them again.

For now they have to content themselves with spending more time without her in the park or behind the library. There is less and less reason for them to come around to the alley in any event. The Penthouse has become a treacherous pit of drunken hostility, its founders outnumbered by strangers. Even Wendy keeps the healthy width of an alley between her and the rumblings of unrest she hears across the way after the sun goes down.

Jake's dream is disintegrating. These days, whenever she sees the aging man, once as agile in gesture as he is in wit, she sees a nervous, spectral creature, hovering outside the entrance to his own home like an interloper, a dispossessed king. In this world of third-hand clothes and the cheapest tobacco one can find, the man had been a savior to many, a sower of rare brotherhood among a band of squatters. Now he is truly homeless.

Early in summer, when he'd returned from his respite stay in the hospital, full of plans for reform, he'd found the Penthouse in a state of near ruin, the furniture wrecked or vanished, and the rubble that remained wet from having been left in the rain. Within days an old friend of Willy's showed up, ready to raise hell, direct from prison, where he'd been locked up for thirteen months. Once more Jake retreated to the fire escape. From there he watched his home decline into irreversible chaos. From his perch on the rusty iron several stories up, he saw rats get in the front door for the first time. They started invading in droves. Soon the Penthouse had a major infestation.

Now, when Willy gets raving drunk, he stumbles into the alley, loud and profane, and staggers out to the street. He turns right, blunders up to the phone booth at the corner, plugs a dime in, and dials the Inn.

"What's up, Willy?" Michael Malone is often at the desk when Willy's calls come in.

"I don't want to see your faces, or your goddamn van in this alley ever again."

Then Willy proceeds to vent a litany of threats that grow more sinister with each call. Michael hangs up, wondering bleakly what is going to become of Jake.

His answer comes sooner than expected.

One night shortly after one of Willy's calls, Holly, on the street, radios in. It's started to pour, and she tells Michael she expects to bring in more than the usual number of men. He'd better see how many beds are available at the Inn and figure out contingencies, if necessary.

After she signs off, Holly realizes that another season is ending, this one on a note of finality for her. In a few weeks she'll be leaving the van to take a job working with emotionally disturbed children in the Boston public schools. She wants to see the daylight again. And, much as she has loved her work on the streets these past two years, she's burned out.

You go along, she thinks, making a small mark here and there. Some situations get better. Some deteriorate and seem to keep going in that direction. Did the van play a role in the Penthouse demise? She believes they have to ask themselves this question. Or was it just bad timing that after thriving for seven years without any interference, suddenly upon their arrival Jake's world started to lose what little protected ground it had occupied? Or was some other, unrelated entropy at work?

She is close to Rat Alley and decides to take a quick look in. The downpour obscures nothing of what is happening as the headlights pick out Willy's form. He is rooted in the alley, soaked through but indifferent, as he bellows up at the figure wound into a blanket on the fire escape. Holly grabs the high-powered flashlight and, leaving the headlights on, gets out of the van.

"I'm going to fuck you up good, you goddamn bastard," Willy's voice pounds through the rain. Very high up, Jake doesn't move a muscle. He must be scared out of his mind, Holly thinks.

"Hey," she calls out, "William!"

He wheels, only now aware of her presence.

"And you," he yells. "You can take your sandwiches and shove them up your ass!"

Holly steps back a pace. Much as she hates to admit it, the moment has come. She knows that the van can't return here. It's no longer safe. More important, they are no longer welcome.

She calls up to the patriarch of the alley, "Hey, Jake, you want to ride with us for a while?"

A head emerges from the blanket and nods grateful acceptance. He labors down three flights, gripping the railing for dear life. Stiffly he crosses the asphalt. He needs Holly's arm to climb inside. He's aged ten years, she realizes, since she met him.

Jake stays on board until dawn, brooding silently, watching the rest of the city wake to another day.

"The fire department wants Will out," he tells Holly as the sun is coming up. "They've cut off the electricity until he goes."

Traveler, realizing he can't reclaim Wendy, returns to Karen, which is fine with Wendy, except for one thing. She hears that Traveler's been calling Karen Wendy II. There's more: Karen has bleached her hair to about the same shade as Wendy's. Already close to the same height and heft, this Wendy II is more than Wendy I intends to take sitting down.

Karen's been a fixture on the street for as long as anyone can remember. She hangs out in doorways late at night, usually with some guy and usually drunk. What little Wendy knows about her, she detests, and after she learns of Traveler's moniker, she starts to tell people that she and Karen did time together at the women's correctional facility in Framingham, fifteen miles west of Boston, in the early eighties. Wendy for assault and battery. Karen, as Wendy has it, for having set one of her children on fire. Rumors say Karen has a husband, a full-time resident at Pine Street, but marriage seems to have had little inhibiting effect on Karen's street conduct.

"She'll have a lesbian encounter in order to get a drink," Wendy is broadcasting with disdain these days from her stoop in the alley. "Even just a little sip. She goes after anyone who has a drink."

Shortly after this pronouncement, word comes back through the grapevine: Wendy II says that she's going to beat the piss out of Wendy I.

"There's only one Wendy," she tells Buddy one afternoon outside of Auditorium station.

"I don't care about them being together. They make a fine couple — totally moronic. But," she glowers, "nobody threatens me. Nobody."

She doesn't have long to wait for the inevitable confrontation to occur. She is stemming at the bottom of the Auditorium station stairs one night alone, and has positioned herself about ten feet from the token booth — a nostalgic spot, she reflects with dark humor, for this is where Traveler stabbed her with a bottle last New Year's Eve. It is a warm night. She's barefoot, wearing only cutoffs and a T-shirt. She tucks up against the worn yellow tiles, draws her legs up under her, and rests her quart of wine behind her against the wall.

Then she sees the two of them coming in, arm in arm. She hasn't laid eyes on her successor since prison days but recognizes her instantly. She knows that Traveler sees her sitting there, and still he brazenly keeps coming on.

Maybe that's what got to her, she tells Kurt the next morning as she pieces together the sequence of events. She doesn't know. Something sure did. Because what happened next did so almost without her thinking about it.

"She comes sauntering in," she tells Kurt. " 'Okay,' I think. 'So, you're gonna beat me up,' I said. Very quietly. When I get like that, run."

She rose and turned her back on Karen, as if she were going to walk away. In truth she was cupping both hands together into a formidable club of knuckles. Tensed, she whipped around and struck.

Karen, hit in the head, crumpled to the floor.

"That's when I used my feet," she tells Kurt. "I beat the piss out of her. I broke her jaw. I broke her nose. Then I stomped her neck with my feet. Then I knocked the living shit out of her. There was blood all over creation."

The first uniforms she saw were those of the MBTA police. Then the Boston police. She'd had her moments with all of them before.

"Hey, buddies," she tells them. "I gotta take a leak."

"Wendy, you did it this time." One of those who know her observes the bloodshed.

"What are you talking about?"

"Trying to steal your wine, huh?" one of them asks, with a sparkle in his eye.

"She hit you first, didn't she?" It is one of the subway cops who used to drive her out of the station with his billy club. He looks her straight in the eye.

An ambulance arrives and takes Karen away.

"She tried to take this poor girl's bottle, and hit her, and cut her," the transit cop defends Wendy as the phalanx of Boston police hustle down. "And all she was trying to do was defend herself. Poor girl, doesn't even have any shoes. Look at her."

Wendy snuffles, trying to look pathetic. When the questioning is over, she signs her name on the complaint form. In an obscure way, she has just won an ounce of justice for the many past sins the system has committed against her.

All along, Kurt's known that he wants something more. Love and spare change won't get them a room and a better life. It's too easy to drink too much, hanging around on the streets all day. In early September he tells Wendy that it's time to get a job, stay sober, and save some money. Reluctantly Wendy watches him go off now in the mornings to lay roofs, leaving her alone once more.

Several weeks pass. The physical work feels good to him. He likes being outdoors on these crisp fall days, wielding a hammer, bringing an old two-story house in Dorchester back to life. It's what he should have been doing all along, he thinks, as he stops intermittently to take in the early autumn foliage. Then one unseasonably steamy afternoon he is called by the foreman to come down off the job. He's got a visitor in the office, he is told by a surly voice.

Kurt's stomach starts to knot. Rounding the corner of the house, he encounters Wendy. She is standing with her arm in a cast and sling, cowering from his eyes. At first he thinks it isn't possible that anything could have happened in the few hours since they parted. But then his sympathy floods these doubts. And finally, in the wake of conflicting emotions, he just feels depressed.

"What happened?"

She is drunk.

She tried to kick Rocko, she tells him tearily. They were stemming at the top of the Auditorium stairs, and Rocko insulted her — she wouldn't say what he said. Only she missed him, and he kicked her instead, sending her on a header down the full flight of stairs. The pain was so bad that an ambulance had to come and take her to City. The bone had broken all the way through her skin.

"You know I'm legally blind!" She starts to weep again, overwhelmed. He pulls her into his arms and almost starts to cry with her, his ambition is so doomed, it seems at this moment. But his frustration is strong enough to gather itself as a form of hope. Nothing is going to stand in his way. He's going to get them out of this place if it kills him.

The sun has blistered fissures into the asphalt courtyard confined by three walls of the prison's locked dorms, but this doesn't deter a few restless men from aiming a basketball at the rusty, netless hoop. Around them emaciated figures shuffle, holding plastic coffee cups filled with water. A solitary old man with a book in his hands has sought out the shade offered by a spindly willow sustained by a patch of green. Most of the men, like Kurt, have found a space on one of the benches along the walls. They sit out the empty recreational hours trying not to make trouble, trying to be left alone in their own worlds until dinner.

Kurt has been at Bridgewater, thirty-five miles south of Boston, for nine days now. Tomorrow he will go back to Boston. When Wendy showed up drunk, he was asked not to return to the construction job. He decided to voluntarily commit himself, and Bridgewater was his only option.

Virtually unchanged since the state decriminalized alcoholism in 1973, the Bridgewater Addiction Center remains a prison within the larger penitentiary complex, which houses the state's criminally insane. It is only one of two long-term facilities in the state for homeless men who want to get sober. Kurt has come here to get straight and to think. To do so, he and his seven hundred–plus fellow alcoholics and drug addicts must accept the conditions: locked wards, thirty-foot-high barbed wire fences and guard dogs, prison uniforms, no personal possessions, and total lack of privacy.

For the past nine nights he's slept in a ward where the windows are so thickened with steel mesh that the world outside is nothing but a dream. Like everyone else, he's lucky to get a shower and a clean change of clothes every other day. Like them, he's allowed to make one ten-minute collect phone call a day from the coin phone on the landing in the stairwell outside the ward. Kurt, for obvious reasons, hasn't used the phone at all.

His days begin promptly at seven, when he is unlocked from the ward, with its painted brick walls, exposed piping, metal beds, and regulation gray woolen blankets. Each inmate is assigned morning work duty, which can earn him prison rewards: cigarettes, private showers, or assignment to one of the smaller dorms.

Until recently, the only thing Kurt would have done with the rest of his day at Bridgewater was vegetate. Despite a treatment law on the books since 1973, it wasn't until 1986 that Bridgewater had any therapeutic program for alcoholics, except for AA meetings. The facility continues to be administered by the state's Department of Corrections, already overtaxed, with the nation's second most severe overcrowding problem. Now four counselors work with up to eight hundred men. Trained social workers, they earn barely more than grocery store clerks: $4.25 an hour. Overworked and underpaid, they see hundreds of men every day and, not surprisingly, some two hundred and fifty of them again before a year is out.

But Kurt isn't here expecting miracles. As he sits in the cell-like ward after dinner, he thinks about Wendy. He hopes she's been looking after her arm. After nine days' reflection, Kurt still can't believe he let things get so out of hand. Drinking all day, skipping work, hanging out for weeks in the alley.

The heat of summer is ebbing. He looks forward to the change of season. It will give momentum, he hopes, to all the changes he has in mind for them. When he gets back, he's going to try and help Wendy get on welfare again. He'll go back to work. They can save a little money. Get a room. That will cost about seventy-five dollars a week, he calculates. And then they have to eat. But they can swing it. They can cut back on booze money, he figures. When it's just the two of them, they can buy a bottle of Canadian Club and it'll keep them for two days, he thinks. And if they have a room, they can get a few jigsaw puzzles. It will be nice. They'll be happy together.

He lies down and tries to relax. Around him men are preparing for sleep. Some, he knows, will hit the streets again and drink the first day out of here. Not him. Never again.

*

Wendy is waiting for him, as he knew she would be. Still the same Wendy, his woman. First off, he wants to know about her arm.

What did the doctor say?

She didn't go.

What does she mean, she didn't go?

Ah, she couldn't be bothered.

Kurt takes her arm and looks at it. An angry corona of red swells the flesh at either end of the cast. There are signs of carelessly wiped-away pus.

She's infected. They've got to get her down to the hospital.

Not tonight.

Yes, tonight.

No, not tonight.

"You know," she tells him, an edge of anger in her voice, "I can't stand feeling controlled."

Now he wants to know when she will apply for welfare. "You're eligible, why don't you do it?"

"Too much horseshit," she answers.

For one thing, she continues after a heavy pause, she doesn't have the necessary identification. Traveler had her last birth certificate, and God knows what he did with it.

Kurt reassures her. It's an easy matter to go downtown and get a copy.

She doesn't want the hassle.

"But Wendy," he pleads, "I want to get you off the streets. You don't deserve the streets."

She wheels.

"What do you mean, I don't deserve the streets? These streets are mine! I know every inch and alley, every cubbyhole you can crawl into, every doorway you can jump into. I know how to stay alive!"

The heavy door is half closed. Jamie, from the lunch canteen, gingerly pushes it open and steps inside. Quiet competence and institutional self-assurance prevail in the hushed, antiseptic cubicle several stories above street level in one of the wards of Mass. General Hospital.

The blinds have been drawn. Only when her eyes adjust to the dim can she finally make out Wendy. She looks so small in the bed, so helpless. So unlike herself. A clutch of transparent plastic tentacles attaches her arm to pouches of saline and nutrients and antibiotics to combat the infection that four days ago, after breeding and spreading through her system for several weeks, almost killed her.

Wendy had been close to unconscious when she and Matt brought her in. And, to make matters worse, drunk. Before the doctors could introduce the medicines she so desperately needed, the staff had to detoxify her body. Now, three days later, she is totally sober, a condition Jamie has never seen her in before. She has been seriously weakened, Jamie observes. In her little hospital johnnie, with the nurse washing her hair over a small pan of water, she looks so helpless and pathetic.

But suddenly Jamie realizes that it is more than physical weakness that is making Wendy's timid, barely audible responses to her inquiries so out of character. She has become withdrawn, almost shy, a sober Wendy whom Jamie literally does not know.

Despite the months of their developing relationship on the street, when Jamie would stop by with their lunches, it comes to her now that she may be trespassing on some essential and private dimension of Wendy's identity, a part of herself that Wendy never wants anyone to see. In the bed lies the vulnerable child beneath the bravado, who persists in seeking love and affirmation and protection against the odds. Jamie steps back from the bed toward the door. She takes one last glance back at Wendy, whispers a farewell, and withdraws.

Shortly after Wendy gets out of the hospital, she and Kurt are awakened one Monday morning by the sound of sledgehammers. Cautiously Kurt crawls to the bomb shelter door and peaks out, while she hastily pulls on some clothes. He motions her to his lookout. A gang of thugs are in the process of smashing everything in the Penthouse to bits. Wendy's first cogent thought is, where is Jake?

The sounds are terrible as the mallets go at chairs, tables, the refrigerator. She hears them smash the TV screen. Who has it in for him? She is incredulous.

In less than an hour it is over. The alley reverts to a deathly silence. She and Kurt watch the gang emerge from the Penthouse. They toss hammers and several other items into a waiting dump truck she hasn't noticed until now. Then with a chilling start she realizes that the thugs are city employees.

Unbeknownst to her and Kurt, the Public Health Department had given Jake notice on Friday. A police officer and a superintendent delivered the eviction, telling him that he had until this morning to remove his personal belongings. That day, the two men said, the department would be sending a dump truck out to clean up the alley and everything that remained behind.

Now it is over. Kurt and Wendy emerge from the bomb shelter to look around, and as they do, they see Willy come out of hiding behind a dumpster farther down the alley. Together the three of them go over to investigate.

The refrigerator door has been torn off its hinges. Food and bottles and the trinkets the men have collected over the years are strewn everywhere. Across the soiled rugs are pieces of broken furniture. Will says nothing. He just walks back and forth, tripping over shards of glass and torn books, as if he's looking for something he misplaced before it all began.

Wendy and Kurt leave him. From across the way, throughout the day they watch police come by repeatedly and tell Will to move on. Each time they leave, she and Kurt watch him return. Well after dark, they see a light inside the hovel. Since there is no longer electricity, they can't imagine where it is coming from. Wendy steals across the alley and peers in. Willy has poured out a bowl full of 10–40 motor oil, placed it on a plastic milk crate, and ignited it. His eyes are glazed, unfocused on the ruin around him. He seems to be staring at the light. There is only the light. He can't bear the darkness, alone. Not tonight.

Cold is coming on. Each morning at Burger King now, a small cadre of the homeless, most of them women unknown to Pine Street, grip cooling coffee cups. Behind heavy sunglasses they stare down their cigarettes or leaf through the morning's *Herald* or work over crossword puzzles. At the Greyhound station it is the same. People with no place to go try to merge with the impatient departing crowds as if they too can't wait forever. When, in fact, waiting is all they will do now until night falls again.

Long before eight on a Monday morning in November, the streets are slick with a layer of ice. First snow has fallen. A security alarm whines wildly in the fastness of frigid streets, coming from E. F. Costello's liquors near the corner of Mass. Avenue. No one seems to notice or care. From the shelter of doorways and heat blowers, the temporary inhabitants of the city have long since departed for the day, leaving behind slabs of cardboard, a blanket, beer cans, and bottles.

Wendy is already gone from the bomb shelter. A disheveled pile of blankets and quilts and a brown suede jacket are all that remain of her presence overnight.

Five inches of snow fall the next night, and at seven A.M. it is still coming down, mixed with sleet, blinding the windshields of creeping cabs and delivery trucks and undermining any incentive on the part of wakened residents to move. Plows began working before it was fully light to make the rush hour navigable. Schools are closed, and the radio has started to announce cancellations of every special event, lecture, and concert of the day. In the alley a frigid wind blows through a crack in the bomb shelter's door. There is no sign of life.

Wendy has left Kurt sleeping and set out in search of a drink. For the first time last night, they slept down in the cellar below the bomb shelter. But Kurt wasn't happy. He only stayed with her because after they spent the evening drinking together, it was too late for him to have a chance of getting a bed. Angrily he'd accused her of distracting him from the time so that he'd have to stay out. He can't sleep in the cold. And when he doesn't sleep, he can't work.

A rift is forming between them, she admits to herself this morning. She considers all the times that she's protected him, the times she's bailed him out or earned their money. Is it too much to ask that he stay with her when she's lonely? She can't stand babies.

She ends up at the grates behind the library, clothed only in a thin black-and-white checked jacket, blue jeans and sneakers, and black-and-blue houndstooth socks. As she settles down, she reminds herself of what her mother told her: if she started drinking again when she came back up here, she wouldn't live to see her thirty-second birthday. She shakes her head. Now her birthday is three weeks away. She has a bad feeling about things this morning.

"I should have been dead years ago," she says out loud.

The rescue van has missed the group for several nights. Peter Hurley, the van's elder statesman, silently combs the shadows as he cruises the deceptively quiet streets, knowing that if he hasn't caught up with them since the snowfall, it's no doubt because there are more important matters of survival being dealt with on the street, like equipping new, sheltered sleeping quarters against the cold, where his sandwiches and coffee would be of minimal use.

Now it is well past midnight as the van noses through the impacted slush along the road behind the library. Ahead he sees Indian Pete, who has actually run into the middle of the road to flag him down.

Peter inches cautiously forward as Pete continues to wave. As he gets closer, the headlights pick up the alarm on Pete's face.

"Here." Indian Pete speaks quietly as he almost pulls Peter out of the van. Pete leads him over to where Buddy and Troy are huddled over the human wreck that is Karen.

"She's in bad shape," he tells Peter. "Take her in."

Karen's face, swollen and lacerated, is almost unrecognizable. Her eyes are so bruised that she can't open them. She can't speak. Dumbly she gropes her way into Peter's arms and sags against his shoulder. Her pain has been blunted by the enormous quantities of alcohol that she's consumed in the past hour. But she continues to feel the wound within. She can't believe what Traveler has done to her.

She reeks of fresh blood, urine, and alcohol. With effort, Peter leads her to the van and gently lifts her into the back seat. He's unsure whether the women's unit will take her in, so late and in such bad shape.

Well, they'll have to, he decides.

When he arrives and carries Karen in, her condition brings tears to the eyes of the two women on shift there.

"Should she go to the hospital?" one of them asks Peter.

He persuades them to let her curl up on one of the vacant sofas in the lobby for the night. See what her face looks like in the morning, he advises them. Then she'll be sober enough to tell a doctor what happened.

Out on the street again, Peter discovers Wendy, alone, sobbing, and close to freezing to death in espadrilles and a single blanket. She tells Peter that Kurt has taken off, with Rockadock's vodka. She has difficulty articulating. She is desperate to go inside, she tells him, but every women's shelter that will allow her in is already full.

"Can I ride with you for a while, just to warm up?" she asks him. "You have no idea how close to suicide I am."

The night before, she tells him once she is settled into the back seat, Kurt left her to go in to Pine Street. That was fine. She decided to go inside too and walked the eight blocks to the intake shelter at Boston City Hospital. Before parting, they agreed to meet in the morning at Auditorium station. But when she got to Auditorium, Kurt wasn't there. She waited for another two hours, but he never showed.

She falls silent, feeling the city rush past in the cold darkness. Then she says, "He blames me for his being on the street."

"Why?" asks Peter.

A sigh comes from the back.

"He claims that he loves me, dearie. But all he cares about is himself." She pauses, then says reflectively, "He's not bad. I've had four years and one month more street life."

Peter has pulled the van up to the curb, where a group of men are waiting to be taken in.

"Oh God," Wendy moans. "You're not going to put Traveler Kroll in here next to me. Oh, come on, man. I got enough stab marks from him. Christ."

Traveler isn't among the group, Peter reassures her.

"You don't know what he did to that girl, Karen," she says. She sits back and closes her eyes. "Alcoholism is the worst affliction," she muses, "because it's so self-alienating."

And now the images of the children come back to her as she closes her eyes and feels the reassuring sway of the vehicle, its warmth inviting a brief reprieve from the concrete realities. If the dance is doomed, there must be at least a shape, a coherence, somewhere in the chaos that is her. And there is. It is in her, and of her, the myth of self that will save her and explain her when love fails to. Otherwise, who could live with such loss?

"By the time I was seventeen," she tells Peter, "I already had two kids. First baby was fathered by my stepfather. The second baby by my brother. First one was born when I was about thirteen. Second one was born when I was fourteen."

Peter focuses on the road. The smooth motion of the van lulls her. Her voice grows soft and dreamy.

"I had custody of Michael, my little boy," she continues. "I was a stubborn little bitch back then, I'm telling you, boy. At one time I really used to be able to drink a man as big as Big Johnny, and bigger, under the table. People used to invite me to parties just to watch me drink. Michael was my sidekick. He was my special little friend. The last party I took him to, I forget how old he was — he was a toddler, anyway — he said, 'Kidju?' That means mother in Indian. 'Kidju, you gonna drink?' I said, 'You better believe it, and you're gonna go to sleep.' "

Peter has never before heard Wendy talk about the children. It is hard to believe that she would have had guardianship of children at such a young age, but now she is telling him that she sent her sons down to Granny to raise.

"My second husband was the father of my last two," she continues.

"Eddie and Lisa. My second husband — we were already divorced and everything — but he adopted my first two as his own. I gotta give the man credit for that. And he treated them just like they were his children.

"I was about twenty-three. This was in Florida, when I met him. We were going together. He had a contract job in Florida. And I got knocked up. I know it's kinda crude to put it that way, but what can I say? It wasn't expected. So he wanted to marry me. I ended up back on the reservation. My reservation. My real reservation. My tribe. And I hated it."

"Where was that?"

"Right outside of Oklahoma City. It's on the outskirts. They never put the reservation in the city proper, because they didn't want the Indians to associate with regular citizens. I'm sorry. I'm very bitter about it. I had this hatred for reservations. I don't mind going there and visiting friends of mine, or a relative once in a while. But, uh-uh. 'Cause they're legalized concentration camps. I don't care what anybody says. I know from my own head, my own experience.

"He was an Indian. Full-blooded Indian. But he could not comprehend alcoholism. I mean he drank now and then, you know, like a New Year's Eve bash. But he wasn't an alcoholic. Just wasn't.

"His mother did not like me. Back on the reservation. I couldn't please her. All I could think of was my mother. It's like you're butting your head against a concrete wall, ya know? And you're getting nowhere."

"What was Michael's last name, Wendy?"

"Gabriel. Michael Gabriel."

"Nice name," Peter says softly.

"Yeah," she pauses. "I didn't hate the man. I was kinda fond of him. But I'm the type of person, don't put no chains on me."

"Agreed."

"The straw that broke the camel's back, Lisa was six or seven months old. He came home from work, and I'm passed out on the floor. Here's this infant that needs changing, hasn't been fed. *That,*" she pauses, "I can understand the anger in that. So the next day he puts me on a plane to Tampa. He says, 'I'm gonna give you thirty days. If you don't clean up your act, I'm filing for divorce.' He gave me money. I had like three grand on me. So I hit Tampa. Granny picks me up. 'Course I drank on the plane, are you crazy?

"I did go to a detox when I first hit St. Petersburg. My third day, I

call him. I thought he'd be pleased that I'm trying to get my act together. 'Cause I loved my kids.

"He says, 'I'm sorry, Wendy. I filed for divorce the same day I put
you on the plane.' Sure as shootin', two days later, I got the notice.
He certainly had.

"I said, 'That's it, baby. Go for broke.' "

But it is getting on toward morning now, the light will be coming
up, and the children will be gone.

"My first son died from drug and alcohol overdose right here in
Boston," she starts to conclude her story. "He came here to look for
me. His name was Michael. My second son, Jacob, who has his father's
name, he committed suicide. He was right behind Mike. Mike died
when he was sixteen. Jacob musta been fifteen. Or going on fifteen.

"Then what happened was, this wasn't that long ago. Three years?
Two? Something like that. My husband was driving. He had Eddie
and Lisa in the car, and a big truck, a rig, hit 'em head on. The guy
was doped up and they were all killed. So I ain't got a single kid
left."

By four in the morning she has finished creating herself. She has
gotten through the night.

"Just drop me off at the Marlboro Market vents," she says to Peter.
"I'll be okay there."

At four in the morning, only the wanderers are about. They watch
for one another, track each other's movements in the night. It won't
be long now before they will start coming out of the night in search
of breakfast. Some come on crutches, some on the arms of their buddies; some come alone, hooded and afraid. Or angry. For most the
morning is bitter, a burden. And God, a grotesque joke.

The burden of solitude grows increasingly heavy for Wendy. At night
now she crawls into the drafty concrete hut and wraps a cocoon of
blanket around her body, until nothing, not even her face, shows, and
she is less than just anonymous. She is invisible.

By now winter has settled in to stay. During the day Wendy moves
between her usual haunts in search of warmth and companionship, at
the library or the subway entrance. She is lonely. Thanksgiving comes
and goes, and one morning early in December, in an alley off Marlborough Street, she is squeezing the pus out of her third-degree burns
and crying over Kurt.

"They're so good to me." She cries, her tears unstanched. "Until I'm raped in my heart. You know?"

Kurt came back and beat her up, then he stole her vodka and swiped her hat. Now, there is little more than three inches left in Rocko's liter. Barely tucked up out of the raw rain that drips from eaves three stories up, she is thinking this morning about the freedom that death could bring.

"Ah, gimme a drink." She reaches for the vodka, then replays the nightmare.

"He says, 'What do you want, you fucking bitch?' "

"I said, 'What did you say? Be nice, you know? If you can't be nice . . .' "

That's when he started to beat her. Since then, she and Rocko have been sitting in the rain.

"A reservation is nothing but a glorified concentration camp," she says suddenly. "Do you know that the blacks had the right to vote before the Native Americans? Did you know it? There are no Indian senators. Nowhere. Or congressmen. Nowhere. Not in this whole country."

She and Rocko sit in silence again, watching the rain. At length Wendy has to pee. Reaching into a small, plastic grocery bag suspended within arm's reach from a bar of rusted iron, she tears off a handful of tissue, excuses herself, dashes several yards into the rain, and squats.

"Why don't you marry me?" Rocko calls after her. "I've been wanting you to marry me for years."

"Nope," she calls back. "Wouldn't work. You can't mix races. You know who pays the price? The kids."

Finished, she hitches her pants, returns to the cubbyhole, and resumes, "You know why the Indians didn't make good slaves? They'd let them kill them instead of being a slave. You know what I'm saying? The Indians would not work. Nope. 'Kill me. Kill me. I'd rather be killed.' "

She starts to choke up again, thinking about racial injustice and about the failed dance. She'd been so full of hope.

"It's not that the Indians couldn't work. They just wouldn't." She starts to cry. " 'I'm not gonna be your slave.' "

"What you don't know about Custer . . . they didn't want to kill his troops. They wanted Custer. Because Custer found gold in their sa-

cred burial ground. There were Arapahos, Crows, Blackfeet. It was
the only time that mortal enemies banded together. Because he des-
ecrated the sacred burial ground. All because he found gold."

Jake resurfaces. Demented with bitterness and rage, he tries to set the
bunker beneath the bomb shelter on fire by igniting a cone of newspaper and throwing the flaming torch inside, hoping the collection of
wood scraps will catch.

A suicide mission or vengeance? None of them will ever know. The
next night he returns with a can of gasoline and tries to saturate the
damp scraps. He puts match after match to them, but the residue,
barely charred, is discovered the next morning by several construction workers nearby. After this Jake disappears completely. The gate
on the Penthouse fence is welded shut.

Kurt curls close to her body, down against the wall at the grates. The
alley is still. Patches of frost here and there pick up the glow from the
street lights. Around them the others are asleep or unconscious, huddled close beneath blankets and coats for warmth.

As he kisses her, his beard grazes her cheek. Beneath coats and
blankets she fumbles for her zipper. Quietly, so as not to wake the
others, she coaxes her jeans down far enough so she can pull her legs
out. A blast of cold wind meets her flesh and she quickly pulls the
blanket back around her. In the raw silence she smiles at her lover.

Now they hear a strange noise coming from off the alley. They lie
back quietly and remain still, their eyes closed. It sounds like singing,
but it can't be. The bars have been closed for hours. Through partially opened eyelids, they observe a curious light at the mouth of the
alley, coming nearer.

The sound has roused the others. They sit up, nudging each other
into wakefulness, and watch. When they are sufficiently alert, they
suddenly realize what's happening, and join in.

> Happy Birthday to you,
> Happy Birthday to you,
> Happy Birthday, dear Wendy,
> Happy Birthday to you.

Wendy and Kurt laugh as J.T. lowers a Hostess apple tart, decorated with four flickering birthday candles, into her lap.

TWENTY-SEVEN

The Chapter to Memory

DAWN IS just around the corner at 4:56 as the van turns off Boylston and onto Dartmouth, but for the crew today, it will seem as if morning never comes.

Michael is driving. J.T., at the desk in the men's unit lobby, is taking calls from men on the street who want to be brought in, and radioing them out. Jill, a counselor in the men's unit, rides shotgun, and a volunteer named Tim is in back.

Michael passes the library and peers down the narrow street behind it. There he sees a couple of people on the grates. He turns and pulls up alongside them. It is Traveler, lying on top of Karen. He is completely covering her, clutching her to him. Close by are several empty liquor bottles. They have no blankets, no wraps of any kind.

Michael gets out of the van and goes over and pokes at Traveler, trying to rouse him. But Traveler, out cold, can't be moved. With Tim's help then, Michael peels Traveler away. Beneath, Karen is white as a sheet. Michael reaches down. Her face is cold. He puts his hand under her nose but feels nothing. He exposes her midriff, hoping to see the rise and fall of her breathing. When he doesn't, he runs back to the van and radios J.T.

"Call 911."

Traveler, who's been guided into the van, has begun to wake up. He is dazed, disoriented, and sick.

"I need a drink," he rasps to Jill, who's stayed with him. His body is quickly losing control as he gains consciousness. Jill finds the bottle of port stowed on board for emergencies, pours some into a Styrofoam cup, and hands it to him.

Traveler tells her how he and Karen were down at Auditorium station earlier, and Karen had had a grand mal seizure. He says he then carried her the eight blocks to the library. At ten o'clock the blowers were turned off, but they decided to stick it out and try to keep each other warm.

The ambulance has arrived by now, and two emergency medical technicians begin to administer CPR to Karen on the grates. But they soon cut short their efforts, strap Karen to a stretcher, and place her in the back of the truck.

"She's been out here too long," one of them tells Michael as she slams the ambulance door shut.

"How's my old lady?" Traveler confronts Michael as soon as he returns to the van. "Don't tell me there's anything wrong with her! Don't tell me she's not going to make it!"

Michael tells him. Karen is dead.

"Don't tell me this!" he cries out. "I can't believe this! You're lying! You wouldn't lie to me. You're lying to me. Tell me it isn't true! How the fuck could this happen? She was right there!"

He begins ranting. "If I find out anything happened to her, if somebody messed with her, I'm gonna get my friends in the Zone, and I'm gonna kill. I really cared about her. She was my old lady and she took care of me."

By now, light is beginning to slant into the street, picking out the soiled snow, the paper bags frozen in ice beside the dumpsters, creating shadows and concrete shapes again, pressing in as a form of time.

"Why don't we take you down to the hospital, Traveler," Michael offers.

"Yeah," he agrees. "I'd like that."

At the emergency room at Tufts/New England Medical Center, few seats are occupied at this early hour on Saturday morning. Ten minutes pass, then a nurse comes out of the swinging doors and tells them that they are still working on Karen. She was very cold when she arrived, the nurse tells them, but she is being kept alive by manual CPR. Her body temperature is 83 degrees. They plan to inject fluids to see if they can get her temperature high enough to give her heart a chance to sustain a beat of its own.

"I've got to see her," Traveler tells the nurse.

"Well, you can't right now," she tells him. "But if you can sit tight we'll give you another report and the doctor will talk to you later."

At eight-fifteen a young doctor comes out to speak with them. He introduces himself, and repeats what the nurse has already said. But by now Traveler has gone back to the van several times for more port. His clothing is filthy and his beard several days grown. He weaves and runs his hand distractedly through his hair, almost demented with concern.

"Let me see her," Traveler pleads. "I've got to see her. I've got to talk to her."

Michael realizes that Traveler is hardly the model of the concerned husband that this young doctor is probably accustomed to seeing. The doctor tries, gently, to put him off. "We have to concentrate on taking care of Karen," he says to Traveler. "It's really not a good idea for you to see her."

But Traveler won't be coaxed. He begins to bellow. "I've got to see her!"

The doctor studies him for a minute, then says quietly, "Okay. But you'll have to understand that she's not going to look like you've seen her look. She has a lot of tubes in her. And she's bloated. You'll get a sense of how serious a situation this is when you see her."

The two men follow the doctor through several swinging doors and hallways until they come to Karen's room. At the door a security officer prevents Michael from going any farther. Traveler advances to the bed alone. Karen is unconscious. At one side of the bed a doctor is massaging her chest, while from the other a nurse is blowing air into her mouth. They have been doing this for nearly four hours.

Traveler takes Karen's hand. He begins to cry. Incoherent, broken words start coming from his mouth, while with barely restrained agitation he strokes her hand. Finally he falls silent, drops her hand back down to her side, and turns toward the door.

"She's going to die," he tells Michael.

Michael, afraid that if Traveler remains at the hospital he'll become violent, offers to take him back to the library. Traveler, shaken, agrees.

It is close to noon, and the van returns to the all-too-familiar place. On the grates sit Pete, Troy, Willy, and Buddy, wrapped in the blankets the crew had used hours earlier to try to warm Karen. They've been drinking all morning, and at the sight of the van they laugh, disoriented and delighted.

"Hey, can we get some sandwiches?" they ask when Michael opens the door.

Traveler stumbles off the van. He is incoherent. But slowly, imperfectly, the news sinks in. The group members pace, not knowing what to do or how to react. Pete thinks that they ought to go over to the Church of All Nations for lunch. Traveler agrees, and all of them crunch together in the back seat of the van for the ride over.

At two o'clock that afternoon Michael finally gets home to sleep. Four hours later, when he wakes, he calls the Inn. Karen was declared dead at 2:53.

TWENTY-EIGHT

What Comes Around

WENDY CAN'T SAY that she is sorry about Karen's death. But in the weeks that follow, it begins to haunt the group. The chaos of their lives now seems irreversible.

The trash becomes impossible to control. One morning Wendy wakes up behind the library earlier than the others and tries to straighten up the icy concrete around them. She gathers the leftover food and containers, dirty newspapers, milk cartons, soiled scarves, mittens, and empty bottles, and starts across the street to the dumpster. She loses her footing and falls, scattering fragments of tin foil and broken glass everywhere. Landing on her face on the pavement, she sustains yet another round of injuries, a badly bruised lip and elbows.

The loneliness is worse, more crushing than ever. She weeps now every day — sudden, violent jags. Indian Pete has burrowed deeper into silence, coming out only to ask a passer-by from time to time, belligerently, "Give me one good reason why I should get sober. Give me one good reason." Kurt, when he's around, broods in an alcohol haze.

Though none of them talk about it much, Karen has become a chilling repudiation of all that they hoped they would find out on the streets. In the incipient madness that is swirling like the pre–New Year's eve snow around them, it has become vital to cling to anything that feels more rooted than themselves. The blanket around one's shoulders. The hard neck of the bottle. The one who says I love you. The book. The doorway. The poem.

One night, as J.T. pulls up in the van, he observes a woman's brown

pump lying on its side in a pool of vodka and spilled Coke. Nearby a
blanket, balled up and tossed against the wall, has knocked over a
stack of containers of cranberry sauce and an open can of beer. Clothing, the foil from cigarette packs, and food, thrown in defense or
contempt, is everywhere.

The huddle of bodies is wrapped tightly together; the wind drives
a freezing rain against them. If they don't get inside tonight, J.T.
fears, they'll go the way Karen did. All of them are sleeping, except
Traveler.

Sitting slightly apart, Traveler clutches a book against his chest. It
is the *Rubáiyát*, the one book he's managed to hang onto since he stole
it from a bookshop in July. Before he and Wendy split up. Before
everything.

"The best poetry there is," he says now as J.T. steps up to him, eyes
stinging from the cold. "You can't beat it."

J.T. frowns. "Hello, everyone!" he calls out.

" 'To grasp this sorry Scheme of Things entire,' " Traveler begins
to recite.

J.T.'s voice rouses a few. Pete and Troy lumber out from under the
sodden, half-frozen blankets and silently climb into the van. Traveler
follows them.

As sleet begins to strike the windshield, J.T. starts back, still worried
about those he's leaving on the grates who wouldn't budge. He pleaded
and cajoled, promising that no one would hassle them once they got
into the shelter. But his efforts had no effect.

As usual, Traveler's first words when J.T. got behind the wheel
were to inform him that he just wanted to drive around for a few
hours. But J.T. doesn't have time for Traveler's antics tonight. There
are too many more people out here to see. Traveler is going to the
shelter and that is that.

Traveler slides his book out of the protective embrace of his jacket
and runs his hand over the elaborately illustrated cover.

"He was a sultan's son, and he gave up millions to be a drunk," Troy
now says to J.T., of Omar Khayyam. "Every poem in here is about
being drunk."

"Have you ever read it, J.T.?" Traveler asks.

"Naw," J.T. answers. "Never did."

"He had seven wives at the same time." He pauses. "Ever since my
old lady died," he starts.

But Troy cuts him off. "She wasn't your wife. Don't say that."

"She was my common-law wife. Same thing."

"She wasn't your legal wife," Troy insists.

J.T. is taken aback by Troy's uncharacteristic assertiveness until he remembers — Troy's wife ditched him while he was in Vietnam.

"Don't you have to be seven years to be common law, J.T.?" Troy now enlists his support.

"Yep."

"As far as I'm concerned," Traveler retorts, "if you love a woman, she's your wife."

The van has arrived at the Inn. J.T. gets out, opens the back door, and as soon as the trio is safely indoors, sets out again.

Forty-five minutes later the two-way radio overhead rasps and the familiar signal summons J.T.

"Hey," a voice comes through. "Do you see a paper bag full of books on the back seat?"

J.T. cranes his neck and checks. Nothing.

"Traveler Kroll thinks he left them there."

"Naw," J.T. radios back. For some reason he clearly remembers Traveler's raw, aimless hands tonight. "He didn't bring them on with him. I'm sure of that."

"Okay," the voice crackles. "Thanks."

J.T. glances at the clock outside of the BayBank. Before long this especially straining shift will be over.

He heads back to the Inn. Inside, he returns the undistributed sandwiches to the cafeteria, the coffee urn to the kitchen. The morning crew has already been up for an hour, pulling together breakfast. Wearily, J.T. nods to them. They grin and exchange a few quiet words.

A quarter of a mile away, battling both blizzard and sleep, Traveler is stalking away from the Inn as fast as he can in wet leather shoes and sockless feet. Bent into the wind, the tails of a second, ill-fitting coat tugged on over the first, flapping like broken wings, his hollow figure is being propelled by the force of obsession. He is seeking the only thing that means anything, without which he is sleepless, insensible, lost. His books. He's got to find his bag full of second-hand books.

Wendy weeps. It is cold and lonely on the grate. From time to time, bundled in a rough gray army blanket, she glances down the street. She pulls blackened hands out of the sleeves of her plaid wool jacket and warms them over the current of hot air. There is nowhere for her to go, unless she wants to sit on a chair at the intake until dawn, two hours away, which she doesn't.

She knows that even if Kurt were with her, it wouldn't be the way it used to be. They don't have sex anymore, or hardly ever. These days his voice is harsh. He's stopped using her Christian name and started calling her "squaw." He knocks her around.

How it's come to this again, she wishes someone could tell her. Covering her head with her blanket, she caves against the concrete. She knows this feeling well. It is fear.

A daily liter of vodka, an infrequent bowl of soup, every few days a sandwich from Burger King. Some days she can't keep any food down. One morning recently she swallowed a pint of milk, only to throw it up again, and with it, blood.

"I puke up so much blood," she says these days, "it makes me sick."

And when sleep finally comes, it brings alcoholic dreams, weird, larger than life, and terrifying.

"It's usually when the booze is coming on," she says. "They're nightmares. They're so horrifyingly real, I jump right out of a sound sleep."

The dreams trace the outermost boundary of what is tolerable. But just barely, for when she wakes with tears in her eyes and her pulse knocking wildly, she knows that, alone and unprotected, she verges on the blue horrors.

Now she fumbles among the orphaned bottles. If she doesn't find a few drops in one of them she'll be in trouble long before post time at Danny's Liquors.

"I have to tell you," her voice quavers. "I've been stabbed. I've been shot. I've been strangled. I've had a lot of things done to me. Physical abuse. But the scariest thing I've ever been through is the D. T.'s. I shit you not. It's the most horrifying experience a human being could ever go through. You can't explain it. It's not the same for everybody. And every time it's not the same. It's always different. You might think you're hearing creatures talking to you and you're looking around for these voices that are saying these things, and there's nobody there. Sometimes sounds will be amplified. A little pin drop will be like a boom. I wouldn't wish it on my worst enemy. I'd rather shoot them outright."

Suddenly she is crying again. Tears run down her cheeks and into her open palms silently for several minutes.

"I'm so afraid," she whispers.

Once more she checks the entrance to the alley. Then, she starts to sob like a little girl.

"I'm losing my soul," she says.

"I don't know." J.T. is thinking out loud the next night as he navigates the peaceful, mostly deserted January streets. "There are probably fifty folks out here today, where last year there were only thirty."

Arctic air has come down from the north, making the midnight sky a cold, clear indigo. This is J.T.'s kind of weather, and he drives with his window wide open, his worn leather flight jacket unzipped, as he sips from a cup of lukewarm coffee and keeps watch.

Ever since he left his large family back in Wisconsin, he's been involved in human service work. He ran a special needs camp for kids, then worked with the elderly, with adolescent truants, and now with the homeless. He likes and respects most of the street people he's met, and though he doesn't put up with as much as some of his colleagues, he knows that he's well liked and respected in return. But he's under no illusions. He's not out here trying to save the world, or even most of those he sees every night.

"There's little sense of measurable failure out here," he says. "All I'm offering is coffee and an occasional trip to the hospital."

Stopping at one of the automatic teller machines, he spots the same face he's been seeing for several nights, an old black man asleep on his back on the floor, his head propped against the radiator, hands folded across his army jacket. Tucked into the laces of his worn shoes again tonight are two one-dollar bills for potential muggers. Quietly J.T. lays two sandwiches by his head and slips out the door.

Behind the library the grates are deserted. So is Kenmore Square. At the Marlborough grates two unfamiliar faces blink as the headlights strike them. They gratefully take coffee and answer J.T.'s question. No, they've seen no one else.

He's beginning to get a strange sense about the city's silence tonight. He hasn't run into any of the group, and he's almost run out of places to look. The last possibility is Rat Alley. In minutes he has pulled in, cut the engine, and jumped out. He strides to the door of the cellar bunker and calls out, "Hello?"

There is no response. Then he thinks he hears someone stirring about, crawling to the opening. A face appears. It is Buddy.

"They've all gone inside," he whispers to J.T. "They're at the Armory."

J.T. stands still for a minute, hands in his pockets. Then he returns to the van to get Buddy a cup of coffee. The Armory, he knows, doesn't take women. When he returns to Buddy, he remarks on this.

For the next hour J.T. scours the city's remaining hideouts. No Wendy. Close to three, he heads back downtown to see the last of the regulars. As he passes South Station, he suddenly pulls over and jumps out. He stalks into the middle of the deserted street, flings his head back, and stares at the full moon as it shines over Boston. Suddenly he is certain that the last thing Buddy told him is true. Wendy has checked herself into detox.

The narrow back street is hardly auspicious, tucked out of the sun within a labyrinth of rundown brick bowfronts that hug the medical area near City Hospital. It is hard to know who lives here, the sidewalks are so forsaken. Not children. Old people, mainly, and poor drunks, who come here to dry out.

The whitewashed stenciled lettering just outside a dim alcove by an unmarked service door, the entrance to one of the six publicly funded detoxes in Boston, seems so unconvincing, so makeshift, so dismal: BOSTON ALCOHOL DETOX PROJECT.

On Sunday afternoons between two and three, visitors are allowed in. A middle-aged black man blocks the door like an amiably belligerent host who wants to make sure all who enter have legitimate business inside. He knows the floor and the ward of anyone who's asked for, so many are regulars. With a nod and a grunt, he allows one after another to pass through.

"She'll be on the third floor," he says of Wendy, a familiar face going years back.

The elevator opens on a short corridor heaped high with used plastic dinner trays and nearly blocked by a cart full of soiled sheets and bedding.

The "ward" is a dingy hallway. Along both walls ashen-faced patients sit, in regulation blue-and-white striped robes, on plastic chairs facing each other. It is so narrow their knees almost touch. There is nowhere else to go. They smoke and stare into space. Some avoid eye contact, some seek it out, and some, with nothing better to do, listen in on a conversation between a female patient and a black man who's just arrived to visit her.

"See, withdrawal would be harder for you," she's explaining to him, "because you use heroin, too."

He nods, intent.

Off the hallway are three rooms, dark, close, and musty, their shades drawn in the middle of the day. Two are dorms — one for women and one for men. The third is a small television room with a TV suspended high up on the wall, always on, the volume high. There is no place to read, no place to reflect, and no place to be alone, except on the toilet, and even then not for long since there is only one stall for men and one for women. Those who aren't sitting and staring at each other, or at the chipped and yellowed woodwork in the hallway, are lying in the darkness and staring at the ceiling.

There is no sign of Wendy, who's been in since late Friday night — not in the room, the hallway, or what can be seen of the nurse's station behind a window occluded by venetian blinds, where on this Sunday afternoon the staff sits, locked in.

When asked, a pasty-faced, puffy, red-haired patient in a faded housecoat drags her dirty scuffs across the linoleum until she arrives at the foot of the only vacant iron bed in the women's dorm. Emerging from the haze of her own illness for the first time in forty-eight hours, she nods.

"Yeah. Oh yeah. Maybe that's hers."

But this is the end of the available information.

Then out of nowhere, an orderly appears. "She's in there," he gestures to the bathroom. "She's leaving. See if you can talk to her."

Wendy, wearing a green men's pajama top and floppy, burlap-colored pajama trousers, is in the ladies' room struggling into a pair of jeans. No way is she staying.

"They're only giving me two Libriums a day," she puffs from the exertion. "It's not enough. I told them that if someone's been drinking twenty-four hours a day for eight months, two Libriums isn't enough. I'm shaking and rattling all over."

She needs a comb. At this moment an attractive black woman pushes her way into the cramped space and accuses Wendy of trying to steal her sweater. Wendy looks down. She has inadvertently added it to the layers of her own garments she took from the heap in the dorm closet.

She backs into the stall to remove it. "Okay. No problem." Emerging, she looks at herself in the mirror and remarks, "You can't win for losing."

No one tries to stop her. When the elevator opens at One, she ne-
gotiates the hallway, passes the efficient sentry, and is back on the
street.

As she sniffs her first waft of fresh air, she admits, "You know, I've
never stayed in that place the whole time. Never."

"Why don't you just admit you don't love me anymore?"

Three days later, Wendy is unable to stop shivering in the brutal
cold. She is perched on Kurt's lap on the library grates, the large
quantities of alcohol in her system after a day's sobriety making her
belligerently drunk. On top of this, the burns she got when she fell
asleep against a radiator several weeks ago have become infected;
swollen purple welts have risen on her forearms. She hasn't had a
single bite of food since she left detox.

"She's been on this for weeks now." Kurt appeals to Indian Pete.

"All right." He turns back to her. "I admit it. Does that make you
feel any better?"

She slides off his lap onto the grate, pushes aside the blanket and
pulls her jeans down so that she can urinate through the grillwork.
Then she starts to cry.

Kurt has had it. He stands on shaky legs and strides off.

"I'm gonna go jump!" she calls after him. "Then no one can take
anything away from me again!"

Kurt doesn't come back that night. Around two-thirty Wendy gathers up the cast-off blankets lying around, drapes what she can over
her shoulders, and makes her way down to intake.

The next morning she staggers past the smudged glass shelter door
into sunshine, takes a few steps forward, then falters. Where she is,
where she has been — the grates, the factory, the rye fields and the
cheap rooms — spin in bits and clues before her, then blow away. She
falls on the ice. Glancing up before she loses consciousness, she sees
only the night.

Tears leak out of her discolored puff of black eye slowly and painfully.

"I'm afraid," she whispers over and over.

The seizure she had outside of City Hospital two days ago nearly
did her in. Kurt sits next to her on a ledge behind the library. His
face, too, is a mess. Blood has congealed around a nasty gash between

his eyes. His upper lip and nose are covered with cuts. He doesn't say a word, to her or to anyone else.

Something has happened.

"What the fuck is he in love with?" Wendy cries softly. "What's so great about me? If I was intelligent, I wouldn't be on the streets, would I? If I was loving, I wouldn't be being beat up half the time."

Nothing adds up anymore.

When she came to on Monday morning, she was in the emergency ward. The doctor who looked her over asked how long it had been since she'd had a gynecological exam.

She didn't know. She'd missed the day's first liquor run, no doubt, she ruminated. She'd start stemming on her way back downtown, maybe stop at Danny's en route.

The doctor came over to her side.

"Well, from my estimate," he told her, "you're two and a half months along."

She stared at him, aghast. "Along what?"

When she got back to the grates and told him, Kurt wept with joy. But Wendy spent the rest of the afternoon and evening by herself. She rounded the corner and sat staring down Stuart Street toward the Howard Johnson's where she and Annie had gotten drunk and stuffed themselves on Dunkin' Donuts so many years before. In the hospital in Tennessee she'd written a poem about the pregnant and wistful girl that she'd been back then.

> I was a child, and he was a child;
> Oh how sweet were the flowers that then grew wild.
> Believing in love, believing in life;
> Forgetting the woes, forgetting the strife.
>
> We clasped hands as we raced through the field,
> Bursting with desire of which we did yield.
> A childish love with childish dreams,
> Never thinking of tomorrow, or what it could bring.
>
> We never said goodbye, nor see you some day,
> We just drifted apart and went our separate ways.
> But a new life had begun to grow inside of me,
> I love it, wanted it, and never was sorry.

> But the rulers of my life wouldn't allow my unborn
>   to live,
> Nor ever have the chance to feel the love I longed
>   to give.
> But I still believe in love, and I still believe in life;
> But *now* I'll never forget the woes, and I'll never
>   forget the strife.

It was such a sad joke. She couldn't even take care of herself anymore, burning herself against radiators.

The next morning, without telling Kurt, she returned to the hospital and signed adoption papers to give the baby away right after its birth.

"Hey," she says now, shifting slightly away from Kurt and fingering the eye that was the first target of his discovery and his shattered hopes. "I'm not responsible. I can't even take care of myself. I know what my destiny is."

On January 15, as a result of a concerted lobbying effort on the part of the concerned van team, Wendy is officially unbarred at the Pine Street Inn. Late that night J.T. finds her on the grates and delivers the good news.

"Hey," he grins. "You can come inside now."

She hugs her bottle close to her. She's sick as a dog.

"Psshhh!" she answers. "You can have it. I'm out here. I got my vodka."

Epilogue

AMANDA'S BID for the dollhouse was the highest one on that Saturday morning in January. Once she got her coveted treasure home, however, she realized that the ramshackle, tacked-together plywood box was battered beyond redemption.

Undaunted, she went out and bought a brand-new, unfinished two-story miniature colonial. The splendid dollhouse dominates her desk these days, awaiting her imprint on its wallpapers, floorings, and doorknobs. She adds pieces of furniture as she finds them: a writing desk, books, a child's crib. The project has come to take up most of her days off from the department store where she now works. After her weekly session with her therapist, and lunch with one or two old shelter friends, she browses the aisles of Woolworth's in search of accessories or returns home and leafs through home decorating magazines, collecting ideas for her still unfurnished rooms.

The rest of the St. Paul's dinner group have all left the shelter. Like Amanda, Genevieve and Alice are tenants in Paul Sullivan Housing Trust homes; Lucky has an apartment in a low-income elderly housing complex. Colette followed her new man, Danny, south to the Carolinas.

Wendy, after a period of particularly heavy drinking upon learning that she was pregnant, miscarried in the alley. She and Kurt separated during the spring thaws, and in the summer Wendy paired up with Billy, another long-time street person, until he decided to get sober. In October Kurt was arrested again — unjustly, Wendy maintains — in connection with the beating death of another homeless man.

They, and the hundreds of thousands of others like them, are symptomatic of the culture of homelessness that pervades American society. They are casualties of eroded family and community life: the attenuation of our personal relationships; our intolerance of (or indifference to) those who fail to fit narrowly prescribed norms; our inability to nurture ourselves, our children, our aged; our reliance on surrogates to do so whenever we can afford them.

Homelessness cuts across lines of class, age, sex, and race. Our shelters are full of people from the suburbs as well as the inner city: the aged, the poor, the misfits, and the victims of family violence. We need to understand how they got there, understand the relationship between some of our most cherished values — achievement, autonomy, the self-absorbed pursuit of status and wealth — and violence — in this case, the violence of homelessness.

Homelessness in America begins at home:

— Where families no longer function as units that emotionally support their members.

— Where family life is continually sacrificed to long hours of work in environments that all but deny the existence of families. The absence of leave and sick-day policies for working parents and indifference to the pressures of child care continue to force adults to make unworkable compromises in the quality of their lives.

— Where these stresses and related ones, such as the lack of skills to command even subsistence-level wages lead adults to inflict their frustration and self-contempt on the weak: beating and raping women and children, shattering in them the psychological coherence essential to self-esteem and full, productive lives.

With few exceptions, the hundreds of homeless women interviewed for this book were raped, beaten, or abandoned as children or adolescents. Childhood abuse sets the stage for low personal expectations and repetition of the same abusive patterns in their adult relationships, often accompanied by early pregnancies, unemployment, and substance dependency. Nothing, not even economic poverty, destroys an individual's ability to function as categorically as early abuse does.

— Where the families that still *do* function have become so insulated from one another that the families next door remain strangers.

Trapped under such pressures in our home lives, we find ourselves attached only provisionally to our communities, which in turn are sapped of the vital energy needed to sustain our more dependent neighbors.

Traditional church-based groups, civic action associations, and local family organizations founder for lack of volunteers. Opportunities for the young to learn social and other skills in after-school clubs, Scouts, and athletic groups have become anemic for lack of adult leadership. Schoolteachers are often uncomfortable as role models, and those who work in large, urban systems are graduating young adults not only ill equipped to participate in the economic mainstream, but functionally illiterate in the art and possibilities of the democratic process.

These young people — along with our mentally and physically disabled and our elderly — are simply left to their own devices, a cruel form of social Darwinism. Too many of them, neglected, are transformed into undesirable vagrants, and worse, on our street corners.

Finally, isolation and insularity increasingly lead to parochialism in public policy, a lack of political will to address issues that don't touch directly on our perceived self-interest. Spouse and child abuse laws remain scandalously lax; drug and alcohol treatment and child care programs absurdly inadequate; the minimum wage on which so many poor mothers rely so low as to be an incentive to go on welfare, and programs for affordable housing underfinanced.

The culture of homelessness is a closed circle that begins in constricted personal lives and completes itself in short-sighted policies.

Arresting homelessness will require a holistic approach — rehabilitating our communities and restoring to them values that the fortunate have benefited from and today are failing to reinvest. All of us have a role to play.

We need to recognize and begin to prevent the preconditions of homelessness in our families and neighborhoods. At the same time we need to address the current crisis, understanding from the start that many of those who are homeless, and alienated for too long, will never return to the mainstream and will require lifelong support.

Revitalized communities will call for grassroots organizations that are guided by three principal convictions:

— That human beings are complex and not responsive to simplistic, undifferentiated relief efforts.

— That the creative participation of individuals in solving their problems is far more effective than paternalistic charity, in whatever guise.

— And finally, that continuity is essential to a personal sense of meaning.

American history is rich with examples of organizations informed by these beliefs. The minds behind these experiments didn't shrink from complexity — from the often subtle interplay among economic poverty, illiteracy, underemployment, social problems, and handicaps. In confronting complex problems with an array of integrated programs, they linked economic well-being and shelter to other vital strands of community: education, mutual support, and care of the young.

The best of them did all of this on a meaningful scale — not through vast, impersonal, and centralized systems with revolving staffs of caseworkers, but in neighborhoods that permitted one-on-one interaction between residents and staff.

The settlement house network and Edgar Helms's Industrial Church were, first, "preventive" organizations, attempting to stem the disintegration of poor, newly immigrant families in the face of cosmopolitan America's unanticipated challenges. They functioned as vital centers of stability and hope in chaotic social settings. They were committed to nurturing individual potential in as many different ways as possible, while simultaneously encouraging employment, fair housing, and group participation in achieving larger neighborhood goals.

Most important in the context of this book, their holistic approach met the especially complex needs of women — as workers, wives, and mothers — far more fully than have more recent social welfare and jobs policies. The latter, by isolating needs into categories — housing, welfare, disability (in the case of maternity leaves) — betray a fundamental blindness to women's realities, and in practice are destroying the ability of millions of American women to live whole, secure, fulfilling lives.

Helms's recognition of the need to work as a necessary element of personal dignity, his vision of worker cooperatives, his belief that citizens should devote several hours a week to community service, his Seavey Settlement, the Eliza Henry House for indigent working women, and the Massachusetts Housing Organization — all are indispensable models that we must reexamine today.

We know what works and what doesn't in so many areas of social and economic development. Programs offered by neighborhood organizations like the settlement houses could eradicate much of the isolation that breeds violence and perpetuates poverty, and could reach out to meet the needs of families in stress before they enter crises.

We know that physical and sexual abuse festers in secrecy. Earlier judicious intervention would have saved Amanda from her worst traumas; decent day care certainly would have helped. Day care would have alleviated Molly's stresses in an already difficult child-rearing situation. An active practice of reaching out to the insulated families of children like Amanda would have identified Renata's need for counseling before her depression intensified into a debilitating psychosis. And a more assertive approach to alcohol counseling on the part of churches, neighbors, and local drug treatment counselors might have caught Jack Daley's — and certainly Wendy's — drinking earlier. Neighborhood organizations ought to be able to help people find local jobs at every skill level. Though neither family was displaced from their home because of economic pressures, they might well have been. A well-organized infrastructure of community agencies should be able to "place" such families close to their old homes, so as not to disrupt work and school routines and other support systems.

The homeless themselves confirm the crucial role that even seemingly secondary community organizations once played in their lives. For Amanda it was Camp Fire Girls; for Wendy, the time spent in church and writing her poetry. Their happy memories aren't very different from Mary Antin's, seventy years earlier. For Antin the Saturday evening musical presentations at Morgan Chapel revealed a longer and a brighter view into her own future. We overlook such opportunities to develop positive personal expectations at our peril.

There is no lack of existing programs working to address these needs. The difficulty is that some of them are isolated in poor communities while others exist only in affluent communities, when the need for them is universal. The programs aren't sufficiently coordinated with each other, and they aren't truly integrated into the communities that they serve. By and large, there is no social contract between social service agencies and their client populations. The result is a detached, paternalistic service system that reacts in rigid, formulaic ways to acute need instead of actively reaching out with flexible, creative programs that enhance the day-to-day lives of the entire population. Women

and men in all walks of life and all classes today need the support
such programs could provide, from child care to family counseling.

A radical transformation is needed in the philosophy and structure
of our service agencies to bring this about. They must become partic-
ipatory, employing the talents and energies of neighborhood residents. And they must become better connected to other local organizations, churches, schools, and merchants that can provide what they
can't, be it a job, housing, or simply a place to talk to other people.

After twenty years of experience with modern shelters, we also have
a clearer idea of the dimensions of the current crisis of homelessness.
Some homeless people just need an apartment they can afford. Some
need long-term treatment for alcohol addiction. Some need work in
supervised workshops. Some need the proper psychotropic medications and living situations that will provide continuing connection to
others. Some just need decent jobs.

Amanda was fortunate. Though she returned to Pine Street in desperation over the state her life had been reduced to in the fall of 1986,
she came through its doors with an active desire to connect — mean-
ingfully and therapeutically — with a counselor there. Though Pine
Street was, and is still, struggling with just how therapeutic it ought to
be, Amanda saw to it that staff involvement (known in shelter parlance as "intervention," a borrowing from the terminology of alcohol
and mental health treatment) in her plight occurred, by seeking out
Jackie, who believed in an activist approach to the women in her care.

That isn't all. Intervention happened early, within Amanda's first
week at the shelter. She began a formal counseling relationship with
a shelter psychiatric nurse a week later. And, though much of the
burden fell on Jackie and on informal, rather than programmed efforts, her low self-esteem was bolstered and gradually reinforced, and
the skill she valued — her essays and songs of praise — encouraged
and nurtured, to the point where she was ready to get another job
and again seek a degree of autonomy — a room of her own.

Very few homeless women come even close to having Amanda's
quality of experience in America's shelters. In many cases shelters
lack staff and funding to make it possible. But they also seriously lack
organization and a clear philosophy about how to best help their populations. They came into existence in the midst of social crisis and
have struggled along valiantly in a crisis mode ever since. If shelters

are going to serve successfully as places where the homeless can find not only a warm bed at night, but also a way back from the roiled eddies of inner conflict (compounded often by years of subhuman existence) to steady, satisfying lives in accordance with their needs and abilities, the institutions must evolve.

The stories in this book limn the contours of what shelters need to become. They must see to it that every homeless woman who comes through their doors is offered, within a day or two of her arrival, a sustained relationship with a staff member who will help her identify her needs and meet her goals. Small shelters like St. Paul's (and specialized shelters) can identify and meet these diverse needs more effectively than can big ones. And they must remain open all day. Shelters for women can't close down during daytime working hours if the needs of their guests are to be met. Group workshops for building self-esteem and individual counseling are necessary services that most shelters currently are staffed to offer. They need to do so, paying particular attention to the hidden histories of abuse that will continue to engender negative relationships in the lives of these women unless their problems are addressed and dealt with. For women who can't be employed, or who aren't, the daytime hours are a time when they can be involved in individually structured routines: skill training, interviewing for jobs and finding apartments, or participating in activities at mental health or elders' centers. Setting daily, weekly and, in time, monthly, goals and, with the daily supervision of a counselor, meeting them will help most of those who are currently in shelters get out of them and stay out. Coopting the resources and talents of existing community agencies in providing these services is also essential. Not only will this approach begin to break down the barriers of disaffiliation and isolation that many homeless women have known for years, but it will be cheaper and more sensible than for shelters to replicate already existing programs, and will safeguard against the institutionalization of shelters — a process that is already occurring.

If, like Amanda, the women in our shelters can be fortunate enough to move into the kind of housing designed by the likes of the Paul Sullivan Housing Trust, which are experienced with the homeless, and can enter into a therapy relationship and, even better, become associated with a local community center that offers them activities and social opportunities, they will stay in housing and develop a more secure sense of belonging in the community.

Americans have quickly grown complacent about the homeless they see on their city streets every day. They assume that these people are all "Wendys," chronically and even intractably resistant to help. I hope the stories in this book dispel this fatal misperception and replace it with the understanding that with committed outreach, like the service the van offers the street homeless of Boston, and a far greater emphasis on one-to-one support and programs inside our shelters and out, the lives of a vast majority of homeless women can be permanently changed for the better.

For those like Wendy, however, who resist what we can currently provide, there is no easy solution. Wendy, and the many chronic alcoholics and drug abusers among the homeless population, can no more be disowned by us (or by advocates for the homeless who all but deny their existence) than they can be sentimentalized. All have been victims of early violence, and most have suffered from the lack of real opportunities to overcome its worst effects. Their families have exhausted their ability to aid them. Their habits are deeply entrenched.

Yet what keeps them most entrenched are the haunting memories of their previous failed efforts to overcome addiction and hold onto meaningful relationships. Wendy has tried sobriety so many times, with such disappointing results, that one voice inside tells her any attempt to change now is doomed from the start.

But there is another voice inside, and it expresses her will to live — in her gregariousness, her poetry, her hunger for people and love, and her fear of loneliness. I believe that this is the true song of Wendy's soul, the song from the alley that is most difficult for us to decipher, and most necessary for us to really hear. For even when Wendy has begun to believe that she's lost herself, we must be able to offer her another chance. One day she will take that chance again. Of this I am certain. And when she does, I want to hope that she'll be given the best treatment we know how to give anyone, rich or poor, for what she herself calls "the most self-alienating affliction." I'd like to hope that she'll have the benefits of a Horizon Hospital and a support system of new, sober friends who can help ease the painful transition into life without booze, and a job and relationships that will encourage intimacy free of the barriers she's erected between herself and the world for decades. I'd like to see her empowered by friendship and love to express her manifold talents, her warmth, and her remarkable perspicacity.

As with all alcoholics, the choice has to be hers. We cannot undermine her, or ourselves, with unreasonable expectations which, should she fail to meet them, will only cause us to punish her with neglect and contempt. We owe her, and the hundreds of thousands of addicts like her, in homes as well as on the streets, a much higher quality of addiction therapy — and beyond, decent job and educational opportunities — than we let ourselves be satisfied with now.

As a society riddled with addictions of numerous varieties, we have our own resistant barriers to break down, and one of the most resistant of them is owning up to the bankruptcy of some of our dominant social values, which foster these addictions.

The holistic approach to homelessness and revitalized communities that I'm advocating would link the tasks of prevention and reintegration to the same neighborhood organizations, clubs, and churches. Continuing to segregate the homeless in a separate system of shelters, ghettoized halfway houses, and rehabilitation programs is not the answer. Our own community involvement must extend to the homeless and to those at risk of becoming homeless, helping them to reconnect to others, giving them reasons to believe in themselves and trust those around them.

Creating healthy communities is going to cost money. Until now, small, private organizations have tried to fill the gap between what our human service system provides and the many unmet needs in our communities. But these organizations can't afford the expensive elements of a comprehensive approach, such as health clinics, day care facilities, and affordable housing. Nor can they each create large-scale employment alternatives like Morgan Memorial/Goodwill Industries. These programs have to be financed by the state and federal governments and by private corporations, franchised to local communities.

Put as simply as possible, grassroots organizations can't do what needs to be done without increased government funding and corporate grants. And conversely, the best-intentioned federal and private human service and housing programs will fail unless they are administered by the real experts, technically able people who work in the neighborhoods.

Local communities and cities will have to mobilize to define goals and obtain the funds and the flexibility to meet them. If they don't, community life won't be resuscitated, and solutions to our current problems will either not be forthcoming at all (in which case we will

all pay a more costly bill down the road), or the problems will be del-
egated once again to surrogates in what will inevitably become impacted bureaucracies incapable of responding to individual needs.

There are no short cuts to community, to support, or to relationship. Families that have been forced to deal with a homeless relative
have long since lost the luxury of complacent detachment or sentimentalized concern. They know that the homeless once had homes
and once belonged to the neighborhoods. They know that the homeless are not an anonymous aggregate but are individuals, each related
to us in a vital and intimate way.

Those who staff and volunteer at shelters know this. Paul Sullivan
knew it. Father Bill Francis and Sister Rita Brereton know it. All of
them know that the only real change occurs when we invest ourselves
in the lives of others: by alleviating the loneliness of a solitary neighborhood child like Amanda; sharing our skills; easing the plight of
Americans who can't buy private solutions to the problems we all share,
such as lack of child care; contributing time and money to educational, housing, and work opportunities for those who haven't had
our good fortune; listening with an open heart to the songs from the
alley. These are the investments that will yield real change. Nothing
else, nothing less. The solution to homelessness begins at home.

Notes

Bibliography

Acknowledgments

Notes

Prologue

1. Robert A. Woods and Albert Kennedy, *The Settlement Horizon* (New York: Russell Sage Foundation, 1922), p. 29.

Chapter 3   Magdalens and Madonnas

1. Carl Seaburg and Stanley Paterson, *The Merchant Prince of Boston* (Cambridge: Harvard University Press, 1971), p. 22.
2. Katharine D. Hardwick, "As Long as Charity Shall Be a Virtue: Massachusetts Charities 1657 to 1800," Simmons College Archives, p. 4.
3. Ibid., p. 27.
4. Ibid., pp. 6–7.
5. Seaburg and Paterson, *Merchant Prince*, p. 44.
6. Oscar Handlin, *Boston's Immigrants* (New York: Atheneum, 1976), p. 8.
7. Harold Kirker and James Kirker, *Bulfinch's Boston* (New York: Oxford University Press, 1964), p. 155.
8. Ralph Waldo Emerson, *Journals*, VIII:339, quoted in *Elias Boudinot's Journey to Boston in 1809*, ed. Milton Halsey Thomas (Princeton: Princeton University Press, 1955), p. 39.
9. Ibid.
10. Brett Howard, *Social Boston* (New York: Hawthorn Books, 1976), p. 25, from the Rev. Russell H. Conwell's "Acres of Diamonds" sermon.
11. Kirker, *Bulfinch*, p. 11.
12. *Brief History of the Rise and Progress of the Penitent Females' Refuge*, ed. the Secretary (Mrs. M. L. O'Brien) (Boston: Wm. D. Ticknor, 1848), p. 4.
13. Ibid.

14. *Bethesda Society Annual Report 1817* (Boston: Lincoln & Emands, 1817), p. 8.
15. Ibid., p. 9.
16. Ibid., p. 9.
17. *Brief History*, p. 4.
18. *Third Annual Report of the Penitent Females' Refuge* (Boston: Lincoln & Emands, 1822) recounts the formal incorporation of the refuge, as well as its first year in operation.
19. Ibid., p. 22.
20. *Appeal to the Public, Annual Report, Bethesda Society, 1839* (Boston: Perkins & Marvin, 1839), pp. 6–7.
21. *Ninth Annual Report of the Directors of the Penitent Females' Refuge, Auxiliary Visitors' Report* (Boston: T. R. Marvin, 1828), p. 16.
22. *Bethesda Society Report 1817*, p. 5.
23. David J. Rothman, *The Discovery of the Asylum: Social Order and Disorder in the New Republic* (Boston: Little, Brown, 1971), p. 114. I am indebted to Rothman for his analysis of the convergence of social change and the desire to control society's least integrated members.
24. *Bethesda Society 1817*, pp. 7 and 8.
25. Rothman, *Discovery*, p. 169.
26. *Ninth Annual Report*, p. 3.
27. Josiah Quincy, *Report of the Committee on the Pauper Laws of this Commonwealth* (Massachusetts General Court, 1821), p. 9.
28. Ibid., p. 4.
29. Ibid., p. 5.
30. Ibid., p. 3.
31. Ibid., p. 8.
32. Rothman, *Discovery*, p. 188.
33. M. B. Katz, *In the Shadow of the Poorhouse* (New York: Basic Books, 1986), pp. 31–32.
34. Rothman, *Discovery*, p. 183.
35. Ibid., p. 205.
36. *Third Annual Report*, p. 3.
37. *Brief History*, p. 12.
38. *Annual Report of the Bethesda Society, Nov. 15, 1854* (Boston: John Wilson & Son, 1854), p. 5.
39. *Reports of the Refuge and Bethesda Society for the year ending February 1900* (Boston: Frank Wood, 1900), p. 18.

Chapter 5   From Margin to Mainstream

1. Jane Addams, *Twenty Years at Hull House* (New York: Macmillan, 1910), p. 111.
2. Frederick A. Bushee, "Population," in *The City Wilderness*, ed. Robert A. Woods (Boston: Houghton Mifflin, 1898). Figures extrapolated from pp. 33–57.

3. Oscar Handlin, *Boston's Immigrants* (New York: Atheneum, 1976), pp. 25–44.

4. Mary Antin, *The Promised Land* (Boston: Houghton Mifflin, 1911), p. 272.

5. Robert A. Woods and Albert Kennedy, *The Settlement Horizon* (New York: Russell Sage Foundation, 1922), pp. 273–74.

6. Addams, *Hull House*, p. 126.

7. Ivan D. Steen, "Building a Foundation for Goodwill Industries: The Activities of the Rev. Henry Morgan," unpublished paper, Department of History, State University of New York at Albany, p. 8.

8. Ibid., p. 3.

9. Antin, *Promised Land*, p. 267.

10. F. C. Moore, *Activities of the Morgan Memorial Co-Operative Industries and Stores, Inc.* (Boston: Morgan Memorial Goodwill Press, 1943), p. 8.

11. John Fulton Lewis, *Goodwill, For the Love of People* (Washington, D.C.: Goodwill Industries of America, 1977), p. 67.

12. Ibid.

13. Edgar J. Helms, *Pioneering in Modern City Missions* (Boston: Morgan Memorial Printing Department, 1927), p. 72.

14. Ibid., p. 73.

15. Souvenir Report of Morgan Memorial, p. 12.

16. Lewis, *Goodwill*, p. 179.

Chapter 7   The Margin Redrawn

1. Bascom N. Timmons, *Portrait of an American* (New York: Henry Holt, 1953), p. 155.

2. Ibid., p. 158.

3. Daniel J. Boorstin, *The Americans*, vol. 2: *The Democratic Experience* (New York: Vintage Books, 1974), p. 216.

4. Letter of Glenn W. Leighbody, excerpted in Lewis, *Goodwill*, pp. 198–99.

5. Martin F. Nolan, "Tracking History," *Boston Globe Magazine*, April 26, 1987, p. 61.

6. Ronald W. Geddes, "Making Drunkenness Legal: The Clash of Multiple Perspectives on Social Control and Treatment," doctoral dissertation, Boston University, 1982. Geddes was the first director of the Boston Alcohol Detox Project; I have drawn on his thorough examination of the decriminalization of public intoxication throughout this chapter.

7. "National Group Formed to Aid the Homeless," *New York Times*, May 9, 1982, p. 14.

Chapter 11   In from the Cold

1. Disputes over homeless census results weren't new. A 1973 Pine Street Inn newsletter claimed there were upward of 10,000 homeless men in Boston. The most famous number dispute occurred early in the 1980s

between those who claimed an estimate of 3 million nationwide, based on educated guesswork by the Washington-based Community for Creative Non-Violence, and HUD's guestimate of 250,000 to 350,000. No one has been able to definitively tally this population; like victims of rape and sexual abuse, these people often resist making themselves known. About the most accurate figures anyone has to go on are census totals that reflect actual head counts in shelters. These, the equivalent to "reported cases" of sexual assault, reflect the number of people actively seeking help. It is safe to assume that there are many more.

Chapter 12   Starting Over

1. Paul McGerigle and Alison S. Lauriat, *More Than Shelter: A Community Response to Homelessness* (Boston: United Community Planning Corporation and the Massachusetts Association for Mental Health, 1983), p. 100.

Chapter 18   The Women's Group

1. I was present at, and included in, countless discussions like the one described here. However, out of respect for the participants' privacy, I did not tape record these sessions. This scene has been reconstructed from taped interviews conducted following the meeting.

Chapter 23   Not Exactly Paris

1. Massachusetts is a good example of poor public policy in this area. Although it is regarded as the forerunner in community-based alcohol treatment facilities, its drug programs lag far behind. In the city of Boston in 1987, with an estimated population of 14,000 intravenous drug addicts (cocaine, heroin, and speedballing), and the highest infant AIDS mortality rate in the country, there was only one twenty-bed inpatient facility in the entire system equipped to detoxify and treat female heroin addicts, the Dorchester Detox Unit. The unit was closed in 1988 as a "cost-saving" measure.

Bibliography

Addams, Jane. *Twenty Years at Hull House*. New York: Macmillan, 1910.
Annual Report of the Bethesda Society, Nov. 15, 1854. Boston: John Wilson & Son, 1854.
Antin, Mary. *The Promised Land*. Boston: Houghton Mifflin, 1911.
Appeal to the Public, Annual Report, Bethesda Society, 1839. Boston: Perkins & Marvin, 1839.
Bethesda Society Annual Report, 1817. Boston: Lincoln & Emands, 1817.
Boorstin, Daniel J. *The Americans*, vol. 2: *The Democratic Experience*. New York: Vintage Books, 1974.
Geddes, Ronald W. "Making Drunkenness Legal: The Clash of Multiple Perspectives on Social Control and Treatment." Doctoral dissertation, Boston University, 1982.
Handlin, Oscar. *Boston's Immigrants*. New York: Atheneum, 1976.
Hardwick, Katharine D. *Massachusetts Charities 1657 to 1800*. Boston: Simmons College, 1964.
Helms, Edgar J. *Pioneering in Modern City Missions*. Boston: Morgan Memorial Printing Department, 1927.
Howard, Brett. *Social Boston*. New York: Hawthorn Books, 1976.
Katz, M. B. *In the Shadow of the Poorhouse*. New York: Basic Books, 1986.
Kirker, Harold, and James Kirker. *Bulfinch's Boston*. New York: Oxford University Press, 1964.
Lewis, John Fulton. *Goodwill: For the Love of People*. Washington: Goodwill Industries of America, 1977.
McGerigle, Paul, and Alison S. Lauriat. *More Than Shelter: A Community Response to Homelessness*. Boston: United Community Planning Corporation and the Massachusetts Association for Mental Health, 1983.
Moore, F. C. *Activities of the Morgan Memorial Co-Operative Industries and Stores, Inc.* Boston: Morgan Memorial Goodwill Press, 1943.

Ninth Annual Report of the Penitent Females' Refuge. Boston: T. R. Marvin, 1828.

O'Brien, Mrs. M. L., ed. *Brief History of the Rise and Progress of the Penitent Females' Refuge.* Boston: Wm. D. Ticknor, 1848.

Quincy, Josiah. *Report of the Committee on the Pauper Laws of this Commonwealth.* Massachusetts General Court, 1821.

Reports of the Refuge and Bethesda Society for the year ending February 1900. Boston: Frank Wood, 1900.

Rothman, David J. *The Discovery of the Asylum: Social Order and Disorder in the New Republic.* Boston: Little, Brown, 1971.

Seaburg, Carl, and Stanley Paterson. *The Merchant Prince of Boston.* Cambridge: Harvard University Press, 1971.

Steen, Ivan D. "Building a Foundation for Goodwill Industries." Unpublished paper, Department of History, State University of New York at Albany.

Third Annual Report of the Penitent Female Refuge. Boston: Lincoln & Emands, 1822.

Thomas, Milton Halsey, ed. *Elias Boudinot's Journey to Boston in 1809.* Princeton: Princeton University Press, 1955.

Timmons, Bascom N. *Portrait of an American.* New York: Henry Holt, 1953.

Woods, Robert A., ed. *The City Wilderness.* Boston: Houghton Mifflin, 1898.

Woods, Robert A., and Albert Kennedy. *The Settlement Horizon.* New York: Russell Sage Foundation, 1922.

Acknowledgments

Songs from the Alley is in many respects a collaboration, and it is my happiest task to acknowledge my indebtedness, first to my patient, gracious teachers, the homeless people of Boston. Without them, their families, and friends, and without the faith and support of the entire staff of St. Paul's and the Pine Street Inn, especially Richard Ring, Ralph Hughes, Sandy Jones, Randy Bailey, Lori Lambert, Jackie Pierce, Holly Ellison, and Michael Malone, these stories could not have been told.

Others, in both dialogue and debate, have helped me shape and test the conclusions drawn from inductive exploration. Sandra Brawders, former director of the House of Ruth, a women's shelter in Washington, D. C., confirmed my belief that most shelters weren't addressing the emotional problems of abused women. J. Robb Bartlett, former director of The Ark, a family shelter in Oklahoma City, was invaluable in helping me articulate the difficult concept of a holistic approach to homelessness. Mitch Snyder and members of the Community for Creative Non-Violence have shown me by example the profound changes that are possible through personal action. And the persistence of the National Coalition for the Homeless and Bob Hayes in obtaining passage of the Stewart B. McKinney Act has overcome in large measure my skepticism toward the possibility of intelligent top-down social change.

Had not my editor, Katrina Kenison, a woman of courage and integrity, listened with an open heart, *Songs* would have remained just a handful of notes. I can't imagine a more engaged and thoughtful advocate, and it is satisfying to know that in a new way, she will be listening and engaged still. My agent, Kristine Dahl, has supported me with far more than conventional services, including judicious reminders that I sleep and eat.

I am indebted to the Massachusetts Historical Society, the Boston Athenaeum, the College Archives of Simmons College, the Archives of the Archdiocese of Boston, and to Marc Widershien of the Massachusetts State Archives, as well as to Janet Silver and to Peg Anderson, gentle restrainer of sentences, whose editing pencil was intelligent and sure.

Truly heartfelt thanks go to the MacDowell Colony, Chris Barnes, its resident director, and the staff there, who provided me with a much-needed and tranquil retreat in which to reflect on the influences of the people named here, and so many others who will remain unnamed, in order to achieve a synthesizing perspective.

That I have a home, still, after journeying so long and for such extended periods on this intensely personal mission is due entirely to the selflessness of my husband, Mark Morrow. From the start he shared a commitment to my project that overrode any concern for personal comfort. He has maintained our household during my absences, and he has endured uncertainty and countless personal sacrifices to help see me home again.

Finally, my thanks to my grandmother, Ann P. Bell, and my parents, William and Shirley Hirsch, whose lifelong example of tenacity, commitment, and irrepressible optimism, even in the face of seemingly insurmountable troubles, have guided all that I have undertaken to accomplish.